尾田栄一郎

I hate it when things are already decided for you by
someone else. From the day you are born, people say
"You're born in the year of the rabbit!" Or "You're a
Capricorn!" No way! Those animals just sound weak!
So I'm changing it myself. I was born in the Man-Eating
Giant Rabbit Year. I'm also an Anaconda-Swallowing Devil
Capricorn. Wow, that's scary. But they sound strong.
Anyway, volume 58 is starting!

-Eiichiro Oda, 2010

Eiichiro Oda began his manga career at the age of
17, when his one-shot cowboy manga **Wanted!**
won second place in the coveted Tezuka manga
awards. Oda went on to work as an assistant to
some of the biggest manga artists in the industry,
including Nobuhiro Watsuki, before winning the
Hop Step Award for new artists. His pirate
adventure **One Piece**, which debuted in
Weekly Shonen Jump in 1997, quickly became
one of the most popular manga in Japan.

ONE PIECE VOL. 58
PARAMOUNT WAR PART 2

SHONEN JUMP Manga Edition

This graphic novel contains material that was originally published in English in SHONEN JUMP #94–97. Artwork in the magazine may have been slightly altered from that presented here.

STORY AND ART BY EIICHIRO ODA

English Adaptation/Lance Caselman
Translation/Laabaman, HC Language Solutions, Inc.
Touch-up Art & Lettering/Vanessa Satone
Design/Fawn Lau
Editor/Alexis Kirsch

Printed in the U.S.A.

Published by VIZ Media, LLC
P.O. Box 77010
San Francisco, CA 94107

10 9 8 7 6 5 4 3 2 1
First printing, September 2011

SHONEN JUMP MANGA

ONE PIECE

Vol. 58
THE NAME OF THIS ERA IS "WHITEBEARD"

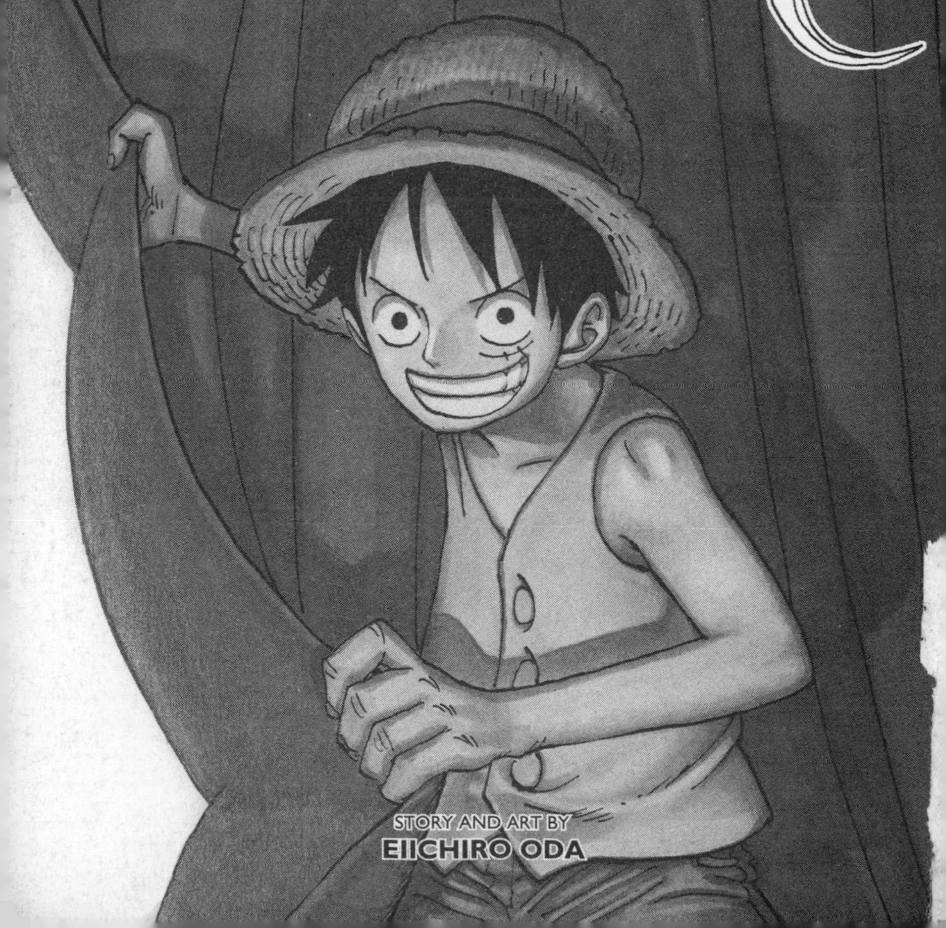

STORY AND ART BY
EIICHIRO ODA

Navy Headquarters
[Marineford]

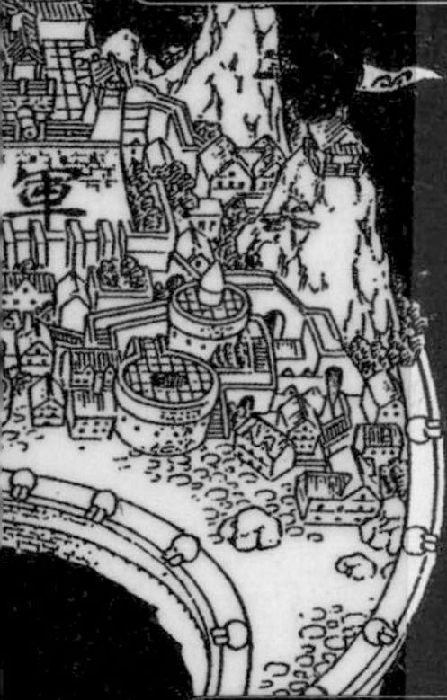

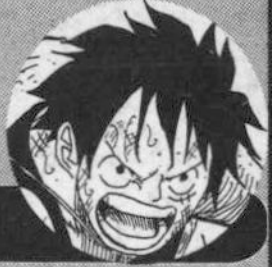

Captain of the Straw Hat pirates. He broke into Impel Down to save his brother, Ace, but now he's arrived at the Navy headquarters.

Monkey D. Luffy

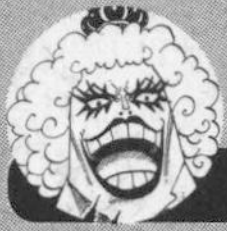

The king of New Kamas known as the Miracle Worker. He is comrades with Dragon the Revolutionary. **[Kamabakka Queendom Queen (Forever Vacant)]**

Emporio Ivankov

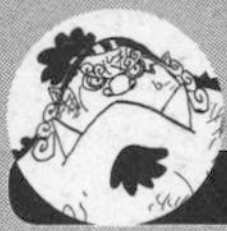

Was Imprisoned in Impel Down where he met Luffy and went with him to save Ace. **[Former Warlord of the Sea]**

Jimbei

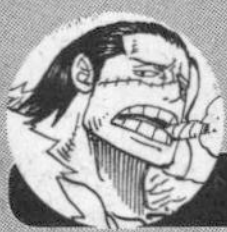

Former member of the Seven Warlords of the Sea and also the former president of Baroque Works as Mr. 0. He has escaped Impel Down with Luffy. **[Pirate]**

Sir Crocodile

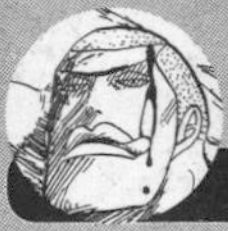

Accompanying Crocodile on his escape after being asked to do so. **[Former B.W. Member, Assassin Daz Bonez]**

Mr. 1

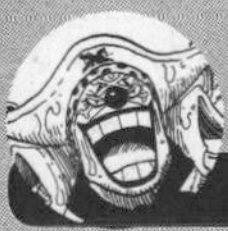

Held at Impel Down, but managed to escape. Currently heading toward the Marine Headquarters with Luffy.

Buggy the Clown

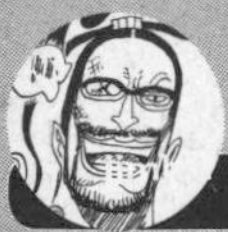

After hitting it off with Buggy, he is also accompanying him on his escape. **[Former B.W. Member]**

Mr. 3

The Navy

Those Assembled at Navy Headquarters at Marineford.

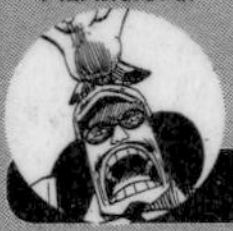

[Navy Fleet Admiral]
"Buddha" Sengoku

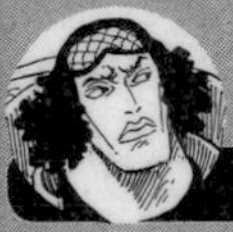

[Navy Admiral]
Aokiji [Kuzan]

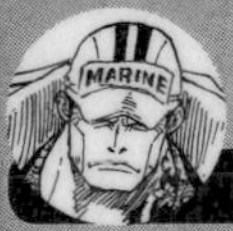
MARINE

[Navy Admiral]
Akainu [Sakazuki]

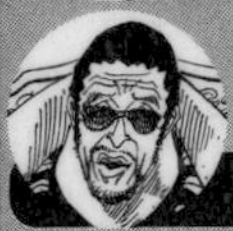

[Navy Admiral]
Kizaru [Borsalino]

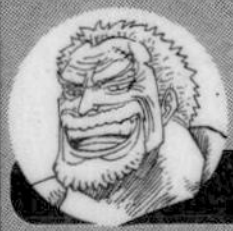

[Navy Vice Admiral]
Garp

[Vice Admiral] Momonga

[Commodore] Smoker

[Captain] Hina the Black Cage, T-Bone

[Ensign] Tashigi

The public execution draws close!

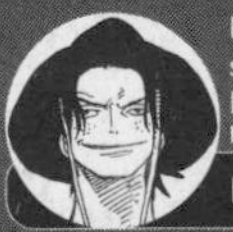

Luffy's older brother. He is the son of the Pirate King Gold Roger. **[Whitebeard Pirates 2nd Division Leader]**

Portgaz D. Ace

PARAMOUNT WAR

ONE PIECE

Vol. 58

The Name of This Era Is "Whitebeard"

CONTENTS

THE STORY OF ONE PIECE

Volume 58

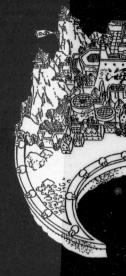

The Four Emperors

Whitebeard Pirates

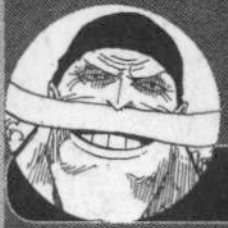

The world's strongest pirate. He has arrived at Navy Headquarters to rescue Ace.
[Captain of Whitebeard Pirates]

Edward Newgate

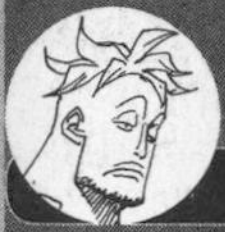

[Whitebeard Pirates 1st Division Leader]

Marco

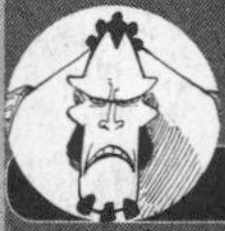

[Whitebeard Pirates 3rd Division Leader]

Jozu

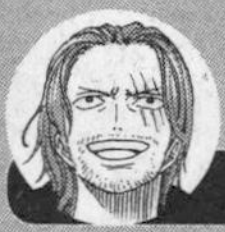

Was involved in a scuffle with Kaido in the New World.
[Captain of the Red-Haired Pirates]

"Red-Haired" Shanks

Luffy infiltrated the Great Prison Impel Down to rescue his brother Ace, but powerful prison guards stood in his way. Upon learning that Ace has already been escorted to the Navy Headquarters, Luffy escapes Impel Down along with many other big name pirates and chases after Ace.
Upon the arrival of the Whitebeard Pirates in Marineford, the war begins! The Three Admirals and the Seven Warlords of the Sea show their strength in battle, staining the Navy Headquarters with blood. Luffy joins the war, but the battle continues to become even fiercer! Ace's execution has been moved to an earlier time! They're running out of time, but suddenly, Whitebeard is stabbed by one of his underlings!

Warlords of the Sea

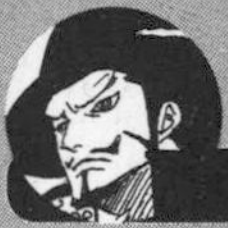

The world's most powerful swordsman. He expresses interest in Luffy and his crew.

Dracule Mihawk

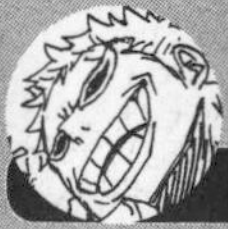

A mysterious man who believes that power is everything.

Don Quixote Doflamingo

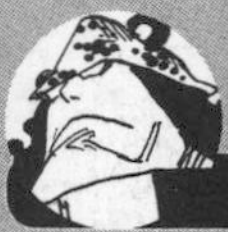

Also known as "the Tyrant." He's acted oddly when it comes to the Straw Hats.

Bartholomew Kuma

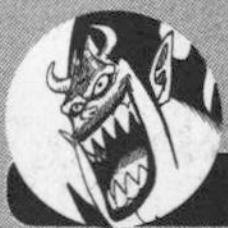

Although he already lost to Luffy once, he answers the call of battle.

Gecko Moria

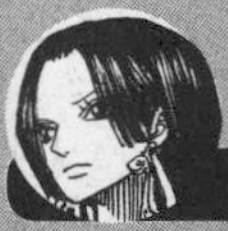

The empress of Amazon Lily and captain of the Kuja Pirates.

Boa Hancock

Chapter 563:
ONE MAN, ONE HEART

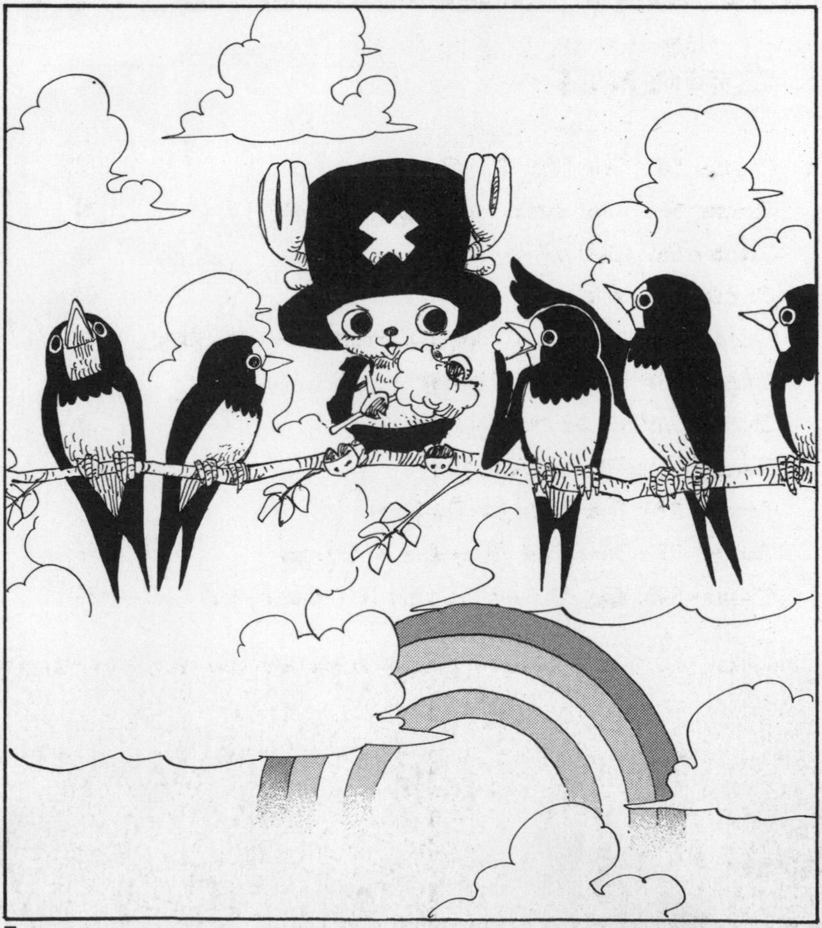

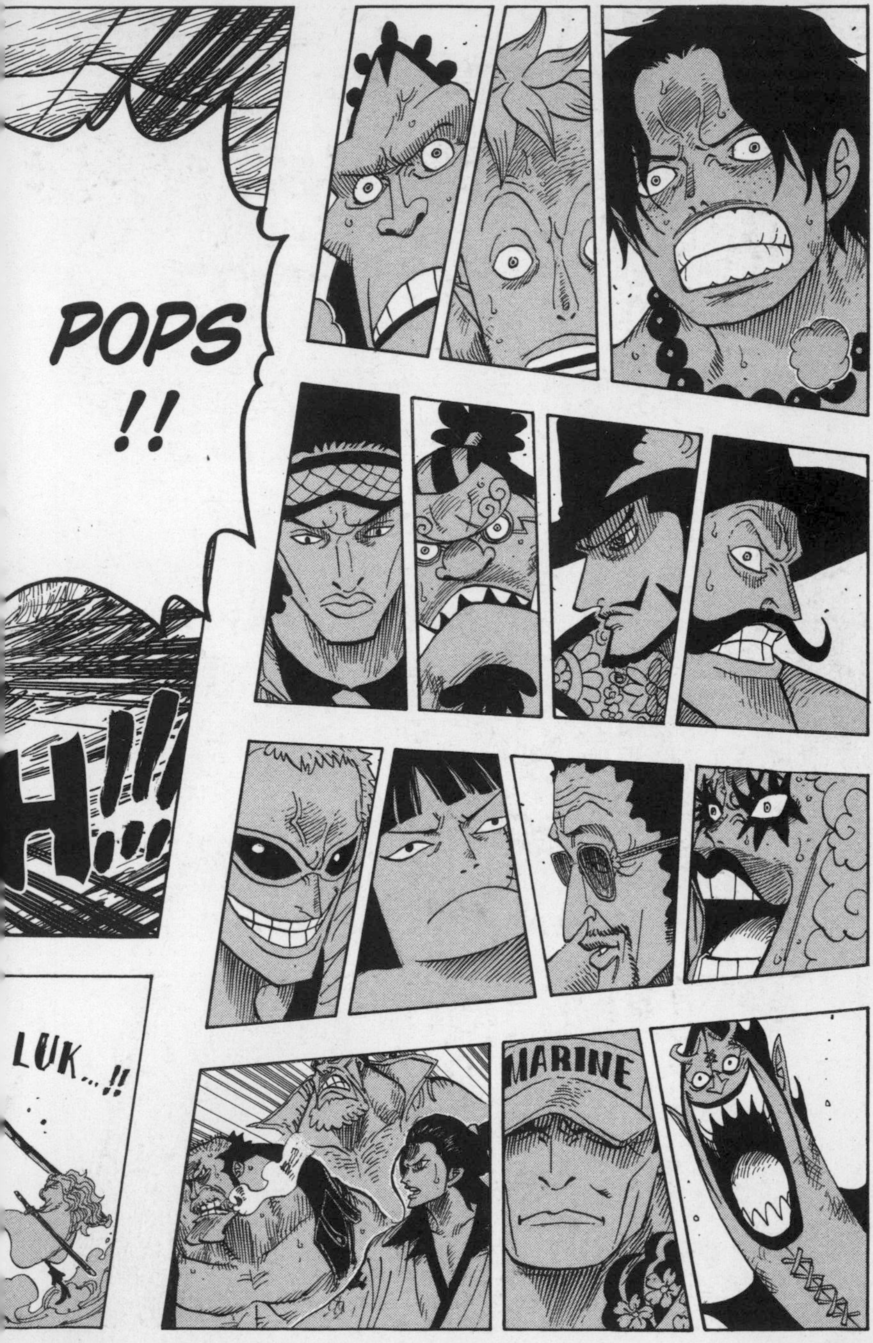
MARINE
POPS !!
H!!!
LUK...!!

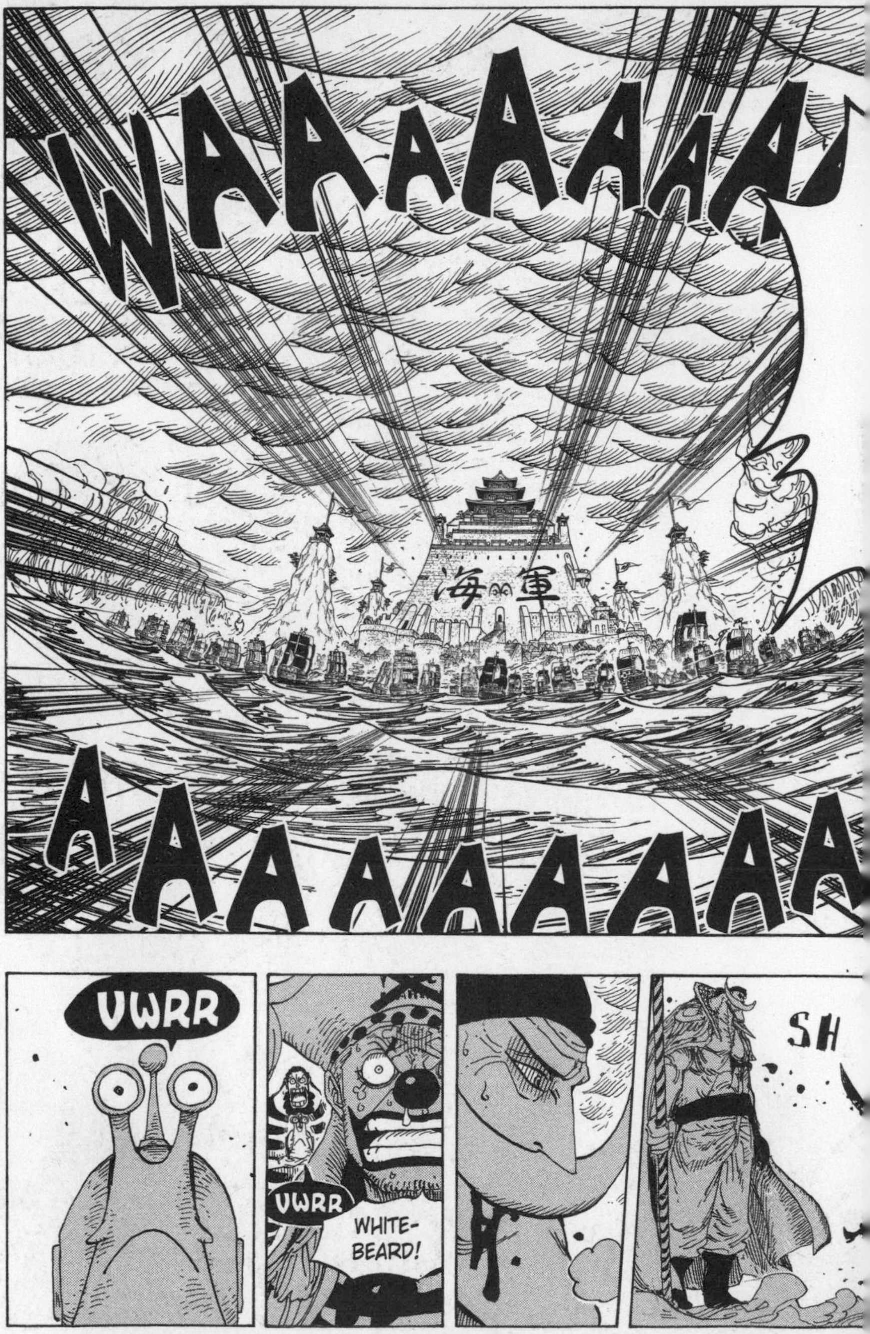
WAAAAAAA
海軍
AAAAAAAAA
SH
UWRR
WHITE-BEARD!
UWRR

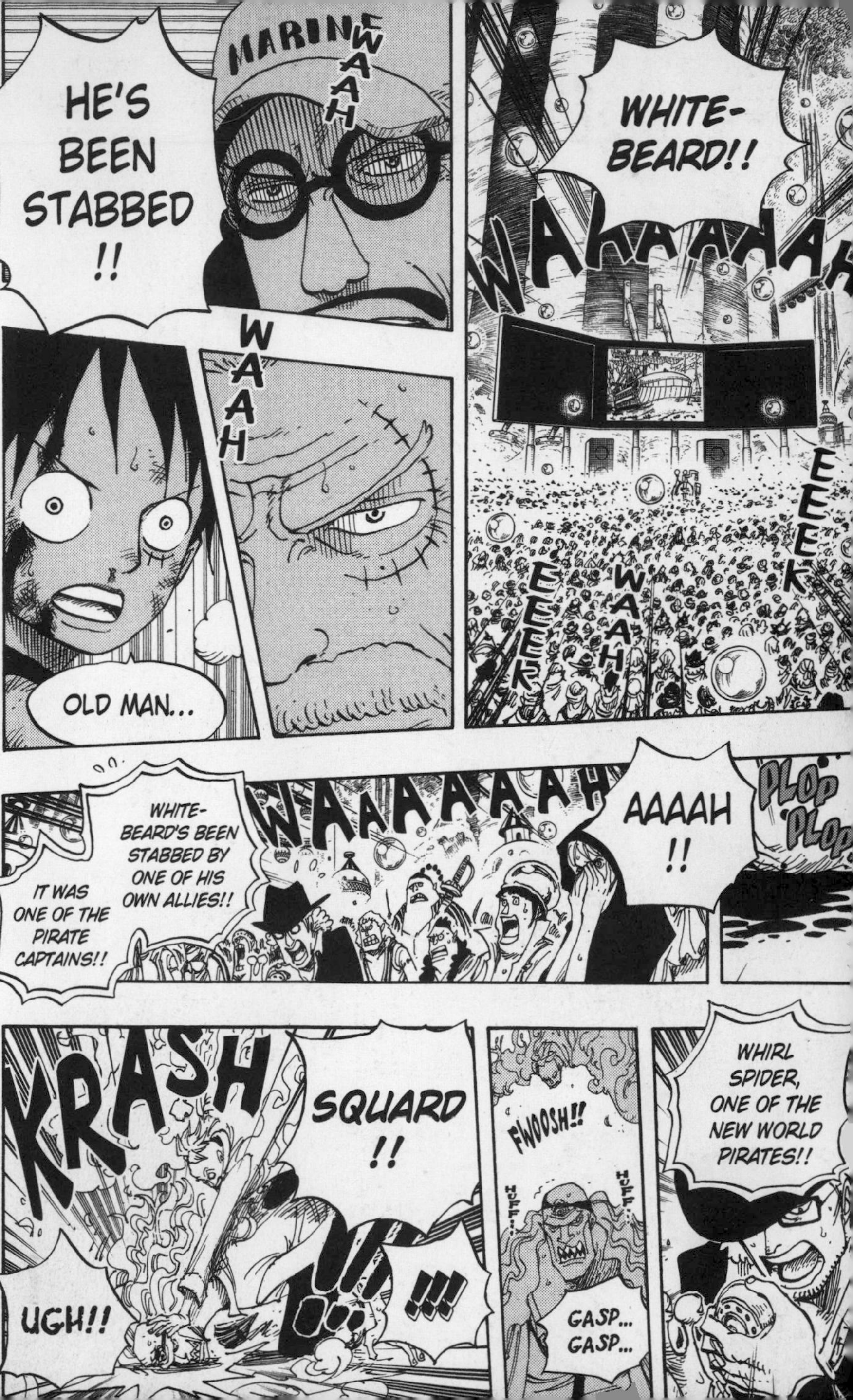

WHITE-BEARD!!
WAAAAAAH
EEEEK
WAAH
EEEEK
MARINE
WAAH
HE'S BEEN STABBED!!
WAAH
OLD MAN...
PLOP PLOP
AAAAH!!
WAAAAAAAH
WHITE-BEARD'S BEEN STABBED BY ONE OF HIS OWN ALLIES!!
IT WAS ONE OF THE PIRATE CAPTAINS!!
WHIRL SPIDER, ONE OF THE NEW WORLD PIRATES!!
FWOOSH!!
HUFF... HUFF...
GASP... GASP...
KRASH
SQUARD!!
!!!
UGH!!

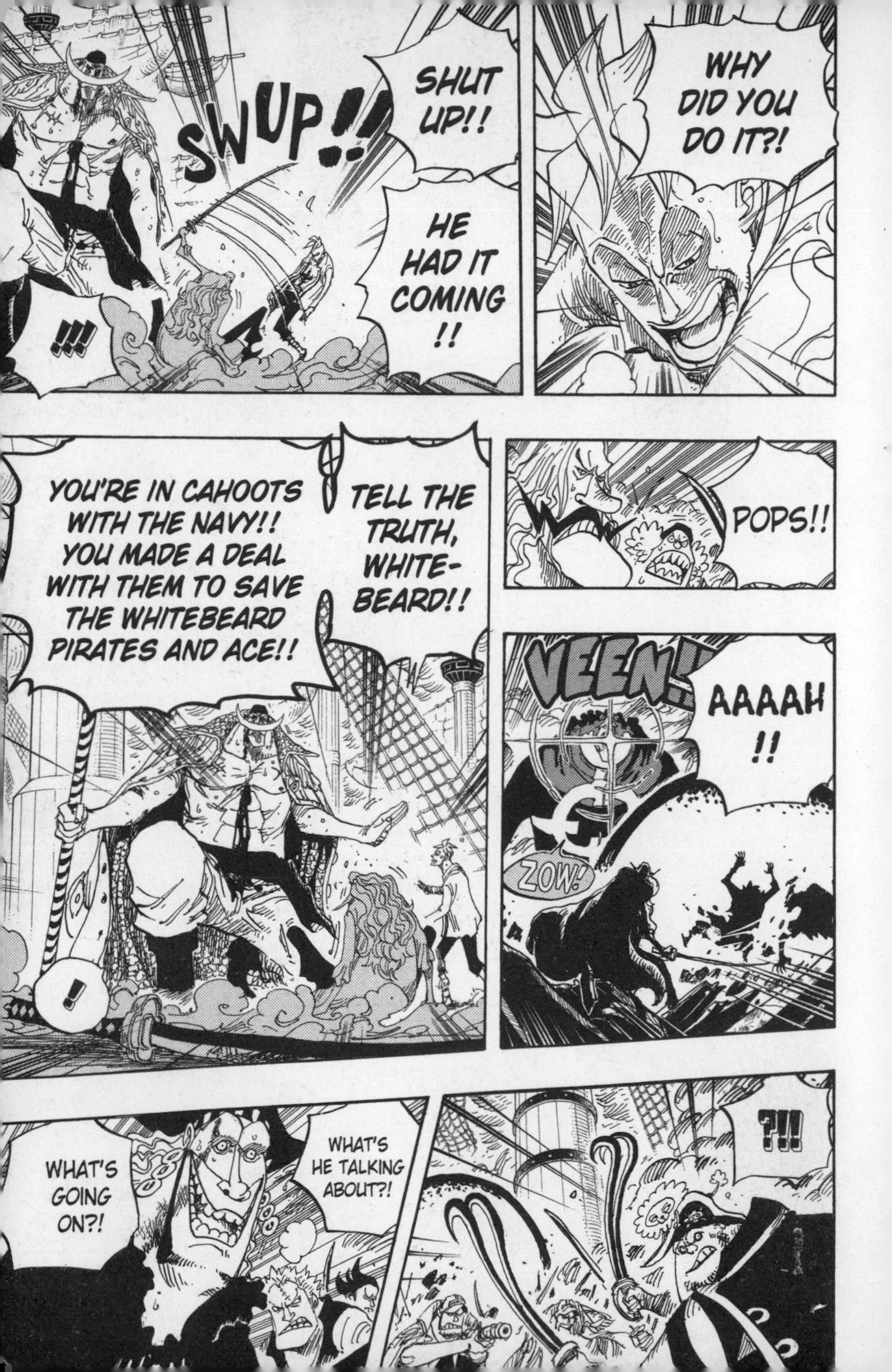
WHY DID YOU DO IT?!
SHUT UP!!
SWUP!!
HE HAD IT COMING!!
!!!
POPS!!
VEEN!!
AAAAH!!
ZOW!
TELL THE TRUTH, WHITE-BEARD!!
YOU'RE IN CAHOOTS WITH THE NAVY!! YOU MADE A DEAL WITH THEM TO SAVE THE WHITEBEARD PIRATES AND ACE!!
!
?!!
WHAT'S HE TALKING ABOUT?!
WHAT'S GOING ON?!

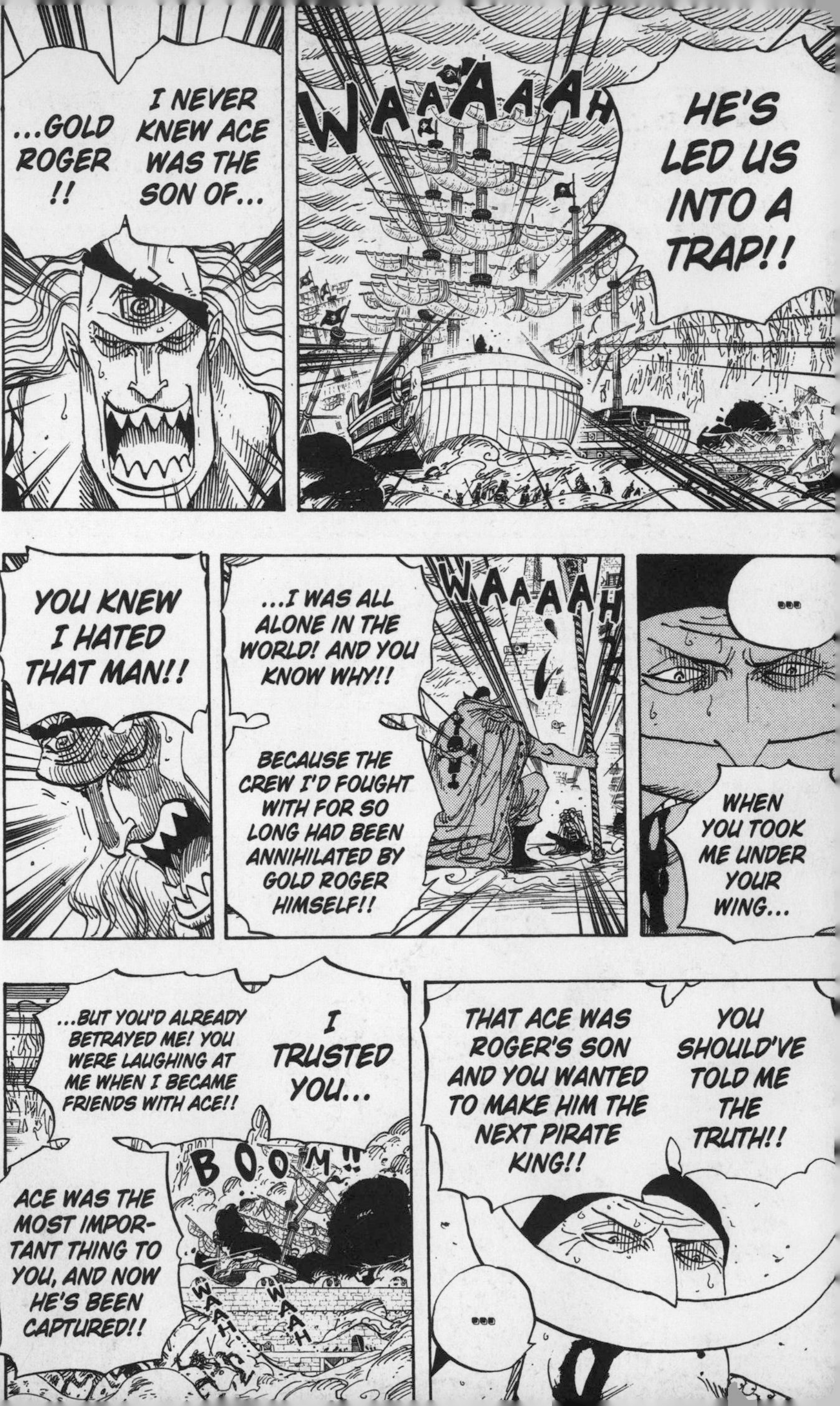

WAAAAAH
HE'S LED US INTO A TRAP!!
I NEVER KNEW ACE WAS THE SON OF...
...GOLD ROGER !!
...
WHEN YOU TOOK ME UNDER YOUR WING...
WAAAAH
...I WAS ALL ALONE IN THE WORLD! AND YOU KNOW WHY!!
BECAUSE THE CREW I'D FOUGHT WITH FOR SO LONG HAD BEEN ANNIHILATED BY GOLD ROGER HIMSELF!!
YOU KNEW I HATED THAT MAN!!
YOU SHOULD'VE TOLD ME THE TRUTH!!
THAT ACE WAS ROGER'S SON AND YOU WANTED TO MAKE HIM THE NEXT PIRATE KING!!
...
I TRUSTED YOU...
...BUT YOU'D ALREADY BETRAYED ME! YOU WERE LAUGHING AT ME WHEN I BECAME FRIENDS WITH ACE!!
BOOM!!
ACE WAS THE MOST IMPOR-TANT THING TO YOU, AND NOW HE'S BEEN CAPTURED!!
WAAH
WAAH

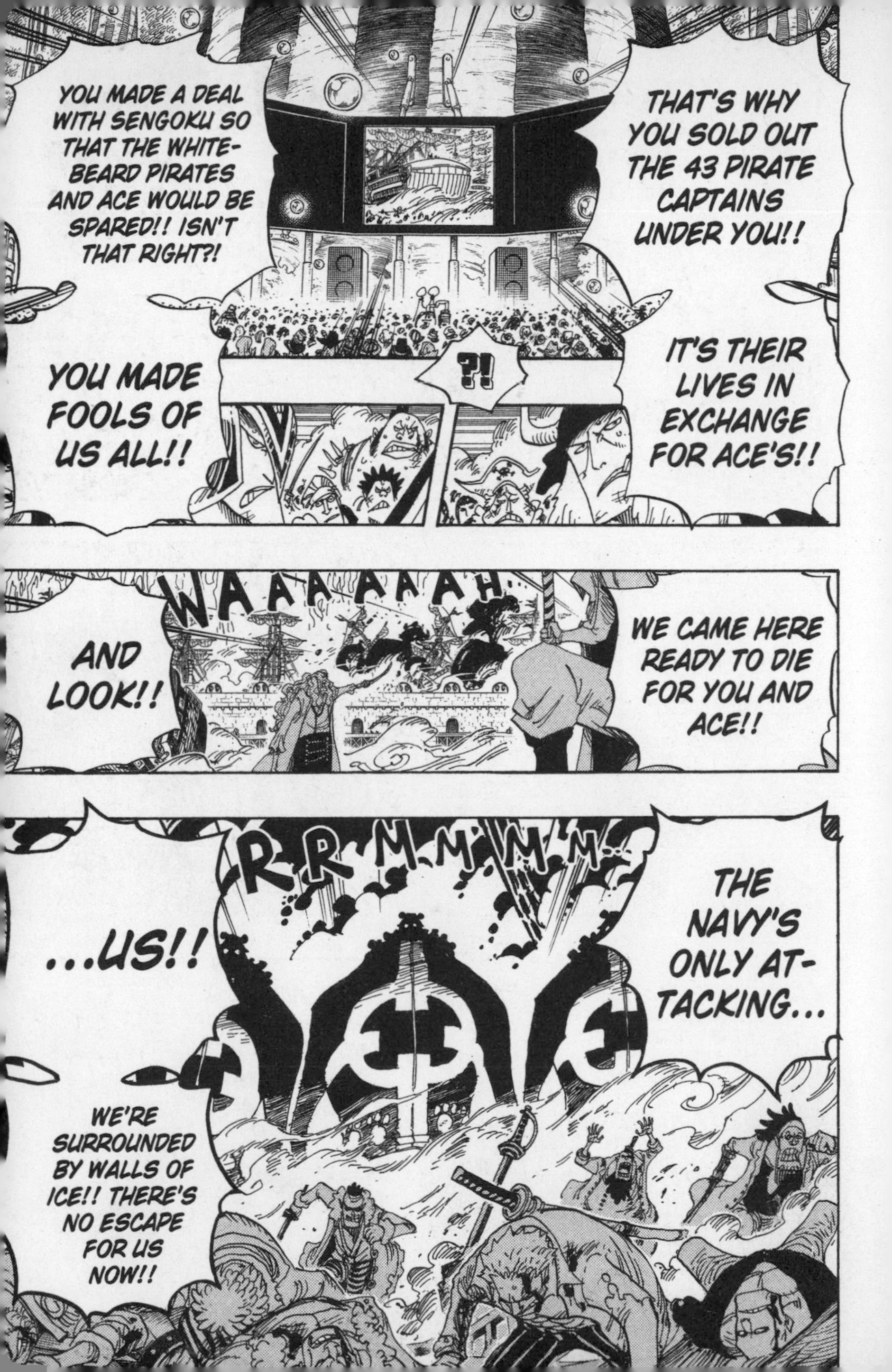
THAT'S WHY YOU SOLD OUT THE 43 PIRATE CAPTAINS UNDER YOU!!
YOU MADE A DEAL WITH SENGOKU SO THAT THE WHITE-BEARD PIRATES AND ACE WOULD BE SPARED!! ISN'T THAT RIGHT?!
?!
IT'S THEIR LIVES IN EXCHANGE FOR ACE'S!!
YOU MADE FOOLS OF US ALL!!
WE CAME HERE READY TO DIE FOR YOU AND ACE!!
WAAAAAAH
AND LOOK!!
RRMMMMM
THE NAVY'S ONLY AT-TACKING...
...US!!
WE'RE SURROUNDED BY WALLS OF ICE!! THERE'S NO ESCAPE FOR US NOW!!

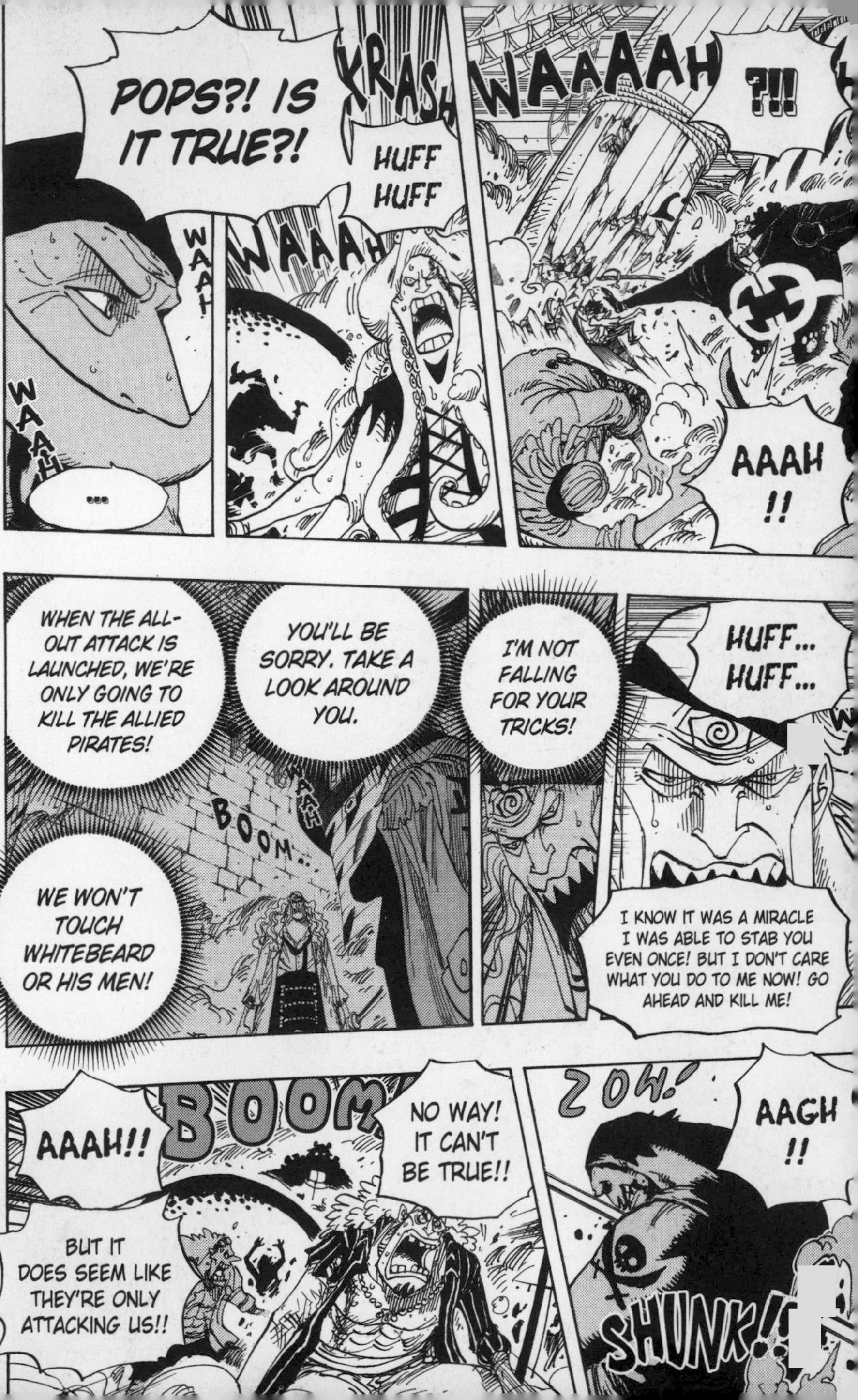
?!!
WAAAAH
AAAH !!
KRASH
HUFF HUFF
WAAAH
POPS?! IS IT TRUE?!
WAAAH
WAAAH
...
HUFF... HUFF...
I KNOW IT WAS A MIRACLE I WAS ABLE TO STAB YOU EVEN ONCE! BUT I DON'T CARE WHAT YOU DO TO ME NOW! GO AHEAD AND KILL ME!
I'M NOT FALLING FOR YOUR TRICKS!
YOU'LL BE SORRY. TAKE A LOOK AROUND YOU.
WHEN THE ALL-OUT ATTACK IS LAUNCHED, WE'RE ONLY GOING TO KILL THE ALLIED PIRATES!
WAAAH
BOOM
WE WON'T TOUCH WHITEBEARD OR HIS MEN!
ZOW!
AAGH !!
SHUNK!
NO WAY! IT CAN'T BE TRUE!!
BOOM
AAAH!!
BUT IT DOES SEEM LIKE THEY'RE ONLY ATTACKING US!!

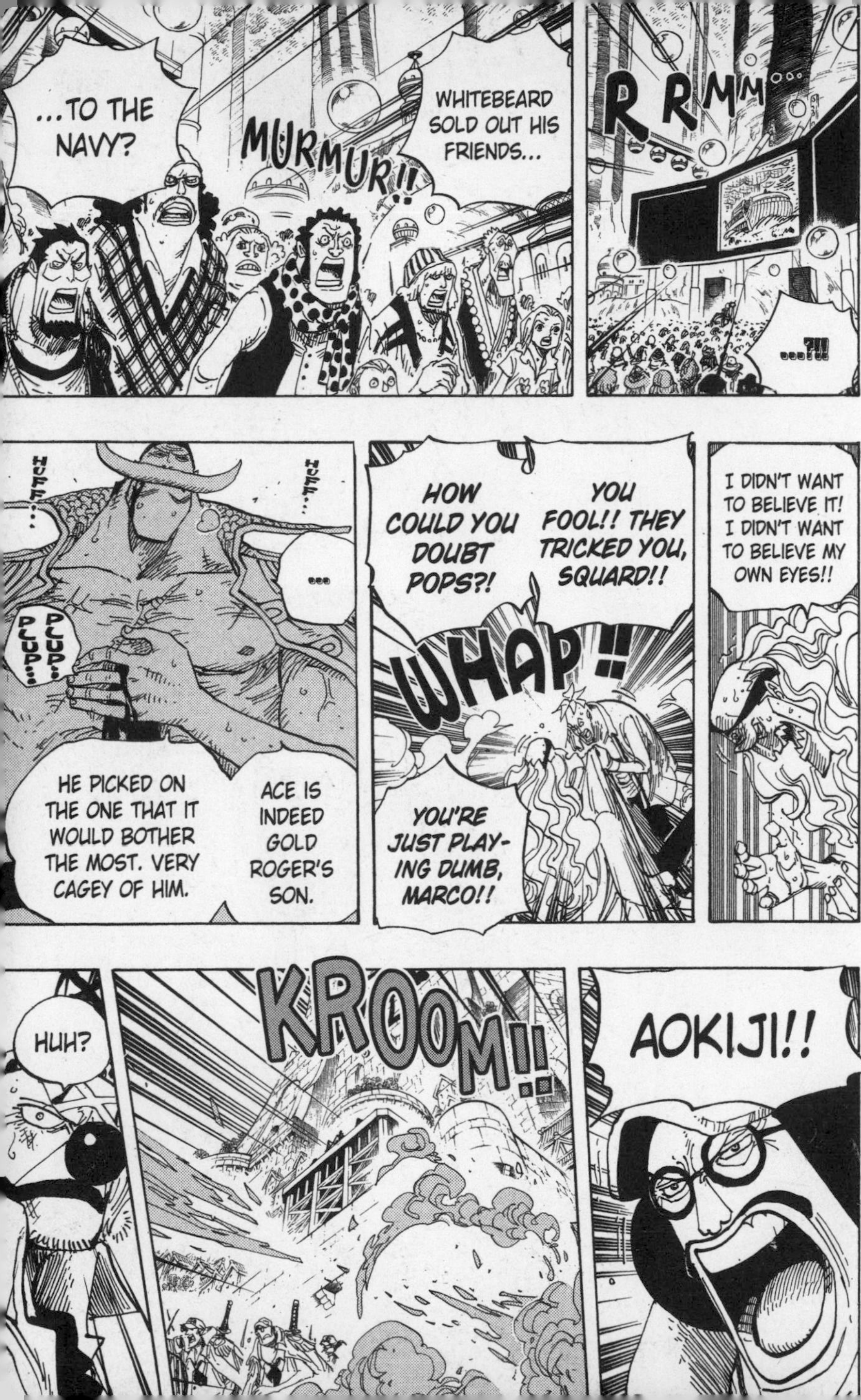
RRMM...
...?!!
WHITEBEARD SOLD OUT HIS FRIENDS...
MURMUR!!
...TO THE NAVY?
I DIDN'T WANT TO BELIEVE IT! I DIDN'T WANT TO BELIEVE MY OWN EYES!!
YOU FOOL!! THEY TRICKED YOU, SQUARD!!
HOW COULD YOU DOUBT POPS?!
WHAP!!
YOU'RE JUST PLAYING DUMB, MARCO!!
HUFF...
HUFF...
...
PLUP... PLUP...
ACE IS INDEED GOLD ROGER'S SON.
HE PICKED ON THE ONE THAT IT WOULD BOTHER THE MOST. VERY CAGEY OF HIM.
AOKIJI!!
KROOM!!
HUH?

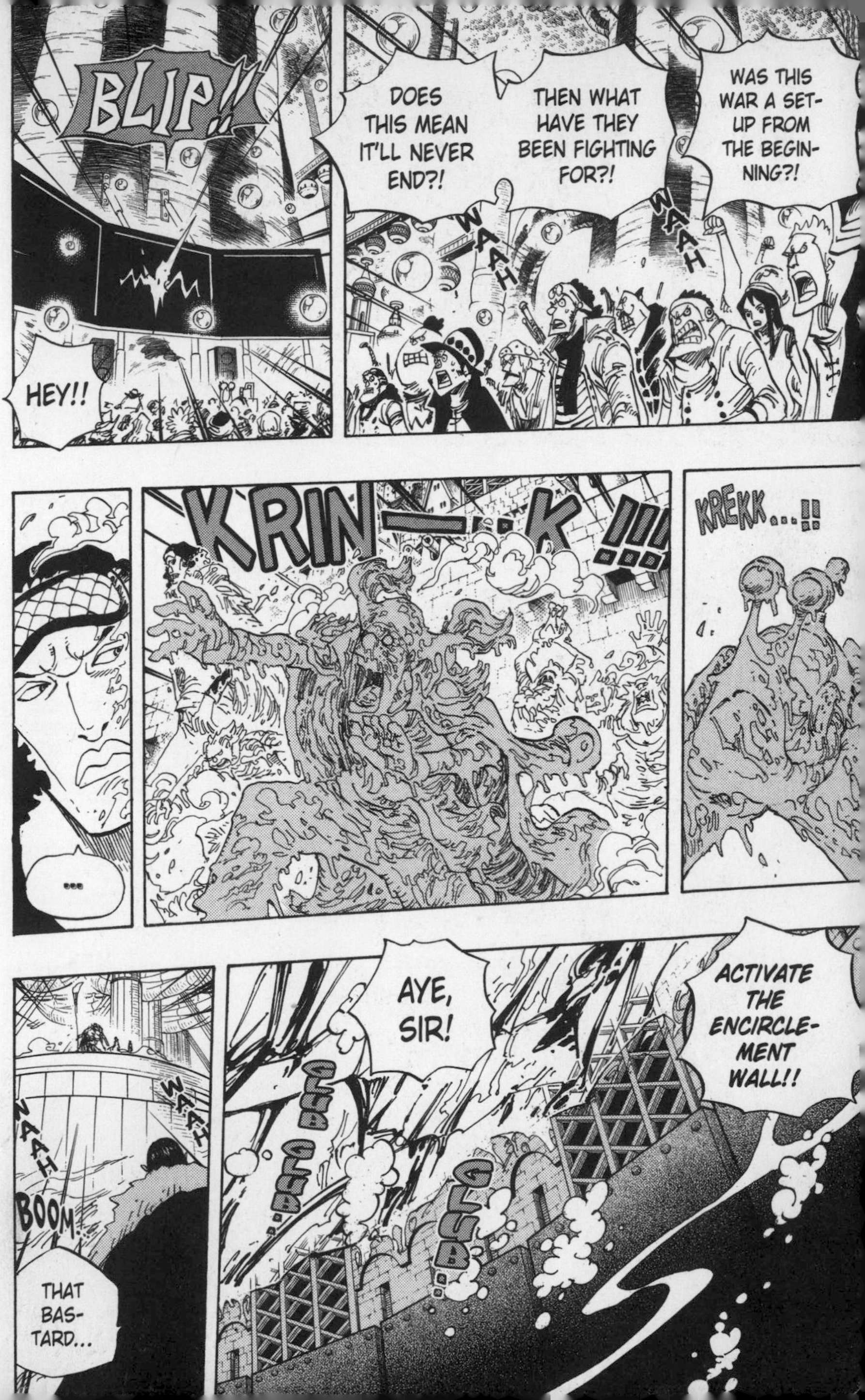
WAS THIS WAR A SET-UP FROM THE BEGINNING?!
THEN WHAT HAVE THEY BEEN FIGHTING FOR?!
DOES THIS MEAN IT'LL NEVER END?!
WAAH
WAAH
BLIP!!
HEY!!
KREKK...!!
KRIN—K!!!
...
ACTIVATE THE ENCIRCLEMENT WALL!!
AYE, SIR!
GLUB
GLUB
GLUB...
WAAH
WAAH
BOOM
THAT BASTARD...

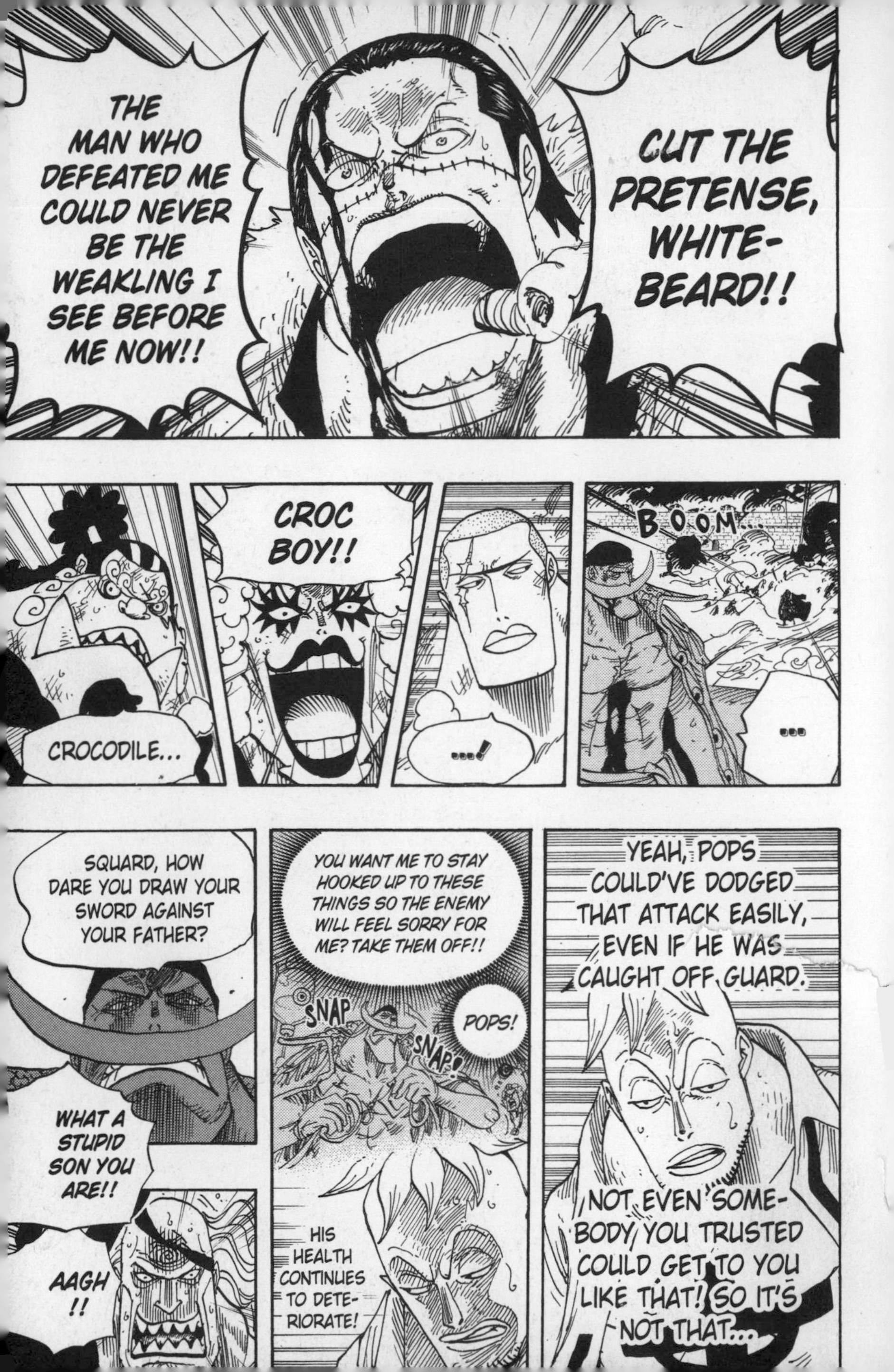
CUT THE PRETENSE, WHITE-BEARD!!
THE MAN WHO DEFEATED ME COULD NEVER BE THE WEAKLING I SEE BEFORE ME NOW!!
BOOM...
...
...!
CROC BOY!!
CROCODILE...
YEAH, POPS COULD'VE DODGED THAT ATTACK EASILY, EVEN IF HE WAS CAUGHT OFF GUARD.
NOT EVEN SOME-BODY YOU TRUSTED COULD GET TO YOU LIKE THAT! SO IT'S NOT THAT...
YOU WANT ME TO STAY HOOKED UP TO THESE THINGS SO THE ENEMY WILL FEEL SORRY FOR ME? TAKE THEM OFF!!
POPS!
SNAP
SNAP!
HIS HEALTH CONTINUES TO DETE-RIORATE!
SQUARD, HOW DARE YOU DRAW YOUR SWORD AGAINST YOUR FATHER?
WHAT A STUPID SON YOU ARE!!
AAGH!!

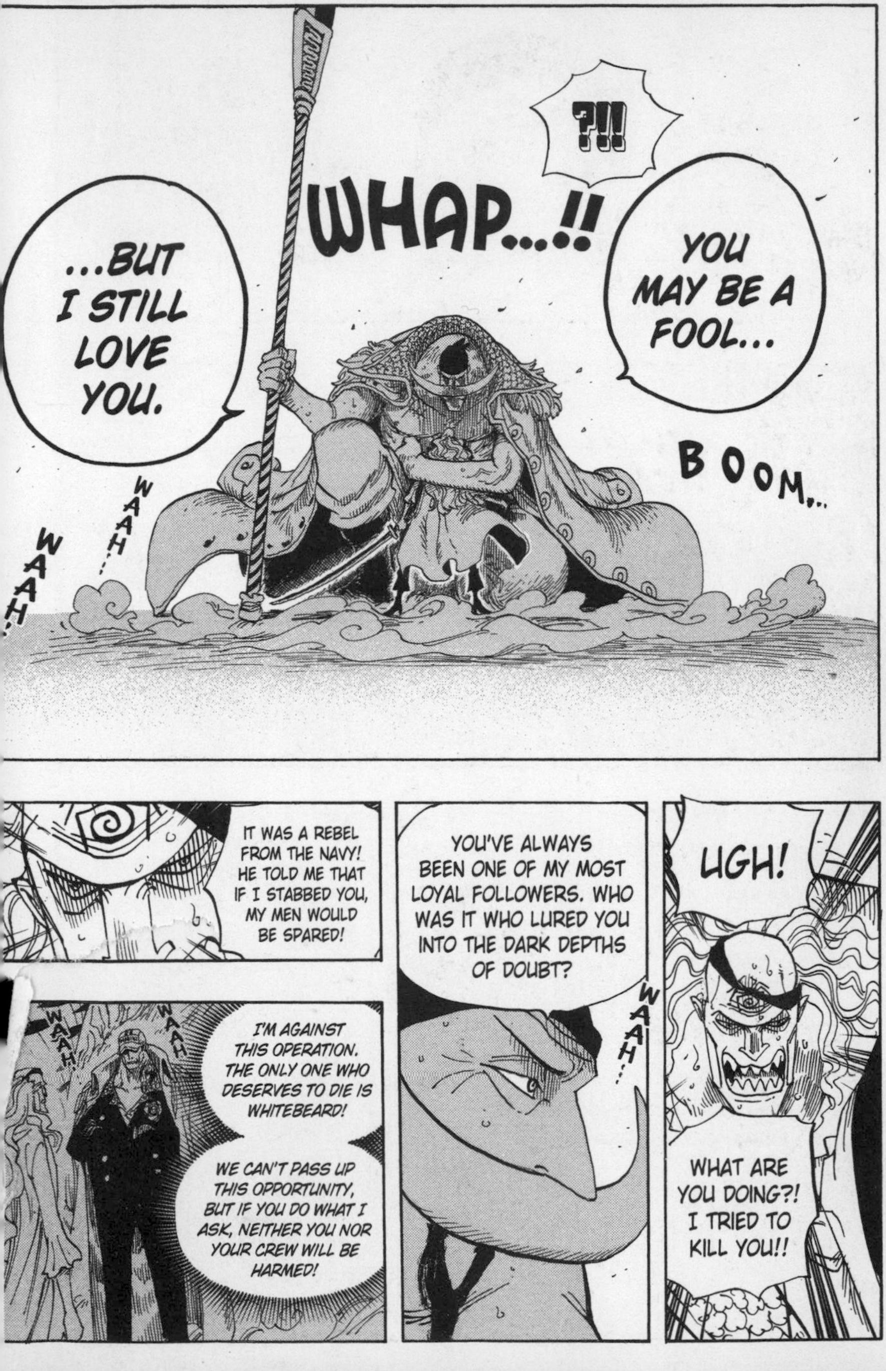
?!!
YOU MAY BE A FOOL...
WHAP...!!
...BUT I STILL LOVE YOU.
BOOM...
WAAH...
WAAH!
UGH!
WHAT ARE YOU DOING?! I TRIED TO KILL YOU!!
YOU'VE ALWAYS BEEN ONE OF MY MOST LOYAL FOLLOWERS. WHO WAS IT WHO LURED YOU INTO THE DARK DEPTHS OF DOUBT?
WAAH...
IT WAS A REBEL FROM THE NAVY! HE TOLD ME THAT IF I STABBED YOU, MY MEN WOULD BE SPARED!
WAAH
WAAH!
I'M AGAINST THIS OPERATION. THE ONLY ONE WHO DESERVES TO DIE IS WHITEBEARD!
WE CAN'T PASS UP THIS OPPORTUNITY, BUT IF YOU DO WHAT I ASK, NEITHER YOU NOR YOUR CREW WILL BE HARMED!

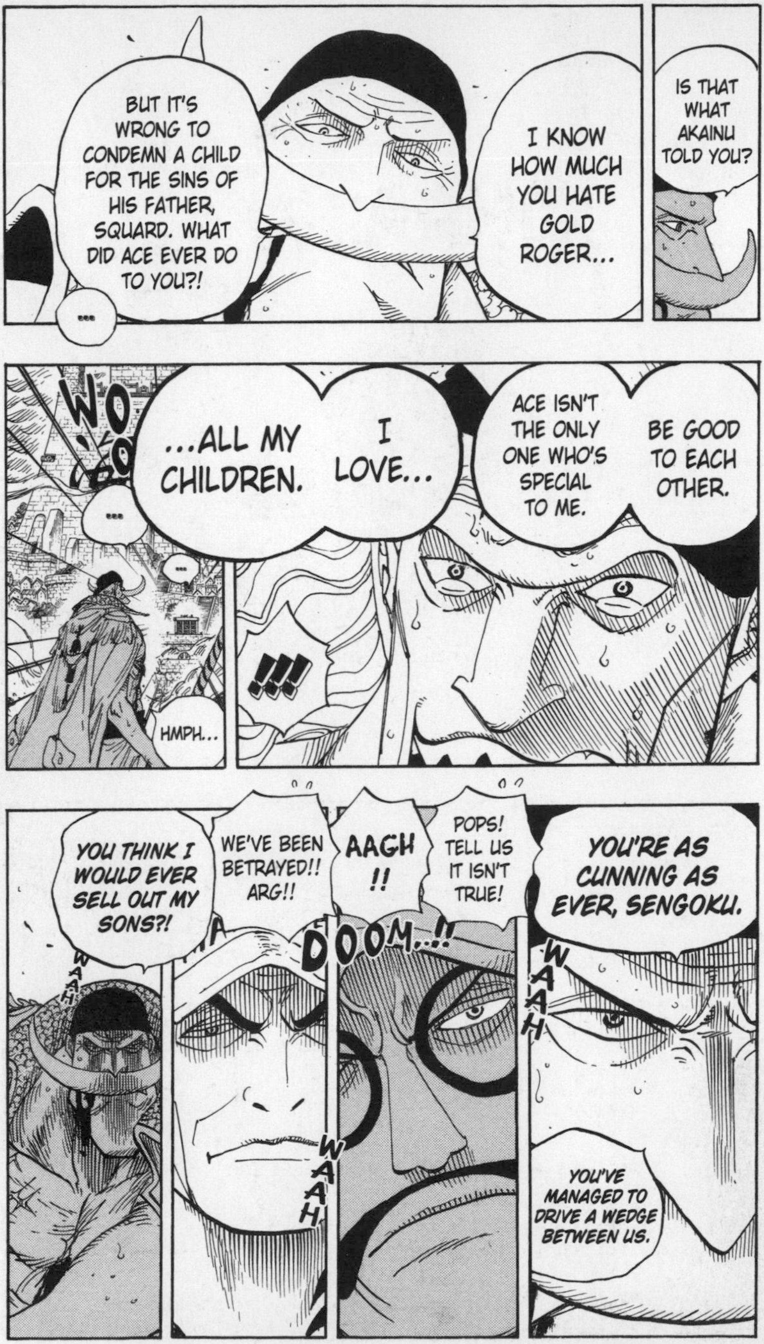
IS THAT WHAT AKAINU TOLD YOU?
I KNOW HOW MUCH YOU HATE GOLD ROGER...
BUT IT'S WRONG TO CONDEMN A CHILD FOR THE SINS OF HIS FATHER, SQUARD. WHAT DID ACE EVER DO TO YOU?!
...
BE GOOD TO EACH OTHER.
ACE ISN'T THE ONLY ONE WHO'S SPECIAL TO ME.
I LOVE...
...ALL MY CHILDREN.
!!!!
WO
...
...
HMPH...
YOU'RE AS CUNNING AS EVER, SENGOKU.
WAAH
YOU'VE MANAGED TO DRIVE A WEDGE BETWEEN US.
POPS! TELL US IT ISN'T TRUE!
AAGH !!
DOOM..!!
WAAH
WE'VE BEEN BETRAYED!! ARG!!
YOU THINK I WOULD EVER SELL OUT MY SONS?!
WAAH

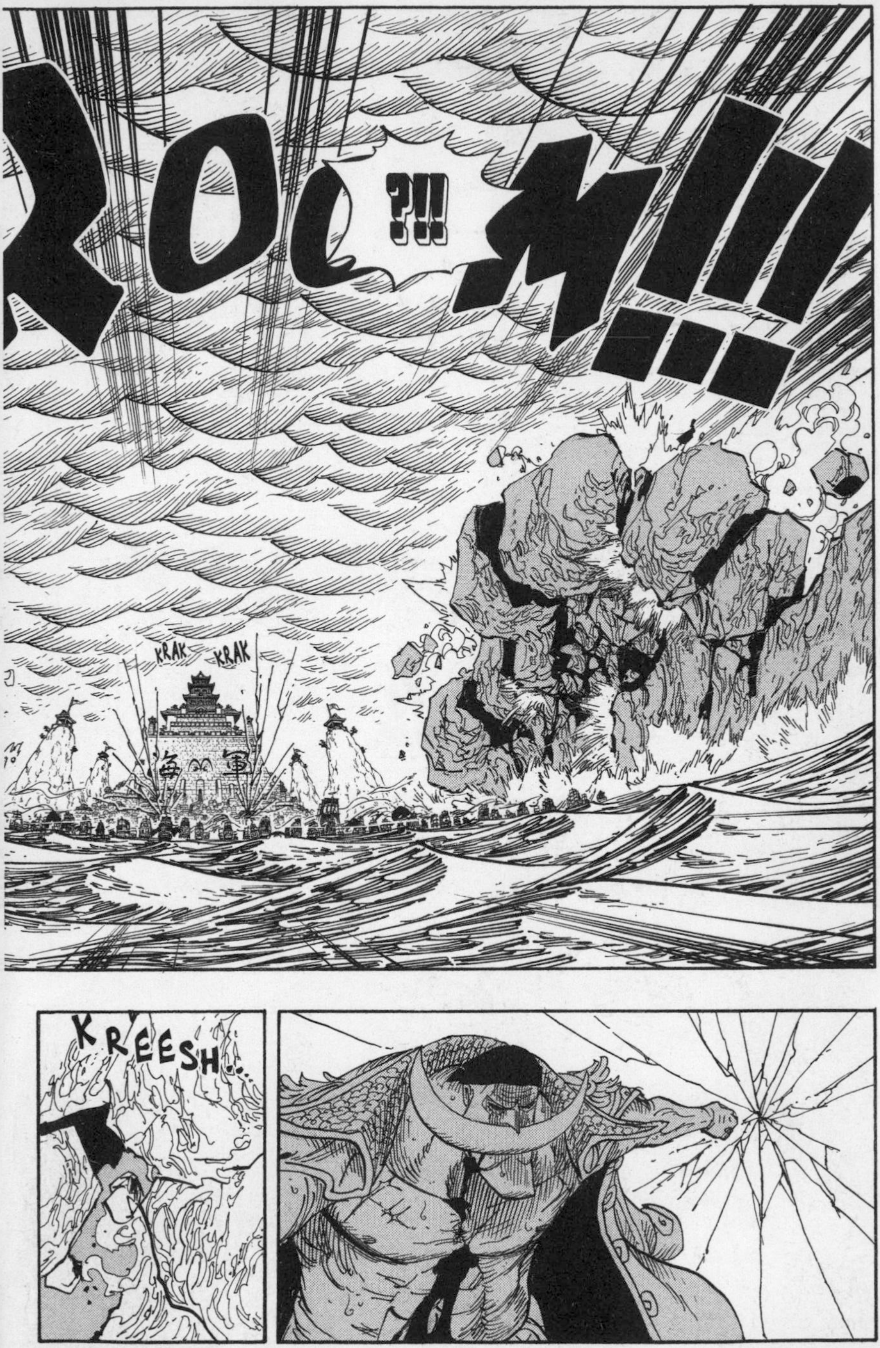
?!!
KRAK
KRAK
海軍
KREESH...

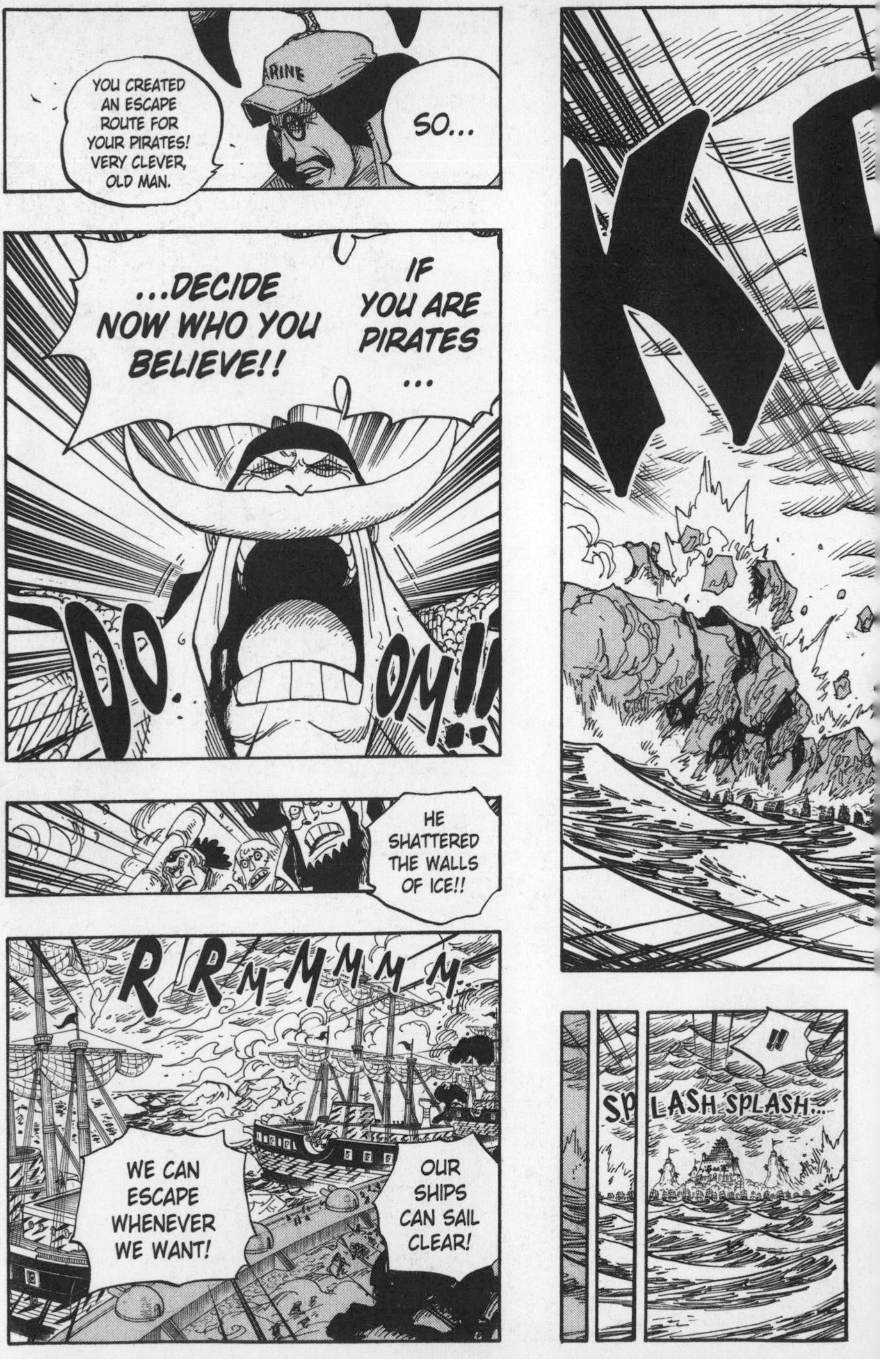
!!
SPLASH SPLASH...
SO...
YOU CREATED AN ESCAPE ROUTE FOR YOUR PIRATES! VERY CLEVER, OLD MAN.
IF YOU ARE PIRATES ...
...DECIDE NOW WHO YOU BELIEVE!!
DOOM!!
HE SHATTERED THE WALLS OF ICE!!
RRRMMMMM
OUR SHIPS CAN SAIL CLEAR!
WE CAN ESCAPE WHENEVER WE WANT!

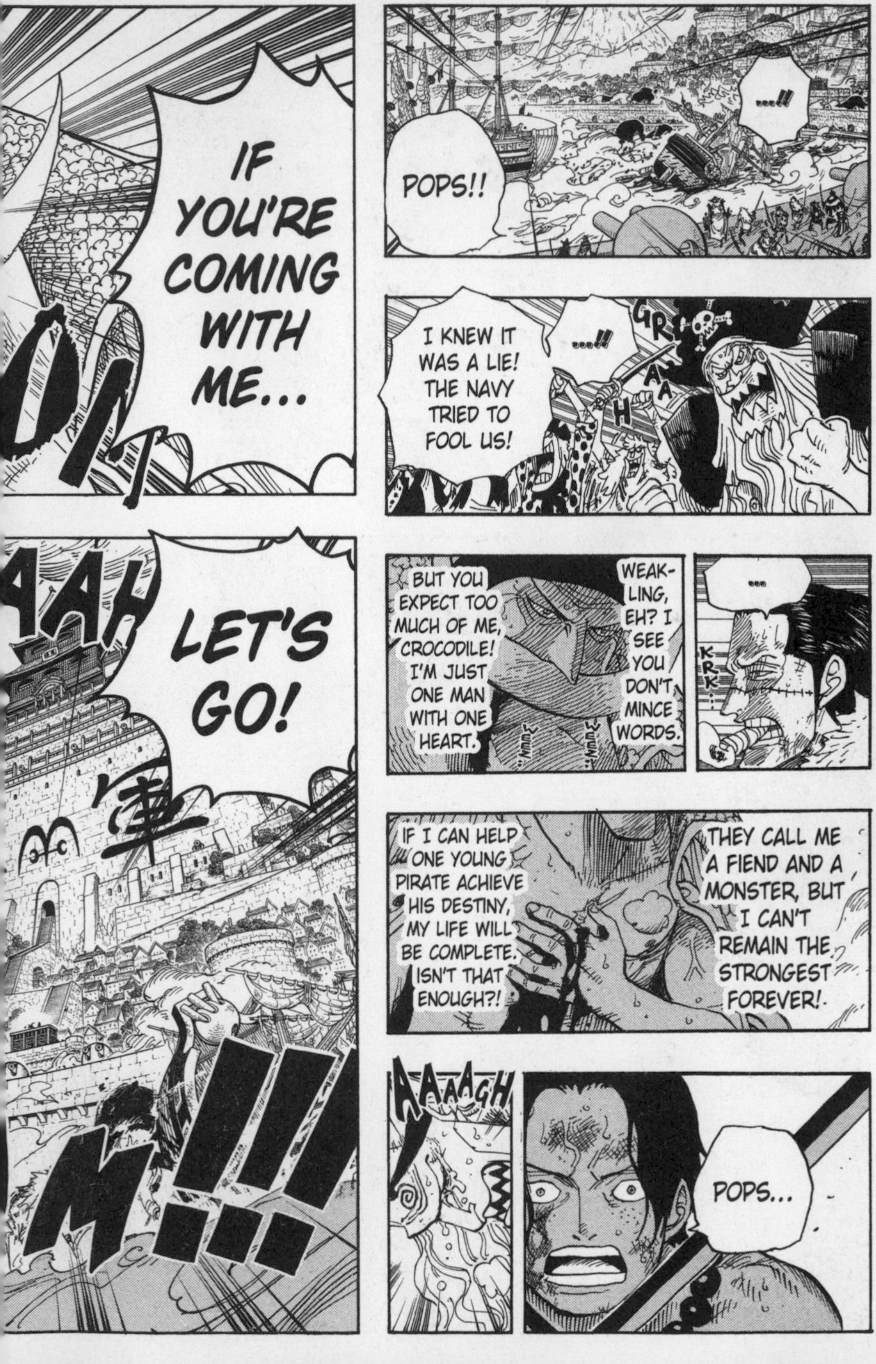

...!!
POPS!!
GRAAAH
...!!
I KNEW IT WAS A LIE! THE NAVY TRIED TO FOOL US!
IF YOU'RE COMING WITH ME...
...
KRK
WEAKLING, EH? I SEE YOU DON'T MINCE WORDS.
BUT YOU EXPECT TOO MUCH OF ME, CROCODILE! I'M JUST ONE MAN WITH ONE HEART.
WEEZ...
THEY CALL ME A FIEND AND A MONSTER, BUT I CAN'T REMAIN THE STRONGEST FOREVER!
IF I CAN HELP ONE YOUNG PIRATE ACHIEVE HIS DESTINY, MY LIFE WILL BE COMPLETE. ISN'T THAT ENOUGH?!
POPS...
AAAAGH
LET'S GO!
AAH

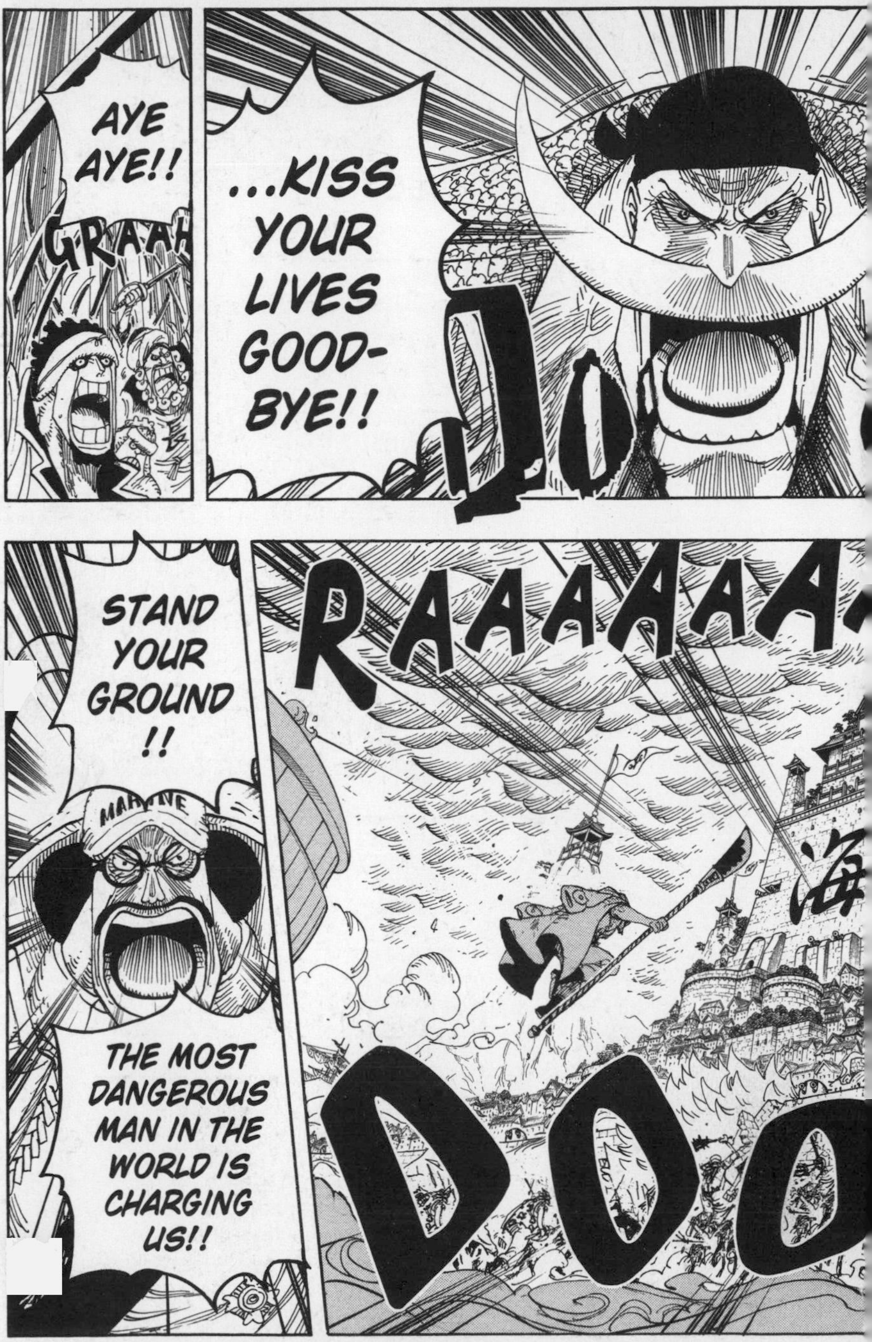
...KISS YOUR LIVES GOOD-BYE!!
AYE AYE!!
GRAAH
RAAAAAA
DOO
海
STAND YOUR GROUND!!
THE MOST DANGEROUS MAN IN THE WORLD IS CHARGING US!!

SBS Question Corner

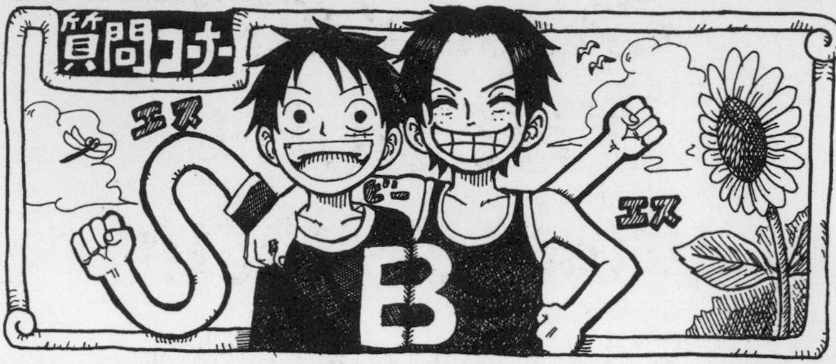
質問コーナー
エス
ビー
エス

(Negi, Saga)

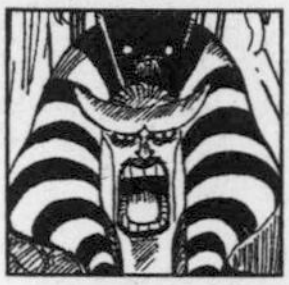

Reader(Q): I'm going to start SBS now.
Whoops, my ambition slipped out.

--Hanko

Oda(A): Ambition? You just granted your wish! It is now officially started.

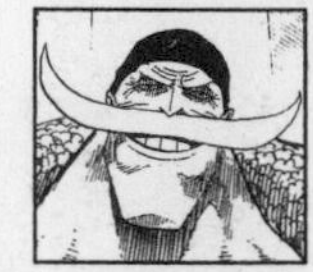

Q: So when is Whitebeard going to use the boomerang under his nose?

--Chi-chan

A: Hmm, well... Probably when he goes to the park with his dog.
"Go get it, Stephen!" *Swirl*
"Woof?!"
"It's not a Frisbee so it comes back! Ga ha ha ha!"
Wait, what?!

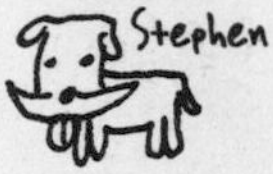
Stephen

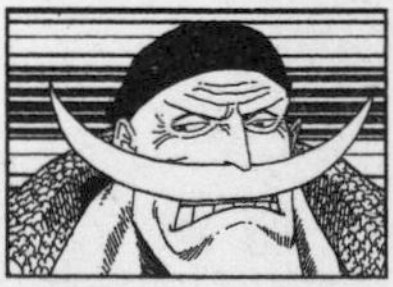

Q: I have a question. Does a banana fit inside Whitebeard's beard? Is that thing like a "banana pouch"?

--Samsam

A: Yup. If you open the zipper on the back, you'll find some bananas. You can line them up, three on the right side and three on the left, bringing it up to a total of six bananas. "Come on, men! It's time for a battle! Have some bananas first! Ga ha ha ha!" What do you people think Whitebeard is, anyway?

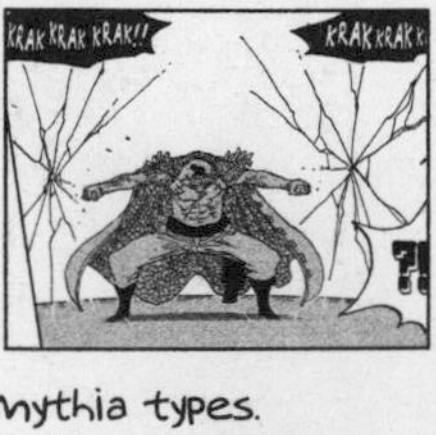
KRAK KRAK KRAK!!
KRAK KRAK K
?!

Q: Hello, Mr. Oda! I have a question. Is Whitebeard, Edward Newgate, a Logia type? Or a Paramythia type? Whitebeard didn't freeze even when he was attacked by Aokiji. Personally, I think he's a Logia.

--NY

A: I guess it's hard to see, but he's a Paramythia type. The Tremor-Tremor Fruit is considered to be one of the most powerful fruits among the Paramythia types. Because he's an "Earthquake Human," you might think he would be a Logia type, but in that case, Whitebeard himself would have to be an earthquake. Whitebeard can cause earthquakes. In other words, he can cause tremors or shaking that start these earthquakes. In short, he's a Paramythia type that's as powerful as Logia types.

Chapter 564: THE MAN WHO SHOOK THE WORLD

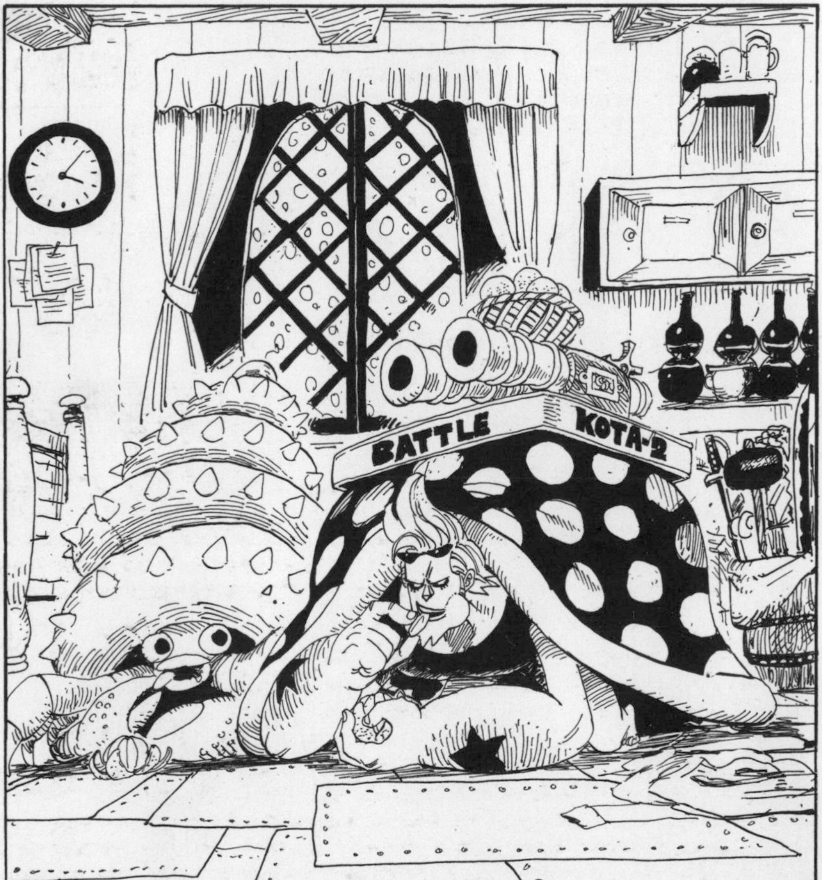
BATTLE KOTA-2

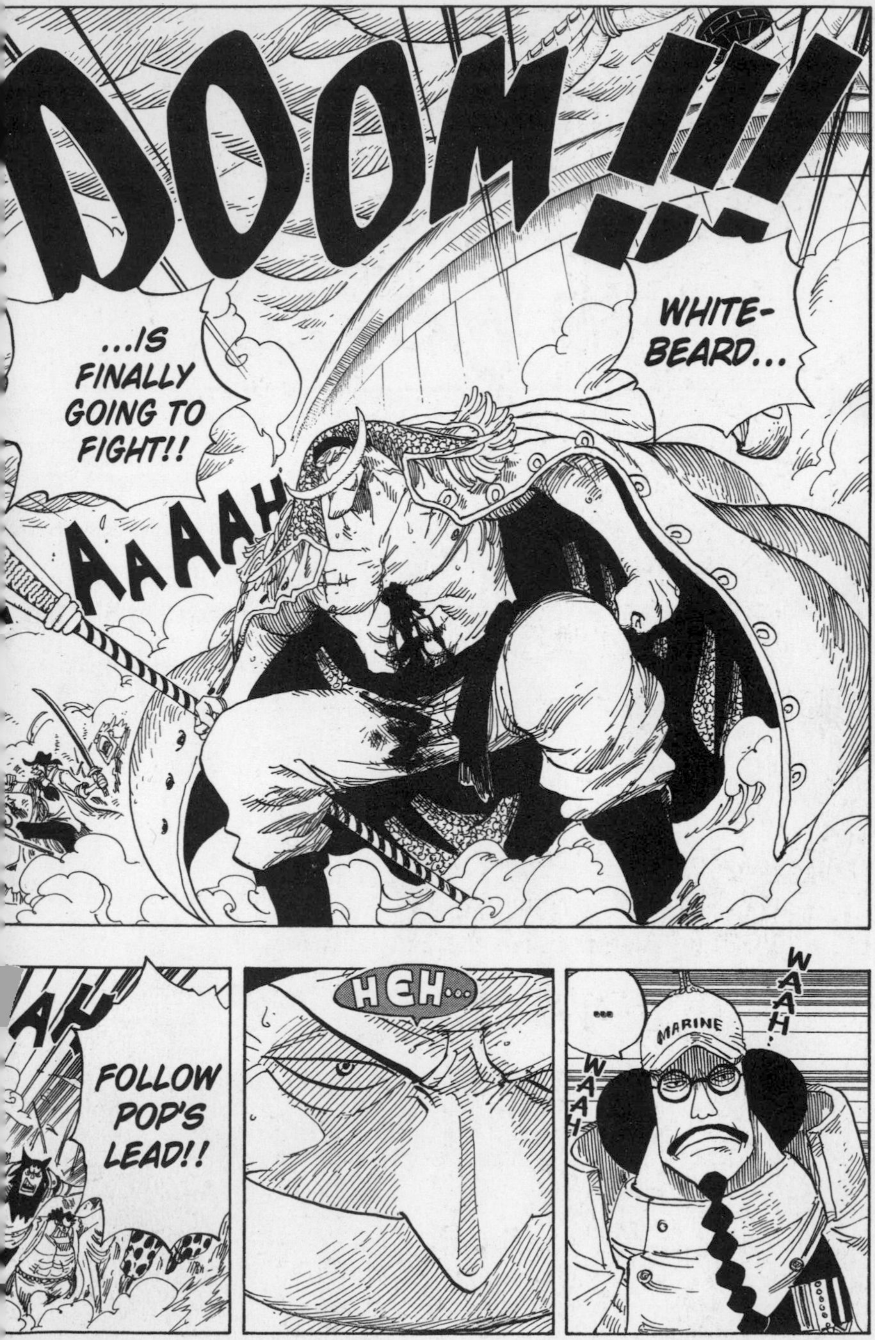
DOOM!!!
WHITE-BEARD...
...IS FINALLY GOING TO FIGHT!!
AAAAH
WAAH..
...
WAAH
HEH...
AH
FOLLOW POP'S LEAD!!

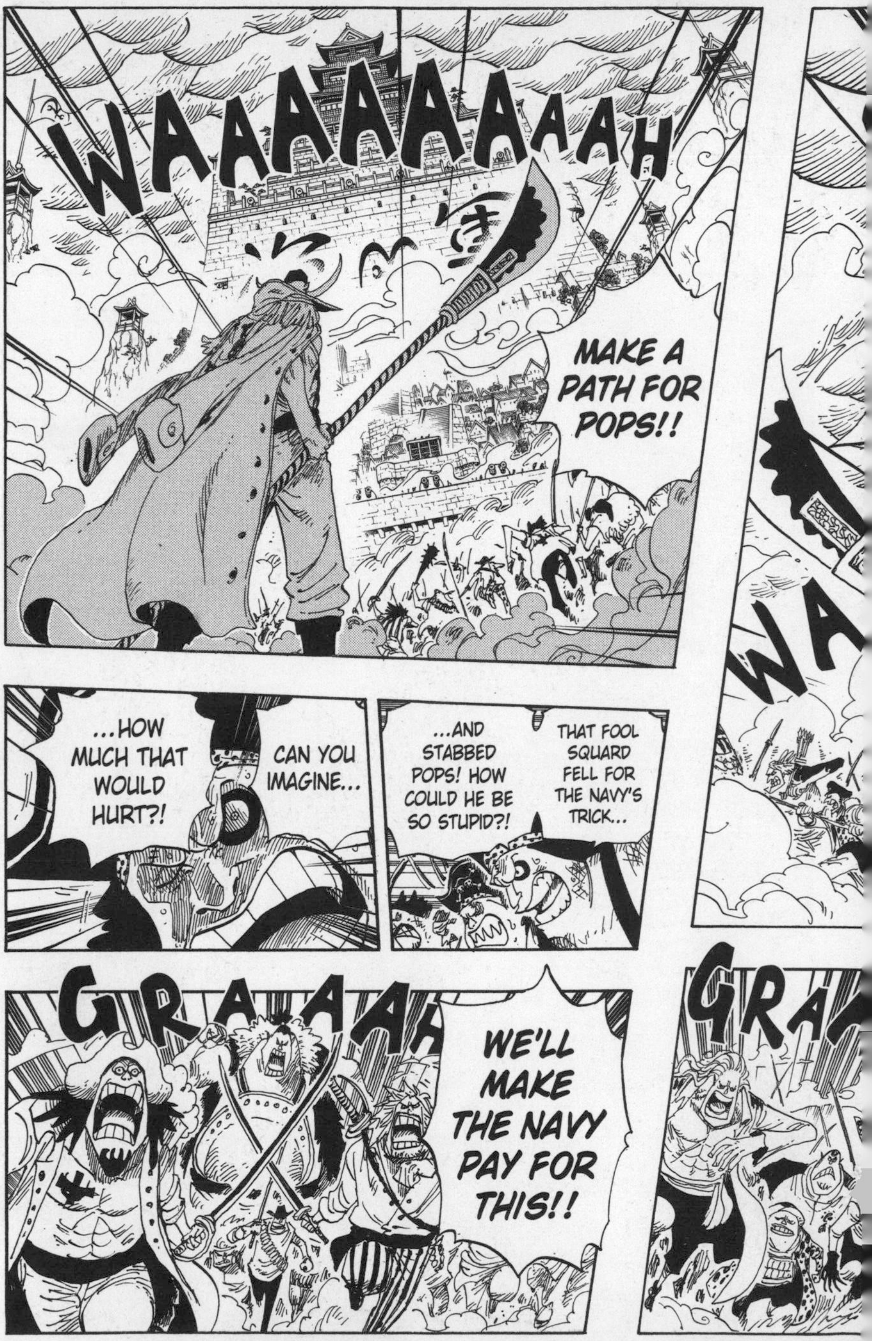
WAAAAAAAAH
MAKE A PATH FOR POPS!!
THAT FOOL SQUAD FELL FOR THE NAVY'S TRICK...
...AND STABBED POPS! HOW COULD HE BE SO STUPID?!
CAN YOU IMAGINE...
...HOW MUCH THAT WOULD HURT?!
GRAAAAH
WE'LL MAKE THE NAVY PAY FOR THIS!!

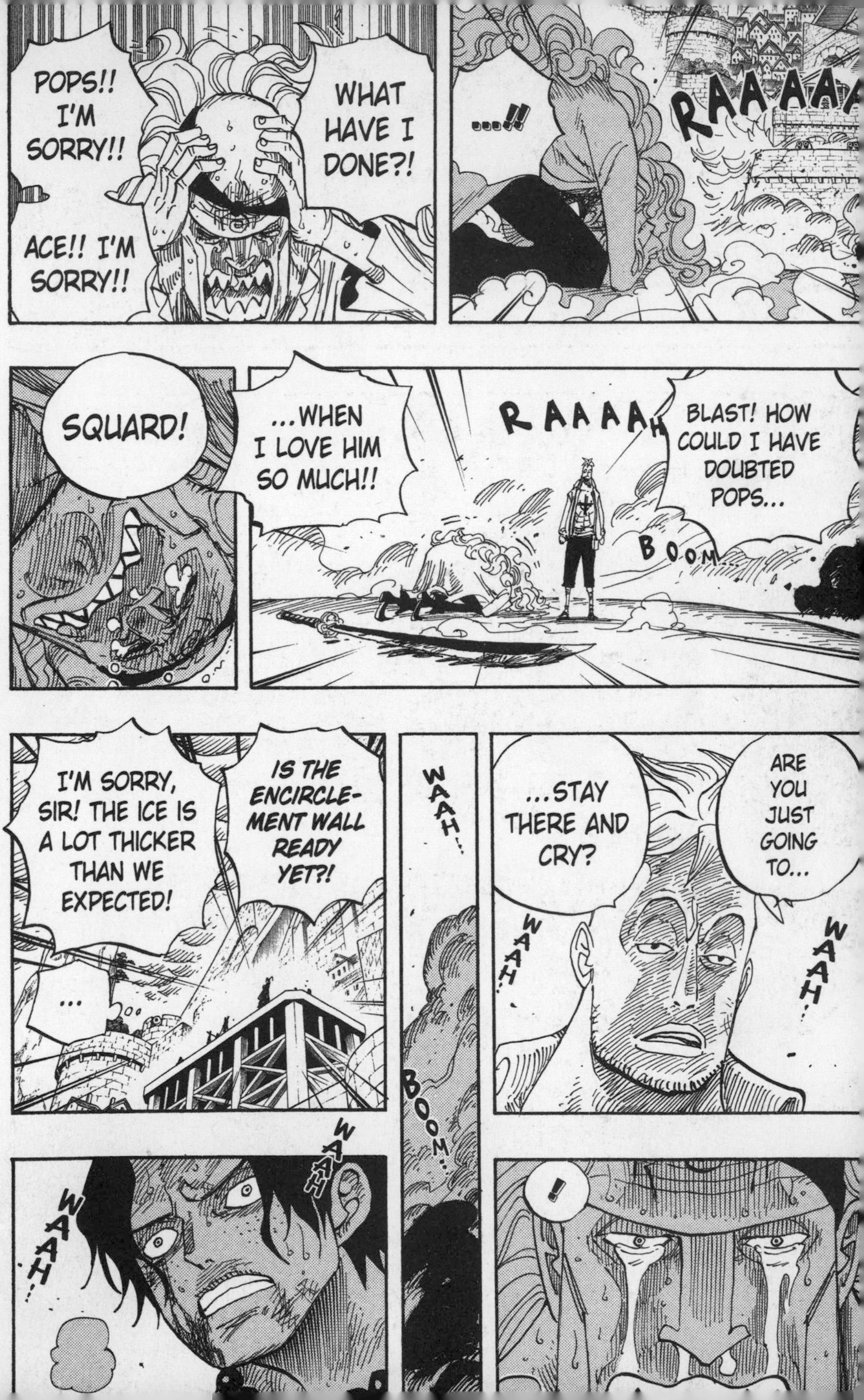

...!!
RAAAA
WHAT HAVE I DONE?!
POPS!! I'M SORRY!!
ACE!! I'M SORRY!!
BLAST! HOW COULD I HAVE DOUBTED POPS...
RAAAAH
...WHEN I LOVE HIM SO MUCH!!
BOOM...
SQUARD!
ARE YOU JUST GOING TO...
...STAY THERE AND CRY?
WAAH...
WAAH...
WAAH...
BOOM...
IS THE ENCIRCLEMENT WALL READY YET?!
I'M SORRY, SIR! THE ICE IS A LOT THICKER THAN WE EXPECTED!
...
!
WAAH
WAAH...

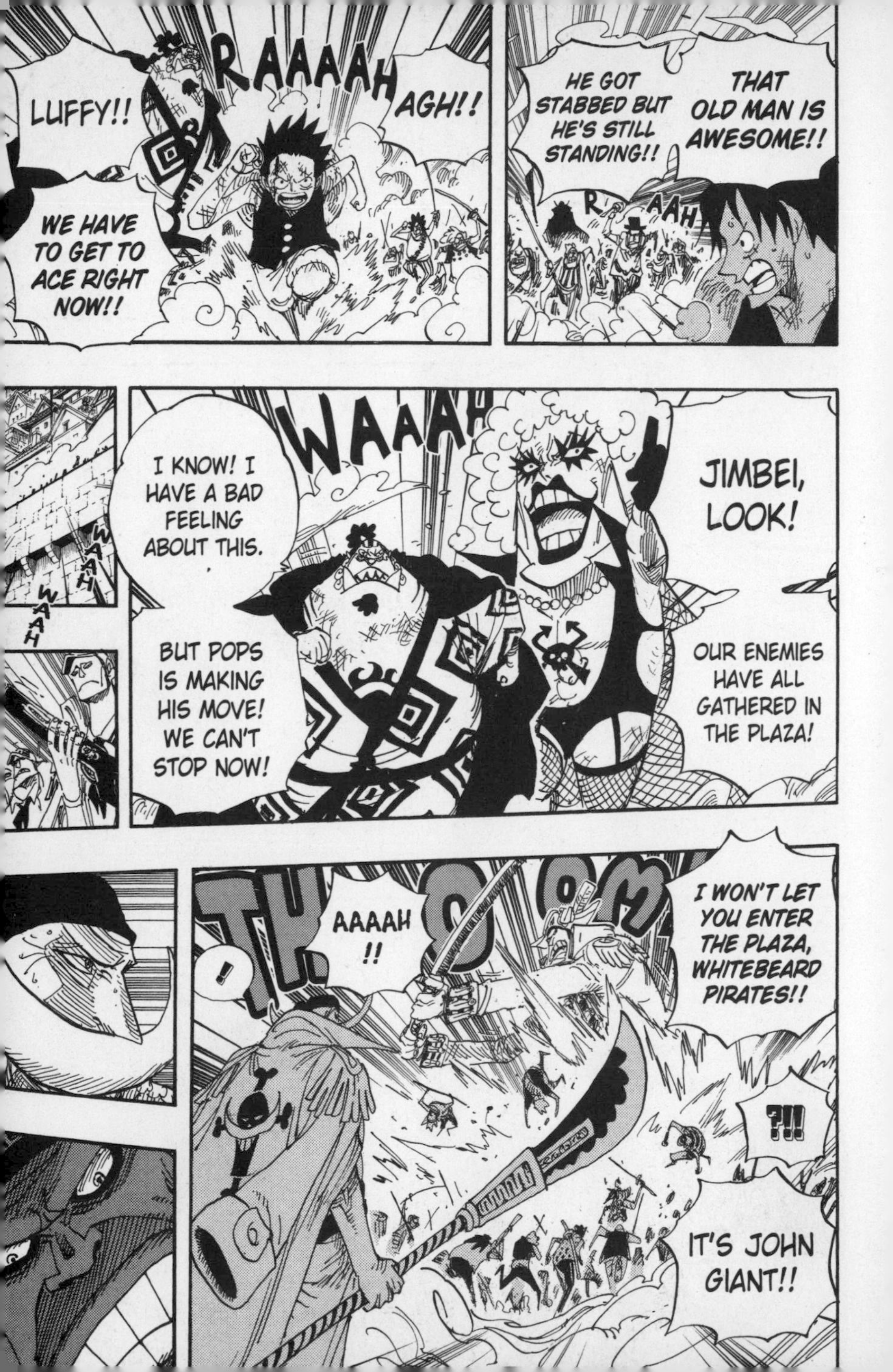
THAT OLD MAN IS AWESOME!!
HE GOT STABBED BUT HE'S STILL STANDING!!
RAAH
RAAAAAH AGH!!
LUFFY!!
WE HAVE TO GET TO ACE RIGHT NOW!!
JIMBEI, LOOK!
WAAAH
I KNOW! I HAVE A BAD FEELING ABOUT THIS.
OUR ENEMIES HAVE ALL GATHERED IN THE PLAZA!
BUT POPS IS MAKING HIS MOVE! WE CAN'T STOP NOW!
WAAH
WAAH
I WON'T LET YOU ENTER THE PLAZA, WHITEBEARD PIRATES!!
THOOM
AAAAH!!
!
?!!
IT'S JOHN GIANT!!

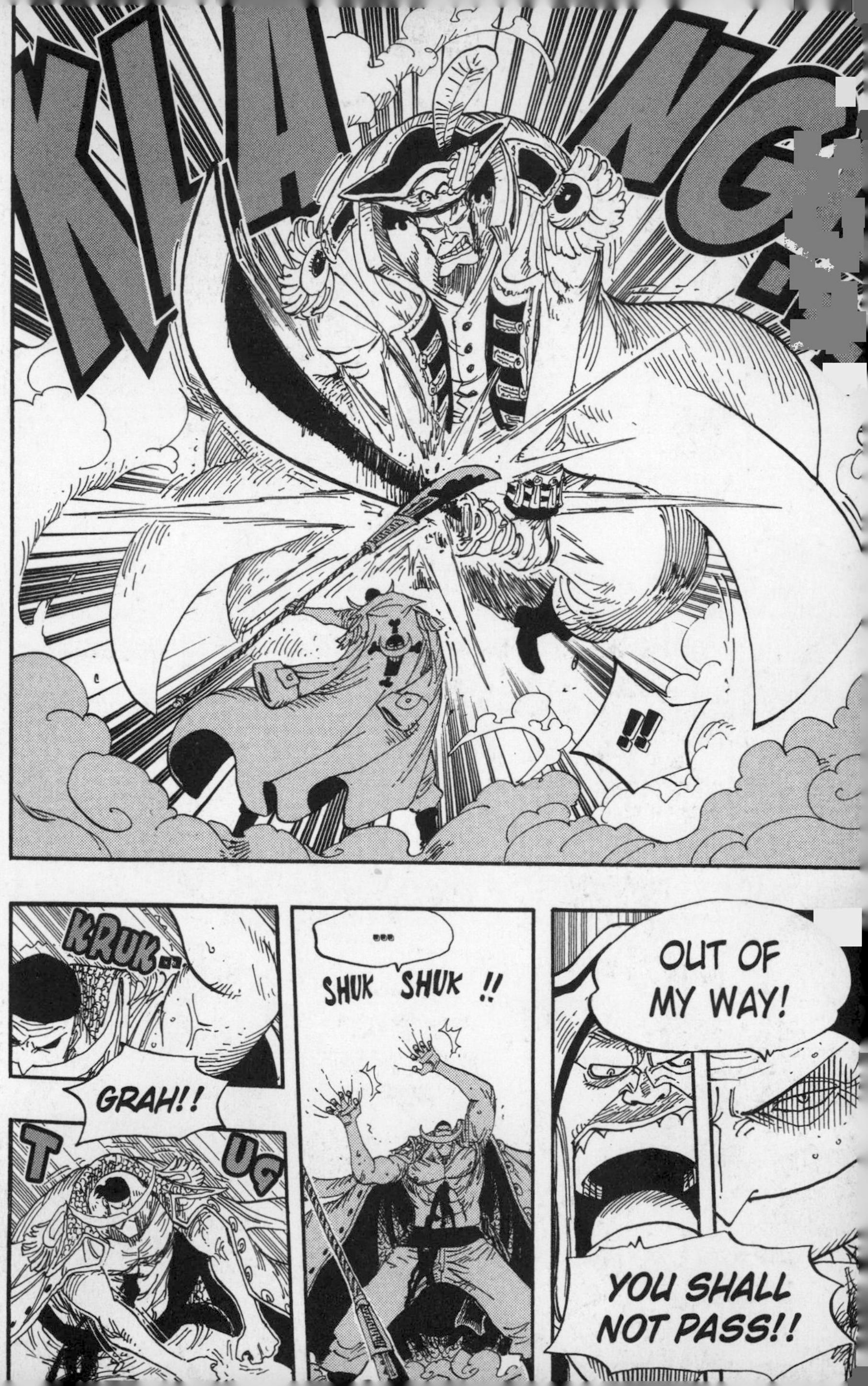
!!
OUT OF MY WAY!
YOU SHALL NOT PASS!!
...
SHUK SHUK !!
KRUK..
GRAH!!
T UG

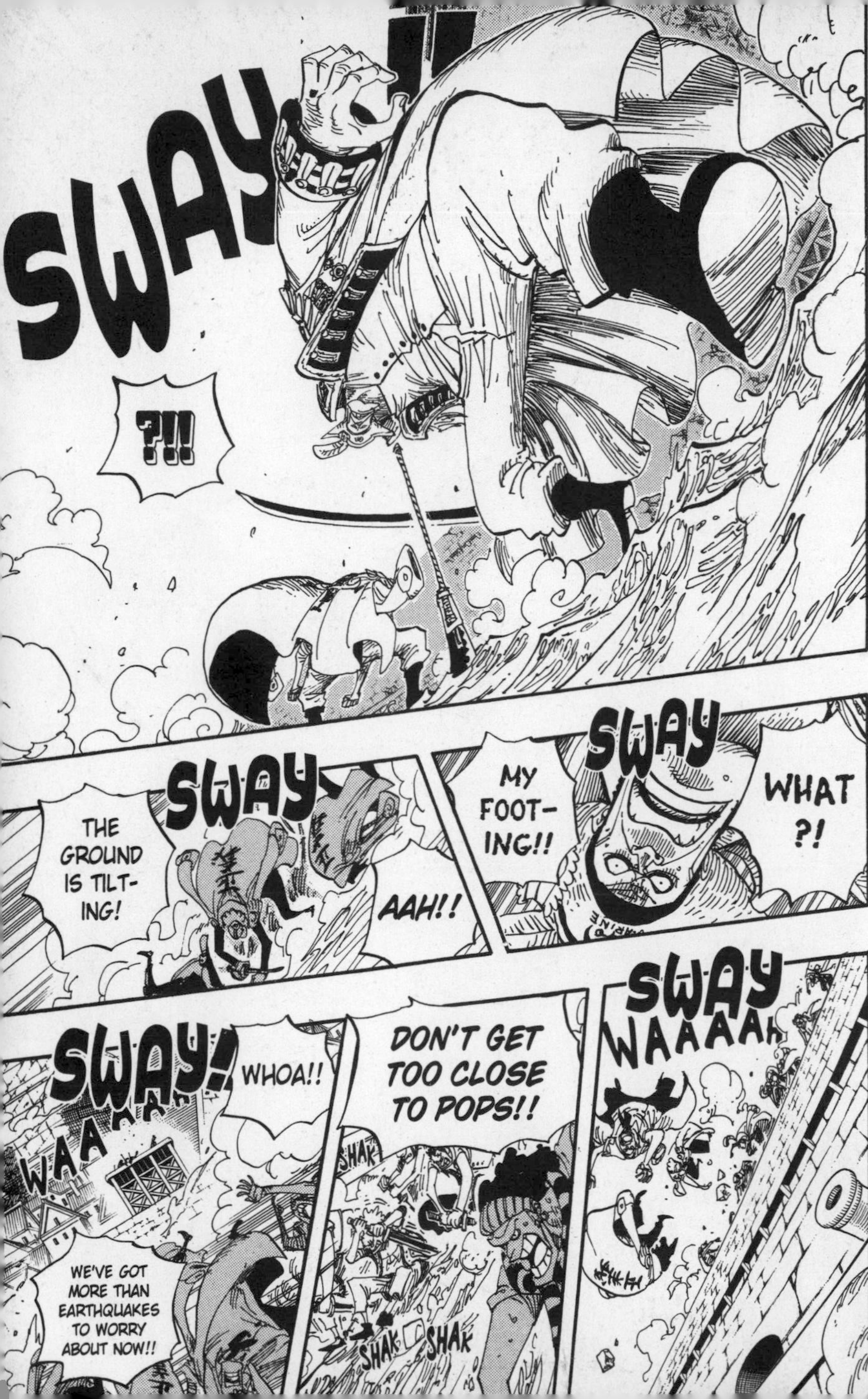
SWAY!!
?!!
SWAY
WHAT ?!
MY FOOTING!!
SWAY
THE GROUND IS TILTING!
AAH!!
SWAY
WAAAAH
DON'T GET TOO CLOSE TO POPS!!
SHAK
SHAK
SHAK
SWAY!
WHOA!!
WAAAA
WE'VE GOT MORE THAN EARTHQUAKES TO WORRY ABOUT NOW!!

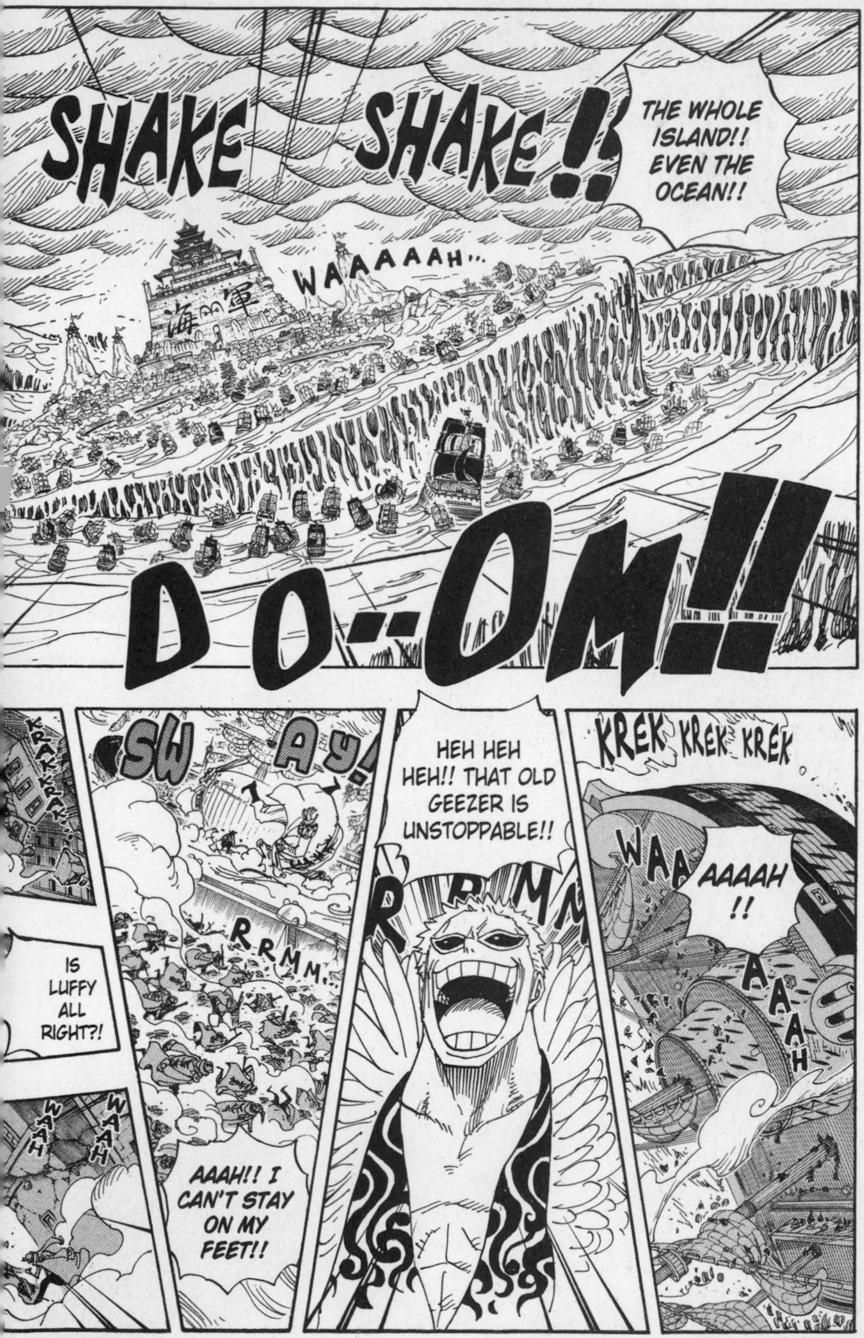
THE WHOLE ISLAND!! EVEN THE OCEAN!!
SHAKE SHAKE!!
WAAAAAH...
D O--OM!!
KREK KREK KREK
WAAAAAAH!!
AAAAH
HEH HEH HEH!! THAT OLD GEEZER IS UNSTOPPABLE!!
RRMM
SWAY!
RRMM...
AAAH!! I CAN'T STAY ON MY FEET!!
KRAKKRAK
IS LUFFY ALL RIGHT?!
WAAH
WAAH

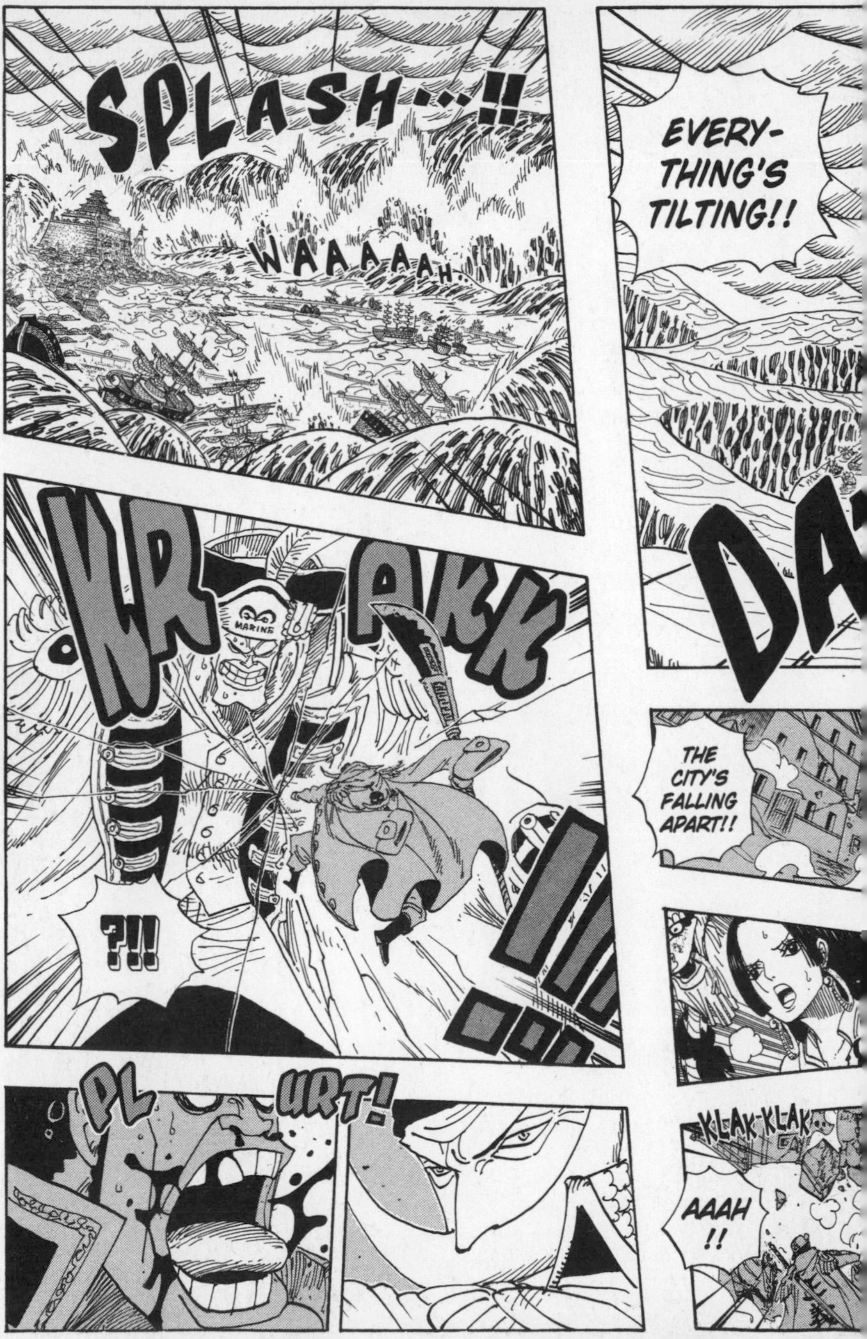

EVERY-THING'S TILTING!!
DA
THE CITY'S FALLING APART!!
KLAK KLAK...
AAAH!!
SPLASH...!!
WAAAAAH...
KRAKK
?!!
PLURT!

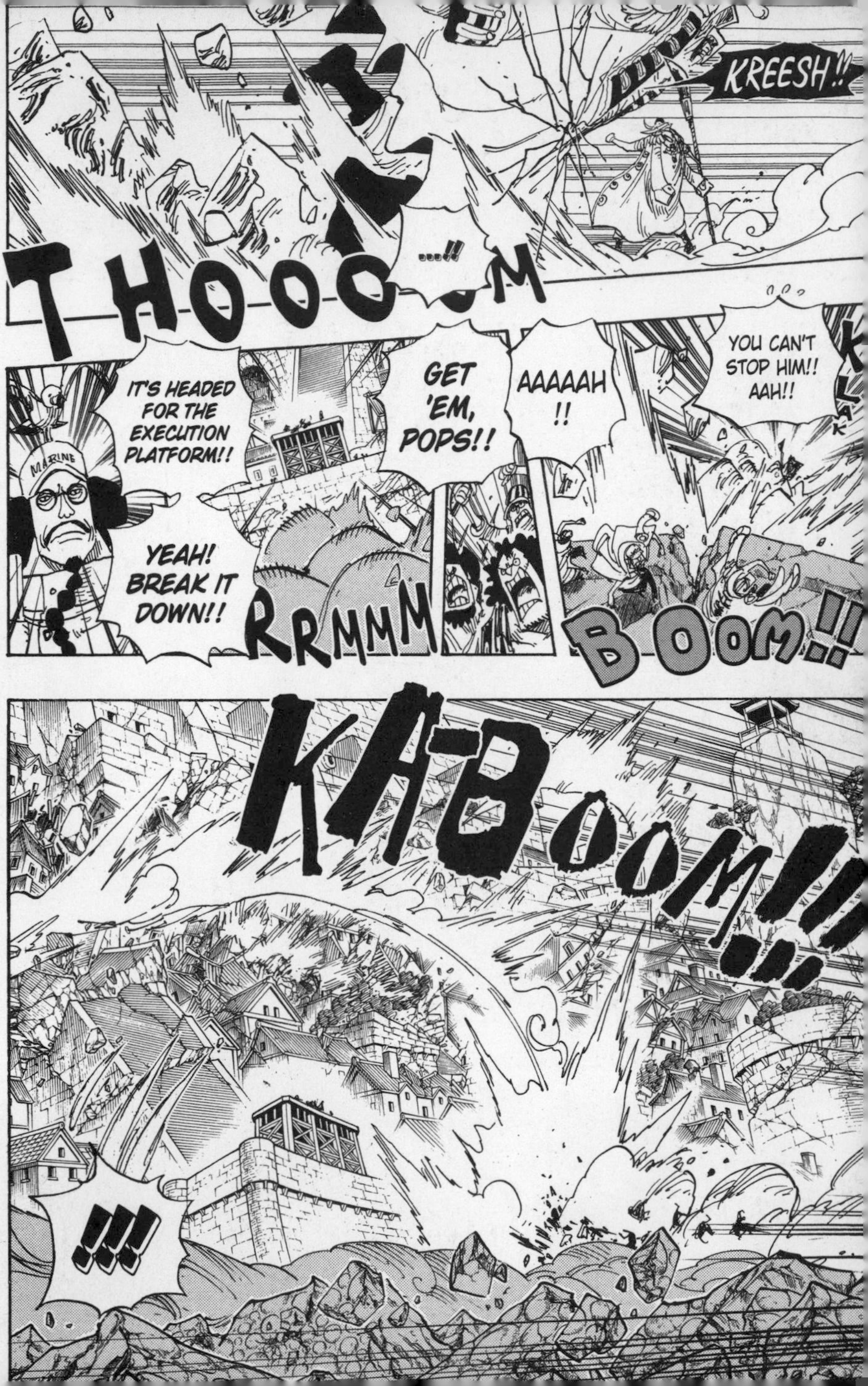
KREESH!!
THOOOM...!!
YOU CAN'T STOP HIM!! AAH!!
KLAK
BOOM!!
AAAAAH!!
GET 'EM, POPS!!
RRMMM
IT'S HEADED FOR THE EXECUTION PLATFORM!!
YEAH! BREAK IT DOWN!!
KABOOM!!!
!!!

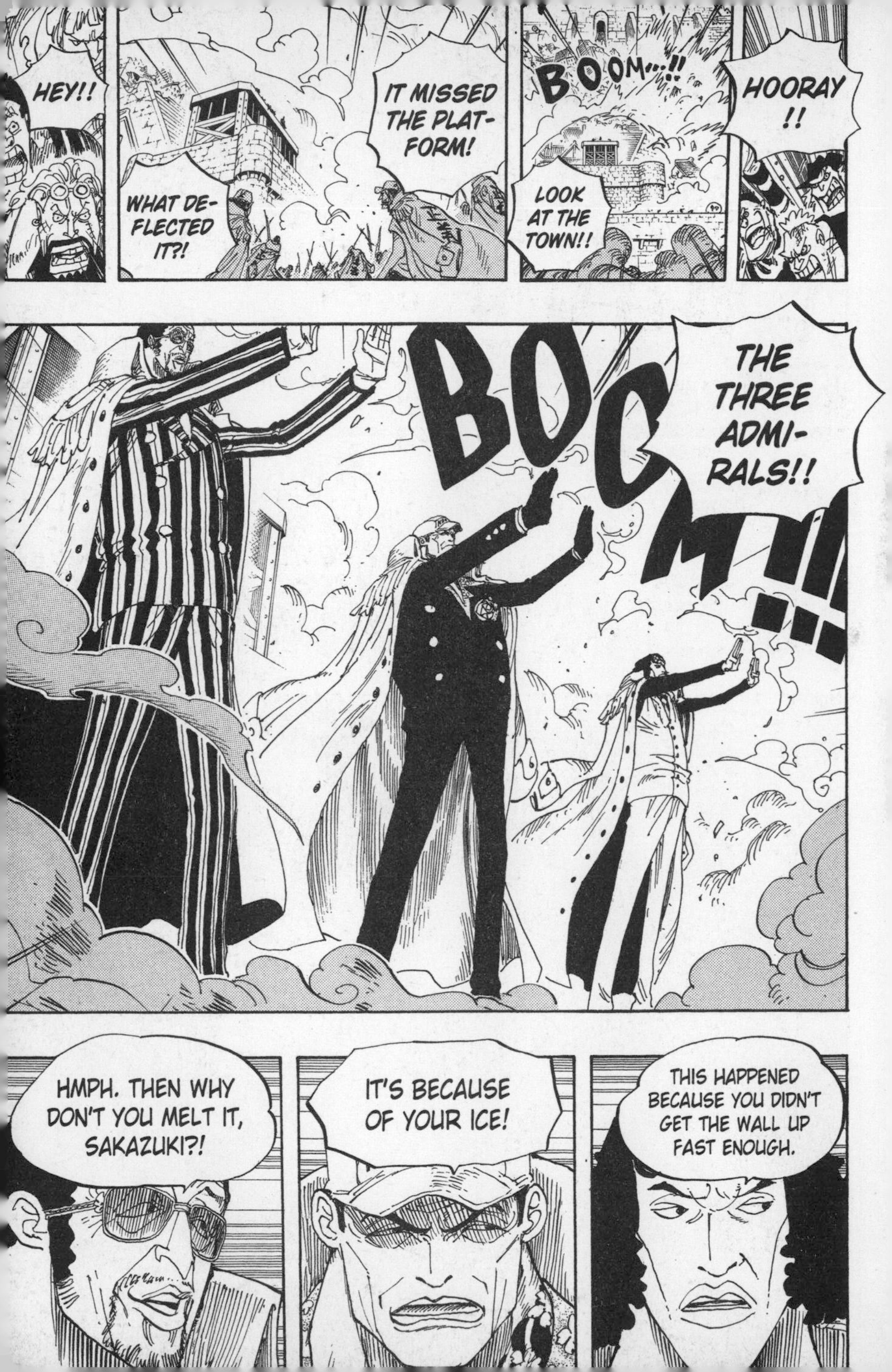
HOORAY !!
BOOM...!!
LOOK AT THE TOWN!!
IT MISSED THE PLAT-FORM!
WHAT DE-FLECTED IT?!
HEY!!
THE THREE ADMI-RALS!!
BOOM!!!
THIS HAPPENED BECAUSE YOU DIDN'T GET THE WALL UP FAST ENOUGH.
IT'S BECAUSE OF YOUR ICE!
HMPH. THEN WHY DON'T YOU MELT IT, SAKAZUKI?!

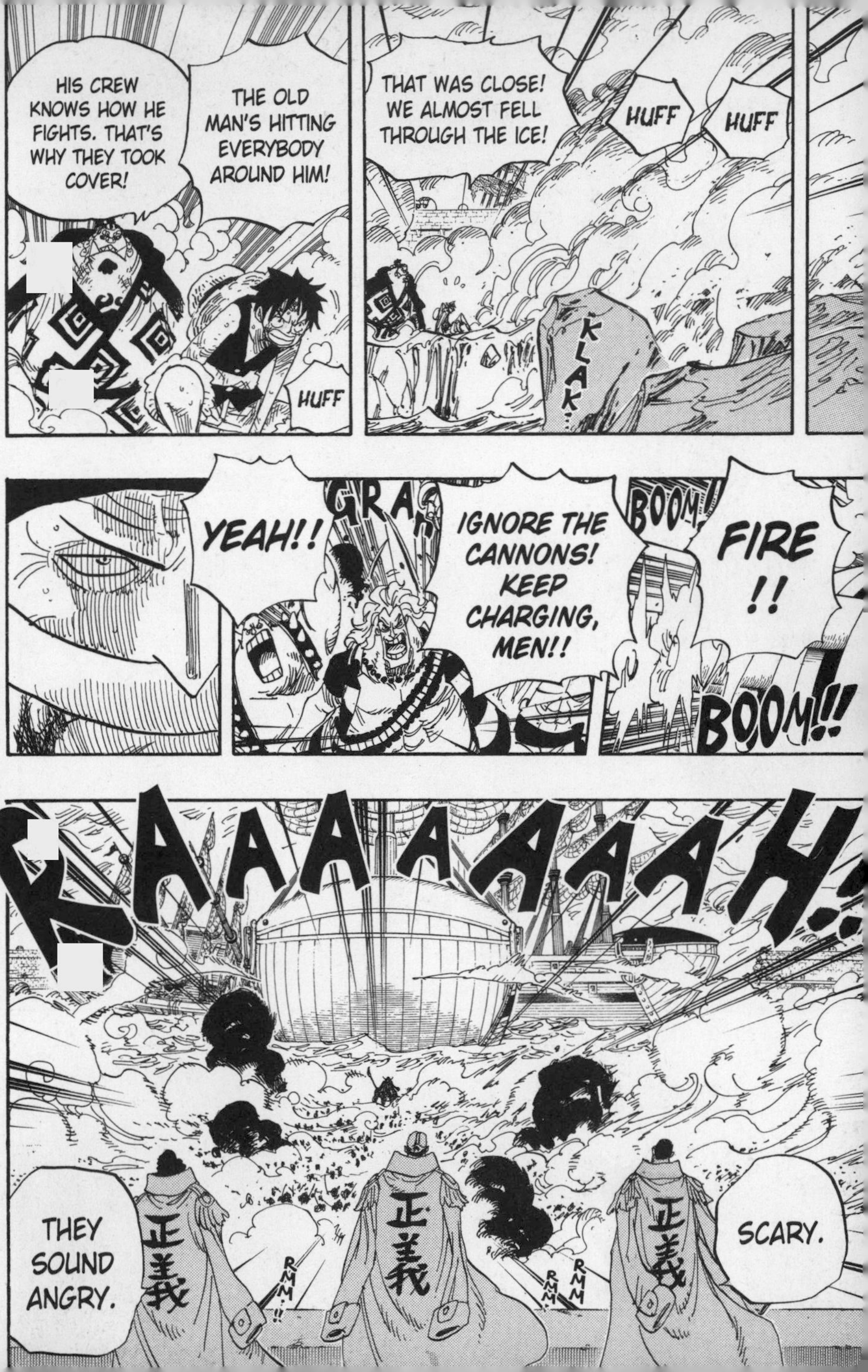
THAT WAS CLOSE! WE ALMOST FELL THROUGH THE ICE!
HUFF
HUFF
KLAK...
THE OLD MAN'S HITTING EVERYBODY AROUND HIM!
HIS CREW KNOWS HOW HE FIGHTS. THAT'S WHY THEY TOOK COVER!
HUFF
BOOM
FIRE!!
BOOM!!!
IGNORE THE CANNONS! KEEP CHARGING, MEN!!
GRAH
YEAH!!
RAAAAAAAH!!
SCARY.
正義
RMM
RMM
正義
RMM!!
正義
THEY SOUND ANGRY.

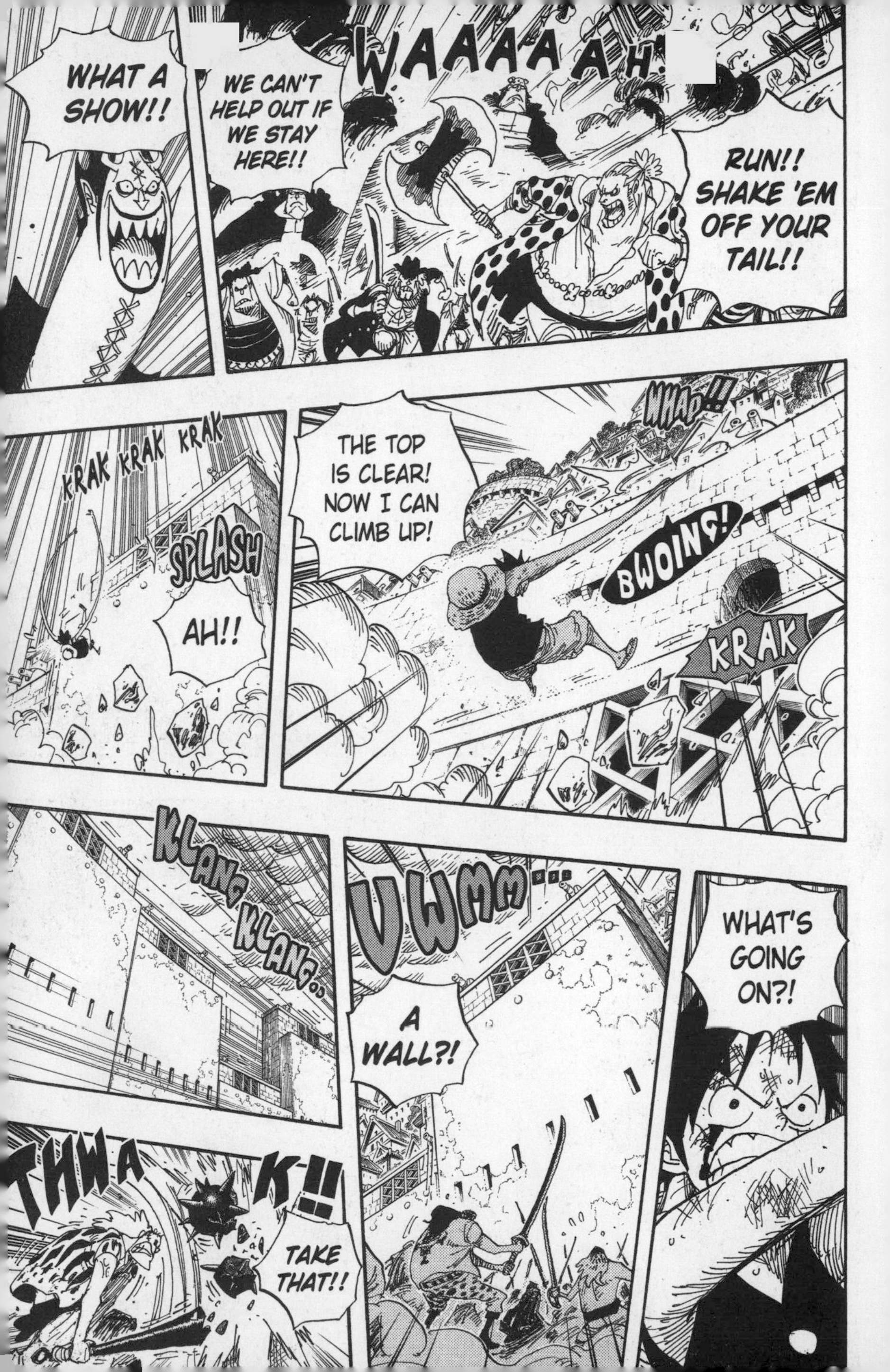

WAAAAAH
RUN!! SHAKE 'EM OFF YOUR TAIL!!
WE CAN'T HELP OUT IF WE STAY HERE!!
WHAT A SHOW!!
WHAP!!
THE TOP IS CLEAR! NOW I CAN CLIMB UP!
BWOING!
KRAK
KRAK KRAK KRAK
SPLASH
AH!!
WHAT'S GOING ON?!
UWMM...
A WALL?!
KLANG KLANG..
THWAK!!
TAKE THAT!!

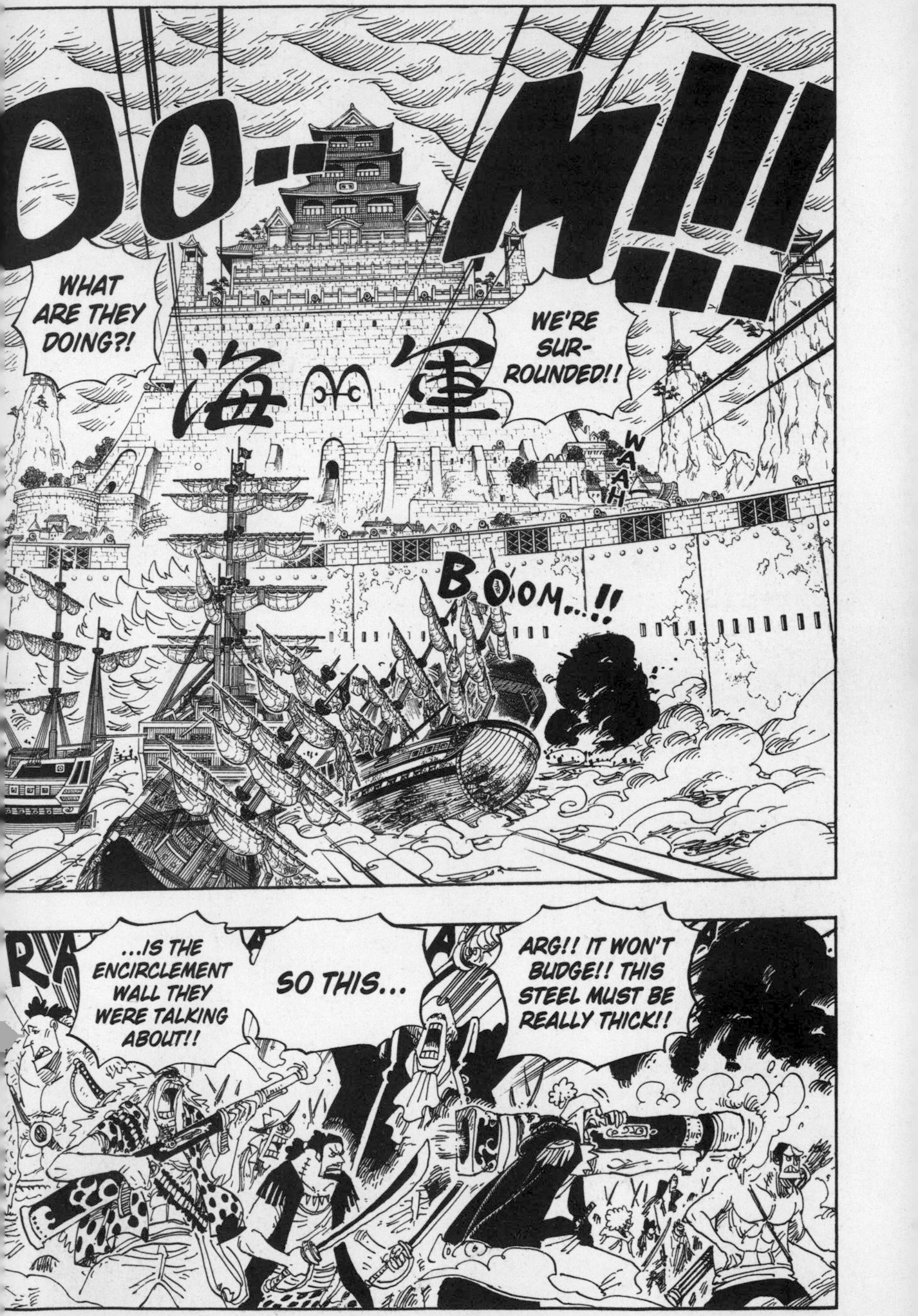
OO-M!!!
WE'RE SUR-ROUNDED!!
WHAT ARE THEY DOING?!
海軍
WAAH
BOOM...!!
ARG!! IT WON'T BUDGE!! THIS STEEL MUST BE REALLY THICK!!
SO THIS...
...IS THE ENCIRCLEMENT WALL THEY WERE TALKING ABOUT!!

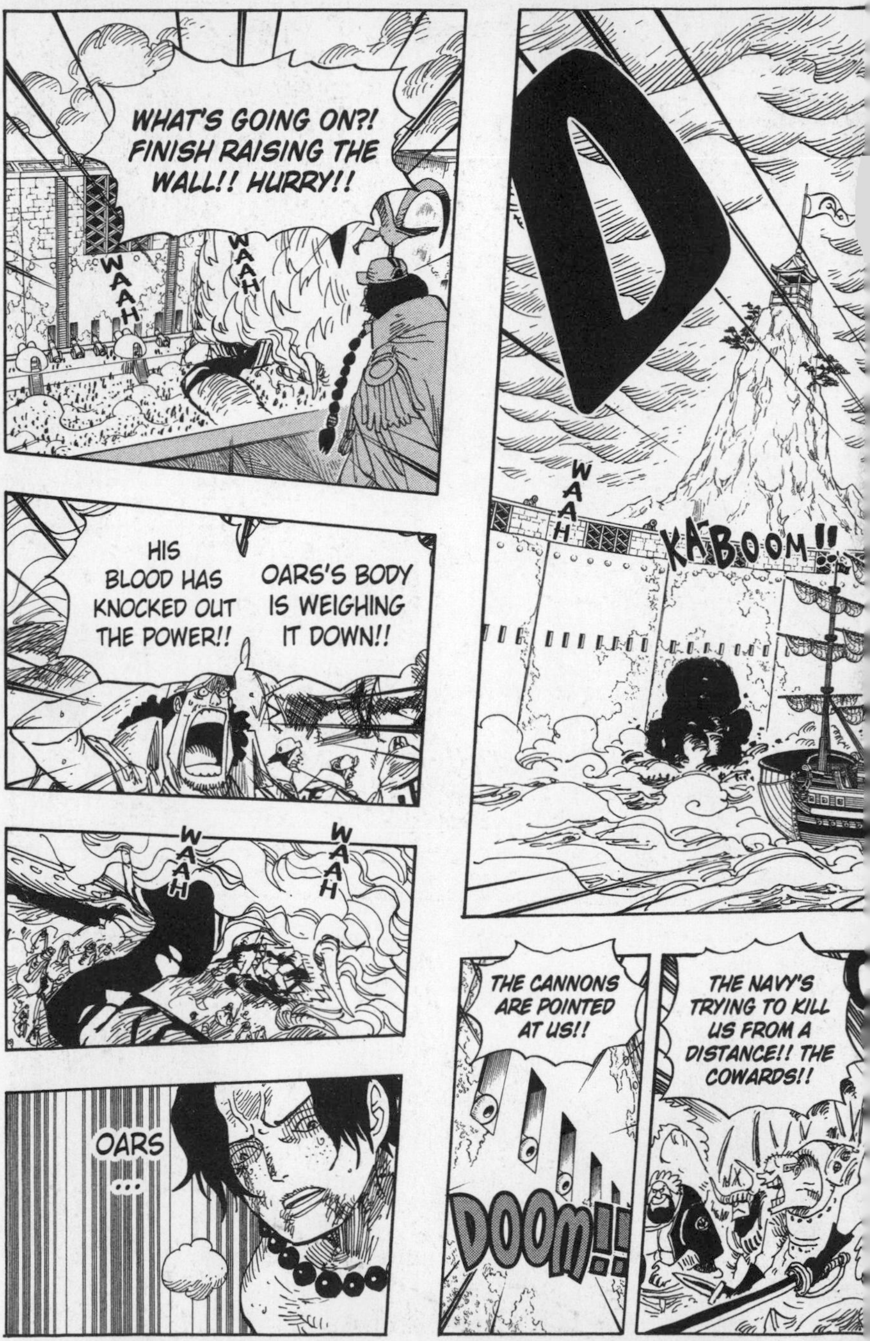
WAAH
KABOOM!!
THE NAVY'S TRYING TO KILL US FROM A DISTANCE!! THE COWARDS!!
THE CANNONS ARE POINTED AT US!!
DOOM!!
WHAT'S GOING ON?! FINISH RAISING THE WALL!! HURRY!!
WAAH
WAAH
OARS'S BODY IS WEIGHING IT DOWN!!
HIS BLOOD HAS KNOCKED OUT THE POWER!!
WAAH
WAAH
OARS ...

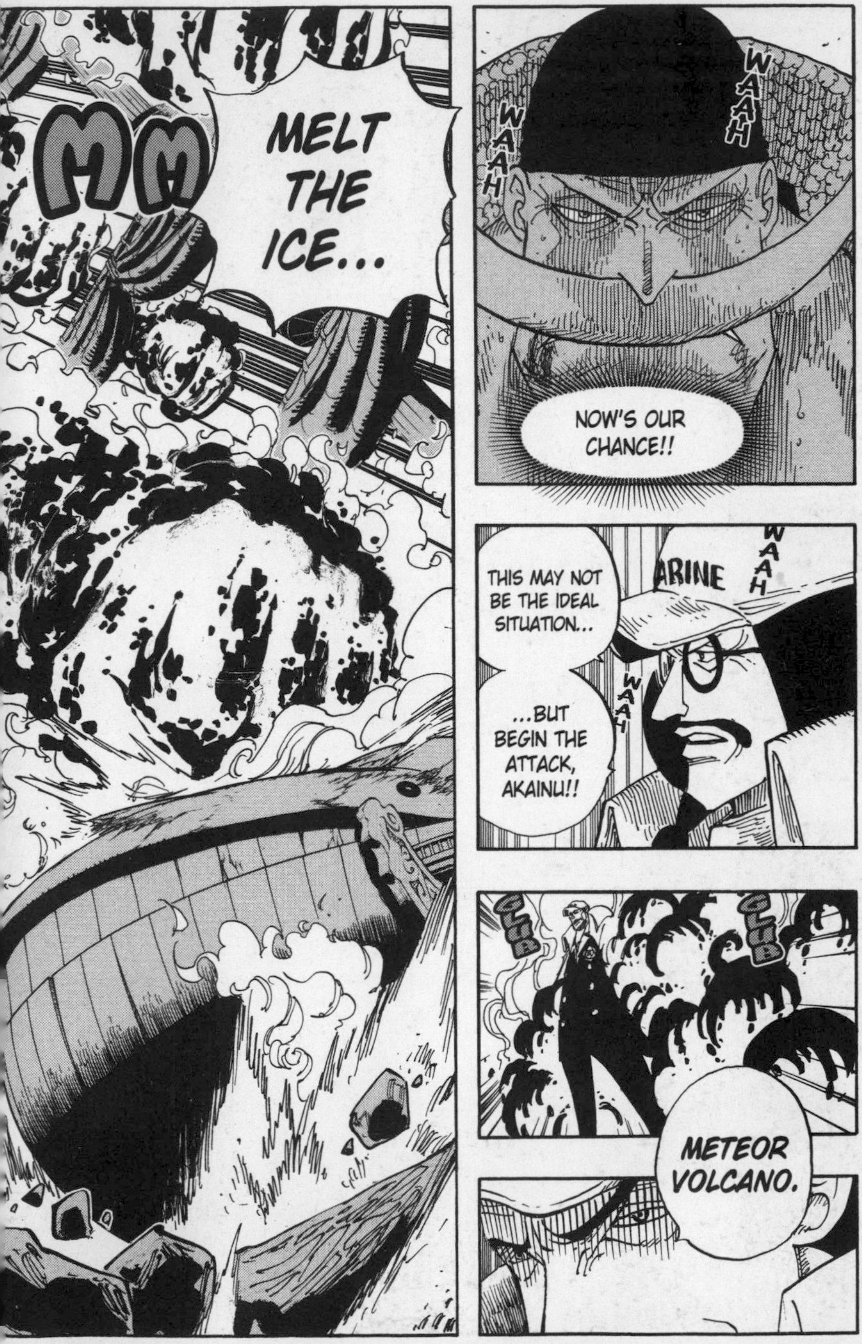
WAAH
WAAH
NOW'S OUR CHANCE!!
WAAH
THIS MAY NOT BE THE IDEAL SITUATION...
ARINE
WAAH
...BUT BEGIN THE ATTACK, AKAINU!!
GLUB
GLUB
METEOR VOLCANO.
MELT THE ICE...
MM

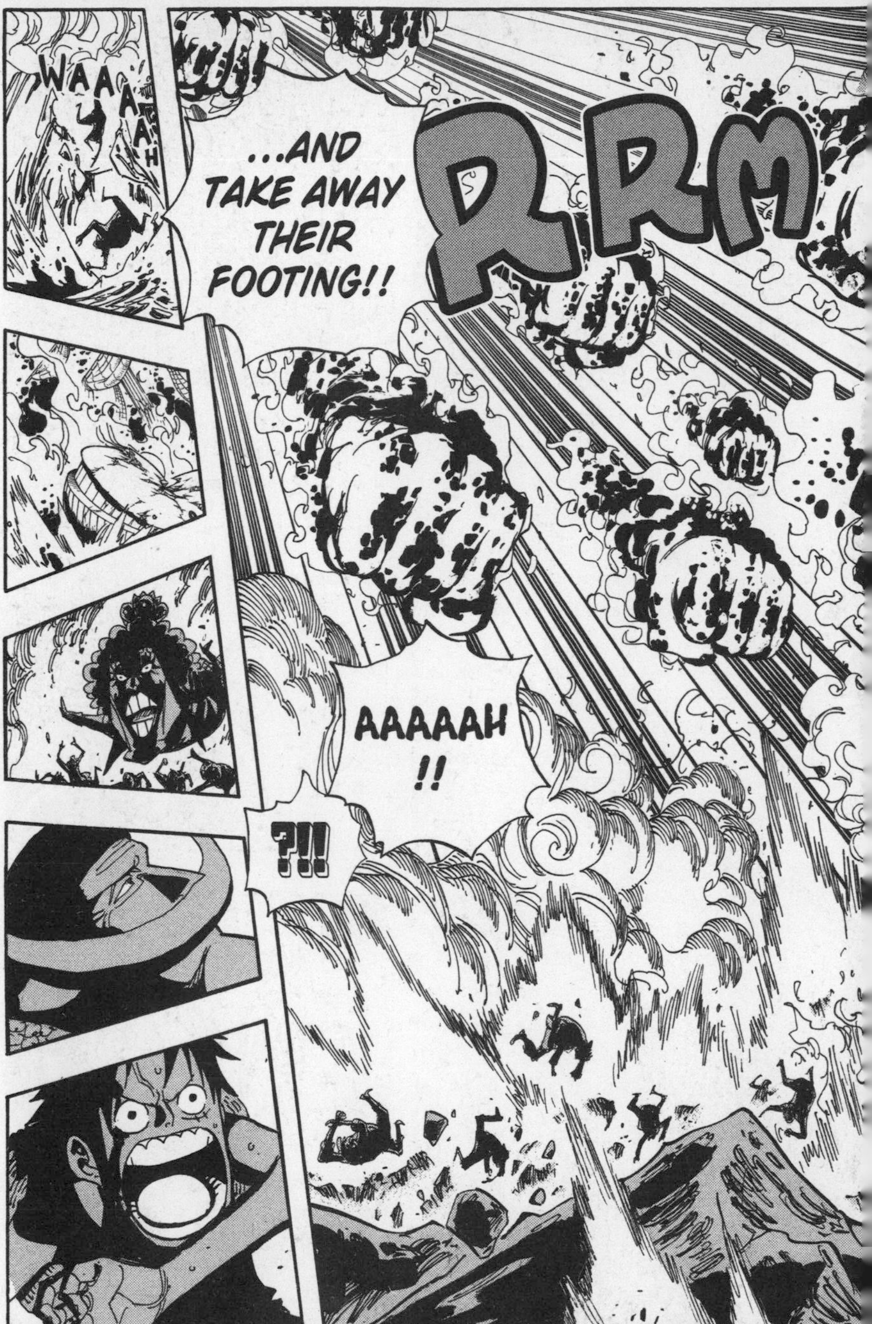
...AND TAKE AWAY THEIR FOOTING!!
RRM
AAAAAH !!
WAAAAAH
?!!

SBS Question Corner

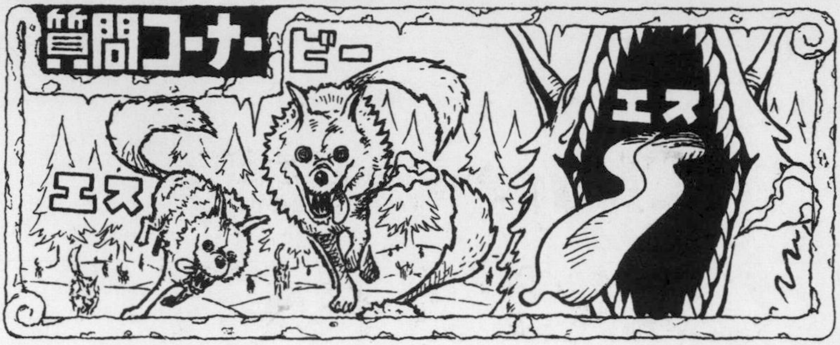
質問コーナー
ビー
エス
エス
(Hiroshi Suyama, Tokyo)

Q: Grrr!

--D. Hosokawa

A: What was that?! Was that some beast growling at me?! Y-You heard that too, right?! Uh-oh! Uh-oh uh-oh! Okay. Moving on

Q: I've turned 28 and every single day, I think about *One Piece*. There's this question I want to ask. In a *One Piece* art book, there was this technique called Face Fleurs where Robin's face appears on the back of Chopper's head. What situation is that supposed to be used in? I couldn't help but laugh when I saw it.

--Tony Tony Chappy

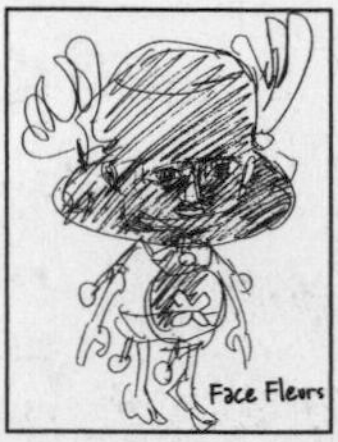
Face Fleurs

A: I see. Well, for the people who don't know, there was a section in an art book that shows parts of my notes and this was one of the things shown. To tell you the truth, there was a scene during the Skypiea arc where Robin had to transport her unconscious crewmates. At that time, I thought that sprouting faces, arms and legs on her crewmates might make transporting them really easy. But it was so creepy that I decided not to do it. But if you really like it, I might do it some other time.

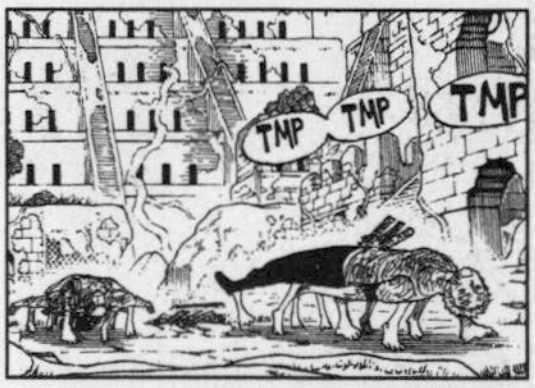
TMP
TMP
TMP

Q: Hello, Mr. Oda! There's one thing that's been bothering me. Why does Ace have freckles? My mother calls him that "freckle-faced guy" all the time. Isn't that terrible?

--Rihosuke

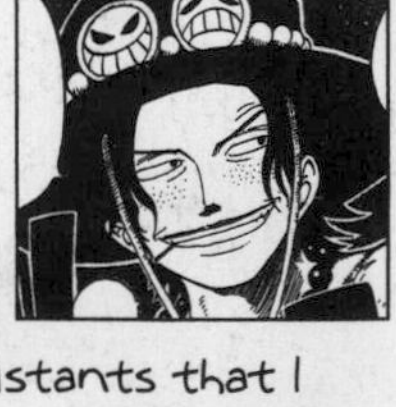

A: Speaking of freckles, it's known among my assistants that I always forget to draw the freckles (about 92% of the time). Well, setting that aside, Ace probably doesn't care about it either. Do you know about the saying from the old show Candy Candy, "I don't care if I'm freckle-faced!"? Yeah. For the people who don't know what I'm talking about, ask your mom or dad.

Chapter 565:
OARS'S PATH

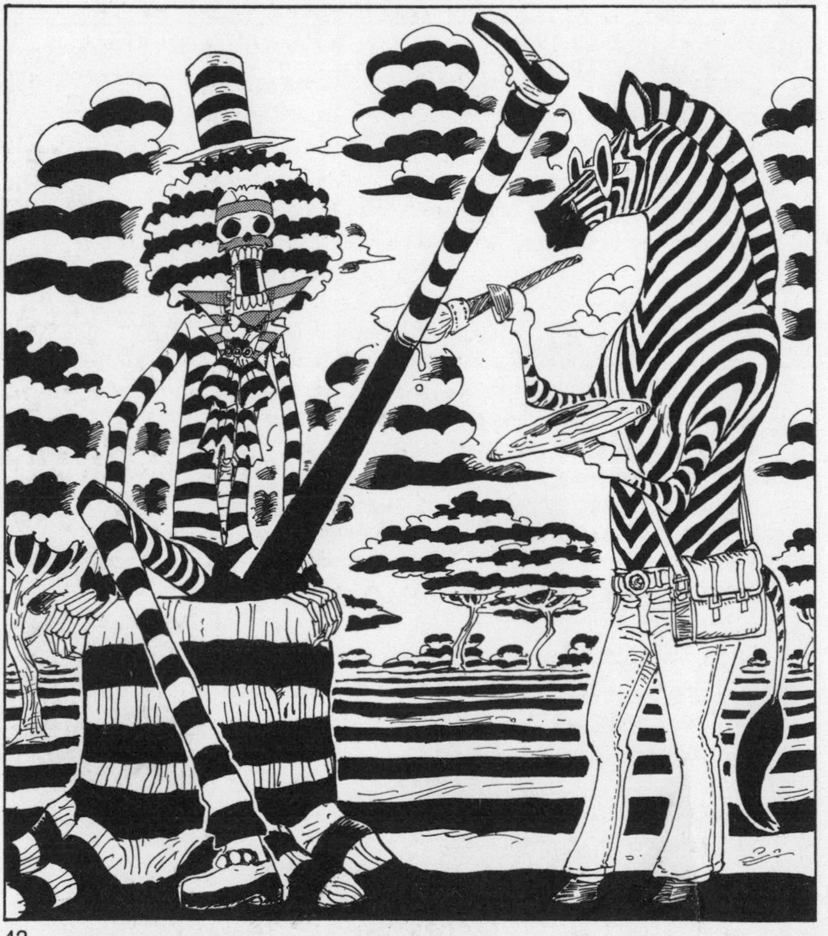

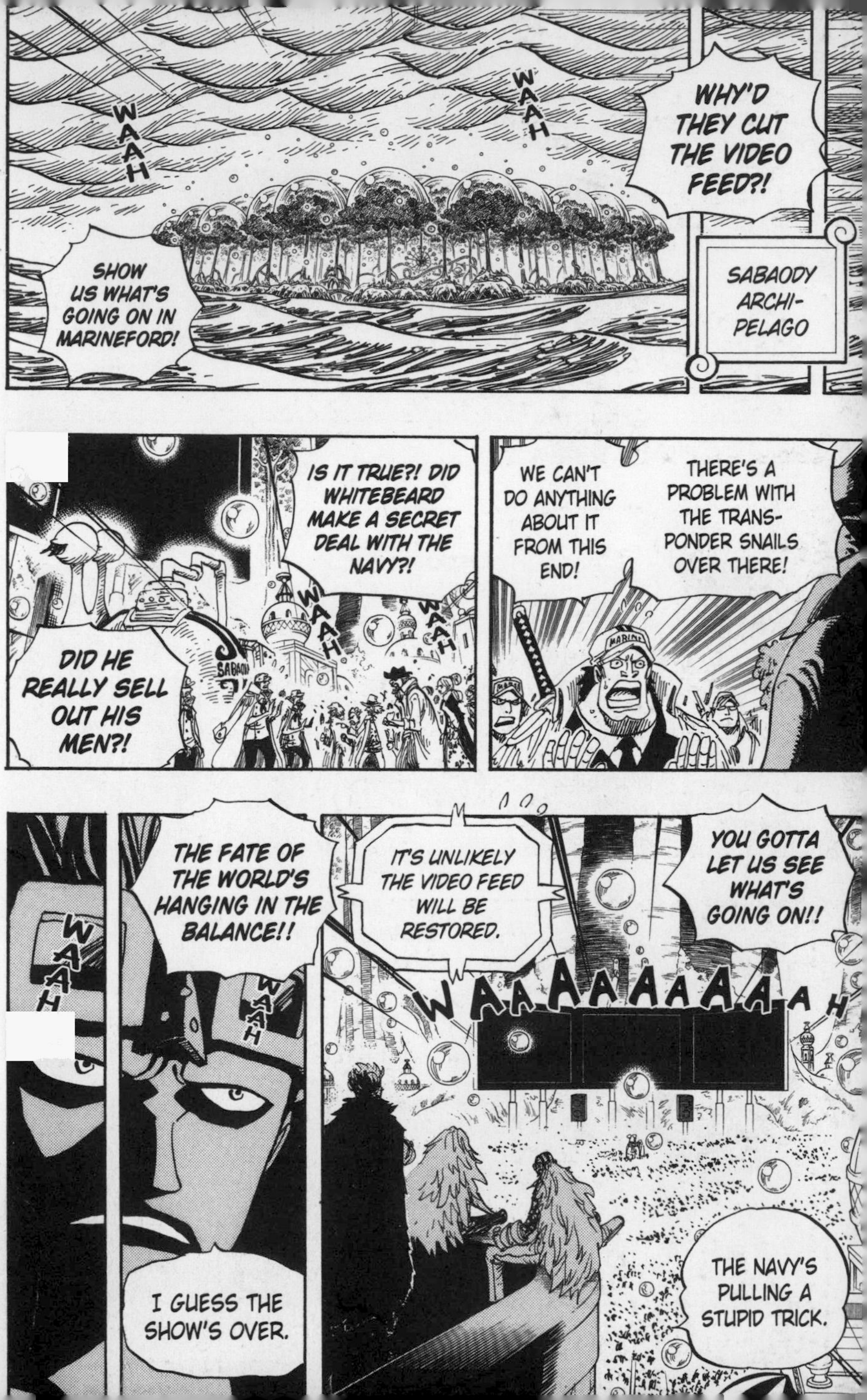
WHY'D THEY CUT THE VIDEO FEED?!
SABAODY ARCHIPELAGO
WAAH
WAAH
SHOW US WHAT'S GOING ON IN MARINEFORD!
THERE'S A PROBLEM WITH THE TRANSPONDER SNAILS OVER THERE!
WE CAN'T DO ANYTHING ABOUT IT FROM THIS END!
IS IT TRUE?! DID WHITEBEARD MAKE A SECRET DEAL WITH THE NAVY?!
WAAH
WAAH
DID HE REALLY SELL OUT HIS MEN?!
YOU GOTTA LET US SEE WHAT'S GOING ON!!
IT'S UNLIKELY THE VIDEO FEED WILL BE RESTORED.
WAAAAAAAAAH
THE NAVY'S PULLING A STUPID TRICK.
THE FATE OF THE WORLD'S HANGING IN THE BALANCE!!
WAAH
I GUESS THE SHOW'S OVER.
WAAH

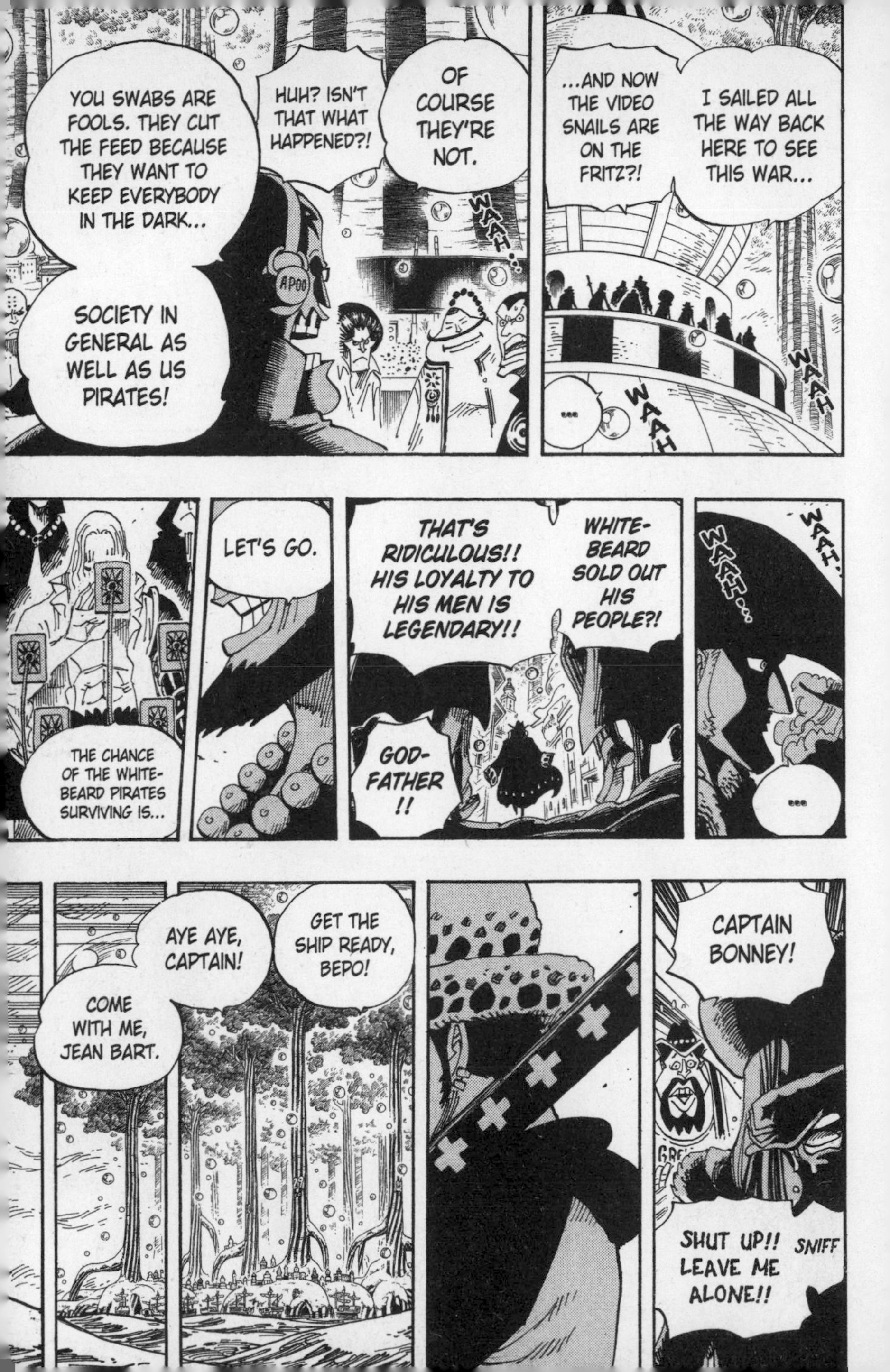
I SAILED ALL THE WAY BACK HERE TO SEE THIS WAR...
...AND NOW THE VIDEO SNAILS ARE ON THE FRITZ?!
WAAH
WAAH
...
WAAH...
OF COURSE THEY'RE NOT.
HUH? ISN'T THAT WHAT HAPPENED?!
YOU SWABS ARE FOOLS. THEY CUT THE FEED BECAUSE THEY WANT TO KEEP EVERYBODY IN THE DARK...
SOCIETY IN GENERAL AS WELL AS US PIRATES!
WAAH
WAAH...
...
WHITE-BEARD SOLD OUT HIS PEOPLE?!
THAT'S RIDICULOUS!! HIS LOYALTY TO HIS MEN IS LEGENDARY!!
GOD-FATHER !!
LET'S GO.
THE CHANCE OF THE WHITE-BEARD PIRATES SURVIVING IS...
CAPTAIN BONNEY!
SHUT UP!! LEAVE ME ALONE!!
SNIFF
GET THE SHIP READY, BEPO!
AYE AYE, CAPTAIN!
COME WITH ME, JEAN BART.

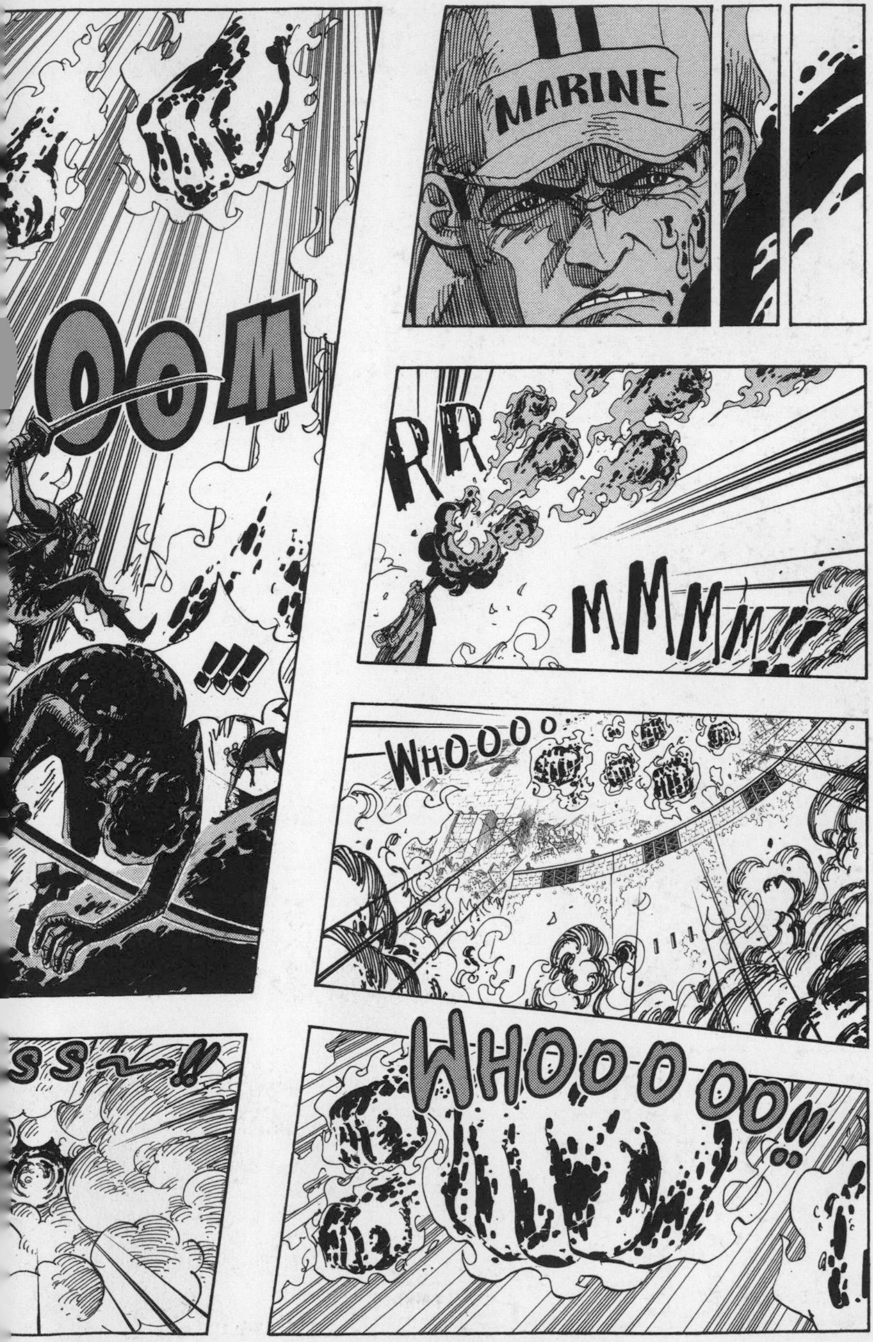
MARINE
RR
MMMM!!
WHOOOO
OOM
!!!
WHOOOOOO!!
SS~!!

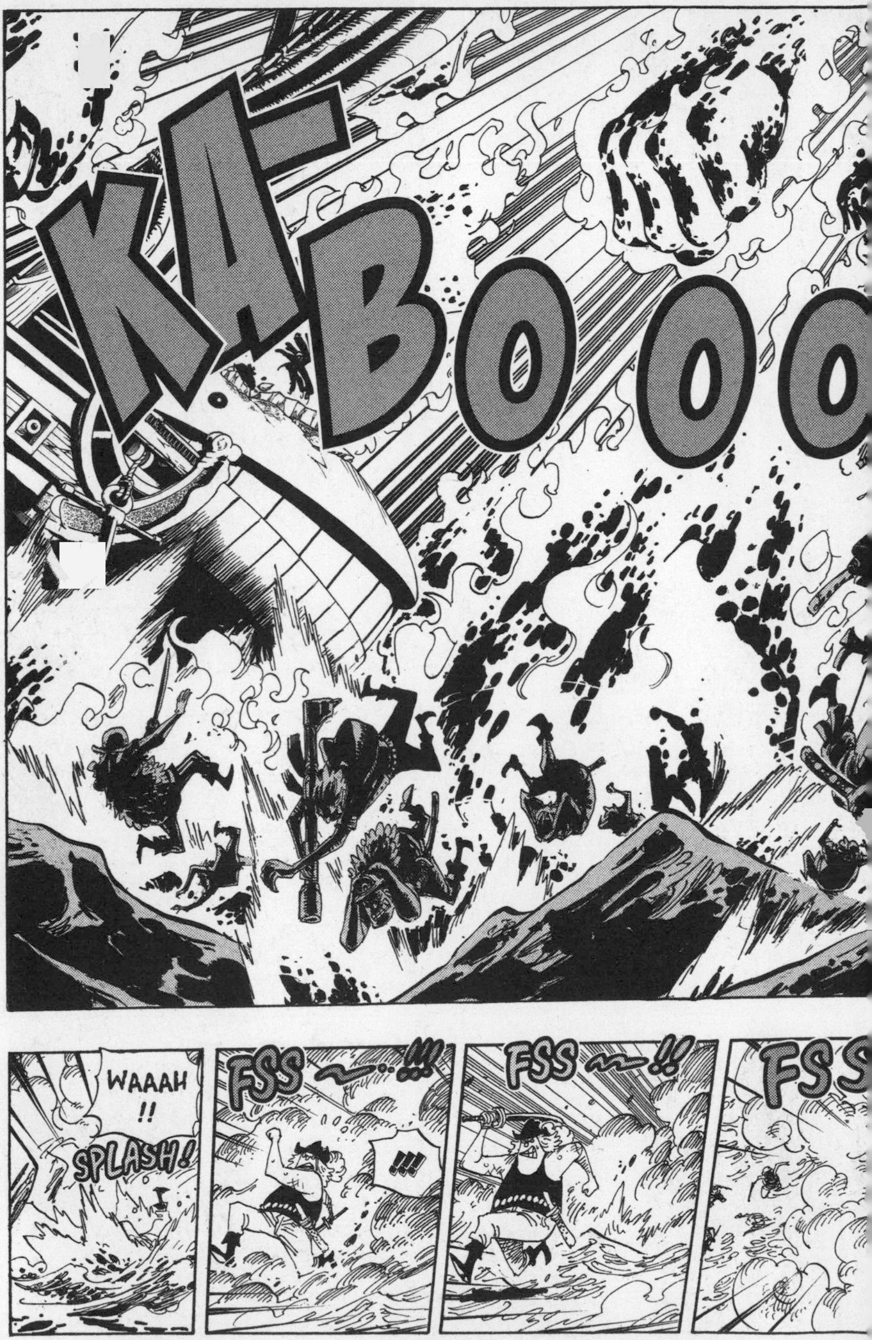
KA-BOOO
FSS
FSS~!!
FSS~..!!!
!!!
WAAAH !!
SPLASH!

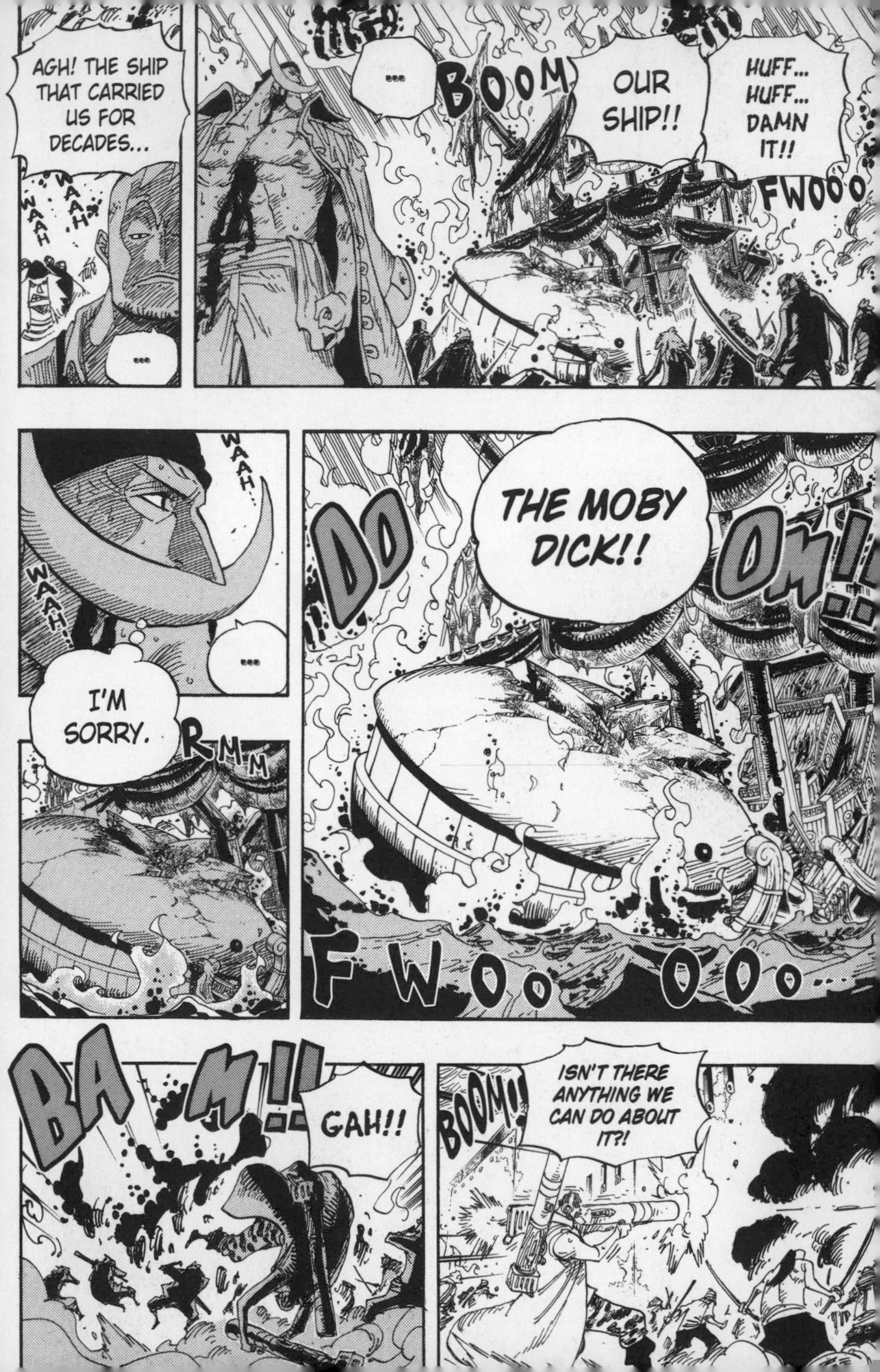
HUFF... HUFF... DAMN IT!!
OUR SHIP!!
BOOM
FWOOO
...
AGH! THE SHIP THAT CARRIED US FOR DECADES...
WAAH
WAAH
...
THE MOBY DICK!!
DO
OM!!
FWOOOOO...
WAAH
WAAH
...
I'M SORRY.
RMMM
ISN'T THERE ANYTHING WE CAN DO ABOUT IT?!
BOOM!!
GAH!!
BAM!!

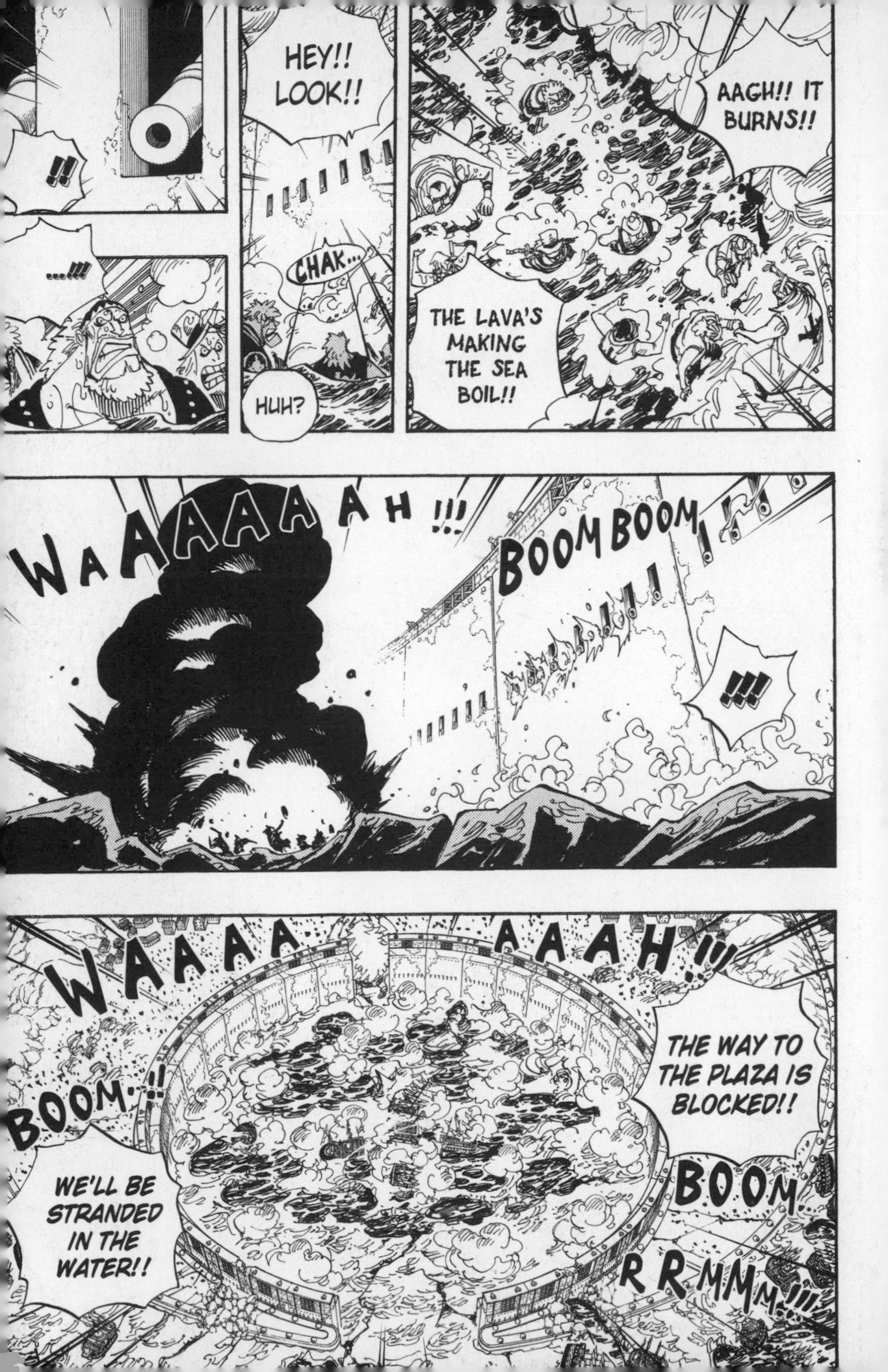
AAGH!! IT BURNS!!
THE LAVA'S MAKING THE SEA BOIL!!
HEY!! LOOK!!
CHAK...
HUH?
!!
...!!!
BOOM BOOM
!!!
WAAAAAAH!!!
WAAAA AAAH!!!
THE WAY TO THE PLAZA IS BLOCKED!!
BOOM...
BOOM...!!
WE'LL BE STRANDED IN THE WATER!!
RRMMM...!!!

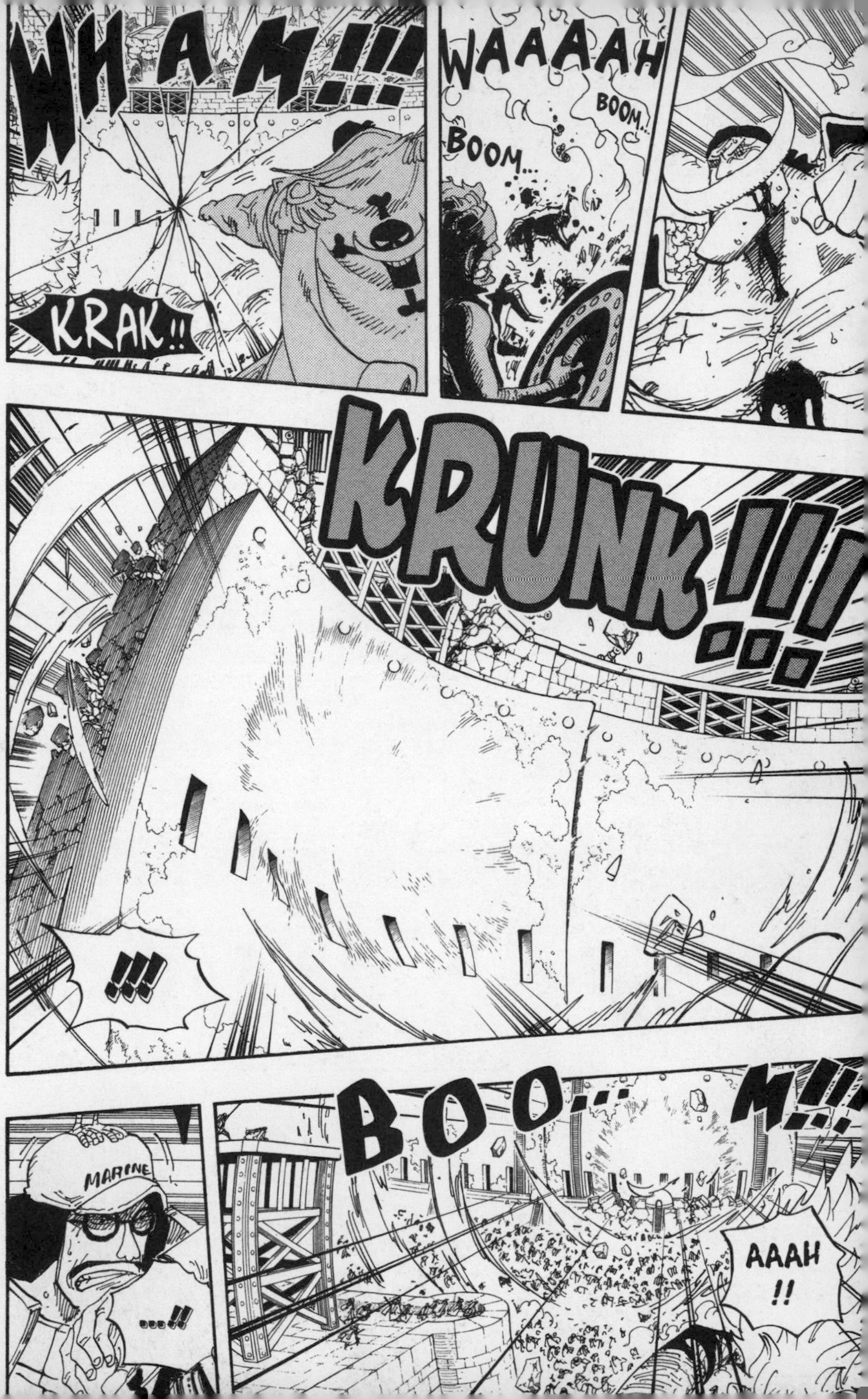
WAAAAH
BOOM...
BOOM...
WHAM!!
KRAK!!
KRUNK!!!
!!!
BOO...M!!
AAAH!!
MARINE
...!!

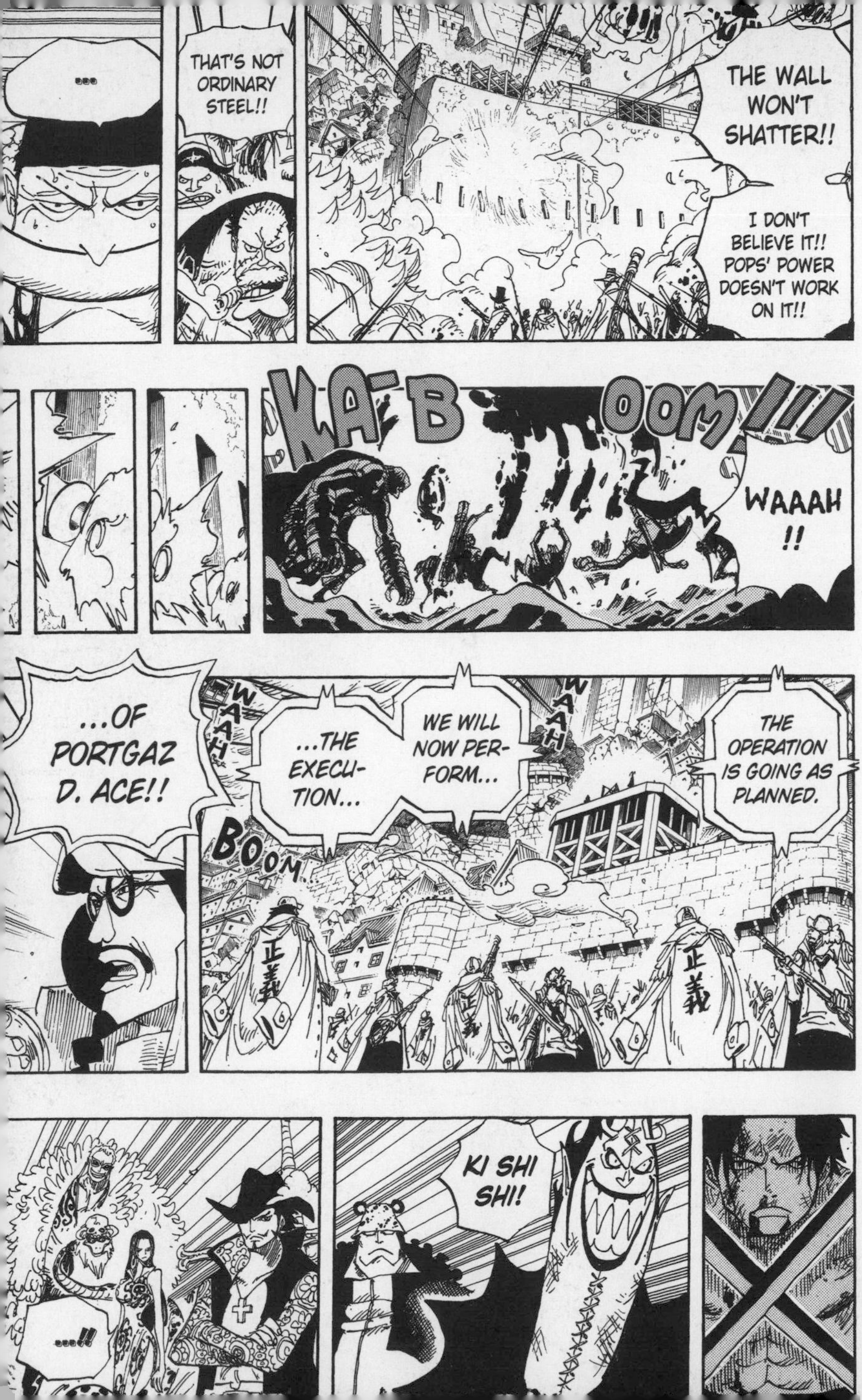
THE WALL WON'T SHATTER!!
I DON'T BELIEVE IT!! POPS' POWER DOESN'T WORK ON IT!!
THAT'S NOT ORDINARY STEEL!!
...
KA-BOOM!!!
WAAAH!!
THE OPERATION IS GOING AS PLANNED.
WAAAH
WE WILL NOW PER-FORM...
WAAAH
...THE EXECU-TION...
BOOM
...OF PORTGAZ D. ACE!!
KI SHI SHI!
...!!

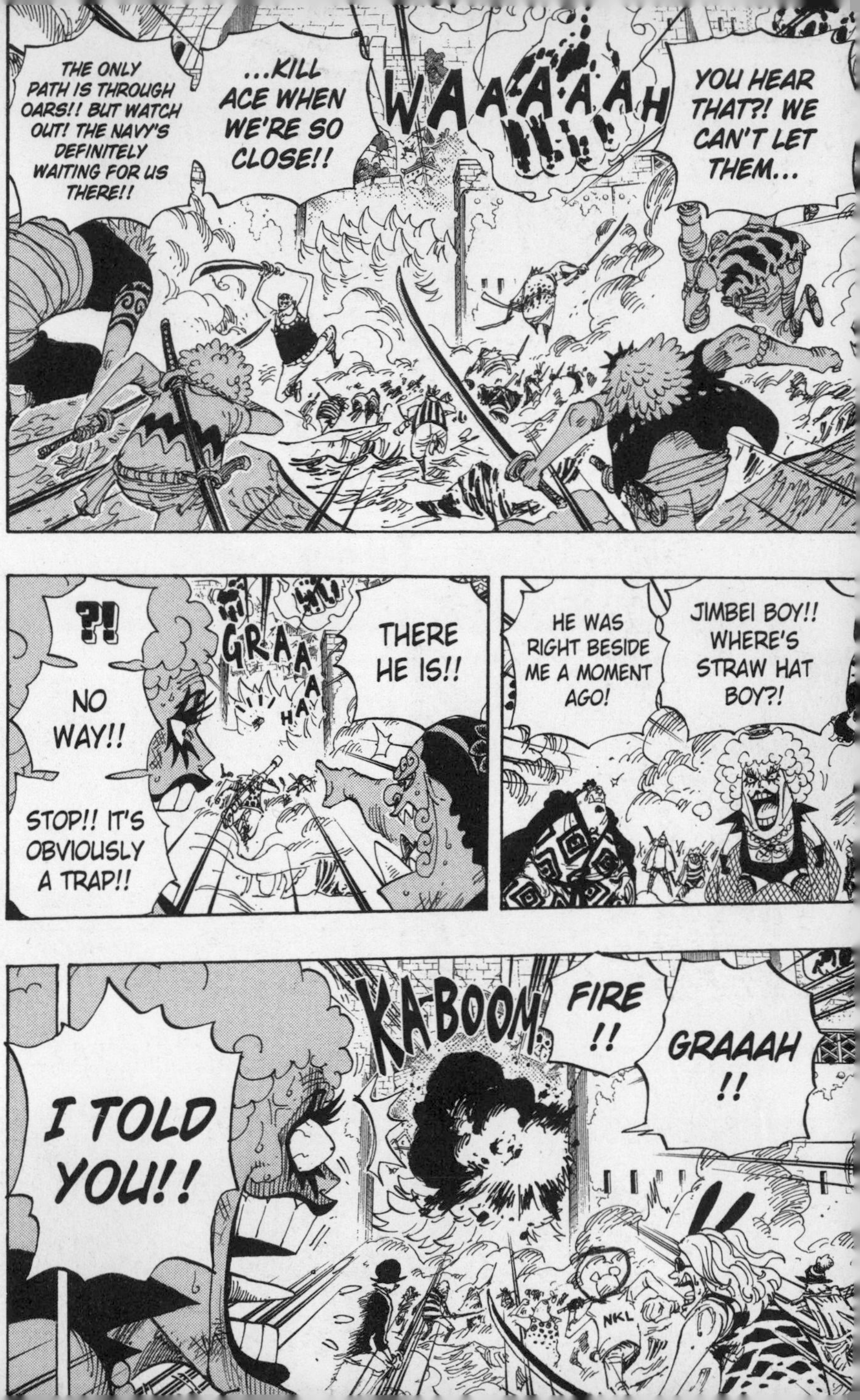
YOU HEAR THAT?! WE CAN'T LET THEM...
WAAAAAH
...KILL ACE WHEN WE'RE SO CLOSE!!
THE ONLY PATH IS THROUGH OARS!! BUT WATCH OUT! THE NAVY'S DEFINITELY WAITING FOR US THERE!!
JIMBEI BOY!! WHERE'S STRAW HAT BOY?!
HE WAS RIGHT BESIDE ME A MOMENT AGO!
THERE HE IS!!
GRAAAAAHA
?!
NO WAY!!
STOP!! IT'S OBVIOUSLY A TRAP!!
GRAAAH!!
FIRE!!
KA-BOOM
I TOLD YOU!!
NKL

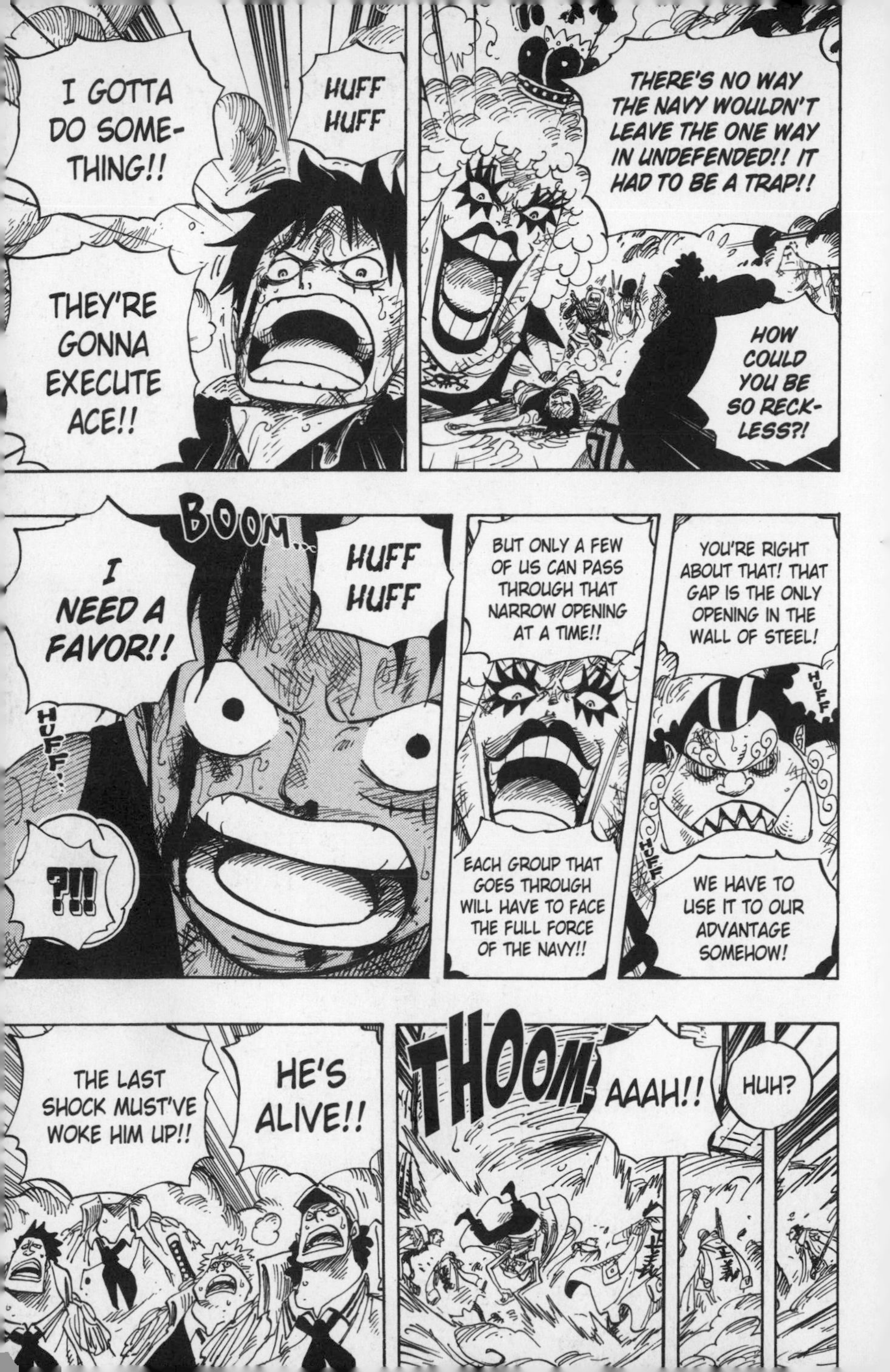
THERE'S NO WAY THE NAVY WOULDN'T LEAVE THE ONE WAY IN UNDEFENDED!! IT HAD TO BE A TRAP!!
HOW COULD YOU BE SO RECK-LESS?!
HUFF HUFF
I GOTTA DO SOME-THING!!
THEY'RE GONNA EXECUTE ACE!!
YOU'RE RIGHT ABOUT THAT! THAT GAP IS THE ONLY OPENING IN THE WALL OF STEEL!
HUFF
HUFF
WE HAVE TO USE IT TO OUR ADVANTAGE SOMEHOW!
BUT ONLY A FEW OF US CAN PASS THROUGH THAT NARROW OPENING AT A TIME!!
EACH GROUP THAT GOES THROUGH WILL HAVE TO FACE THE FULL FORCE OF THE NAVY!!
BOOM
HUFF HUFF
I NEED A FAVOR!!
HUFF...
?!!
HUH?
AAAH!!
THOOM
HE'S ALIVE!!
THE LAST SHOCK MUST'VE WOKE HIM UP!!

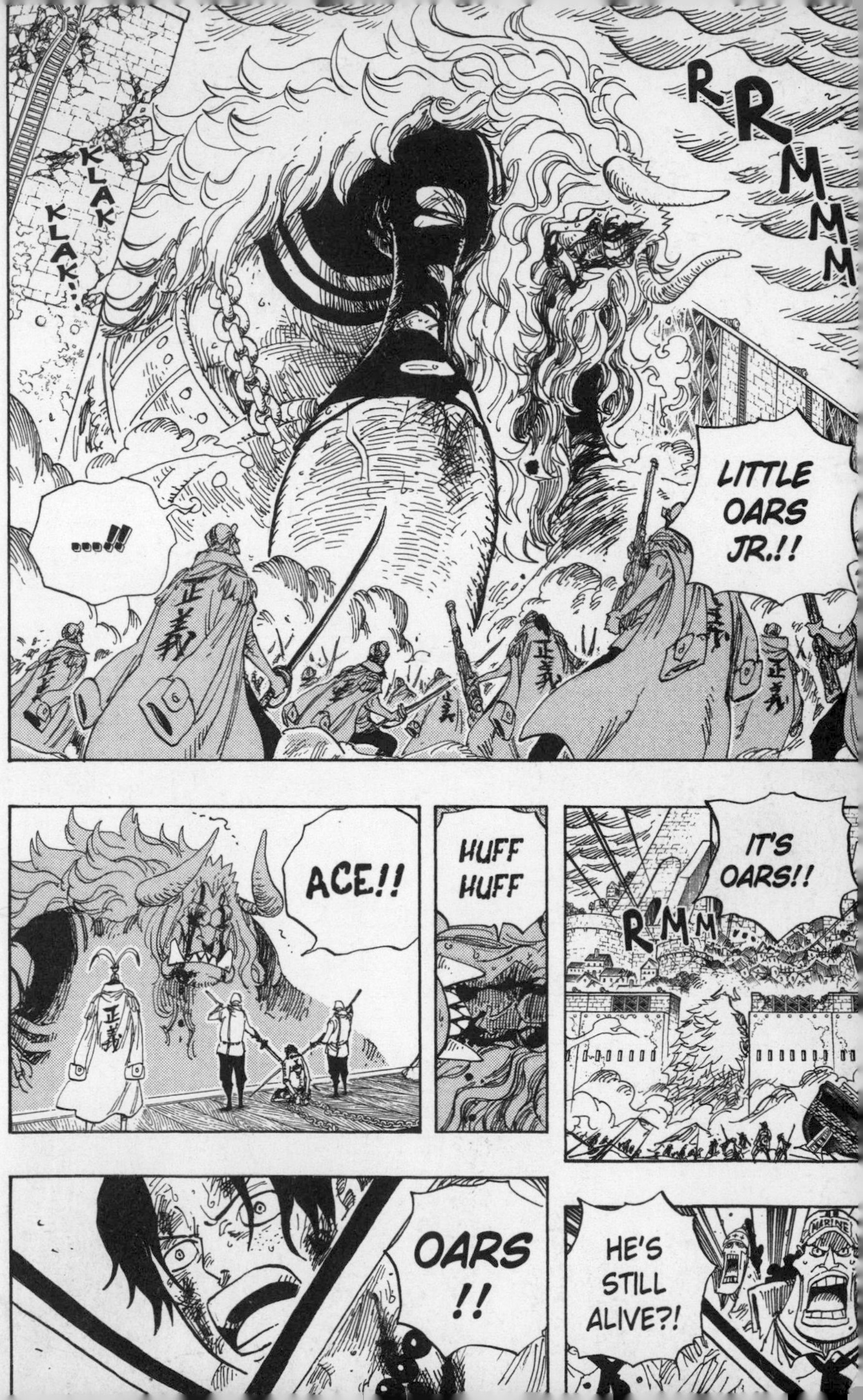
RRMMM
LITTLE OARS JR.!!
...!!
KLAK KLAK!!
IT'S OARS!!
RMM
HUFF HUFF
ACE!!
HE'S STILL ALIVE?!
OARS!!

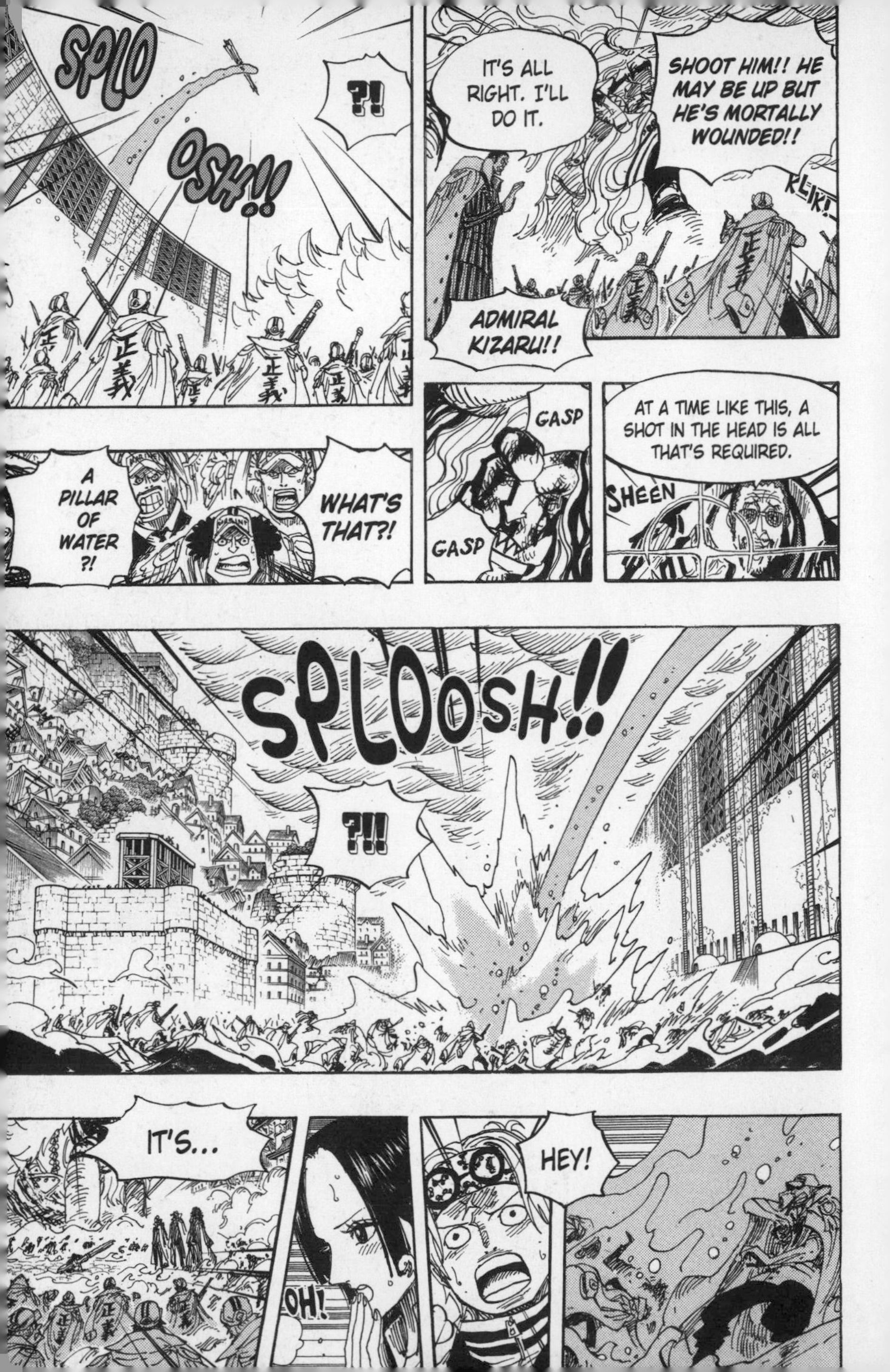
SHOOT HIM!! HE MAY BE UP BUT HE'S MORTALLY WOUNDED!!
IT'S ALL RIGHT. I'LL DO IT.
KLIK!
ADMIRAL KIZARU!!
?!
SPLO OSH!!
AT A TIME LIKE THIS, A SHOT IN THE HEAD IS ALL THAT'S REQUIRED.
SHEEN
GASP
GASP
WHAT'S THAT?!
A PILLAR OF WATER ?!
SPLOOSH!!
?!!
HEY!
OH!
IT'S...

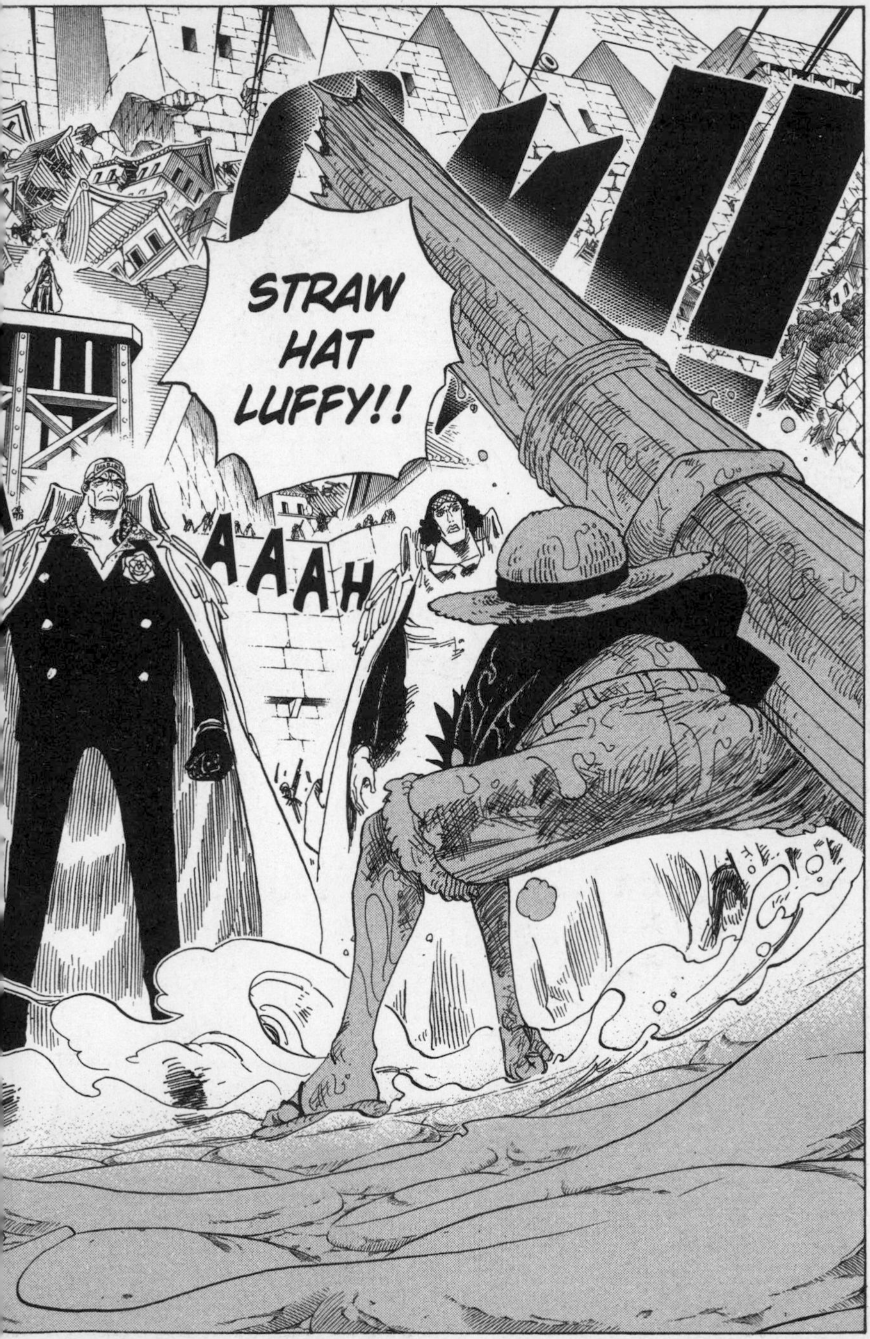
STRAW HAT LUFFY!!
AAAAH

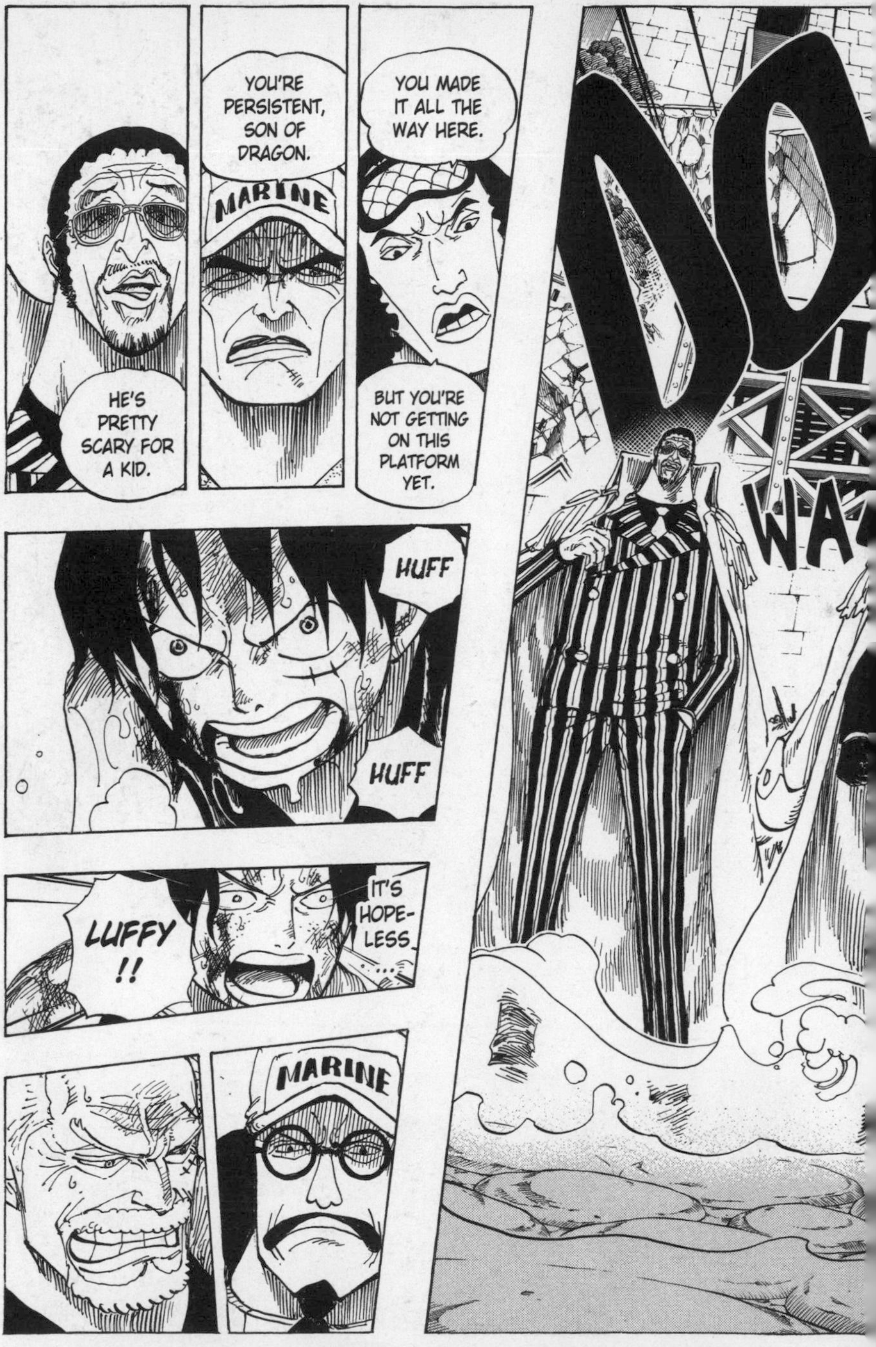

DO
WA
YOU MADE IT ALL THE WAY HERE.
BUT YOU'RE NOT GETTING ON THIS PLATFORM YET.
YOU'RE PERSISTENT, SON OF DRAGON.
MARINE
HE'S PRETTY SCARY FOR A KID.
HUFF
HUFF
IT'S HOPE-LESS......
LUFFY!!
MARINE

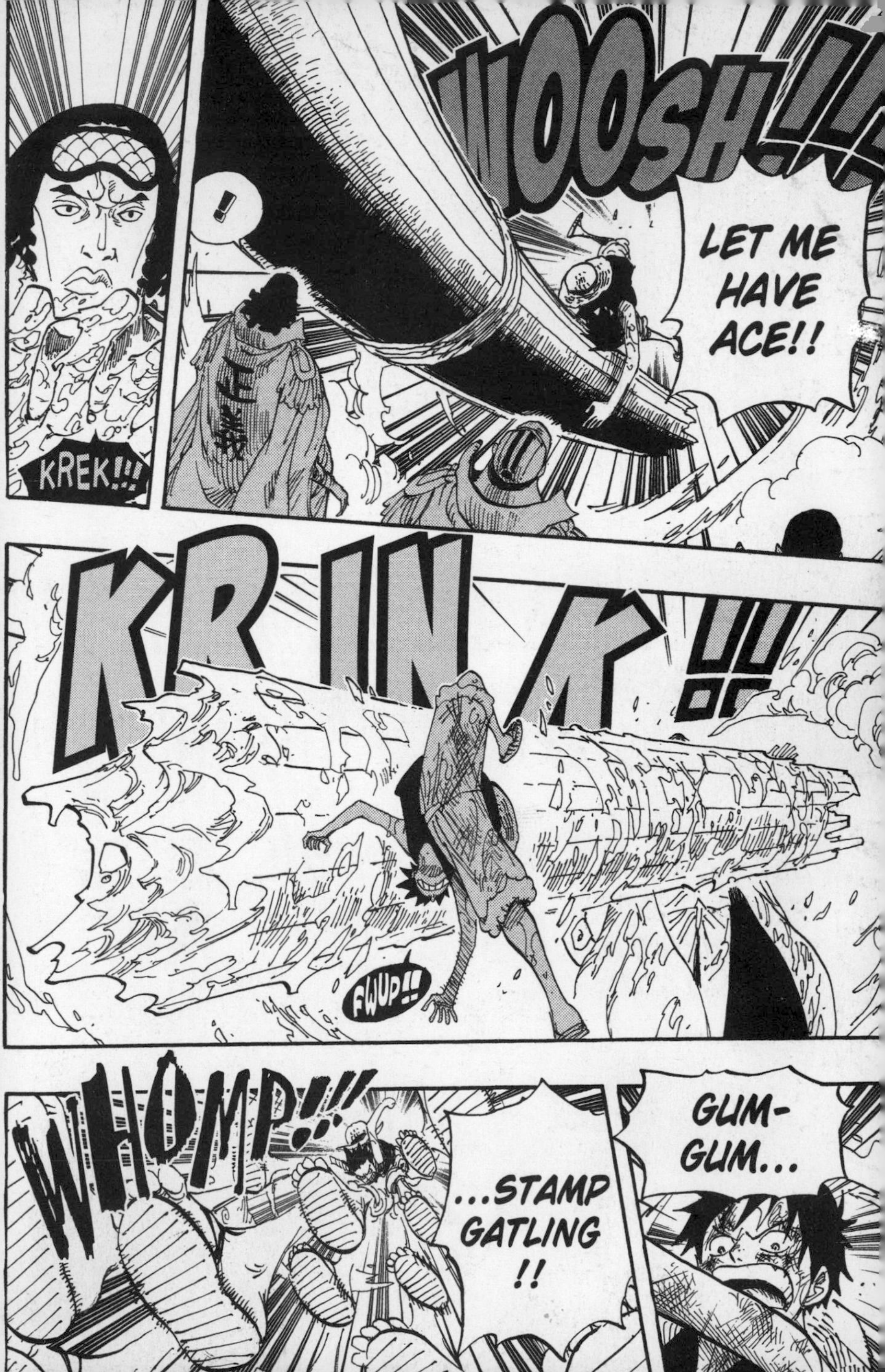
WOOSH!!
LET ME HAVE ACE!!
!
KREK!!!
KRUNK!!
FWUP!!
GUM-GUM...
...STAMP GATLING!!
WHOMP!!!

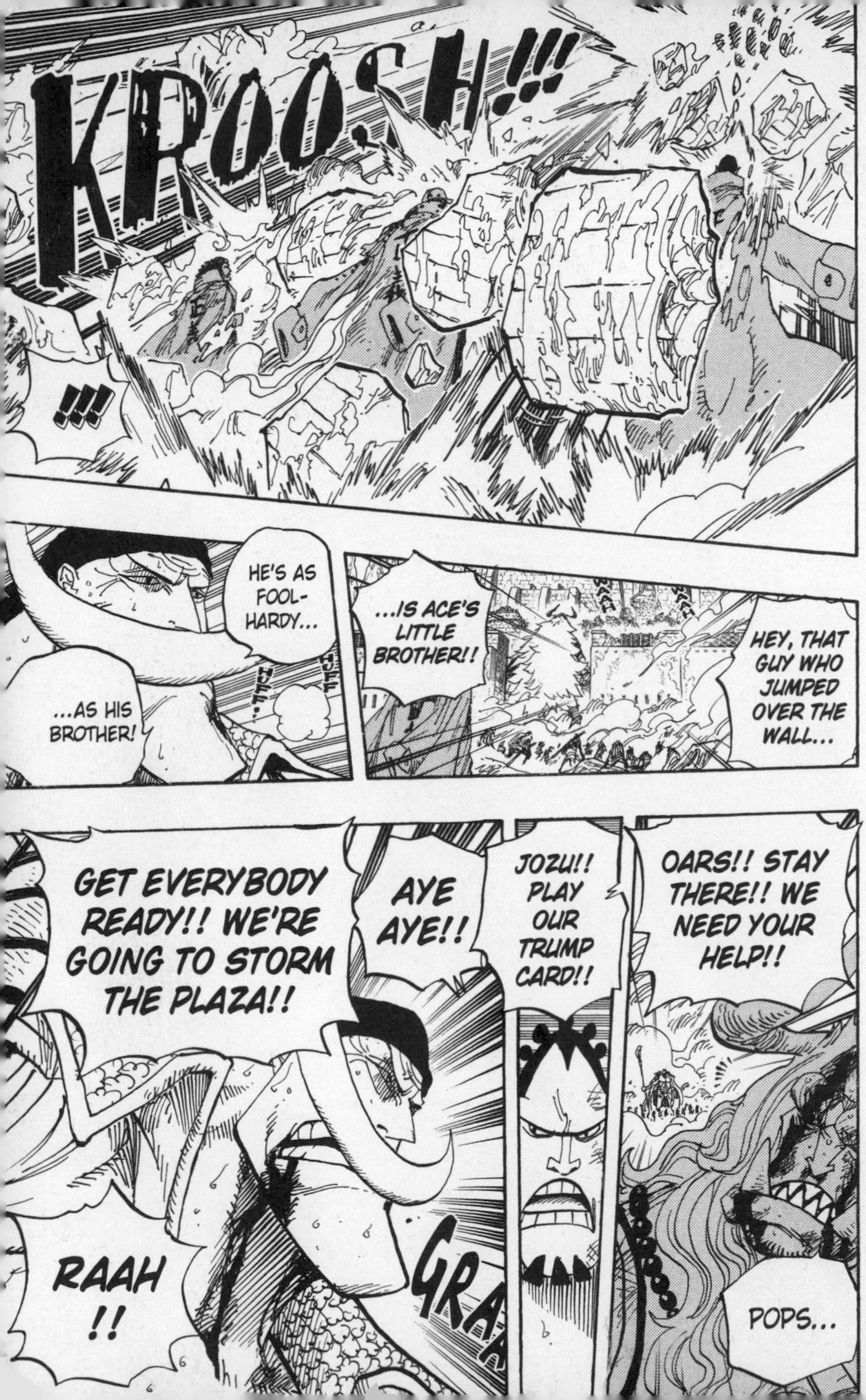
KROOSH!!!
!!!
HEY, THAT GUY WHO JUMPED OVER THE WALL...
...IS ACE'S LITTLE BROTHER!!
WAAH
WAAH
HE'S AS FOOL-HARDY...
HUFF
HUFF
...AS HIS BROTHER!
OARS!! STAY THERE!! WE NEED YOUR HELP!!
POPS...
JOZU!! PLAY OUR TRUMP CARD!!
AYE AYE!!
GRA
GET EVERYBODY READY!! WE'RE GOING TO STORM THE PLAZA!!
RAAH !!

Chapter 566: RAID

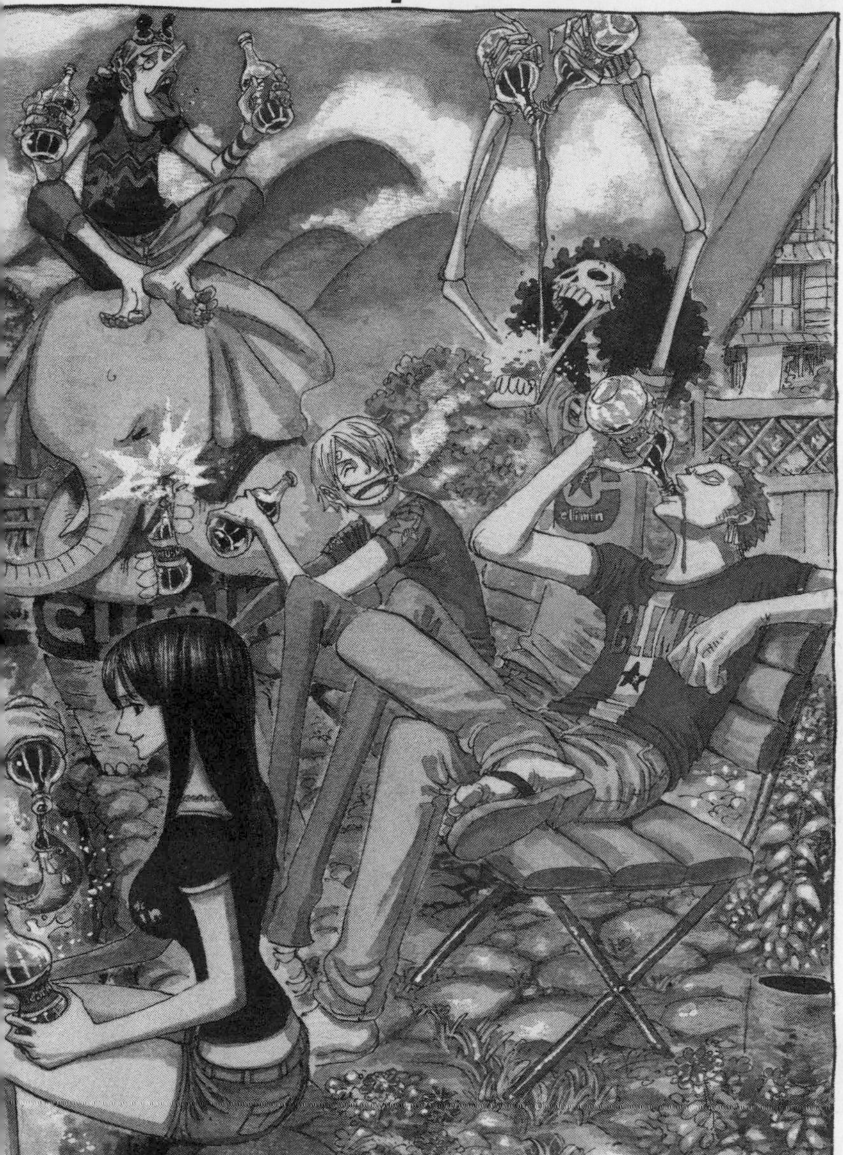

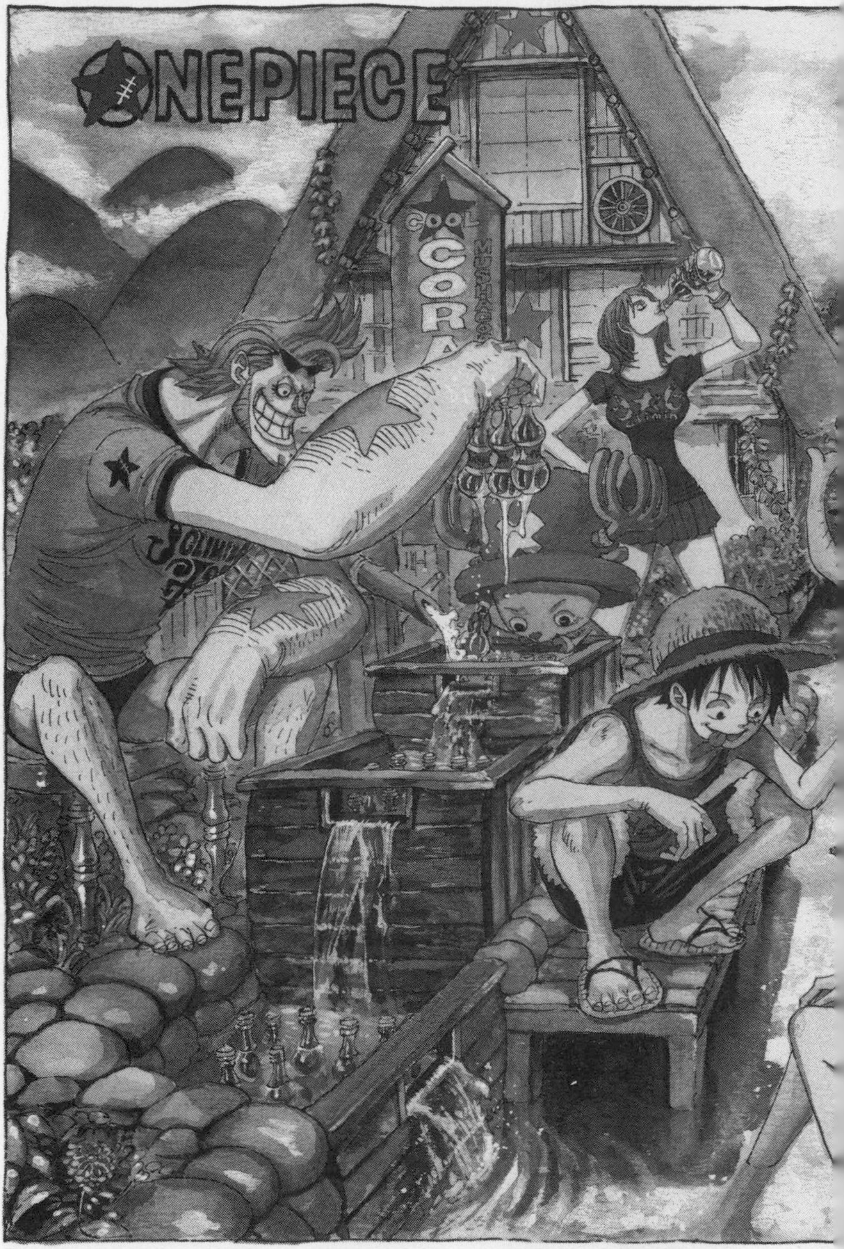
ONEPIECE
COOL
CORA

vol.58
ONE PIECE

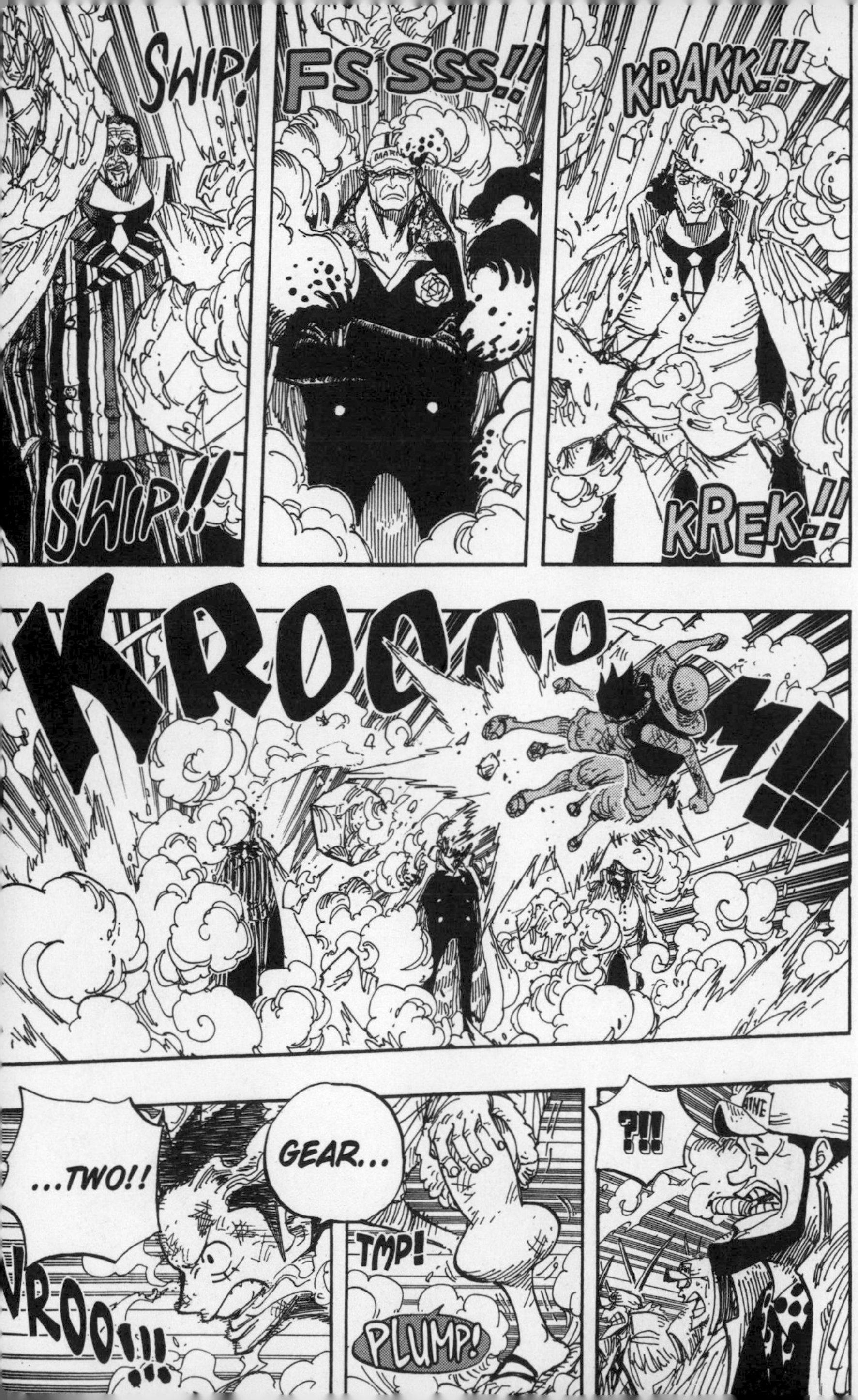
KRAKK!!
KREK!!
FS SSS!!
SWIP!
SWIP!!
KROOOOM!!!
?!!
GEAR...
TMP!
PLUMP!
...TWO!!
VROO!!!

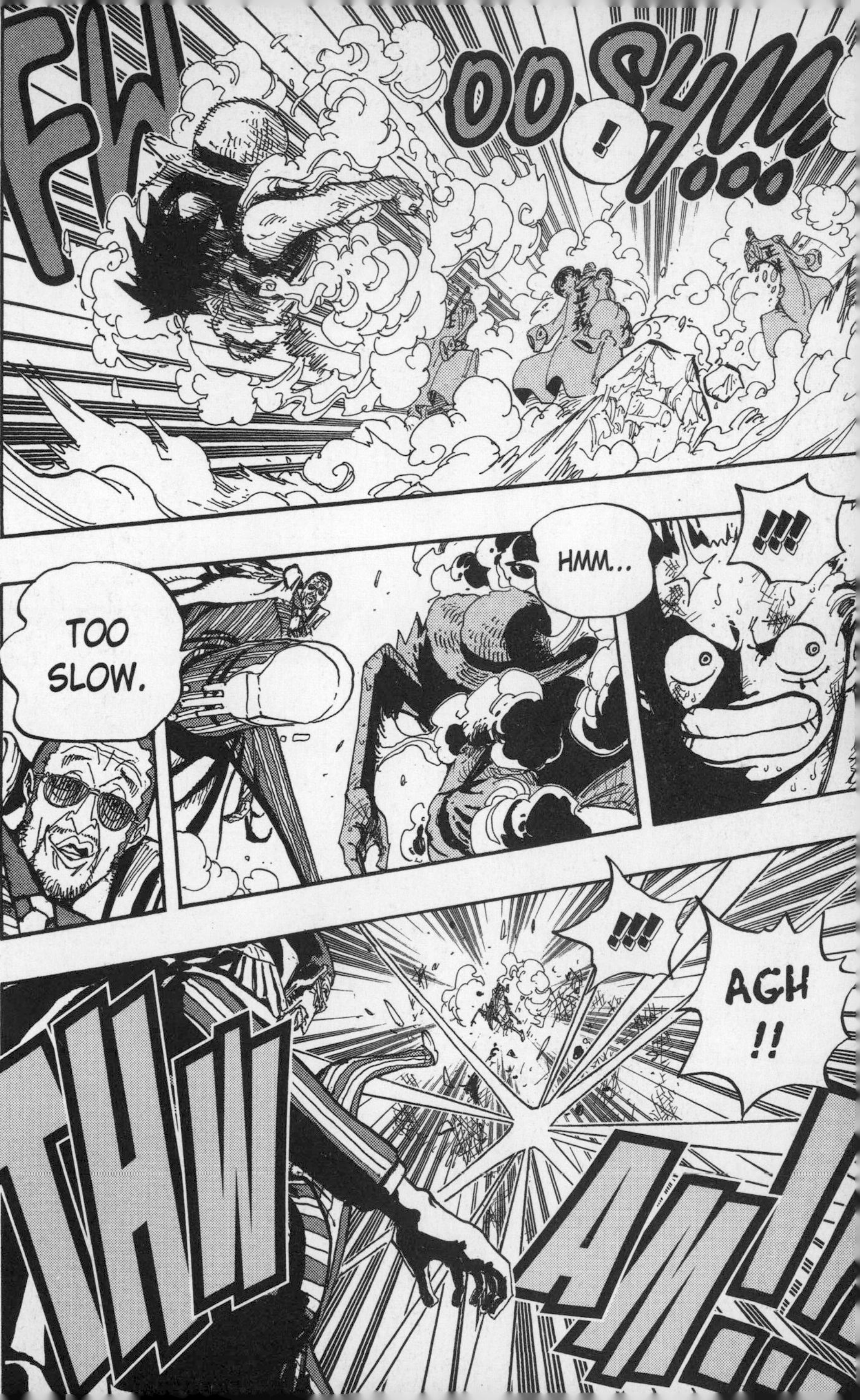
FW
OOSH
!
OOO
!!!
HMM...
TOO SLOW.
AGH !!
!!!
THW
AM...

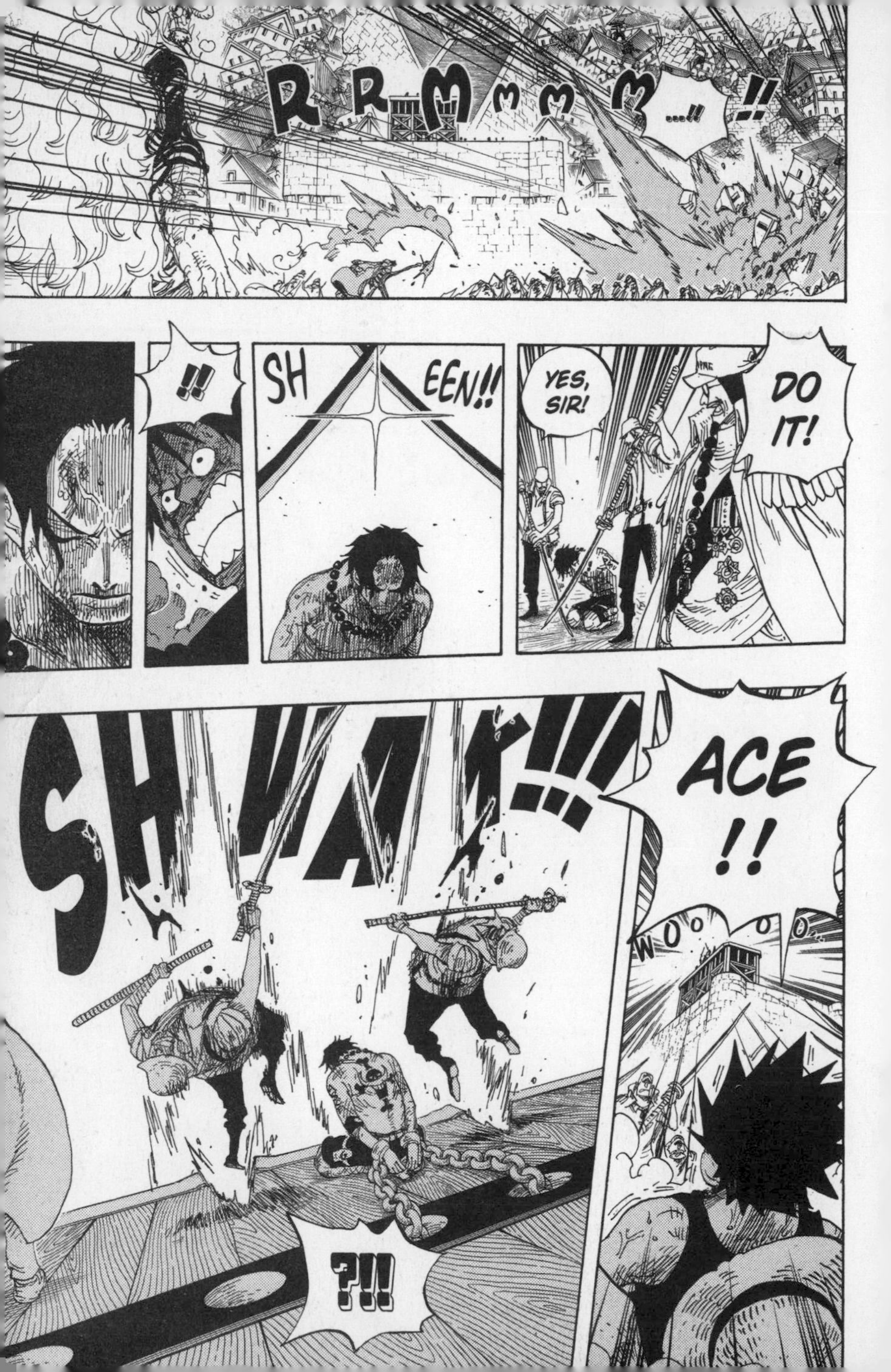
RRMMMM...!!
DO IT!
YES, SIR!
SH EEN!!
!!
ACE!!
WOOOO
SHUNK!!!
?!!

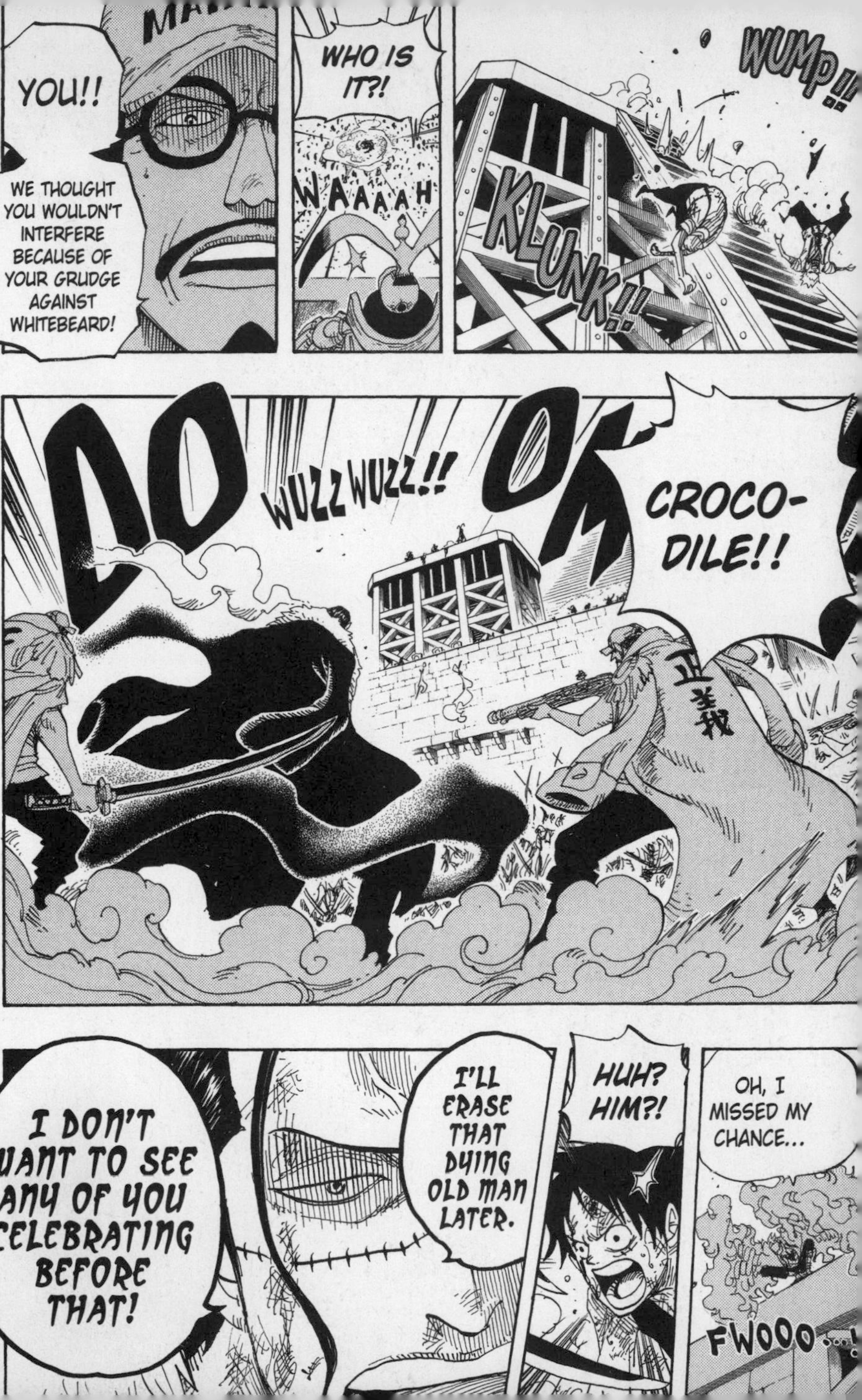
WUMP!!
KLUNK!!
WHO IS IT?!
WAAAAH
YOU!!
WE THOUGHT YOU WOULDN'T INTERFERE BECAUSE OF YOUR GRUDGE AGAINST WHITEBEARD!
CROCO-DILE!!
DOOM
WUZZ WUZZ!!
正義
OH, I MISSED MY CHANCE...
FWOOO...!
HUH? HIM?!
I'LL ERASE THAT DYING OLD MAN LATER.
I DON'T WANT TO SEE ANY OF YOU CELEBRATING BEFORE THAT!

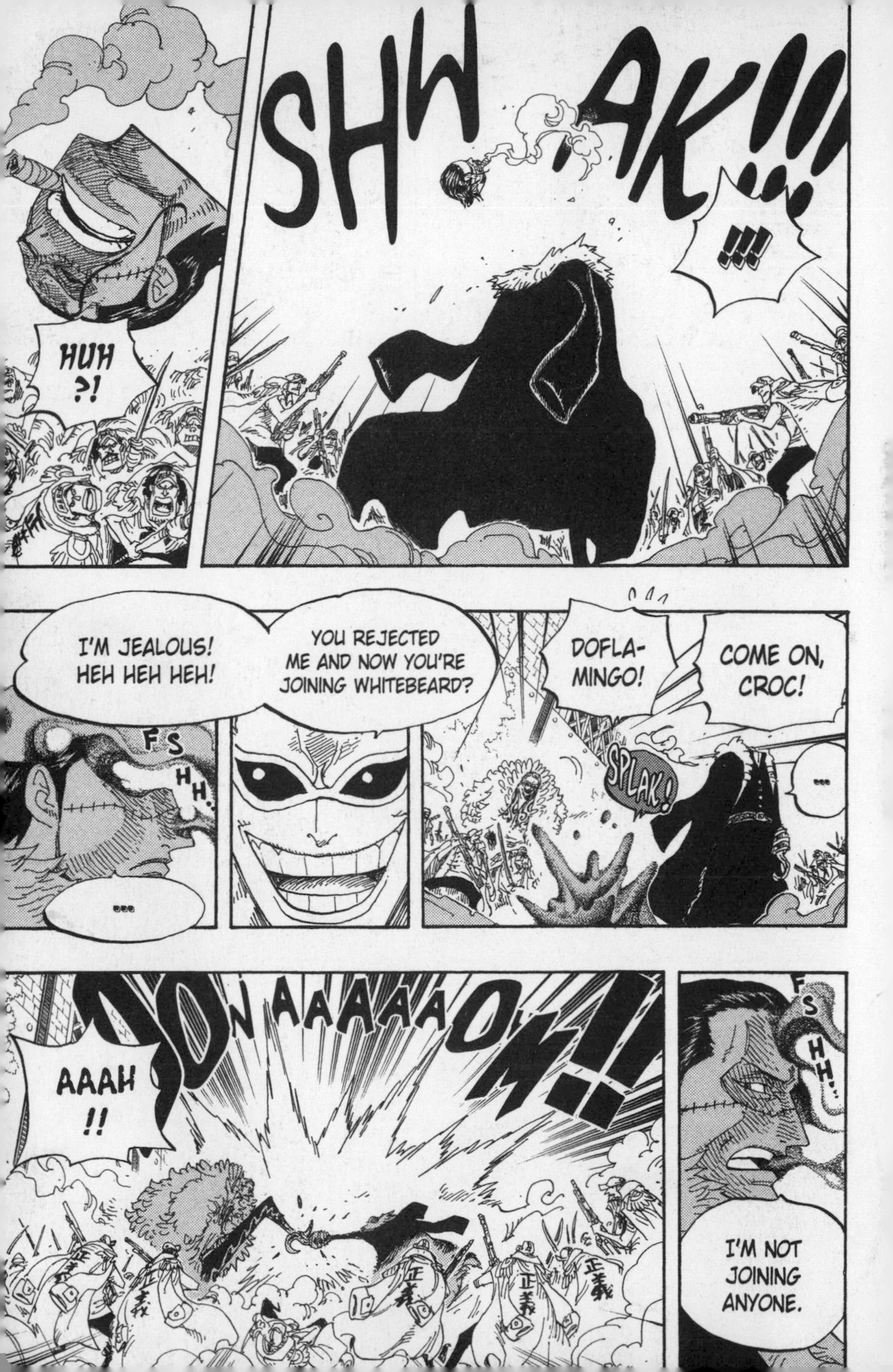
SHWAK!!!
!!!
HUH ?!
COME ON, CROC!
DOFLA-MINGO!
SPLAK!
...
YOU REJECTED ME AND NOW YOU'RE JOINING WHITEBEARD?
I'M JEALOUS! HEH HEH HEH!
FSHH...
...
FSHH...
I'M NOT JOINING ANYONE.
ON AAAAAOM!!
AAAH !!

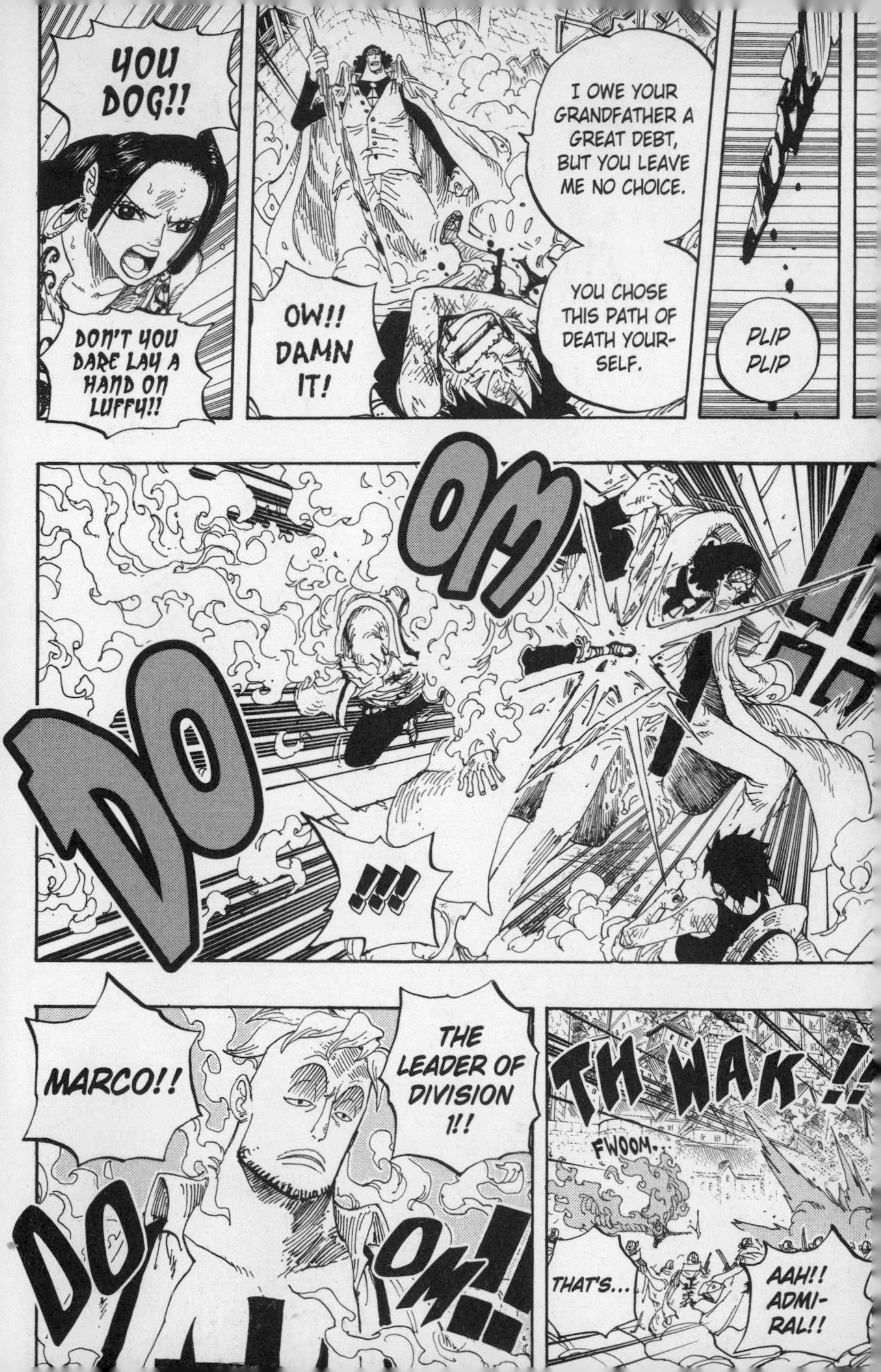
PLIP PLIP
I OWE YOUR GRANDFATHER A GREAT DEBT, BUT YOU LEAVE ME NO CHOICE.
YOU CHOSE THIS PATH OF DEATH YOURSELF.
OW!! DAMN IT!
YOU DOG!!
DON'T YOU DARE LAY A HAND ON LUFFY!!
OM
DO
!!!
THWAK!!
FWOOM...
AAH!! ADMIRAL!!
THAT'S...
THE LEADER OF DIVISION 1!!
MARCO!!
DOOM!!

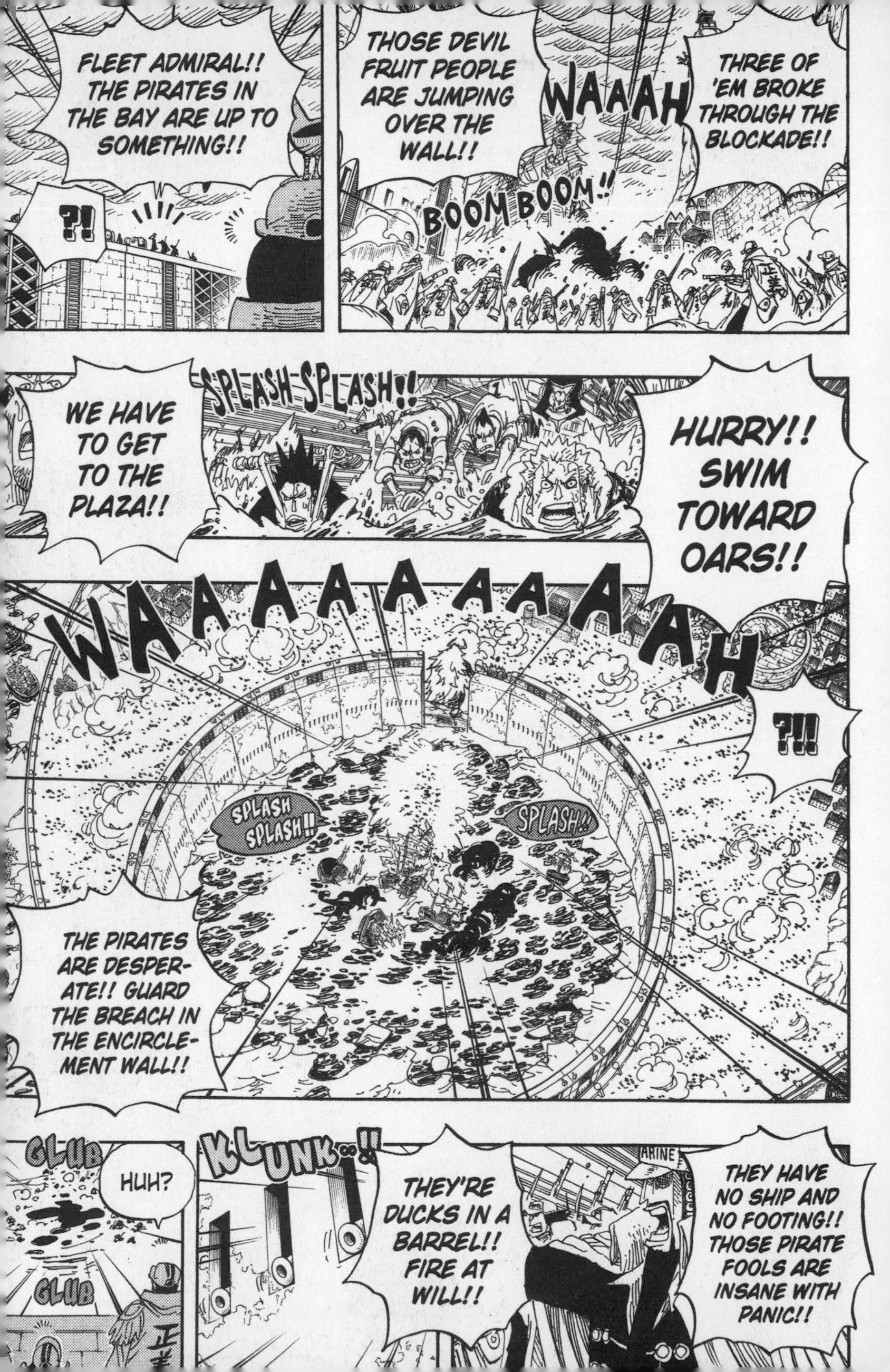
THREE OF 'EM BROKE THROUGH THE BLOCKADE!!
WAAAH
THOSE DEVIL FRUIT PEOPLE ARE JUMPING OVER THE WALL!!
BOOM BOOM!!
FLEET ADMIRAL!! THE PIRATES IN THE BAY ARE UP TO SOMETHING!!
?!
HURRY!! SWIM TOWARD OARS!!
SPLASH SPLASH!!
WE HAVE TO GET TO THE PLAZA!!
WAAAAAAAAAAH
?!!
SPLASH!!
SPLASH SPLASH!!
THE PIRATES ARE DESPERATE!! GUARD THE BREACH IN THE ENCIRCLEMENT WALL!!
THEY HAVE NO SHIP AND NO FOOTING!! THOSE PIRATE FOOLS ARE INSANE WITH PANIC!!
THEY'RE DUCKS IN A BARREL!! FIRE AT WILL!!
KLUNK..!!
HUH?
GLUB
GLUB

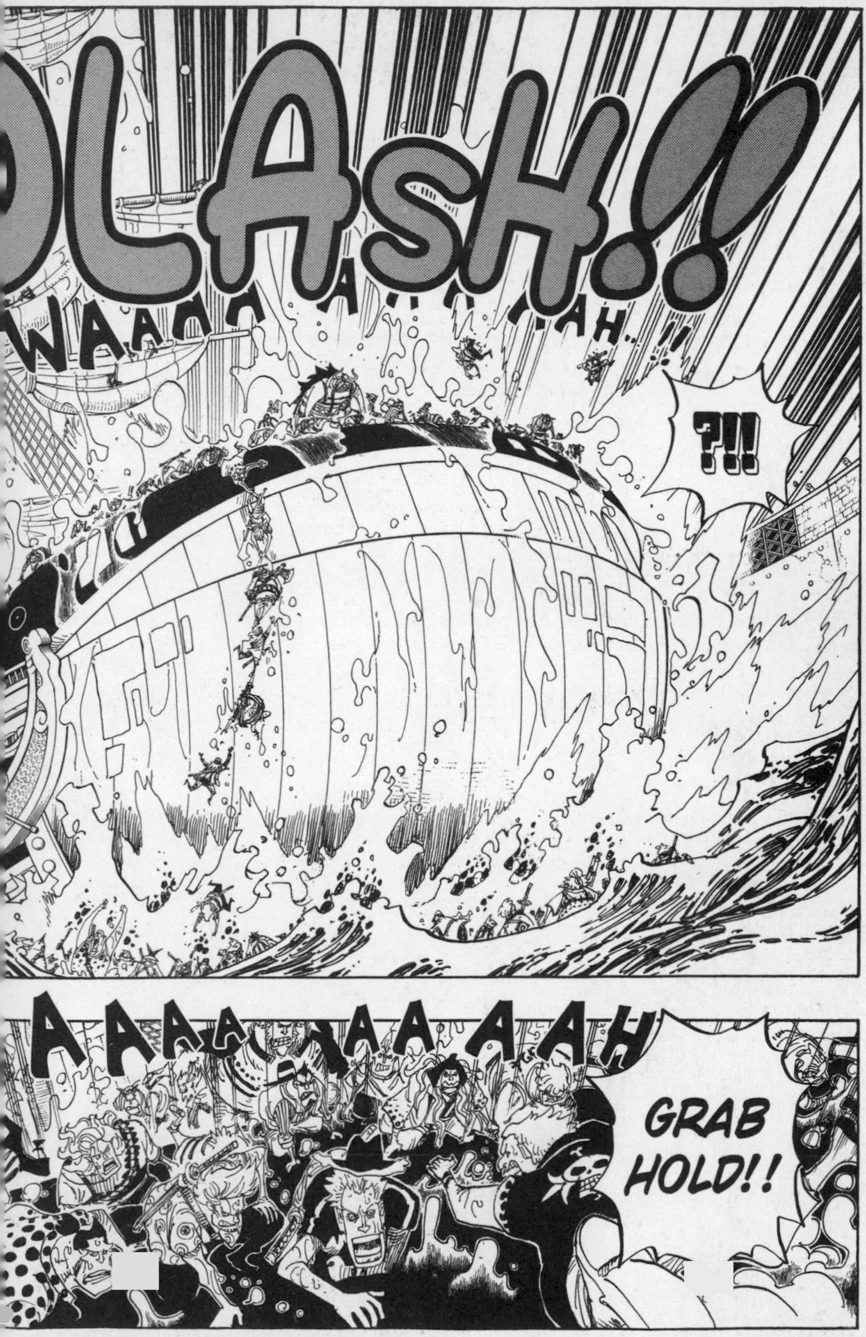

LASH!!
?!!
WAAAAAAAAAH..!!
GRAB HOLD!!
AAAAAAAAAH

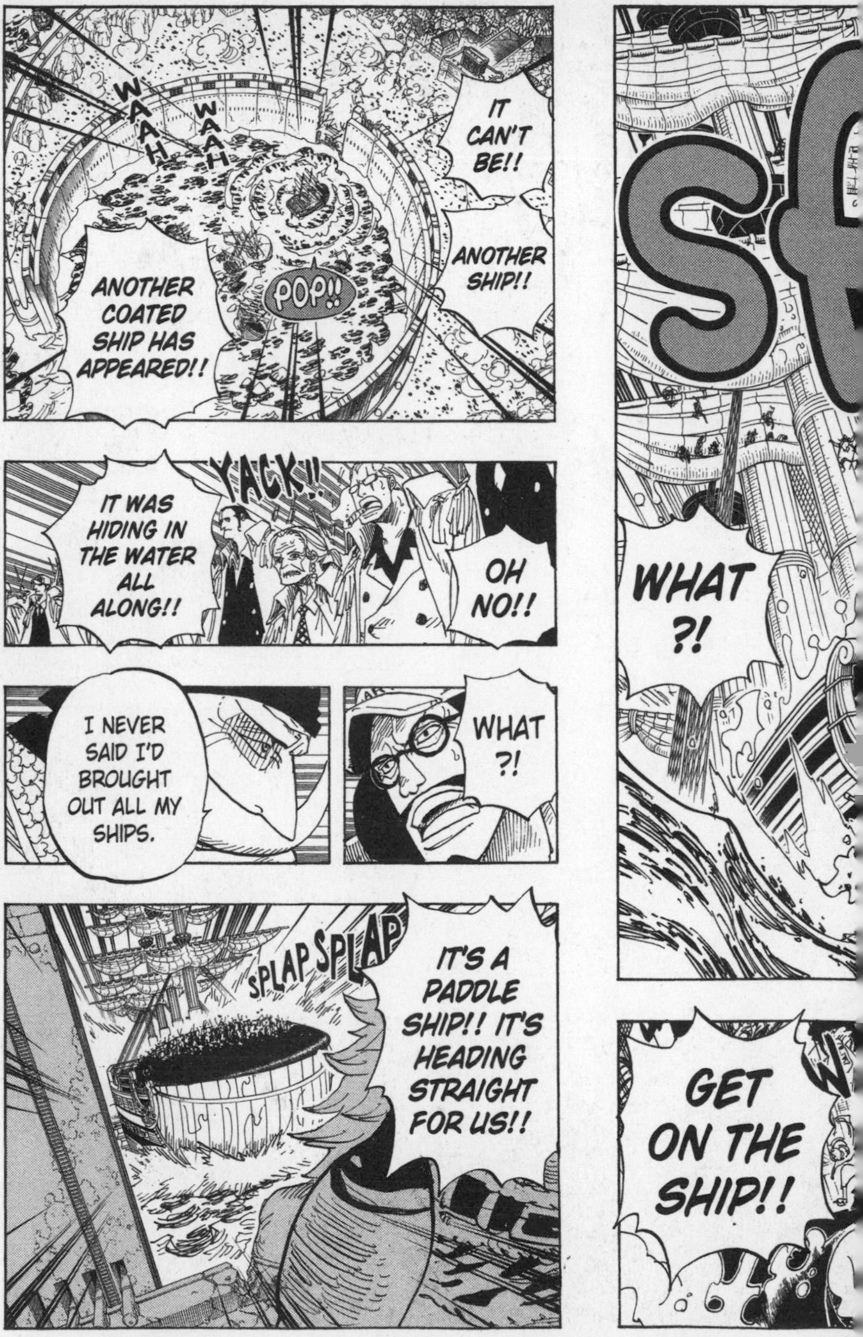
WHAT ?!
GET ON THE SHIP!!
IT CAN'T BE!!
ANOTHER SHIP!!
WAAH WAAH
POP!!
ANOTHER COATED SHIP HAS APPEARED!!
OH NO!!
YACK!!
IT WAS HIDING IN THE WATER ALL ALONG!!
WHAT ?!
I NEVER SAID I'D BROUGHT OUT ALL MY SHIPS.
IT'S A PADDLE SHIP!! IT'S HEADING STRAIGHT FOR US!!
SPLAP SPLAP

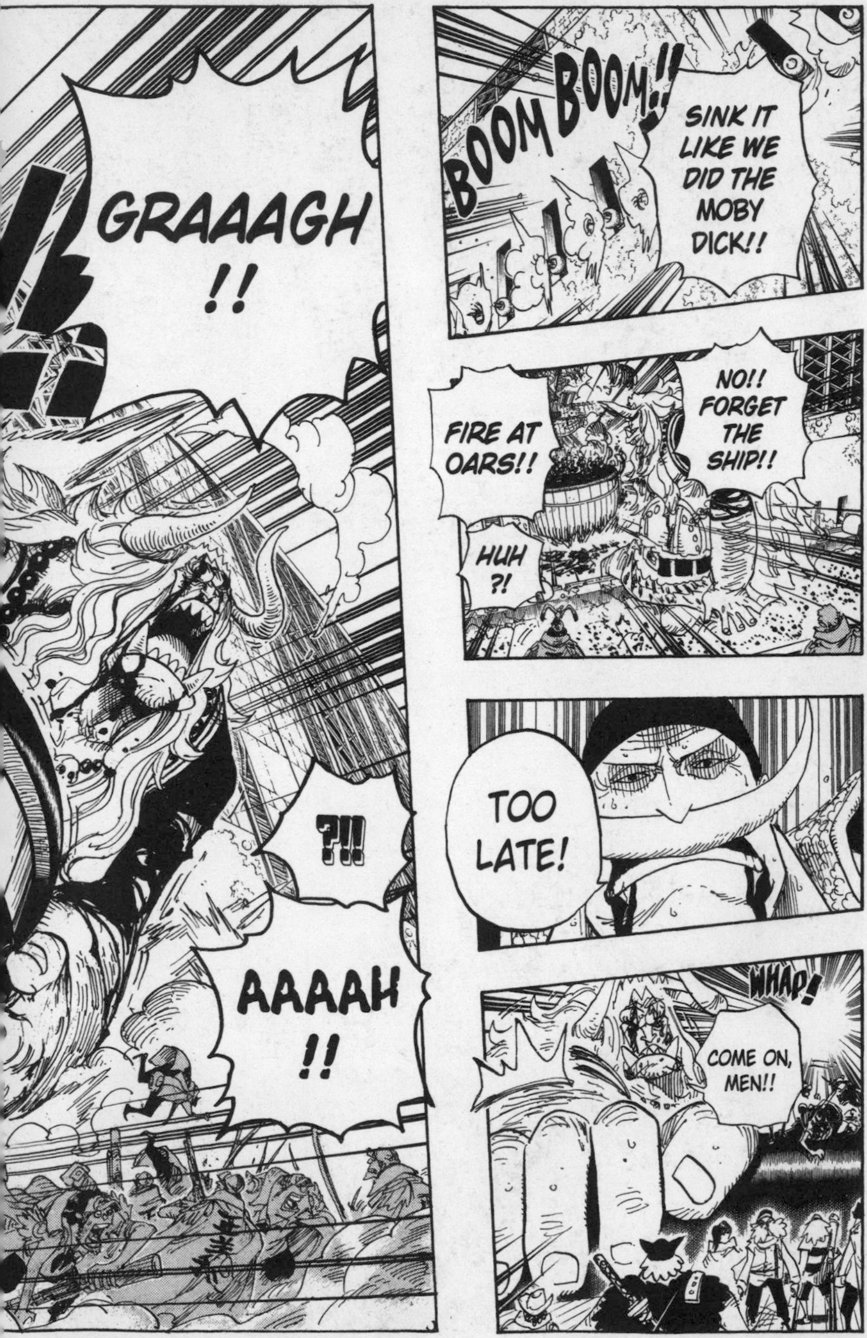
BOOM BOOM!!
SINK IT LIKE WE DID THE MOBY DICK!!
NO!! FORGET THE SHIP!!
FIRE AT OARS!!
HUH ?!
TOO LATE!
WHAP!
COME ON, MEN!!
GRAAAGH !!
?!!
AAAAH !!

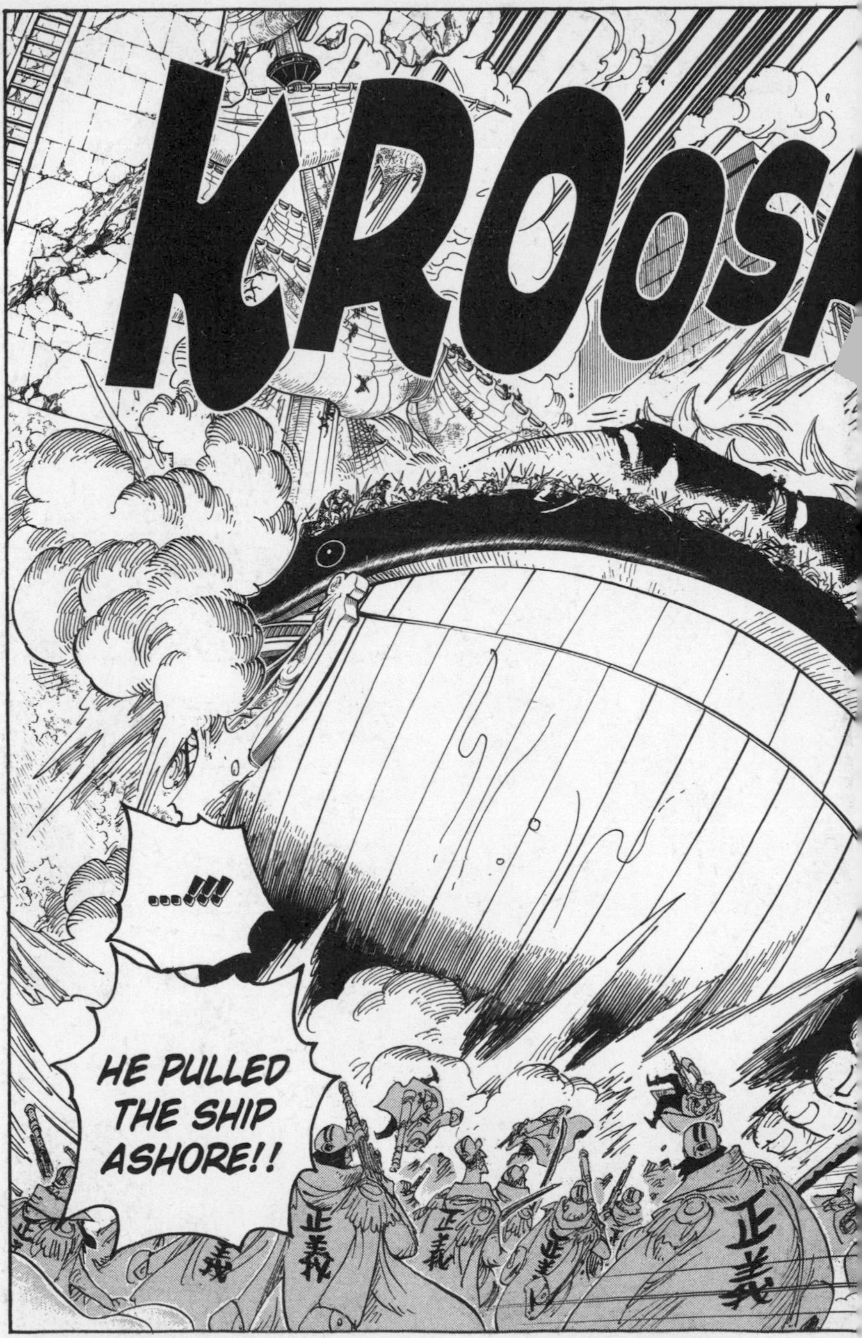
KROOS
...!!!
HE PULLED THE SHIP ASHORE!!

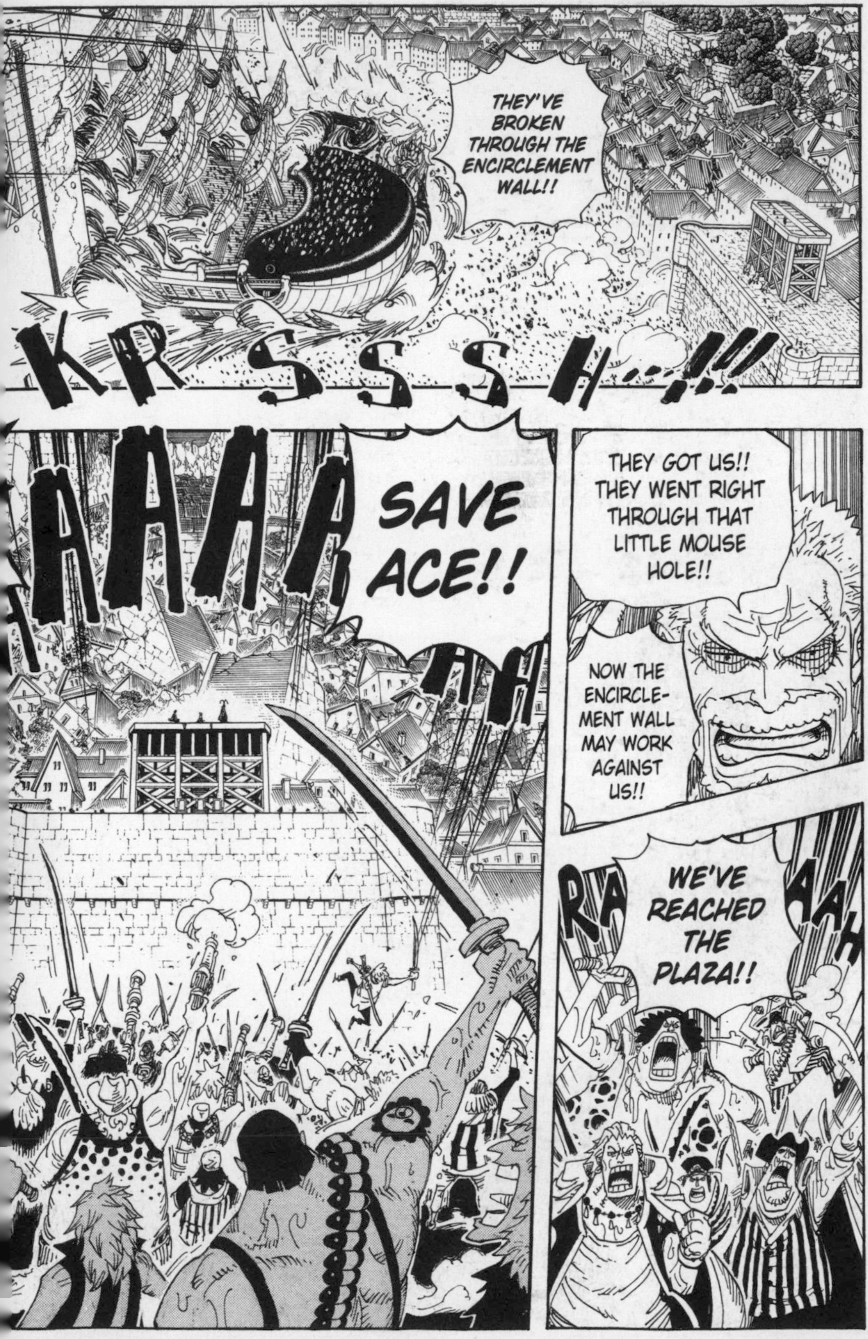
THEY'VE BROKEN THROUGH THE ENCIRCLEMENT WALL!!
KRSSSH...!!!
THEY GOT US!! THEY WENT RIGHT THROUGH THAT LITTLE MOUSE HOLE!!
NOW THE ENCIRCLEMENT WALL MAY WORK AGAINST US!!
RA
AAH
WE'VE REACHED THE PLAZA!!
AAAAA
SAVE ACE!!
AH

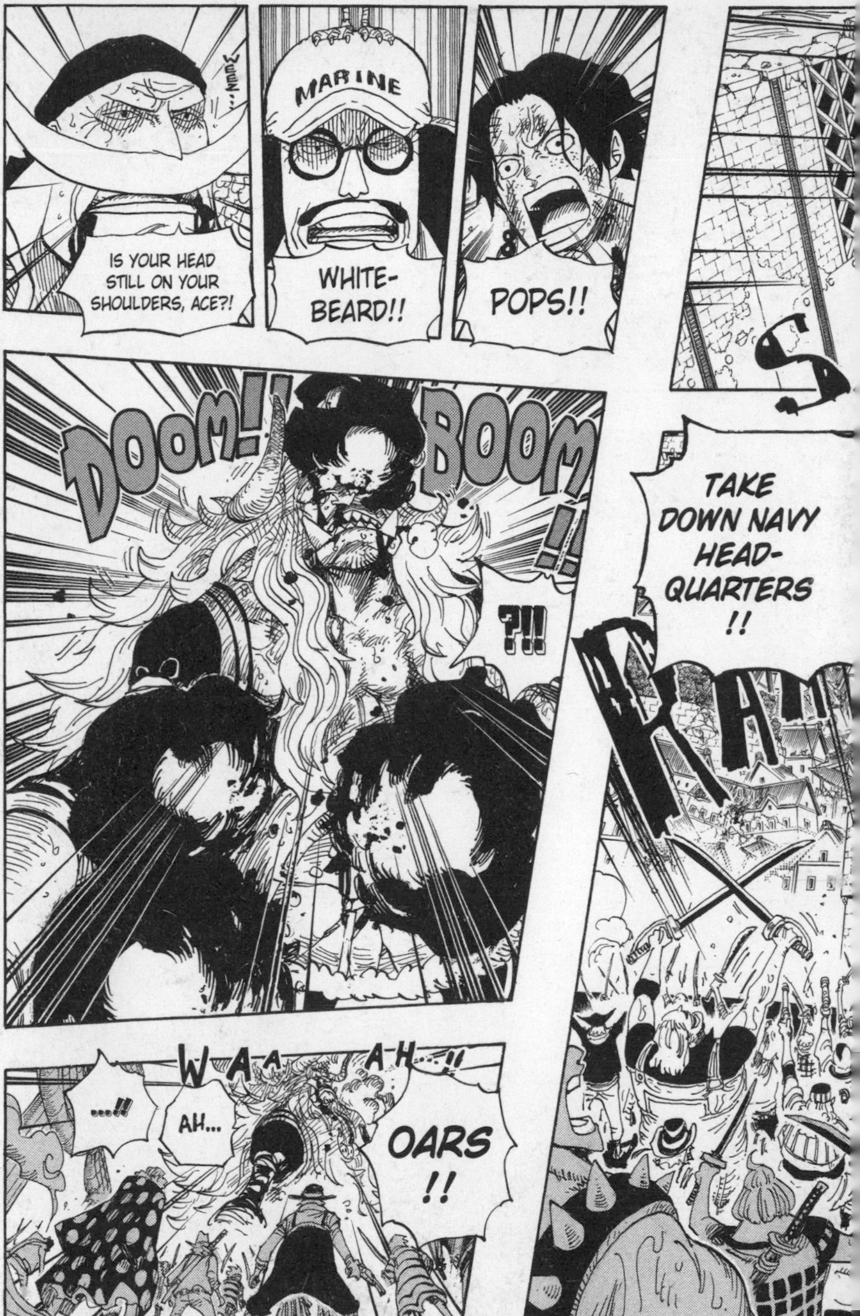
POPS!!
WHITE-BEARD!!
WEEN...
IS YOUR HEAD STILL ON YOUR SHOULDERS, ACE?!
TAKE DOWN NAVY HEAD-QUARTERS!!
RAM
DOOM!! BOOM!!
?!!
OARS!!
WAA AH...!!
AH...
...!!

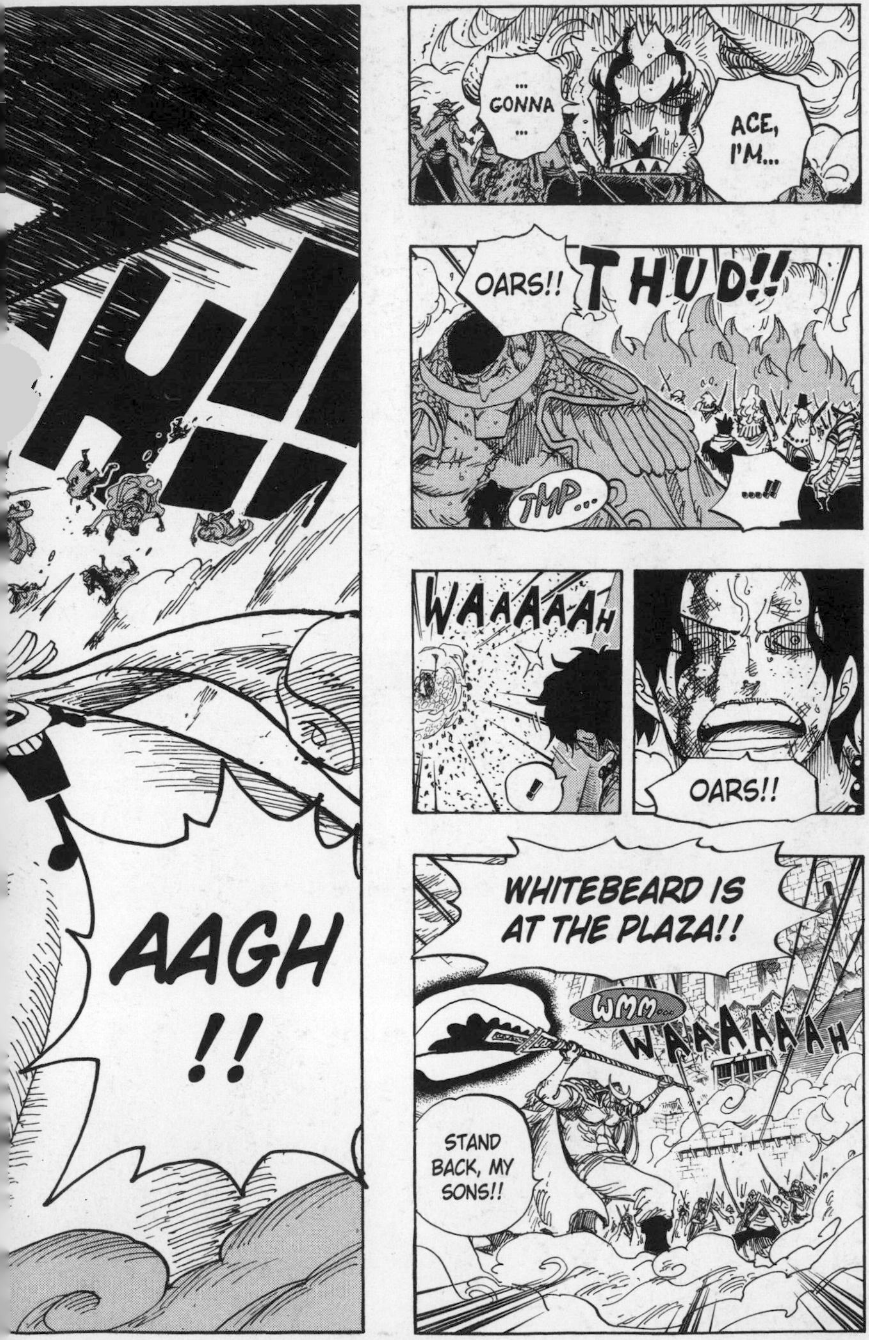
ACE, I'M...
... GONNA ... ...
THUD!!
OARS!!
...!!
TMP...
OARS!!
WAAAAAH
!
WHITEBEARD IS AT THE PLAZA!!
WMM...
WAAAAAAH
STAND BACK, MY SONS!!
AAGH !!

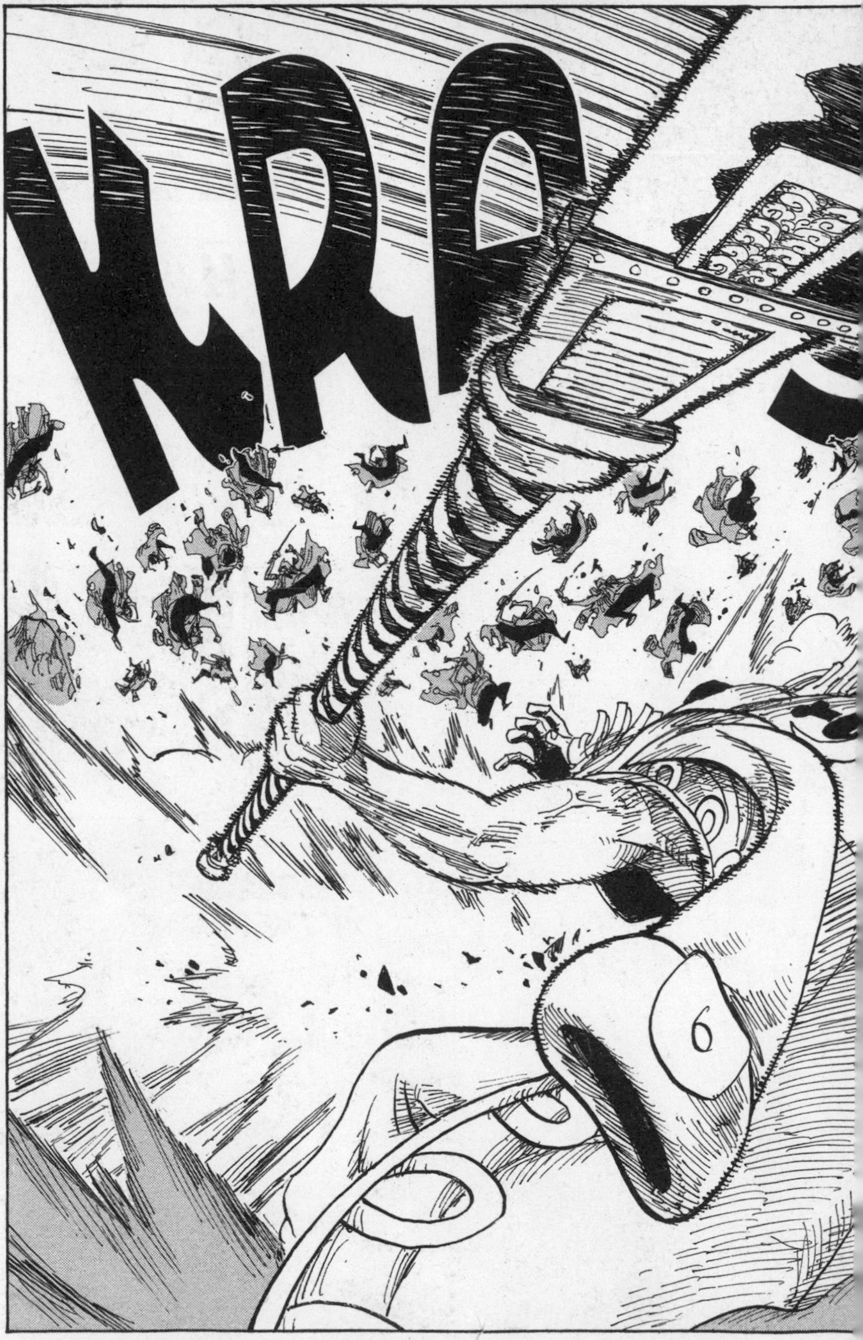
KRA

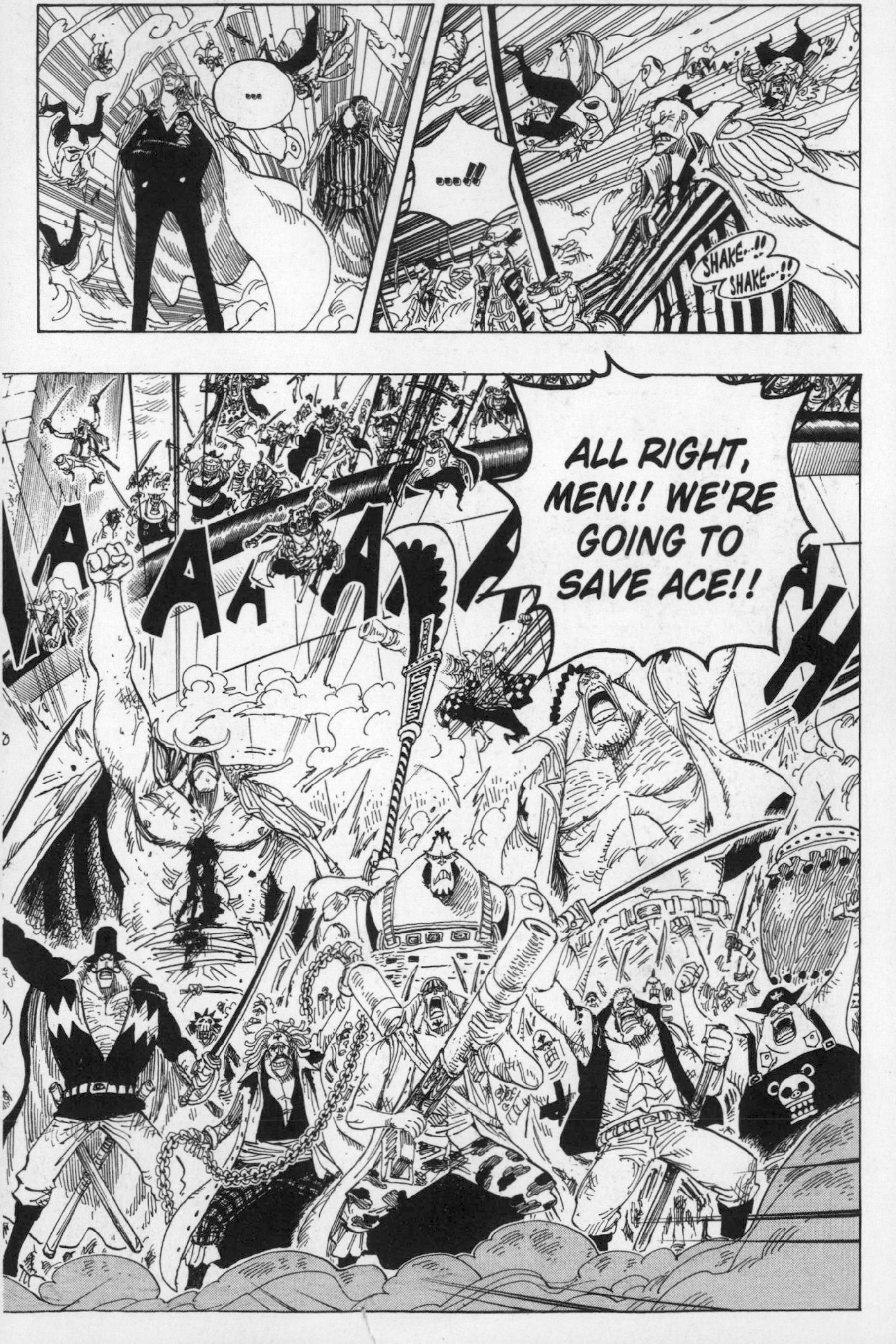
...!!
SHAKE...!!
SHAKE...!!
...
ALL RIGHT, MEN!! WE'RE GOING TO SAVE ACE!!

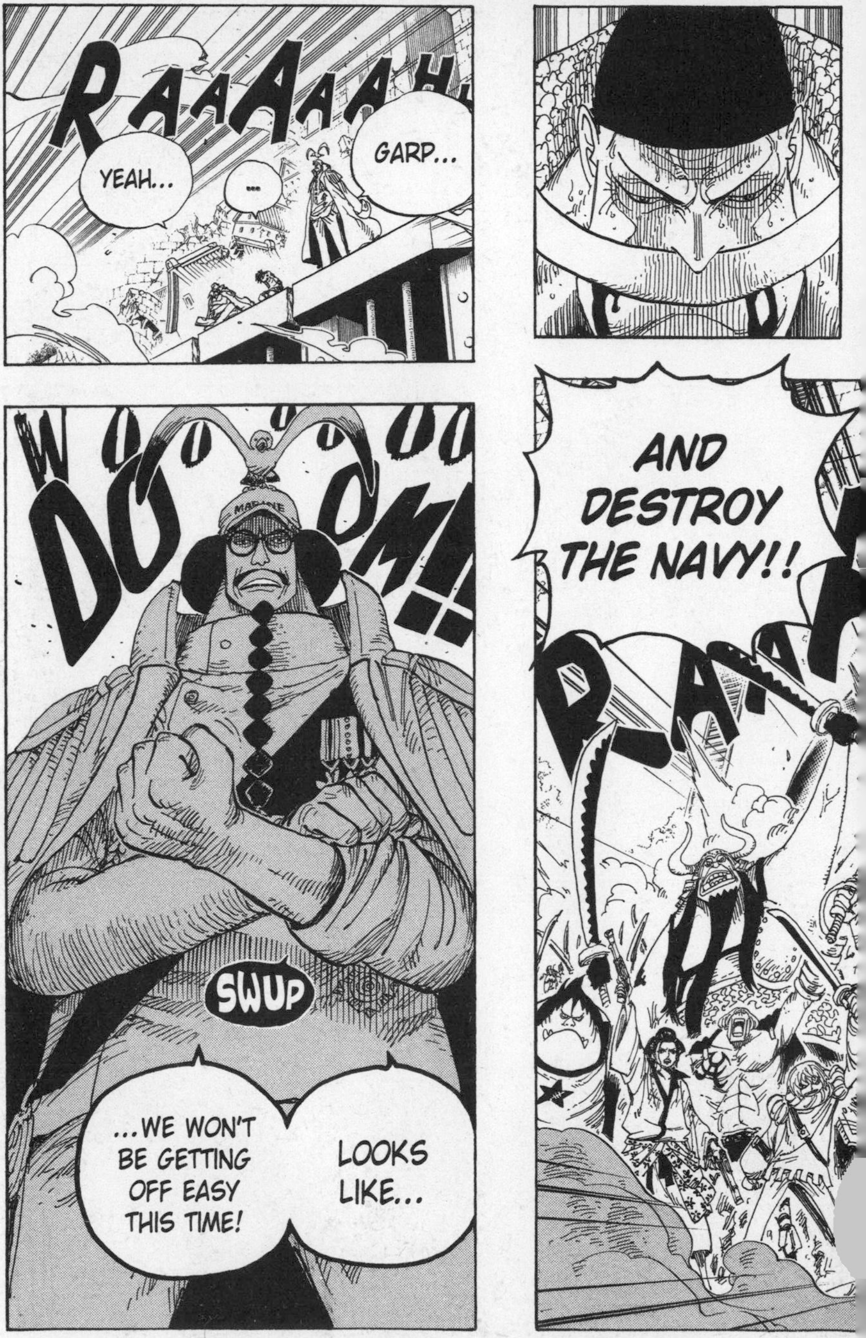
RAAAAAH
GARP...
...
YEAH...
AND DESTROY THE NAVY!!
WOOOOOO
DOOM!!
SWUP
LOOKS LIKE...
...WE WON'T BE GETTING OFF EASY THIS TIME!

HEADQUARTERS—ORIS PLAZA

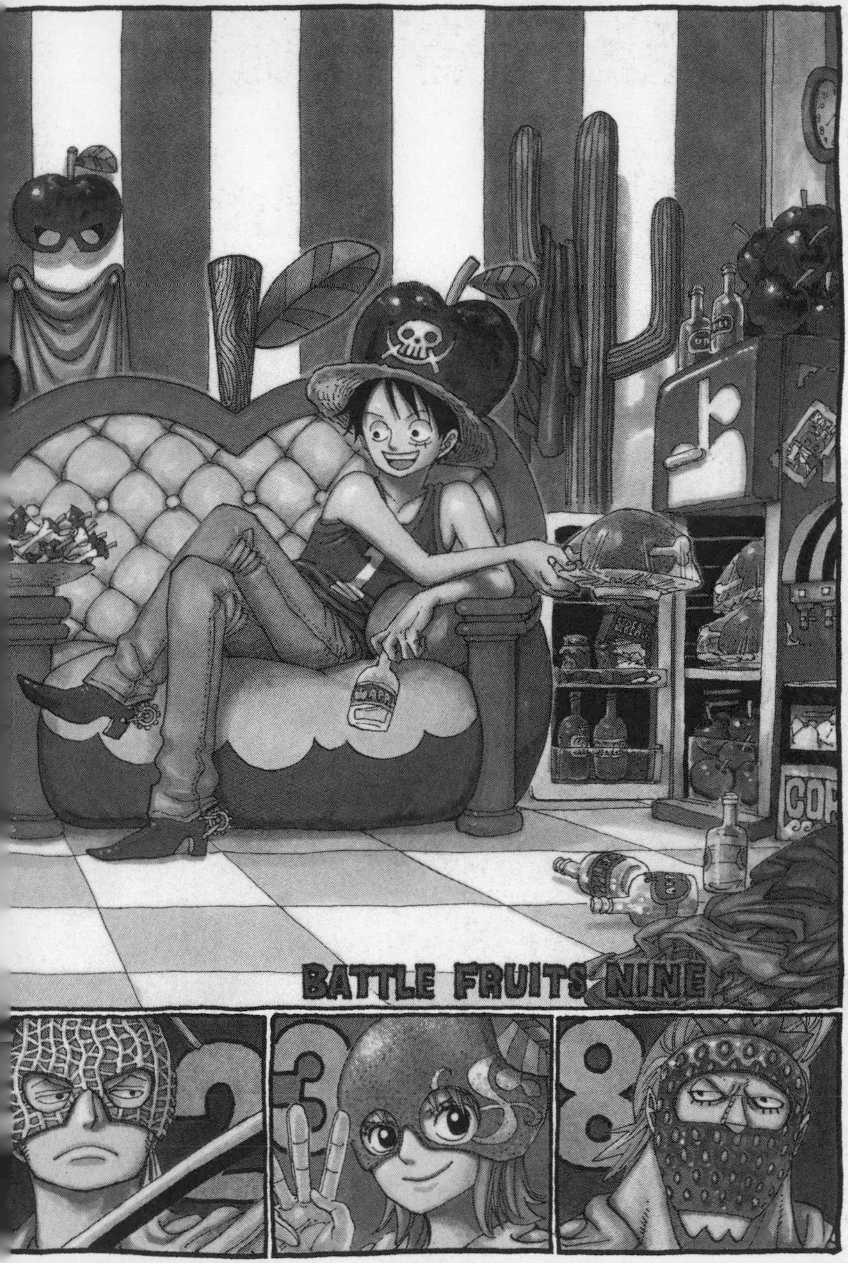
BATTLE FRUITS NINE
8
3
2

Chapter 567: MARINEFORD NAVY

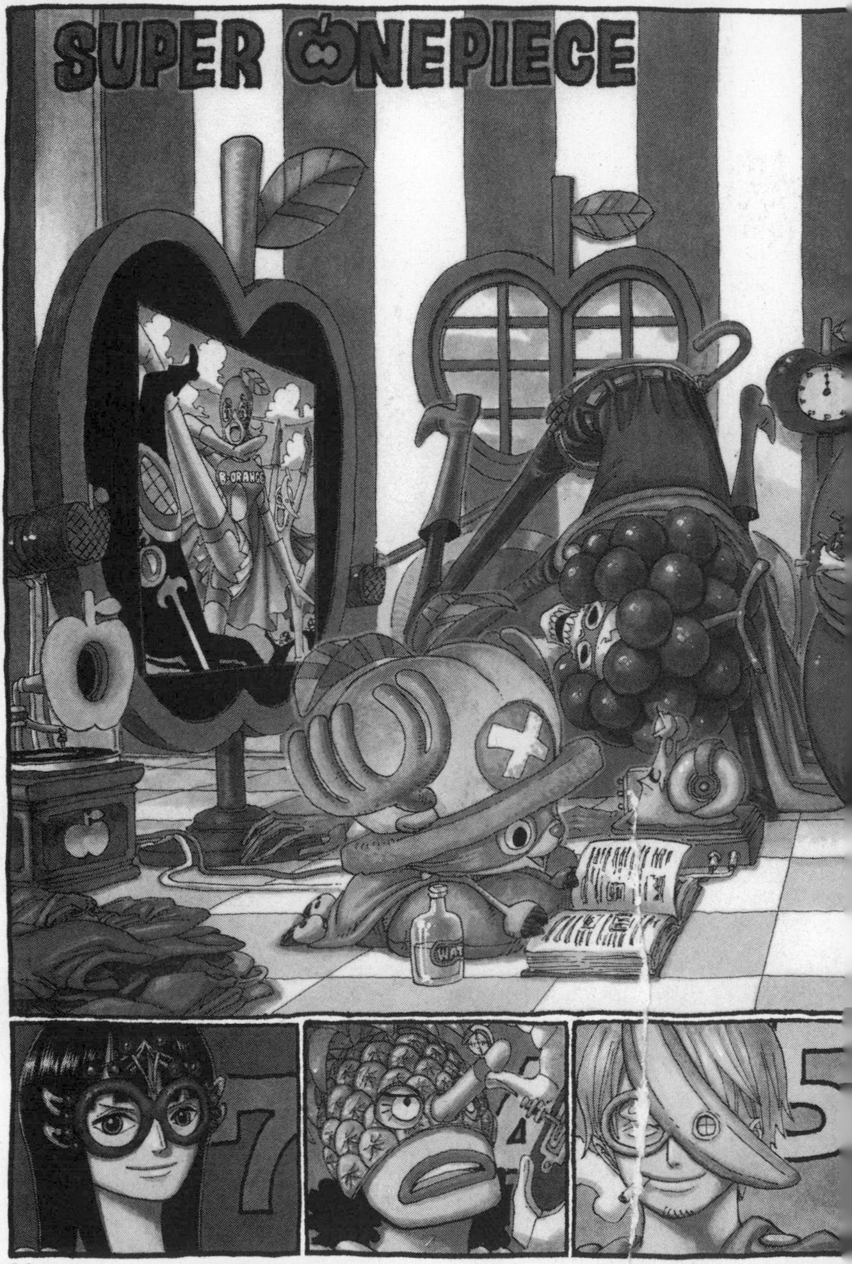
SUPER ONEPIECE
B-ORANGE
5
4
7

vol.58

ONE PIECE

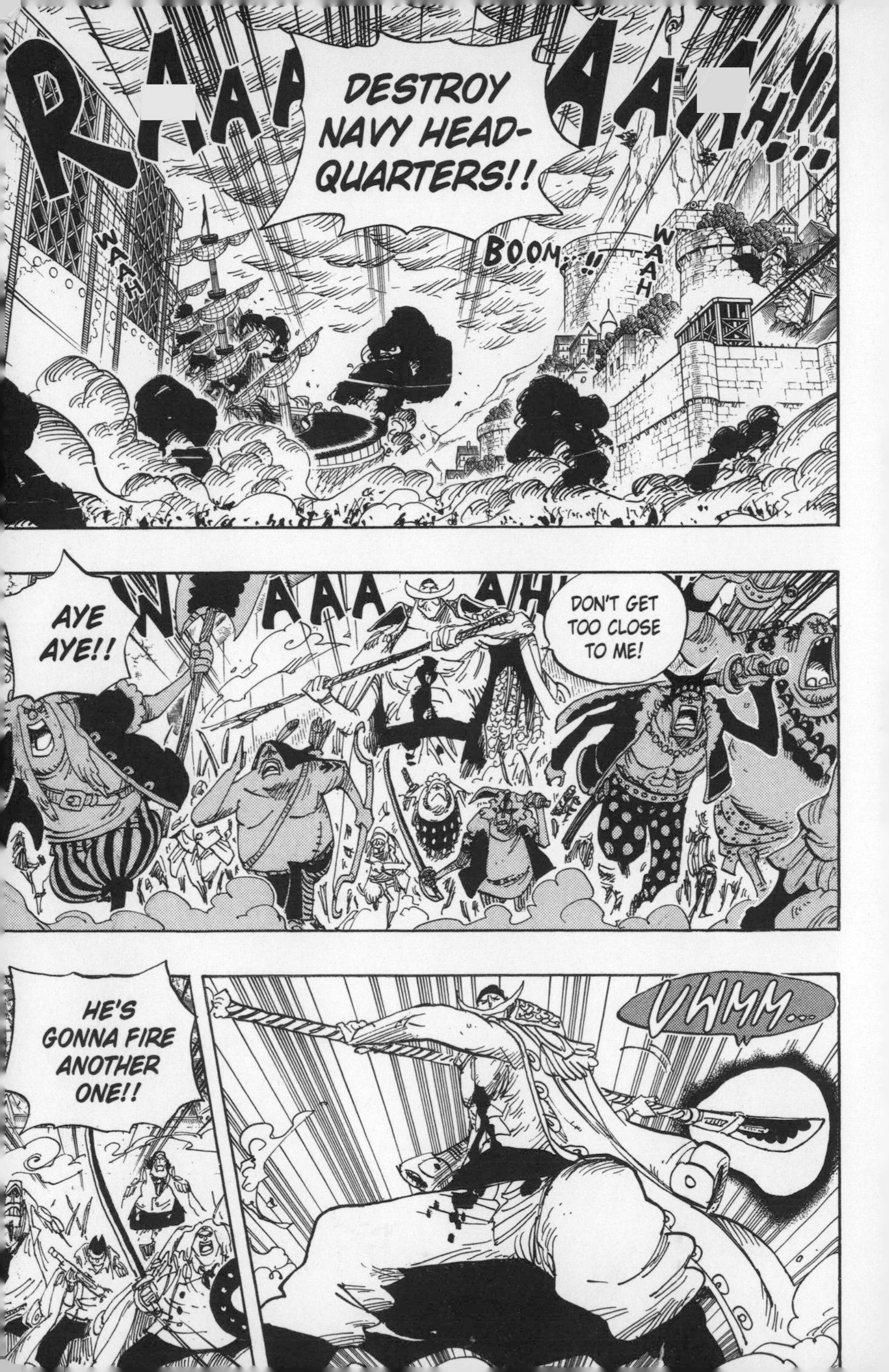
RAAA
AAAH!!!
DESTROY NAVY HEAD-QUARTERS!!
BOOM...!!
WAAH
WAAH
WAAA AH
DON'T GET TOO CLOSE TO ME!
AYE AYE!!
UWMM...
HE'S GONNA FIRE ANOTHER ONE!!

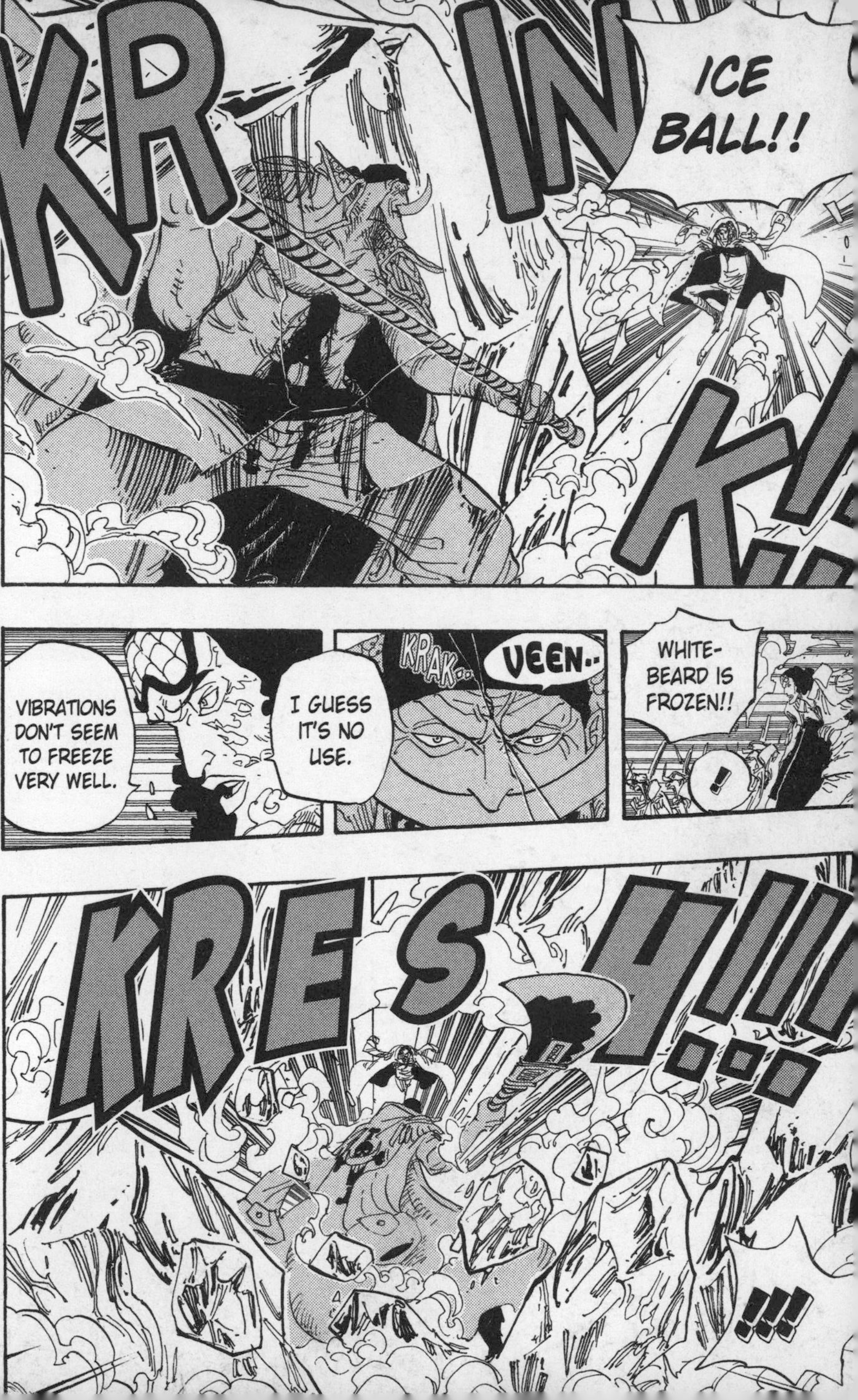
ICE BALL!!
KR IN
WHITE-BEARD IS FROZEN!!
!
KRAK..
VEEN..
I GUESS IT'S NO USE.
VIBRATIONS DON'T SEEM TO FREEZE VERY WELL.
KRESH!!!
!!!

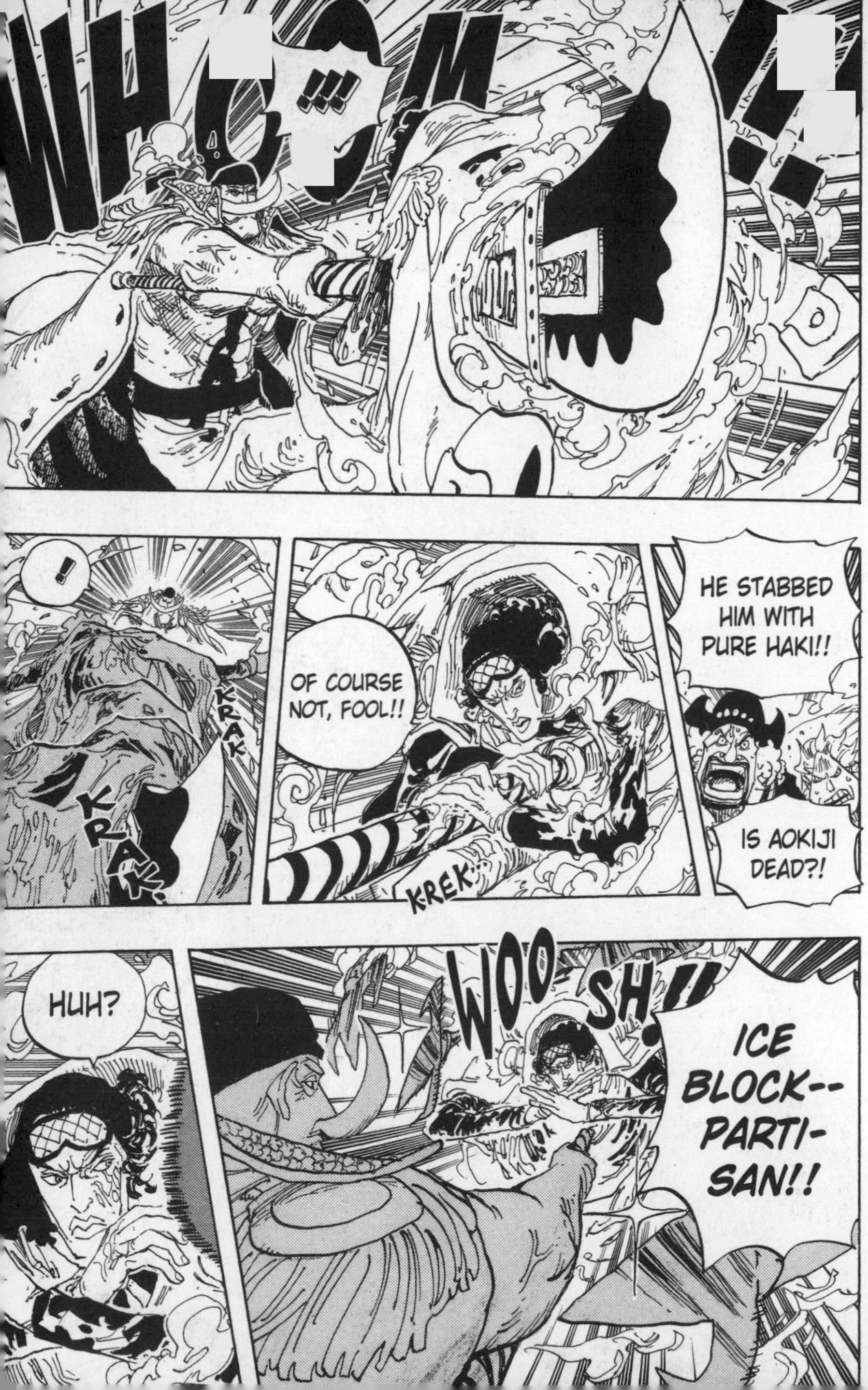
WHOOM!!
HE STABBED HIM WITH PURE HAKI!!
IS AOKIJI DEAD?!
OF COURSE NOT, FOOL!!
KREK
!
KRAK
KRAK
WOOSH!!
ICE BLOCK-- PARTI-SAN!!
HUH?

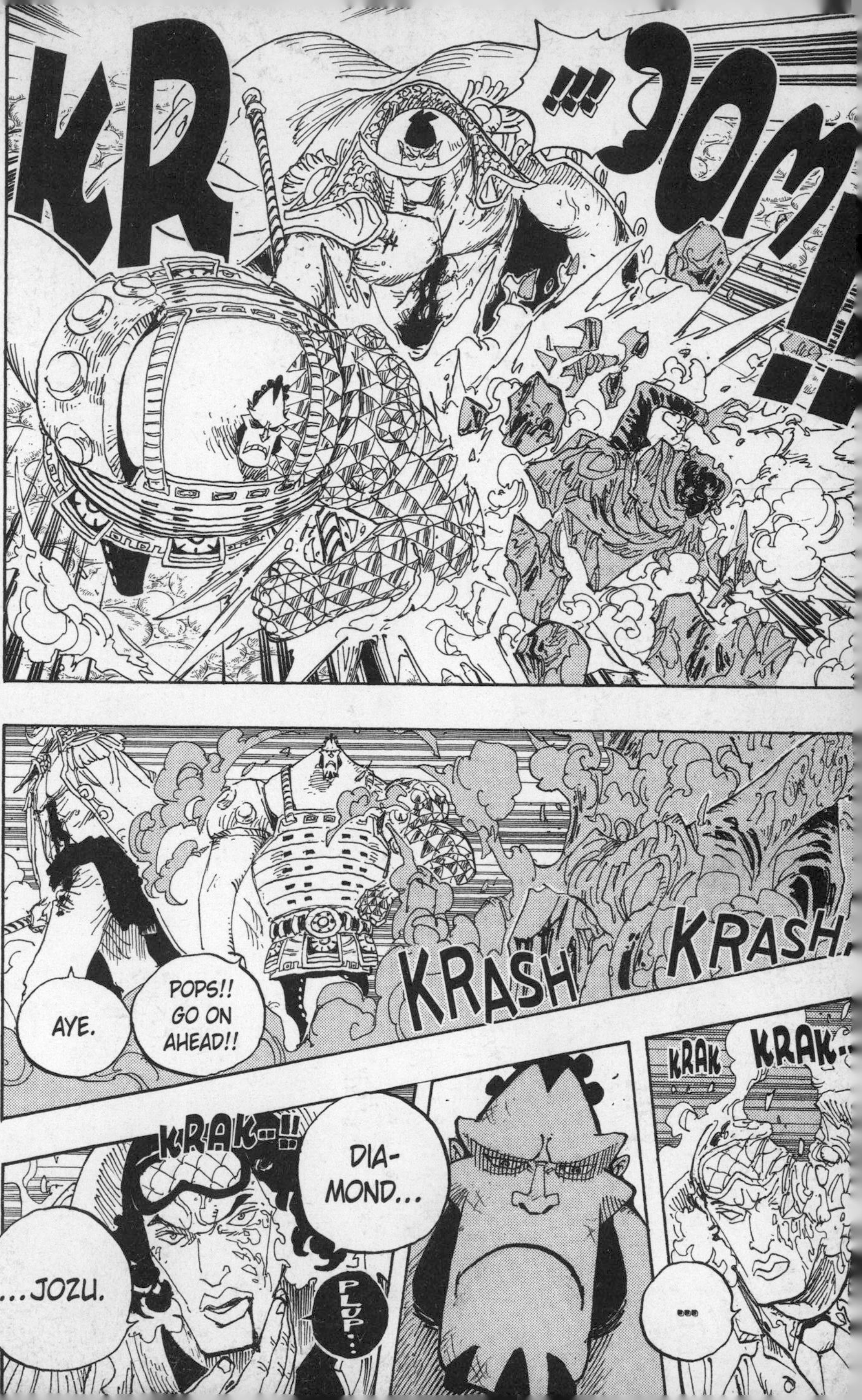
KR
KRASH
KRASH
POPS!! GO ON AHEAD!!
AYE.
KRAK...
KRAK
...
DIA-MOND...
KRAK-!!
...JOZU.
PLUP...

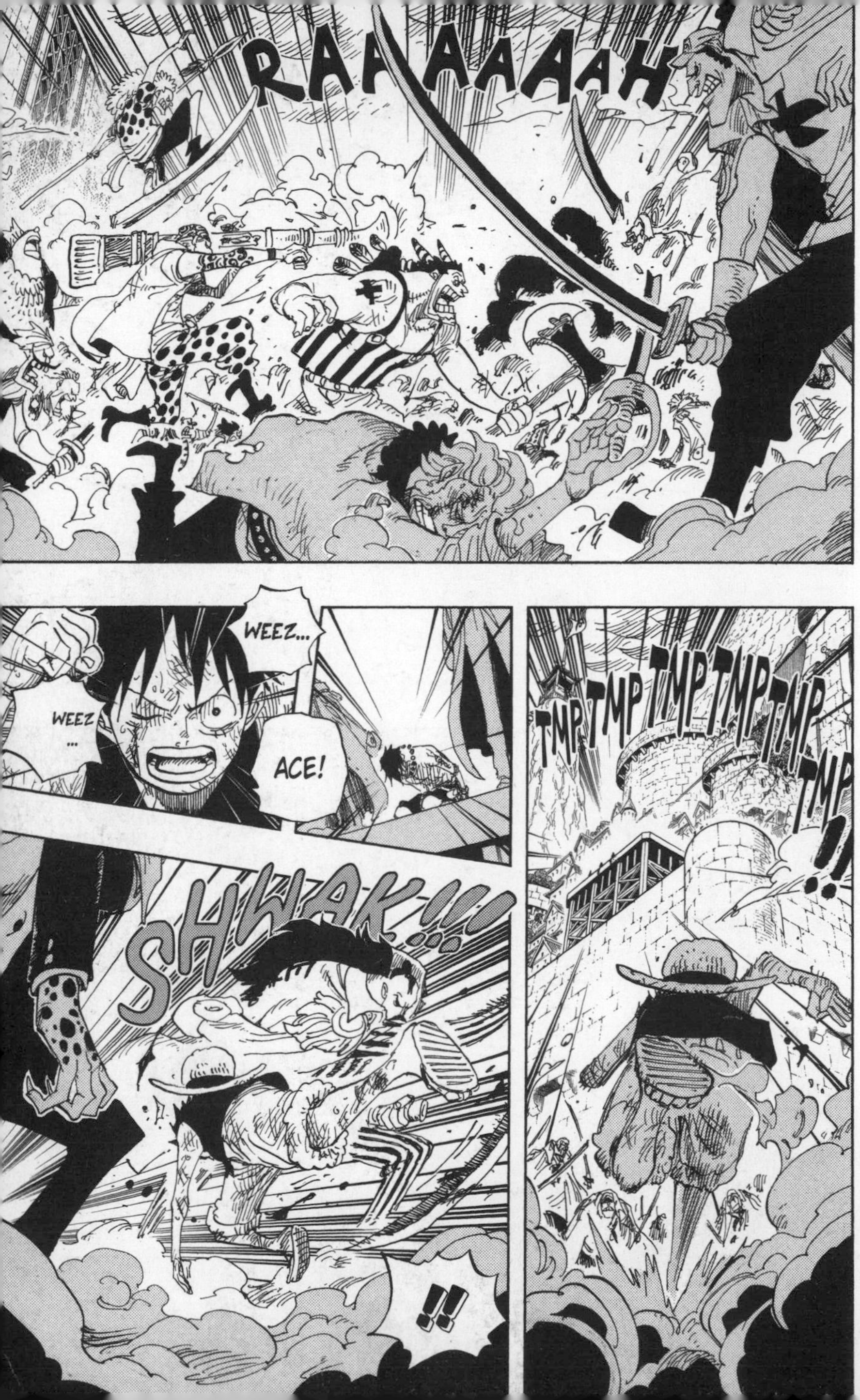
RAAAAAAH
TMP TMP TMP TMP TMP TMP TMP!!
WEEZ...
WEEZ ...
ACE!
SHWAK!!!
!!

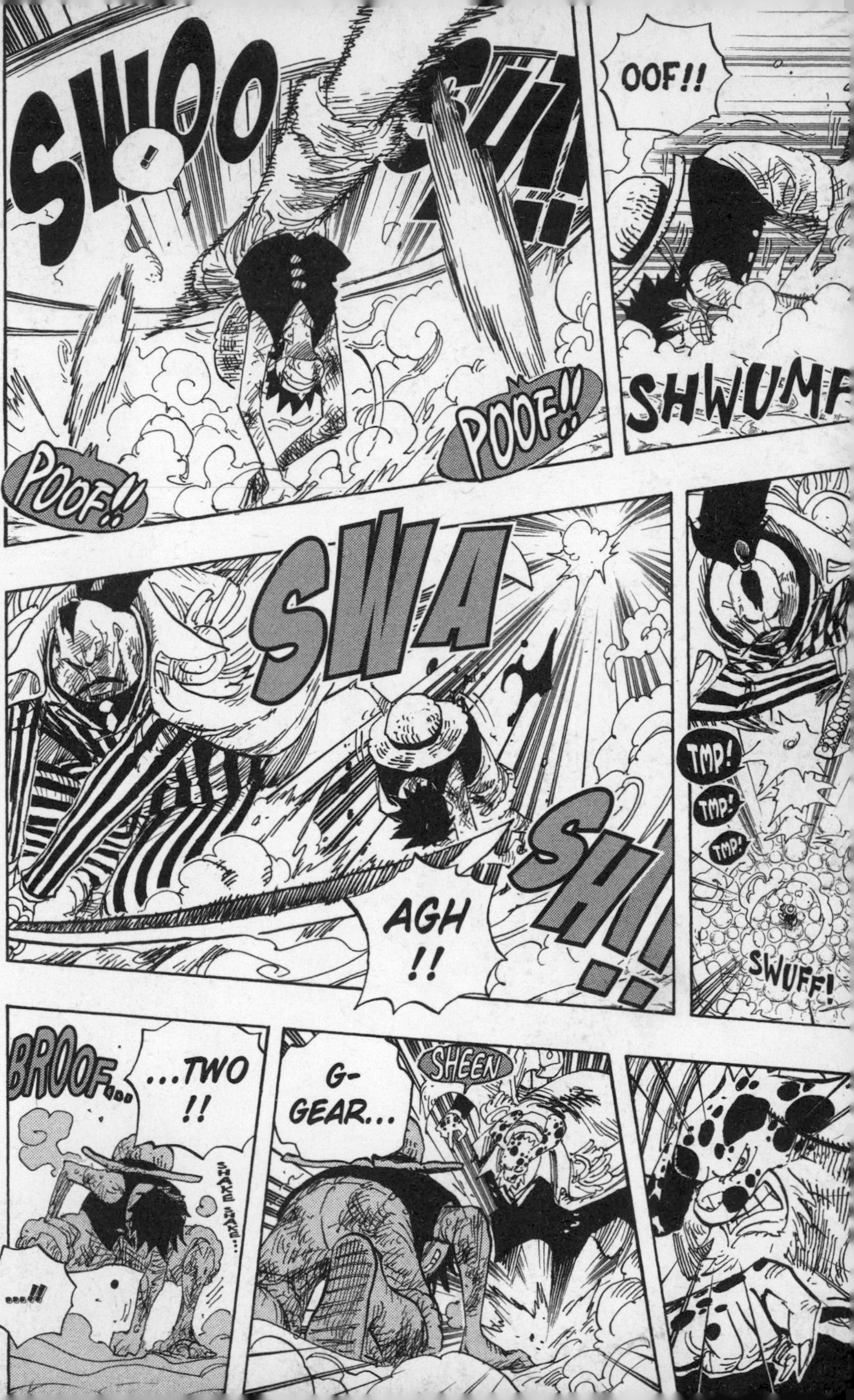
OOF!!
SHWUMF
SHOO
!!
POOF!!
POOF!!
TMP!
TMP!
TMP!
SWUFF!
SWA
SH!!
AGH !!
SHEEN
G- GEAR...
BROOF...
...TWO !!
SHAKE SHAKE...
...!!

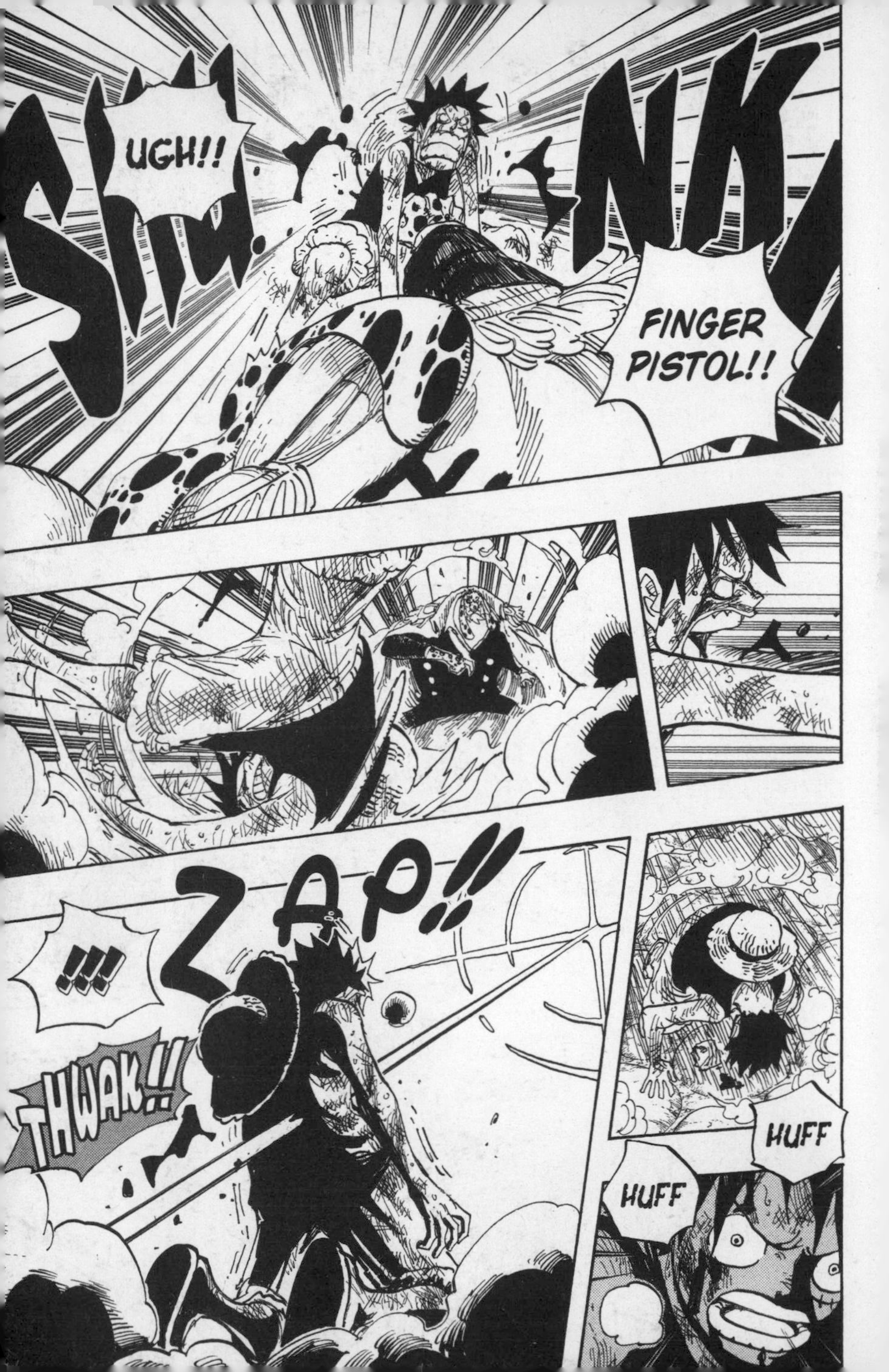
FINGER PISTOL!!
UGH!!
HUFF
HUFF
ZAP!!
!!!
THWAK!!

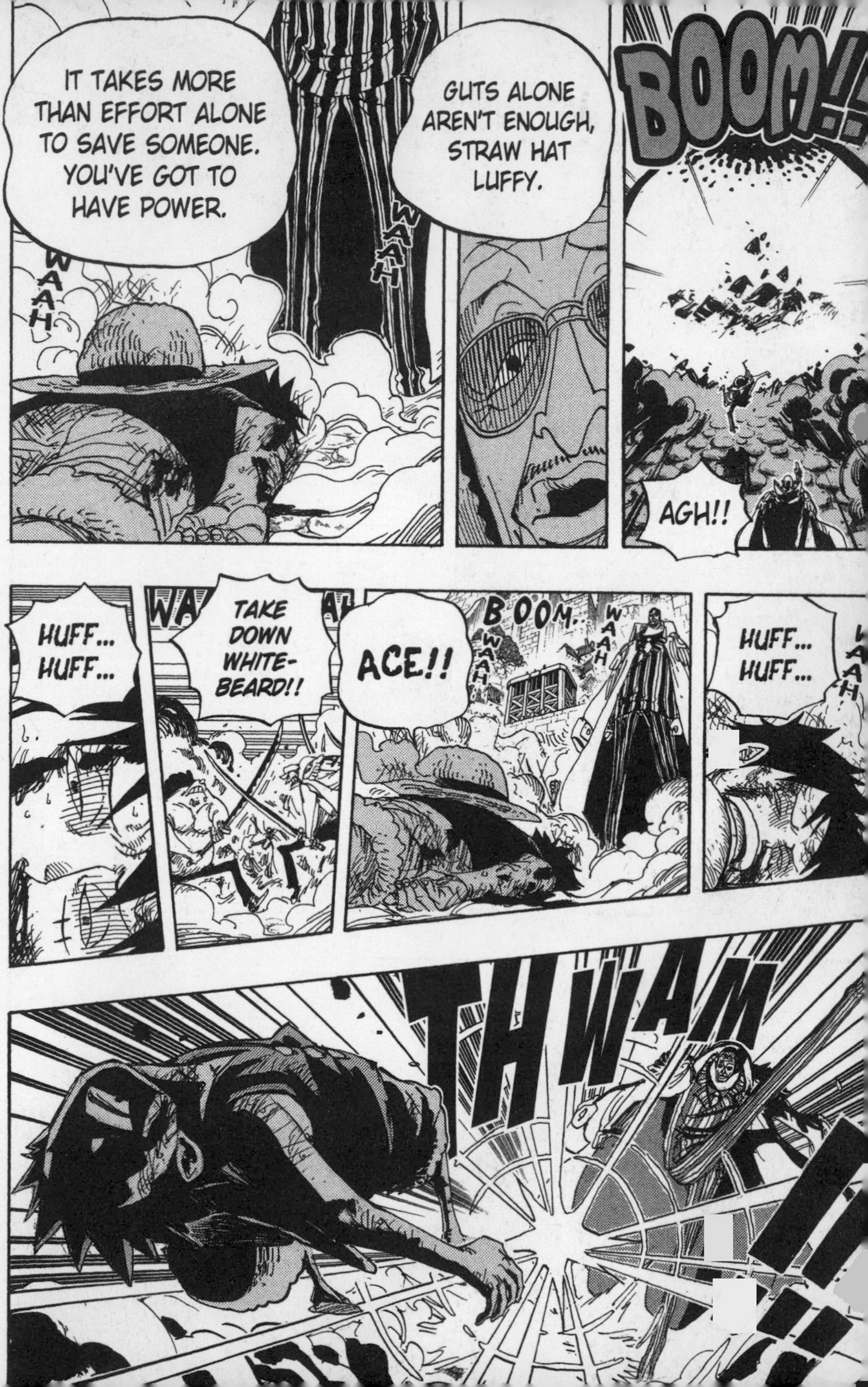
BOOM!!
AGH!!
GUTS ALONE AREN'T ENOUGH, STRAW HAT LUFFY.
WAAH
IT TAKES MORE THAN EFFORT ALONE TO SAVE SOMEONE. YOU'VE GOT TO HAVE POWER.
WAAH
WAAH
HUFF... HUFF...
BOOM..
WAAH
WAAH
ACE!!
TAKE DOWN WHITE-BEARD!!
HUFF... HUFF...
THWAM

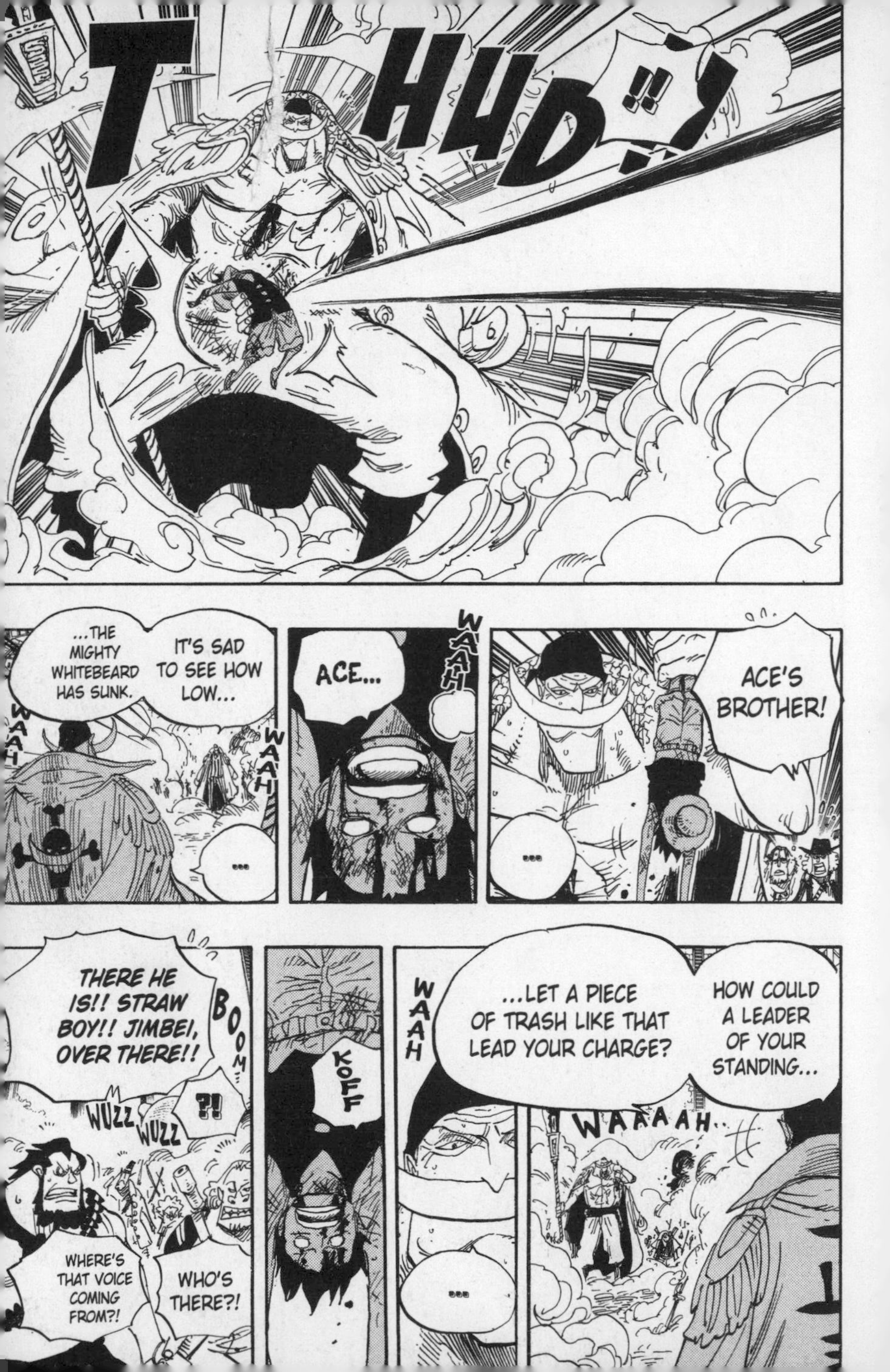
THUD!!
ACE'S BROTHER!
...
WAAAH
ACE...
IT'S SAD TO SEE HOW LOW...
...THE MIGHTY WHITEBEARD HAS SUNK.
WAAH
WAAH
...
HOW COULD A LEADER OF YOUR STANDING...
...LET A PIECE OF TRASH LIKE THAT LEAD YOUR CHARGE?
WAAH
WAAAAH...
...
KOFF
BOOOM
THERE HE IS!! STRAW BOY!! JIMBEI, OVER THERE!!
WUZZ WUZZ
?!
WHO'S THERE?!
WHERE'S THAT VOICE COMING FROM?!

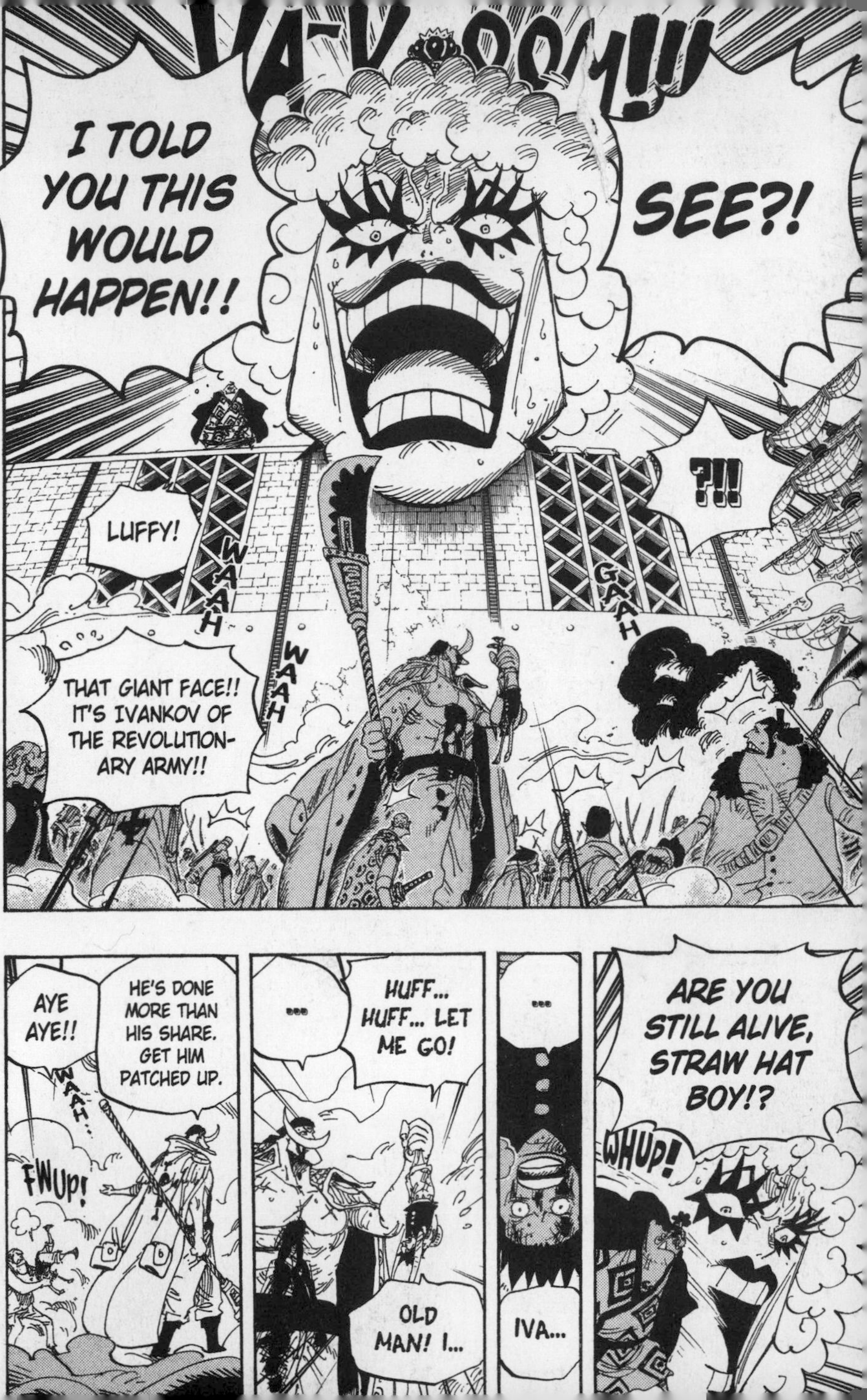
VA-VOOM!!
SEE?!
I TOLD YOU THIS WOULD HAPPEN!!
?!!
GAAAH
LUFFY!
WAAAH
WAAAH
THAT GIANT FACE!! IT'S IVANKOV OF THE REVOLUTION-ARY ARMY!!
ARE YOU STILL ALIVE, STRAW HAT BOY!?
WHUP!
...
IVA...
HUFF... HUFF... LET ME GO!
...
OLD MAN! I...
HE'S DONE MORE THAN HIS SHARE. GET HIM PATCHED UP.
AYE AYE!!
WAAAH...
FWUP!

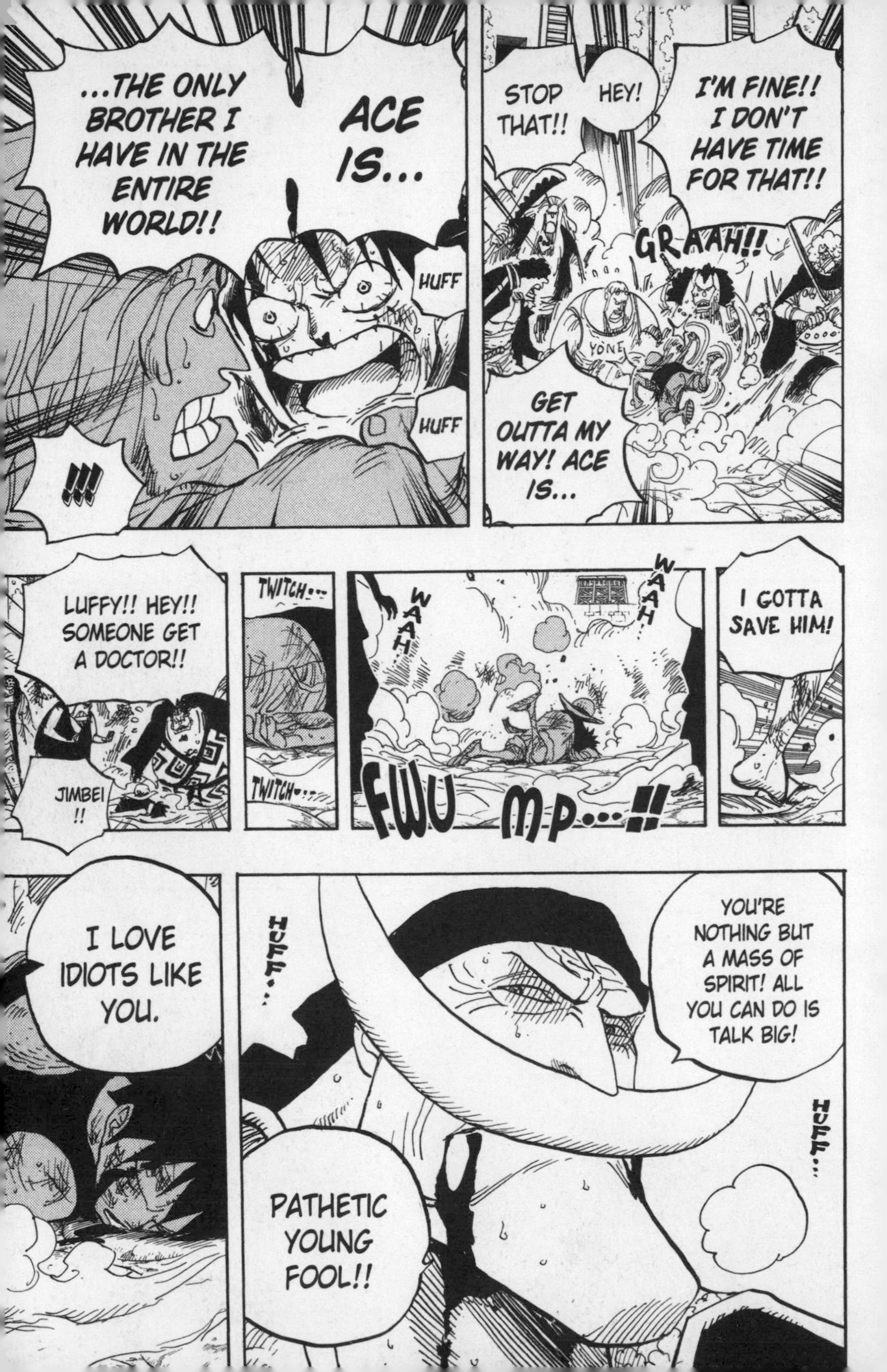
I'M FINE!! I DON'T HAVE TIME FOR THAT!!
HEY!
STOP THAT!!
GRAAH!!
YONE
GET OUTTA MY WAY! ACE IS...
ACE IS...
...THE ONLY BROTHER I HAVE IN THE ENTIRE WORLD!!
HUFF
HUFF
!!!
I GOTTA SAVE HIM!
WAAAH...
WAAH...
FWUMP...!!
TWITCH...
TWITCH...
LUFFY!! HEY!! SOMEONE GET A DOCTOR!!
JIMBEI !!
YOU'RE NOTHING BUT A MASS OF SPIRIT! ALL YOU CAN DO IS TALK BIG!
HUFF...
HUFF...
PATHETIC YOUNG FOOL!!
I LOVE IDIOTS LIKE YOU.

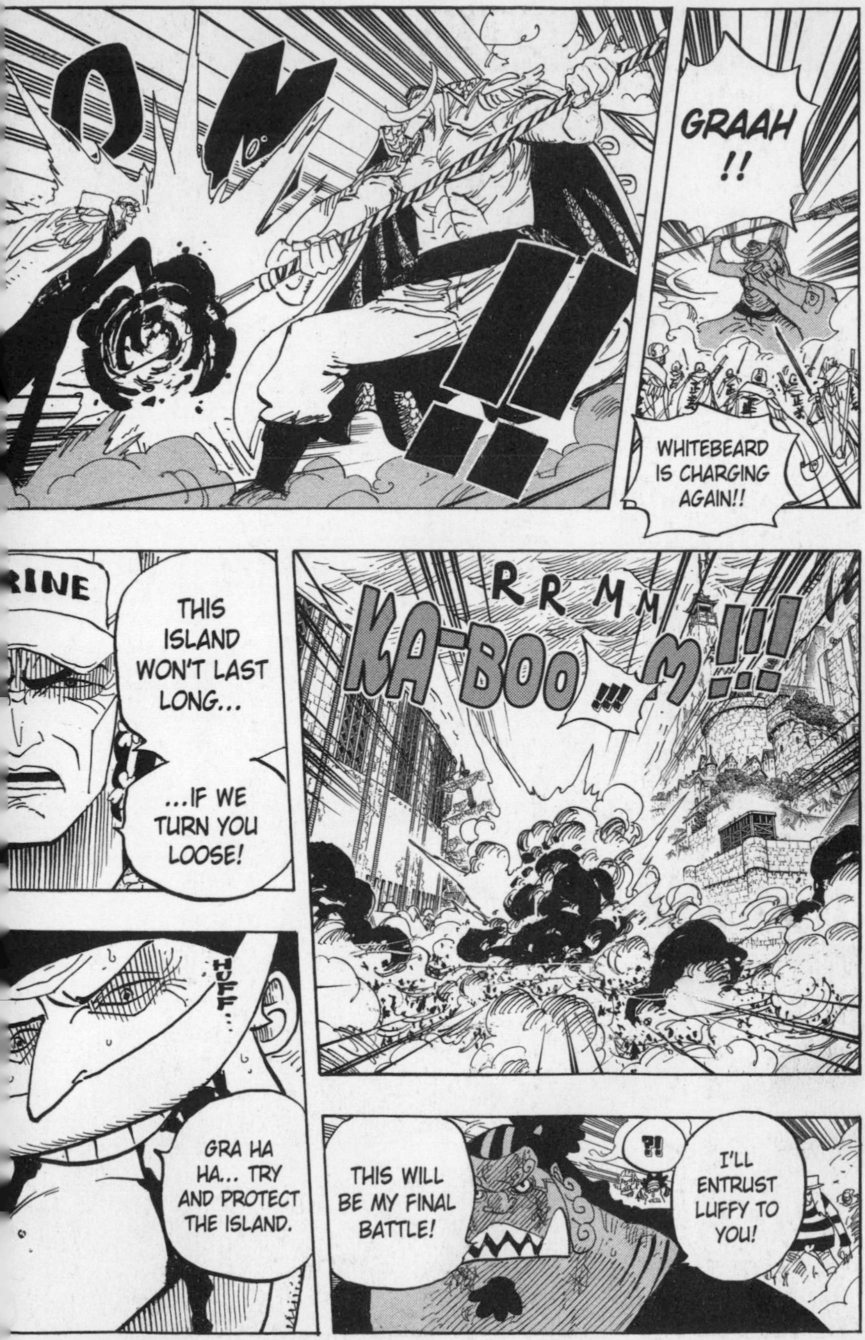
GRAAH !!
WHITEBEARD IS CHARGING AGAIN!!
RRMM
KA-BOOM!!!
!!!
RINE
THIS ISLAND WON'T LAST LONG...
...IF WE TURN YOU LOOSE!
HUFF...
GRA HA HA... TRY AND PROTECT THE ISLAND.
THIS WILL BE MY FINAL BATTLE!
?!
I'LL ENTRUST LUFFY TO YOU!

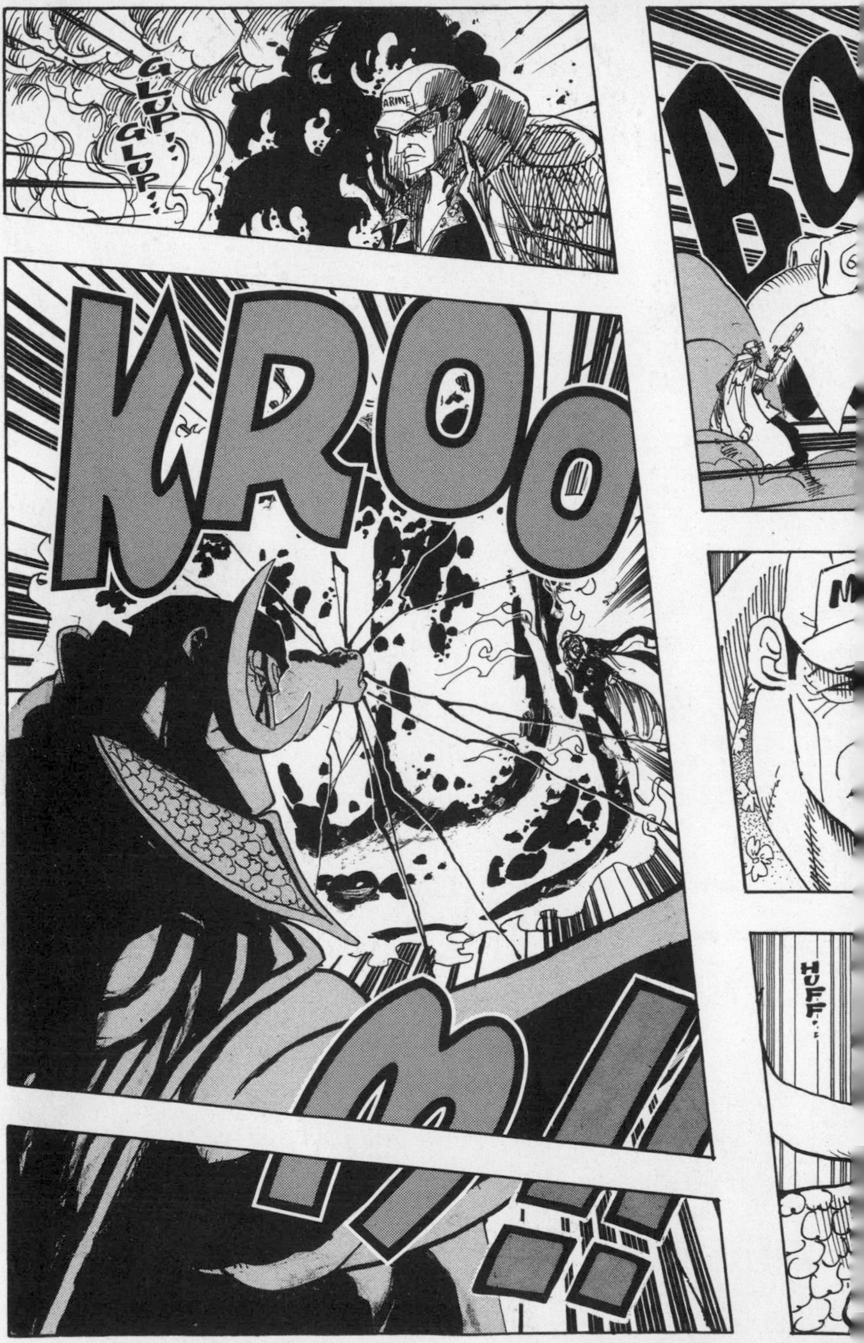

BO
HUFF...
GLUP... GLUP... GLUP...
KROOM!!!

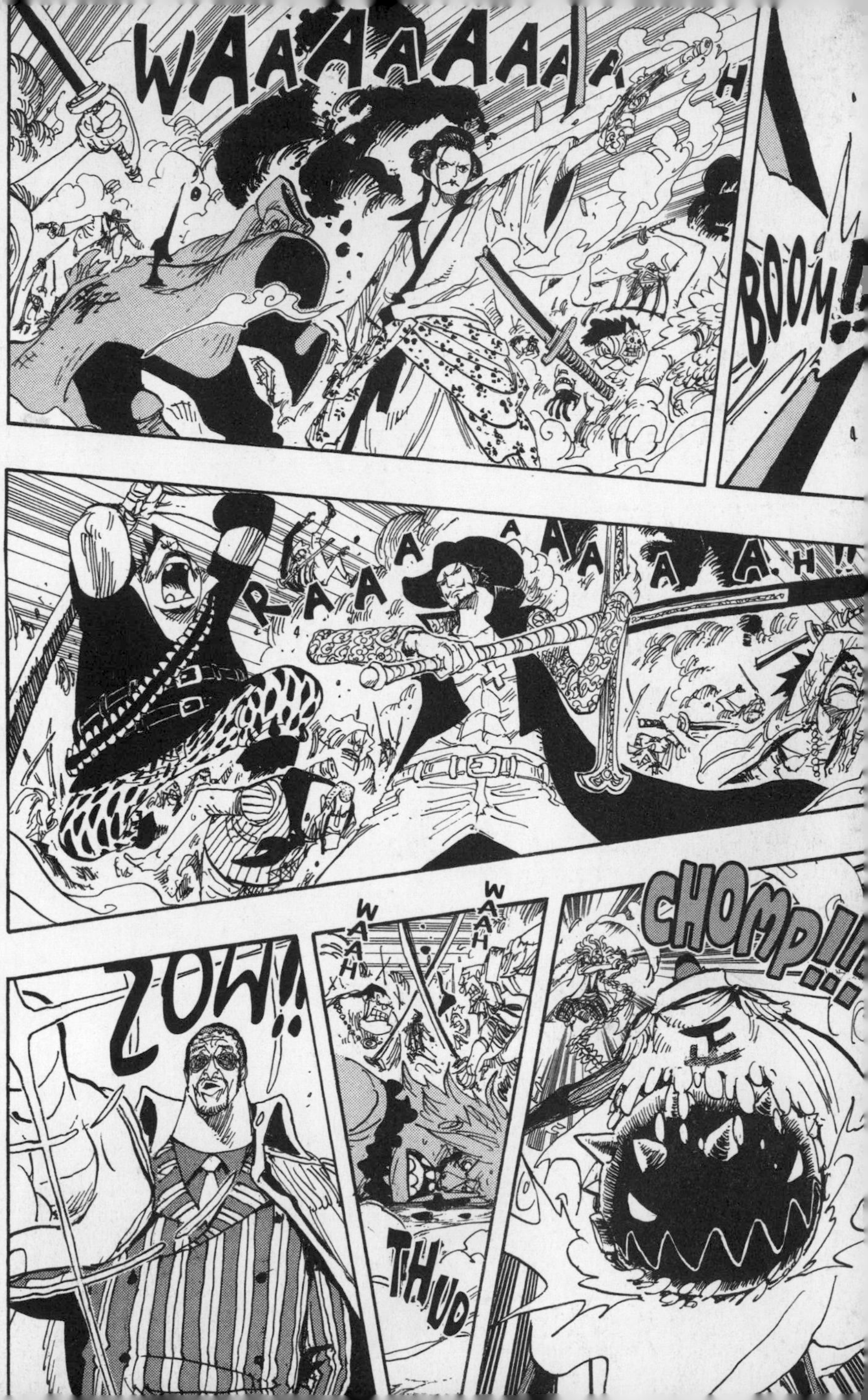
BOOM!!
WAAAAAAAAAH
RAAAAAAAAAAAH!!
CHOMP!!!
WAAH
WAAH
THUD
ZOW!!

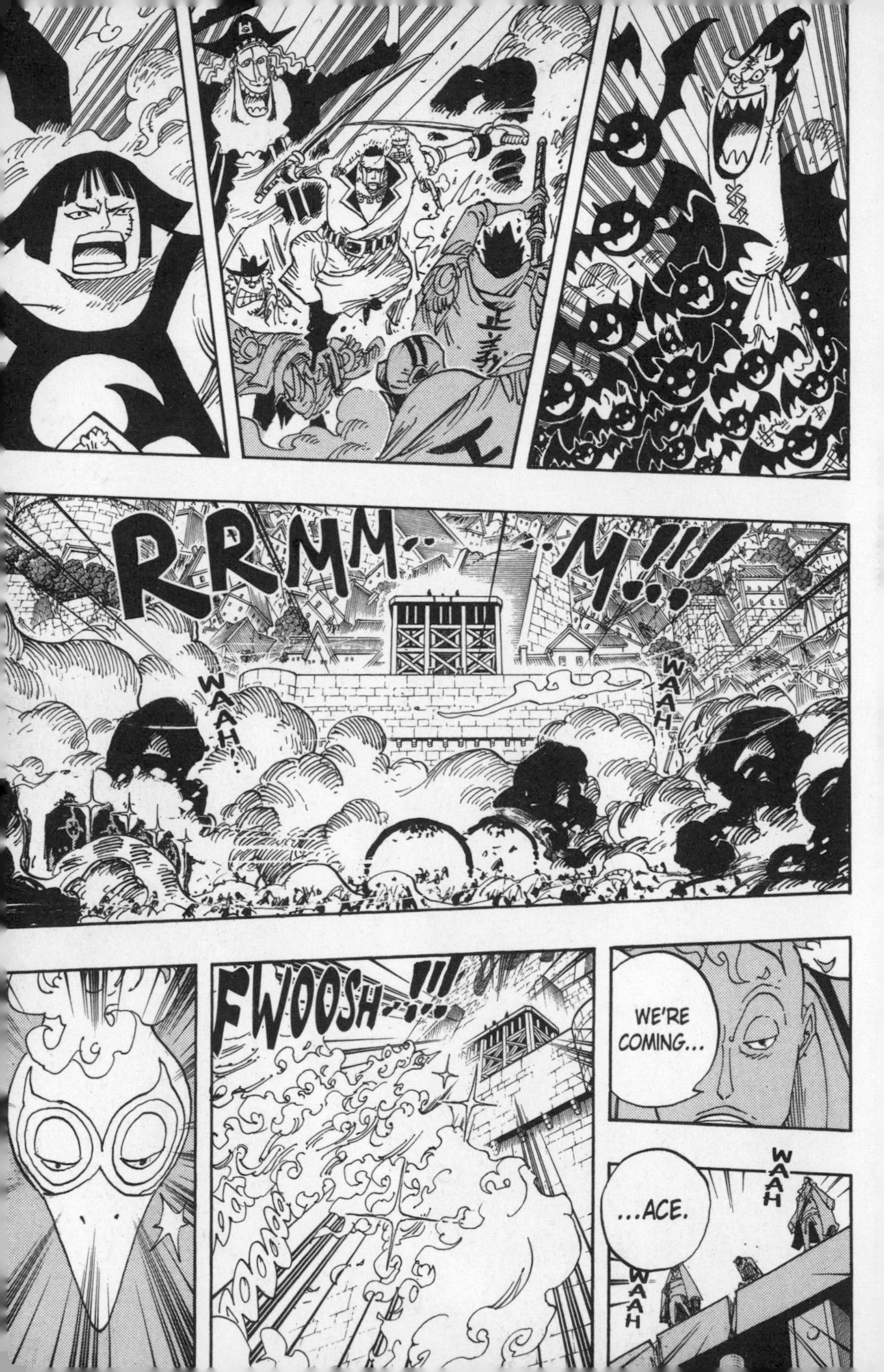
RRMM...M!!!
WAAH
WAAH
WE'RE COMING...
...ACE.
WAAH
WAAH
FWOOSH...!!!

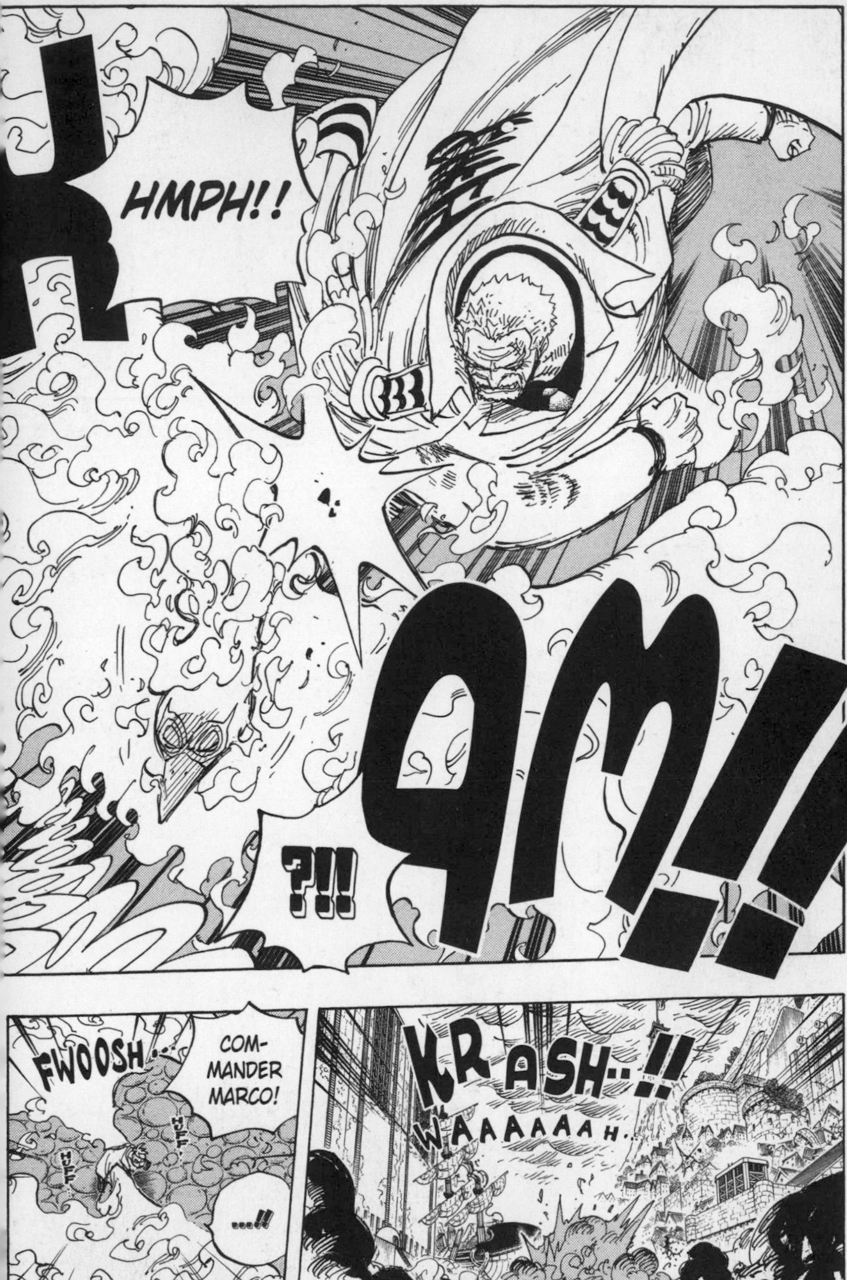
HMPH!!
?!!
KRASH..!!
WAAAAAAH..
FWOOSH...
COM-
MANDER
MARCO!
HUFF
HUFF
...!!

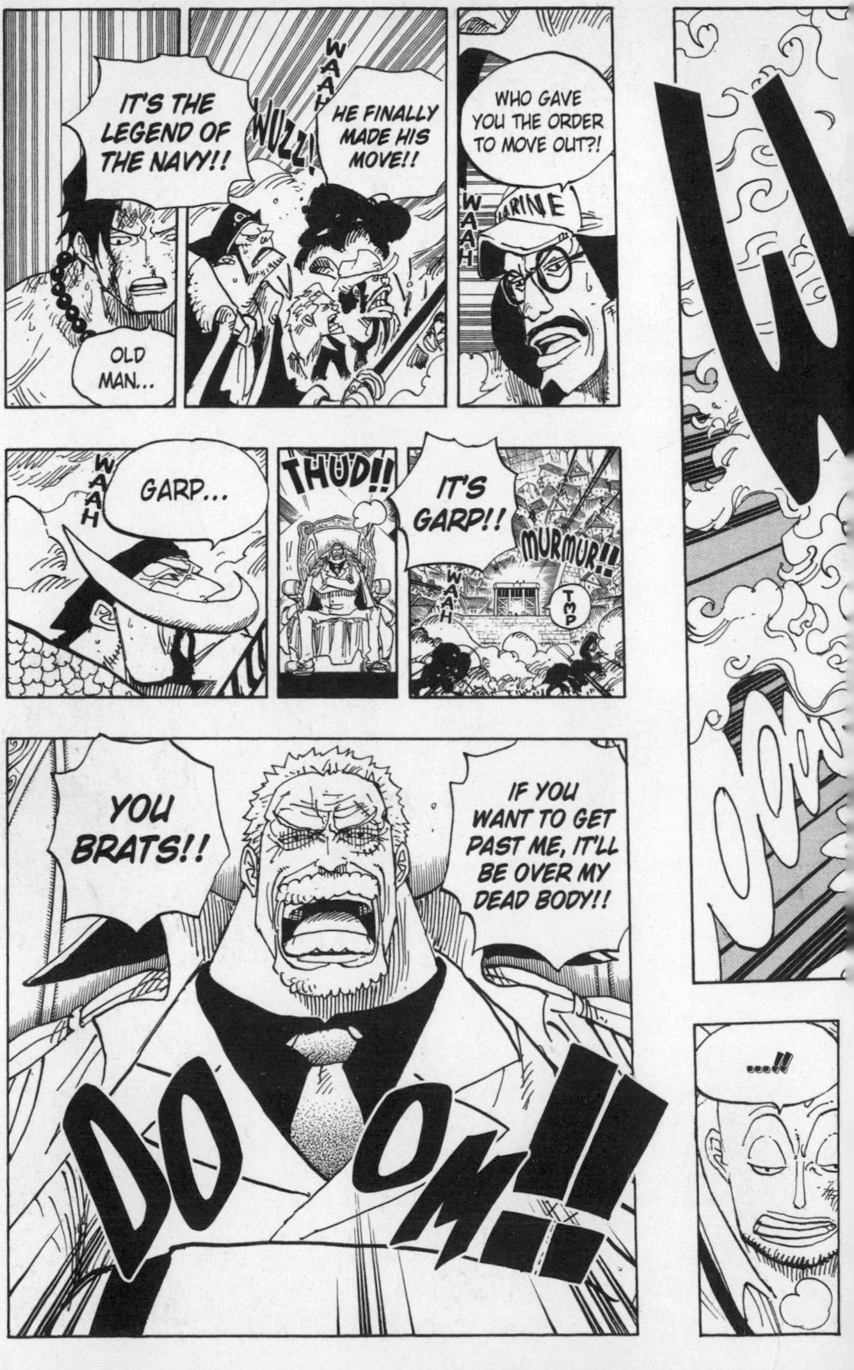
...!!
WHO GAVE YOU THE ORDER TO MOVE OUT?!
WAAH
HE FINALLY MADE HIS MOVE!!
WAAH
WUZZ!
IT'S THE LEGEND OF THE NAVY!!
OLD MAN...
IT'S GARP!!
MURMUR!!
WAAH
TMP
THUD!!
GARP...
WAAH
IF YOU WANT TO GET PAST ME, IT'LL BE OVER MY DEAD BODY!!
YOU BRATS!!
DOOM!!

質問コーナー

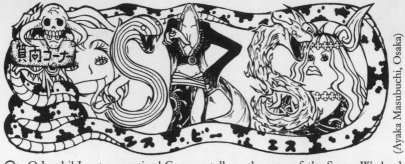

(Ayaka Masubuchi, Osaka)

Q: Odacchi! I got a question! Can you tell me the ages of the Seven Warlords of the Sea?!! --Jaichael Mackson

THEY ARE PIRATES, THE FIVE REMAINING WARLORDS OF THE SEA.
...READY TO DECIDE THE OUTCOME OF THE BATTLE.

Q: I have a question for Odacchi! On Volume 56, Page 172-173, the Seven Warlords of the Sea look really tall. Can you tell me their heights?! --Keita

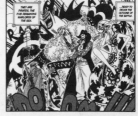

A: Sure thing. You want their age and height, right? I'll just add in Crocodile with them and we'll go with the tallest first.

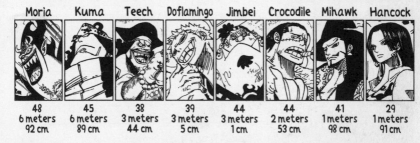

Moria	Kuma	Teech	Doflamingo	Jimbei	Crocodile	Mihawk	Hancock
48	45	38	39	44	44	41	29
6 meters 92 cm	6 meters 89 cm	3 meters 44 cm	3 meters 5 cm	3 meters 1 cm	2 meters 53 cm	1 meters 98 cm	1 meters 91 cm

Q: Odacchi! What's up! It might be sudden, but can you tell me Hancock's measurements?! --Amoeba Pirates Division One, Ii-chan

Q: Odacchi! This is my first time writing to you! There's something I want to ask you, but…what's Hancock's cup size? (Personally, I hope that she's a J-Cup.) --Erogappa

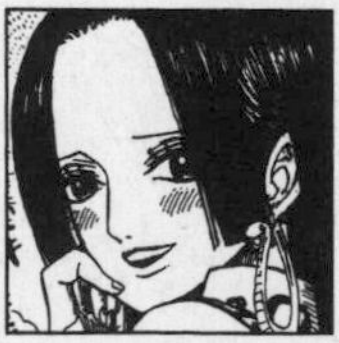

A: Well then, I got these letters above. You perverts! On top of that, Erogappa also had a message saying that he always enjoys my comics with his whole family. Erogappa's mother and father, your son sent me this kind of mail! He's a pervert! Anyway, I got the Snake Princess's measurements from Sanji! Here they are! Bust: 111 cm! Waist: 61 cm! Hip: 91 cm! Mmm! Amazing!♡♡ And for her cup size, Erogappa wanted it to be a J-cup, so J-cup it is!♡ How do you like that, Erogappa's parents?!

Chapter 568:
HAVE IT YOUR WAY!

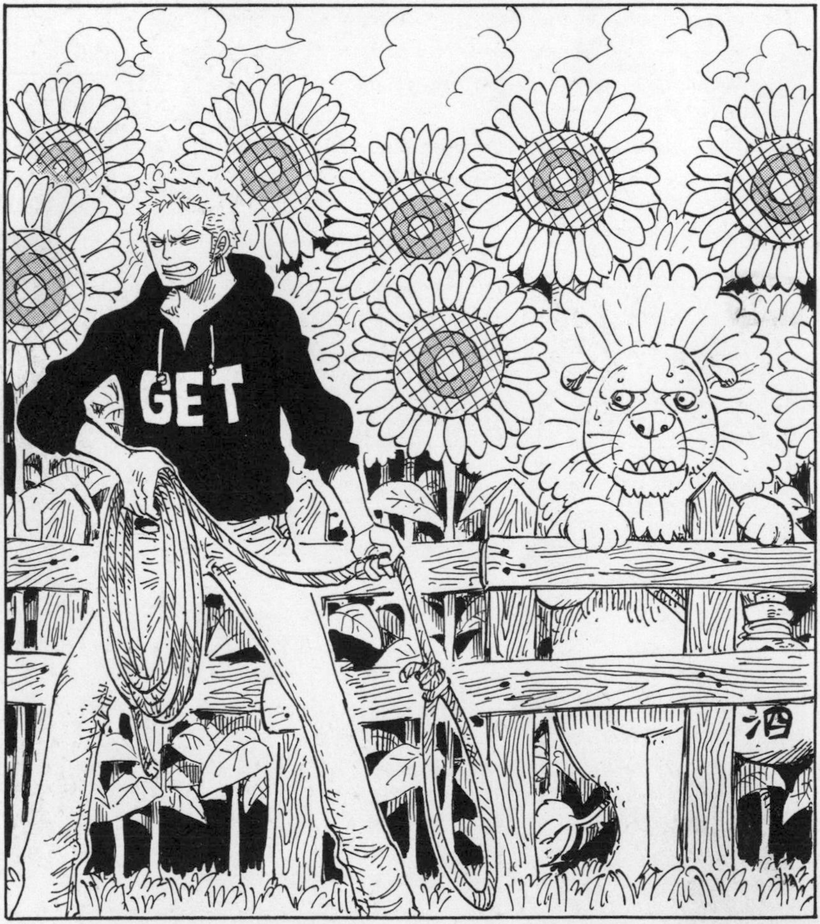
GET
酒

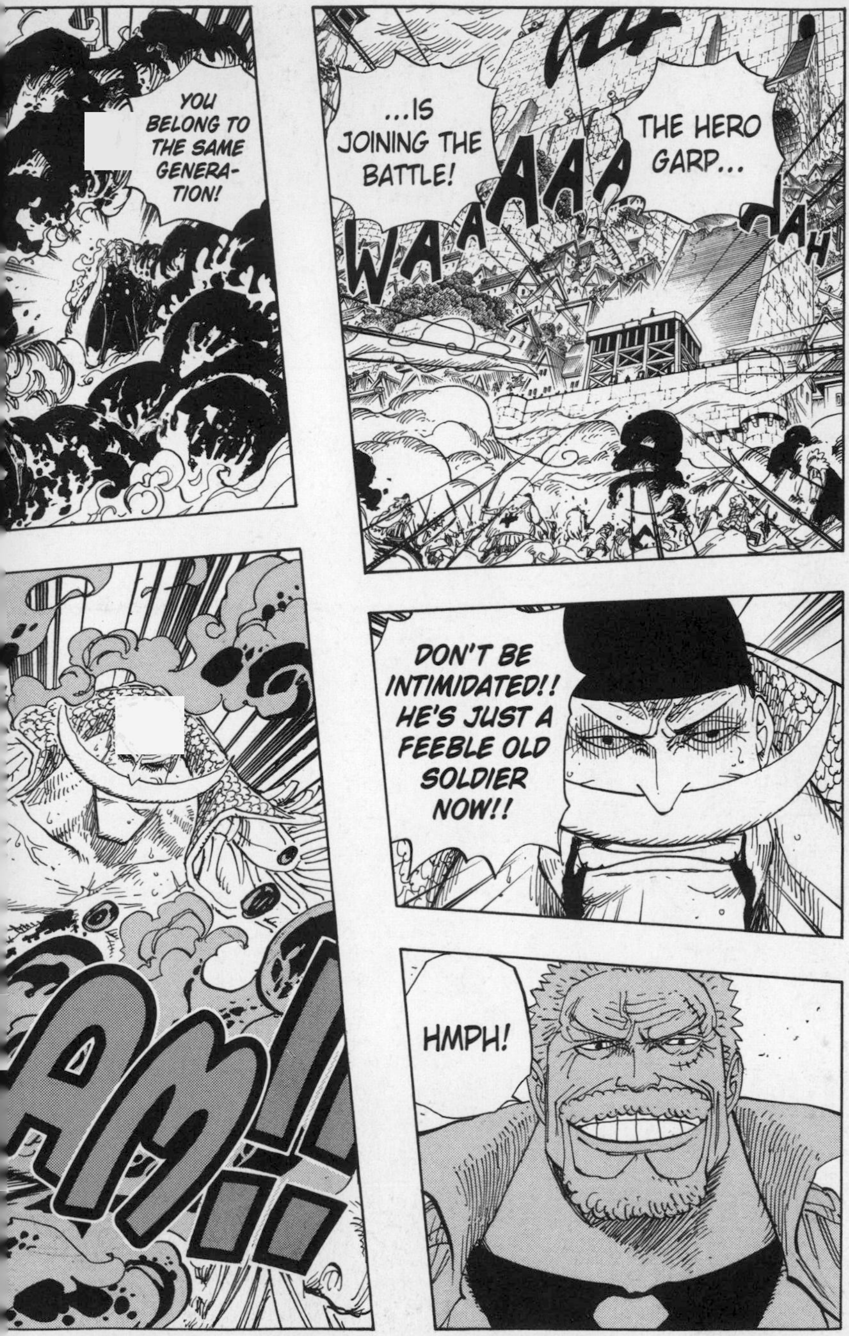
THE HERO GARP...
...IS JOINING THE BATTLE!
WAAAAA
AH
YOU BELONG TO THE SAME GENERATION!
DON'T BE INTIMIDATED!! HE'S JUST A FEEBLE OLD SOLDIER NOW!!
HMPH!

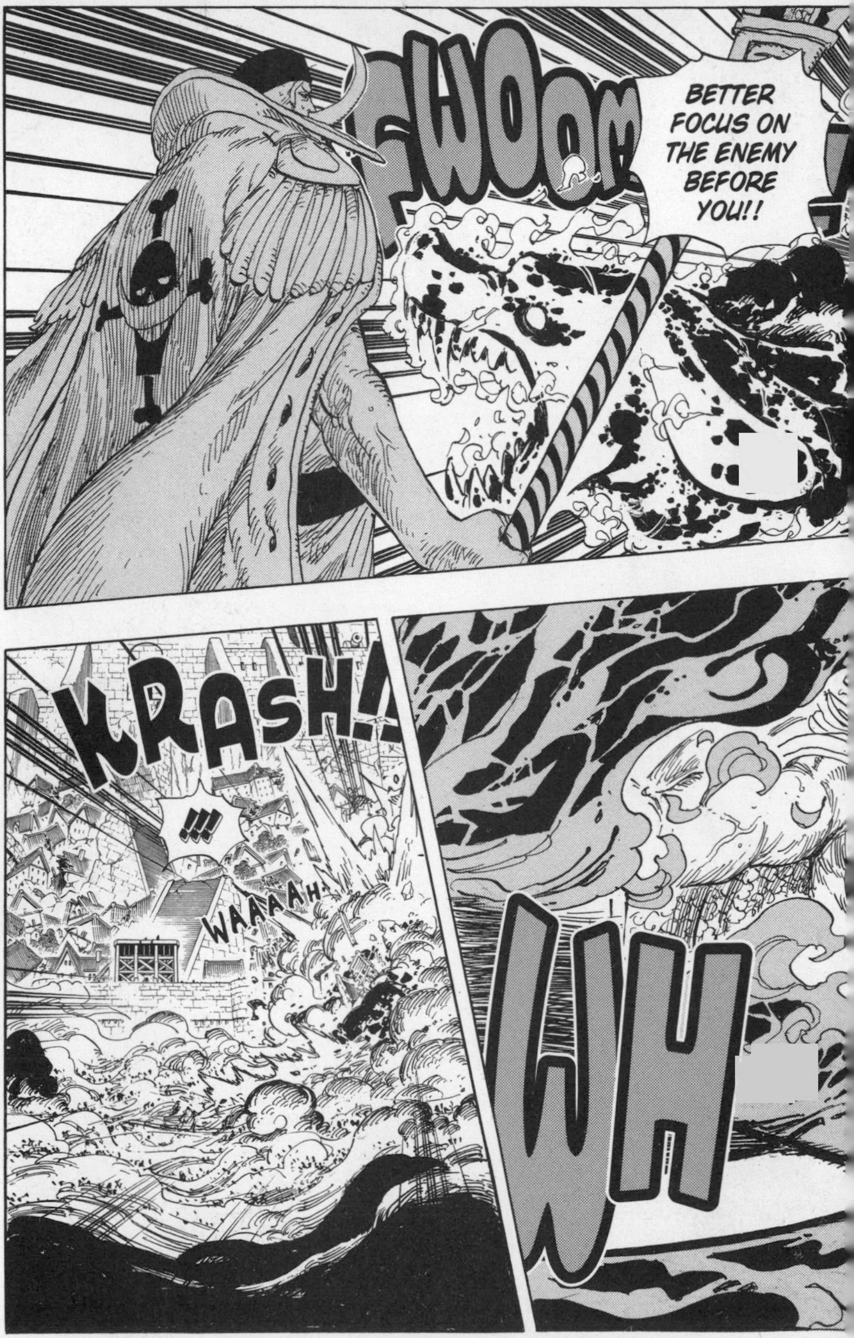
BETTER FOCUS ON THE ENEMY BEFORE YOU!!
WOOM
WH
KRASH!!
!!!
WAAAAH

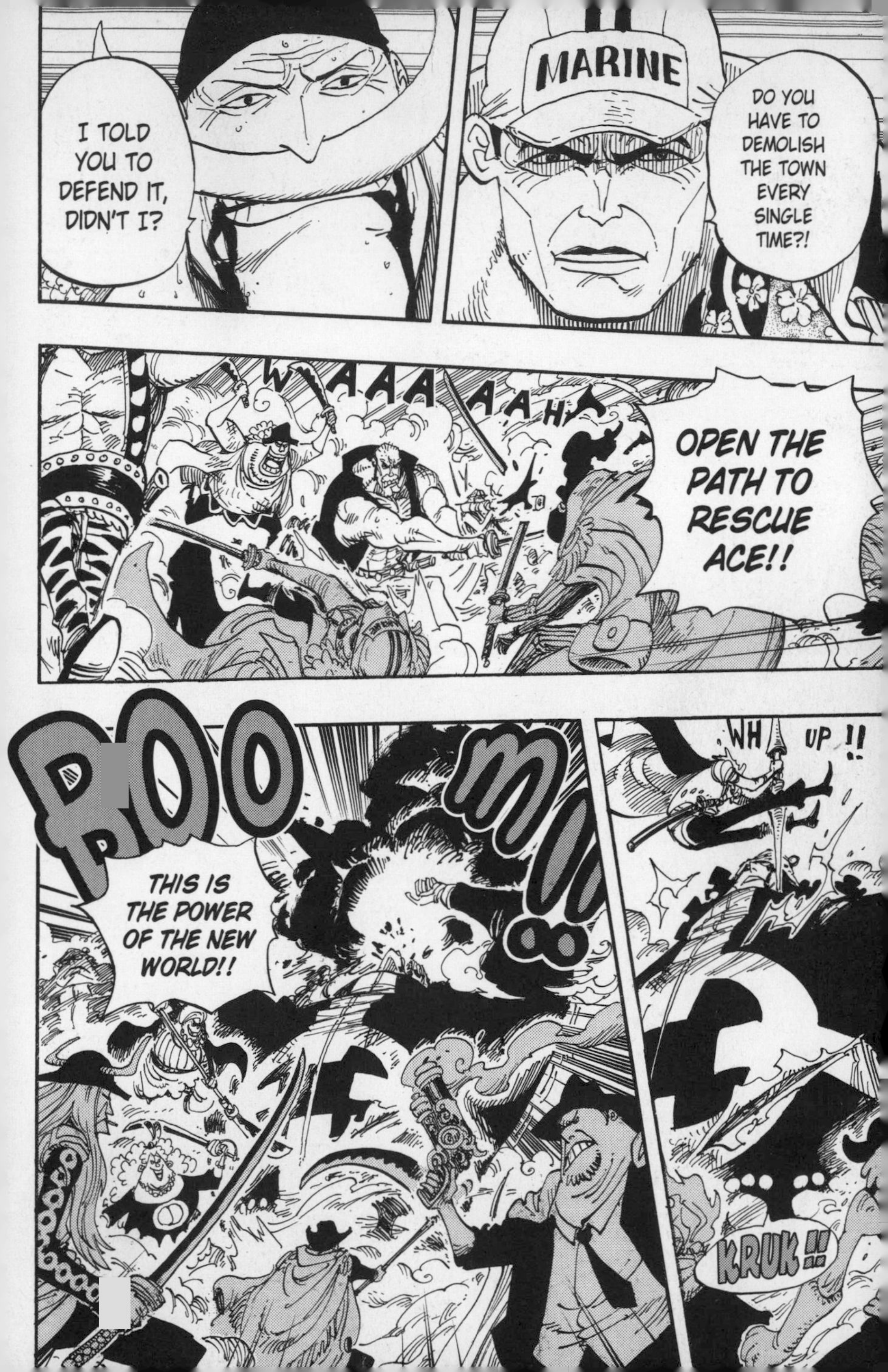
DO YOU HAVE TO DEMOLISH THE TOWN EVERY SINGLE TIME?!
I TOLD YOU TO DEFEND IT, DIDN'T I?
WAAAAAAH
OPEN THE PATH TO RESCUE ACE!!
WHUP!!
KRUK!!
BOOM!!
THIS IS THE POWER OF THE NEW WORLD!!

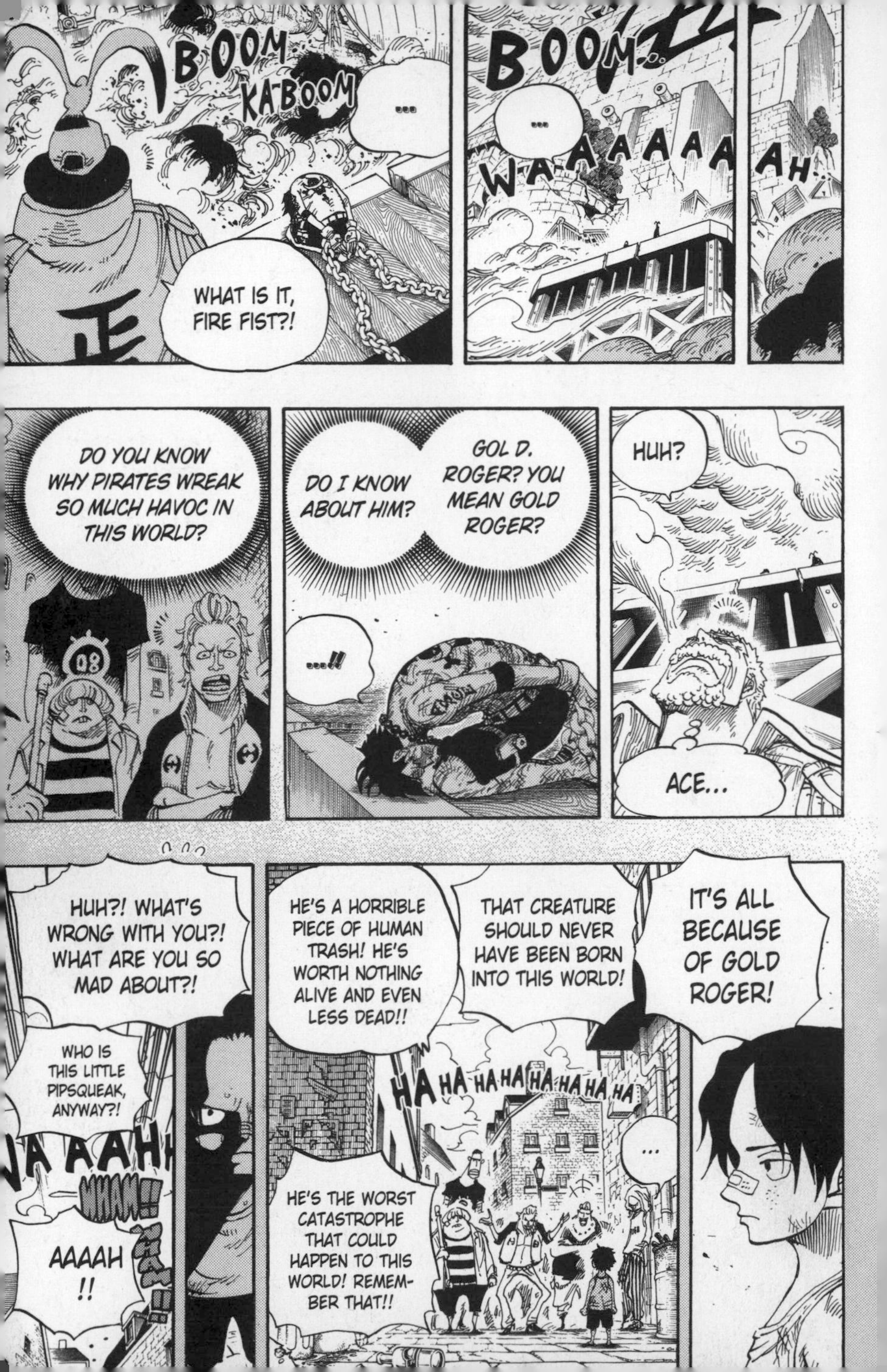
BOOM
...
WA-AAAAAAAH
BOOM KABOOM
...
WHAT IS IT, FIRE FIST?!
HUH?
ACE...
GOL D. ROGER? YOU MEAN GOLD ROGER?
DO I KNOW ABOUT HIM?
...!!
DO YOU KNOW WHY PIRATES WREAK SO MUCH HAVOC IN THIS WORLD?
IT'S ALL BECAUSE OF GOLD ROGER!
THAT CREATURE SHOULD NEVER HAVE BEEN BORN INTO THIS WORLD!
HE'S A HORRIBLE PIECE OF HUMAN TRASH! HE'S WORTH NOTHING ALIVE AND EVEN LESS DEAD!!
HA HA HA HA HA HA HA HA
...
HE'S THE WORST CATASTROPHE THAT COULD HAPPEN TO THIS WORLD! REMEMBER THAT!!
HUH?! WHAT'S WRONG WITH YOU?! WHAT ARE YOU SO MAD ABOUT?!
WHO IS THIS LITTLE PIPSQUEAK, ANYWAY?!
WHAM!!
AAAAH !!

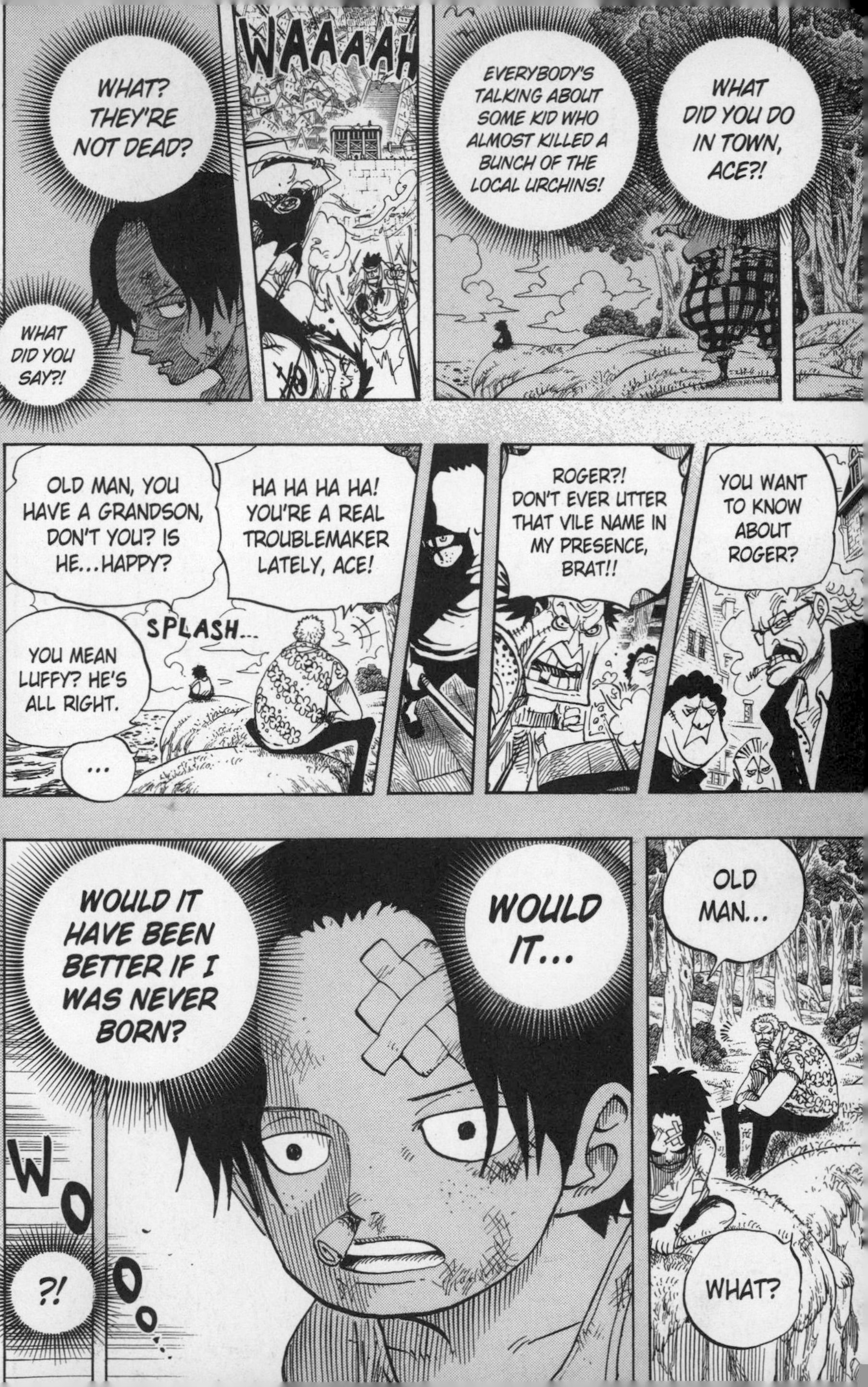
WHAT DID YOU DO IN TOWN, ACE?!
EVERYBODY'S TALKING ABOUT SOME KID WHO ALMOST KILLED A BUNCH OF THE LOCAL URCHINS!
WAAAAH
WHAT? THEY'RE NOT DEAD?
WHAT DID YOU SAY?!
YOU WANT TO KNOW ABOUT ROGER?
ROGER?! DON'T EVER UTTER THAT VILE NAME IN MY PRESENCE, BRAT!!
HA HA HA HA! YOU'RE A REAL TROUBLEMAKER LATELY, ACE!
OLD MAN, YOU HAVE A GRANDSON, DON'T YOU? IS HE...HAPPY?
SPLASH...
YOU MEAN LUFFY? HE'S ALL RIGHT.
...
OLD MAN...
WHAT?
WOULD IT...
WOULD IT HAVE BEEN BETTER IF I WAS NEVER BORN?
?!
WOOO

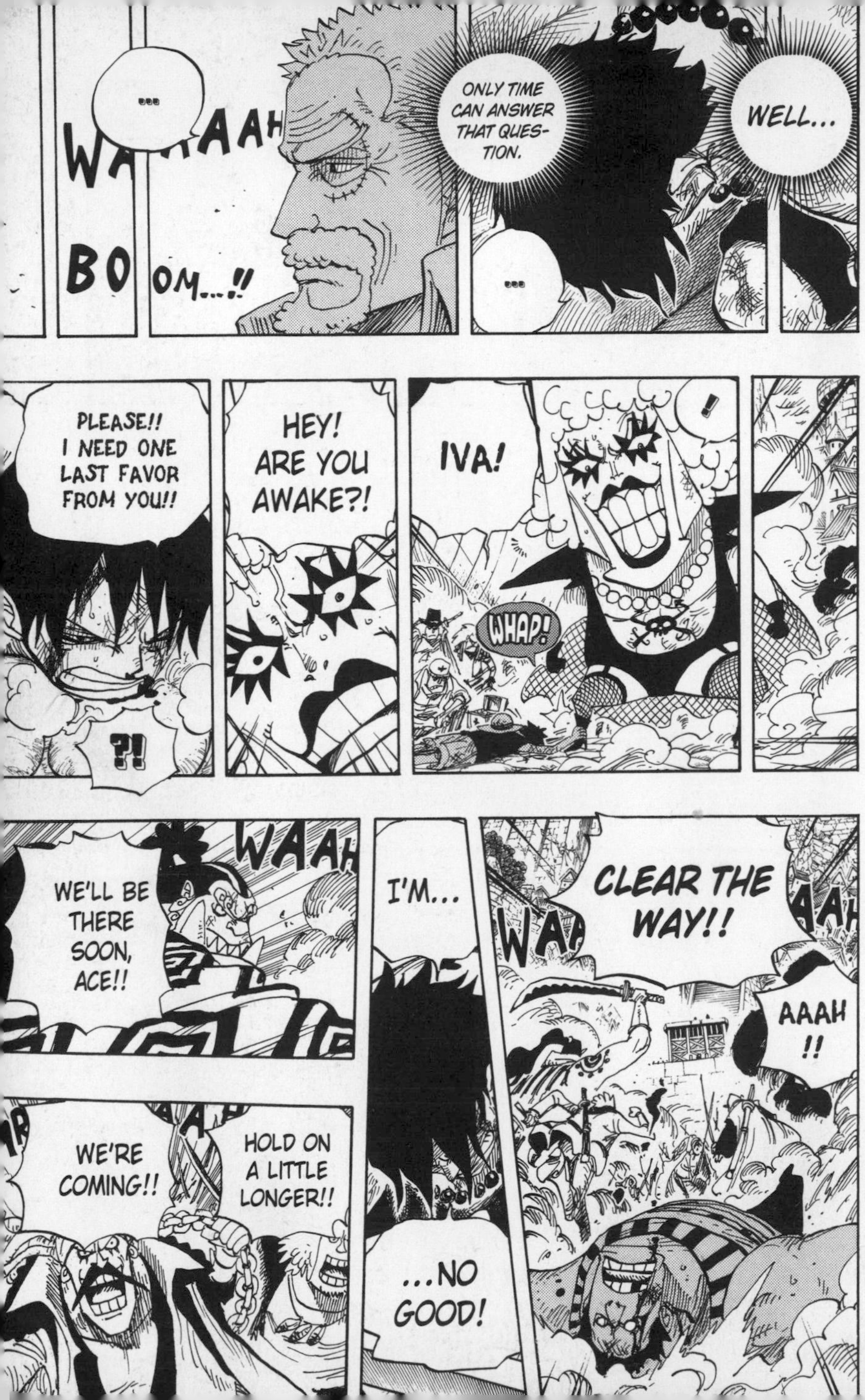
WELL...
ONLY TIME CAN ANSWER THAT QUESTION.
...
...
BOOM...!!
!
IVA!
WHAP!
HEY! ARE YOU AWAKE?!
PLEASE!! I NEED ONE LAST FAVOR FROM YOU!!
?!
CLEAR THE WAY!!
AAAH !!
I'M...
...NO GOOD!
WE'LL BE THERE SOON, ACE!!
HOLD ON A LITTLE LONGER!!
WE'RE COMING!!

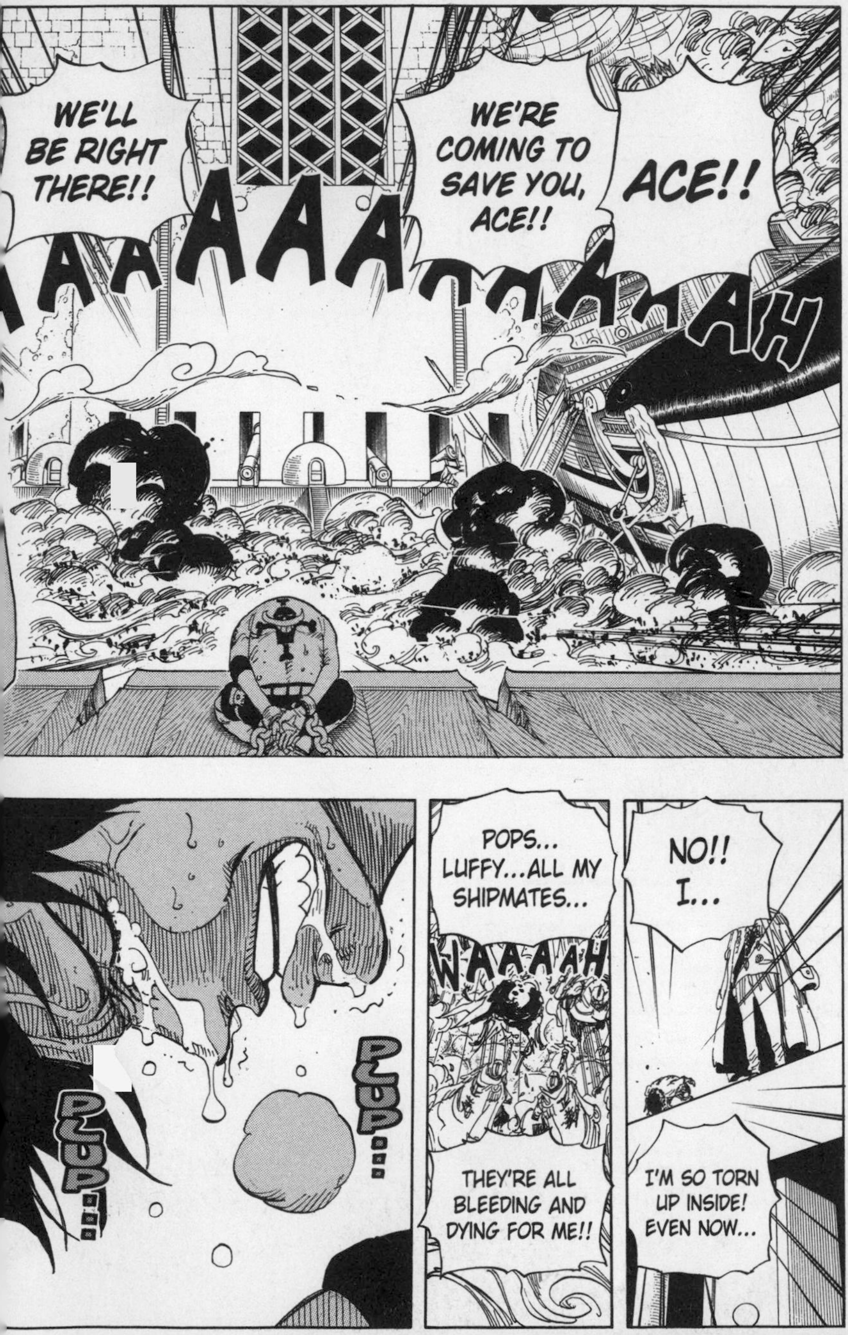
ACE!!
WE'RE COMING TO SAVE YOU, ACE!!
WE'LL BE RIGHT THERE!!
AAAAAAAAAAAAH
NO!! I...
I'M SO TORN UP INSIDE! EVEN NOW...
POPS... LUFFY...ALL MY SHIPMATES...
WAAAAH
THEY'RE ALL BLEEDING AND DYING FOR ME!!
PLUP...
PLUP...

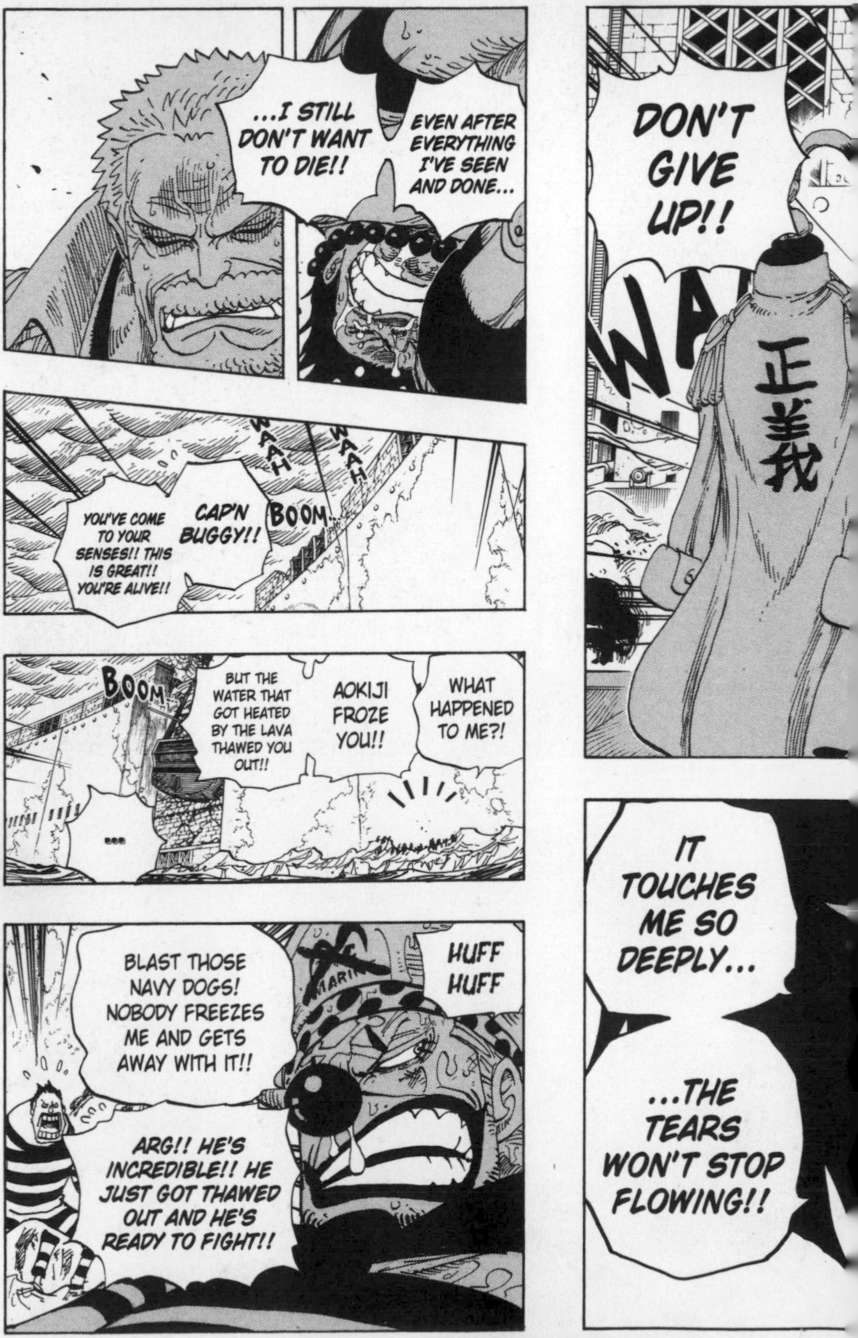
DON'T GIVE UP!!
WA
正義
IT TOUCHES ME SO DEEPLY...
...THE TEARS WON'T STOP FLOWING!!
EVEN AFTER EVERYTHING I'VE SEEN AND DONE...
...I STILL DON'T WANT TO DIE!!
WAAH
WAAH
CAP'N BUGGY!!
BOOM
YOU'VE COME TO YOUR SENSES!! THIS IS GREAT!! YOU'RE ALIVE!!
WHAT HAPPENED TO ME?!
AOKIJI FROZE YOU!!
BUT THE WATER THAT GOT HEATED BY THE LAVA THAWED YOU OUT!!
BOOM
...
HUFF HUFF
BLAST THOSE NAVY DOGS! NOBODY FREEZES ME AND GETS AWAY WITH IT!!
ARG!! HE'S INCREDIBLE!! HE JUST GOT THAWED OUT AND HE'S READY TO FIGHT!!

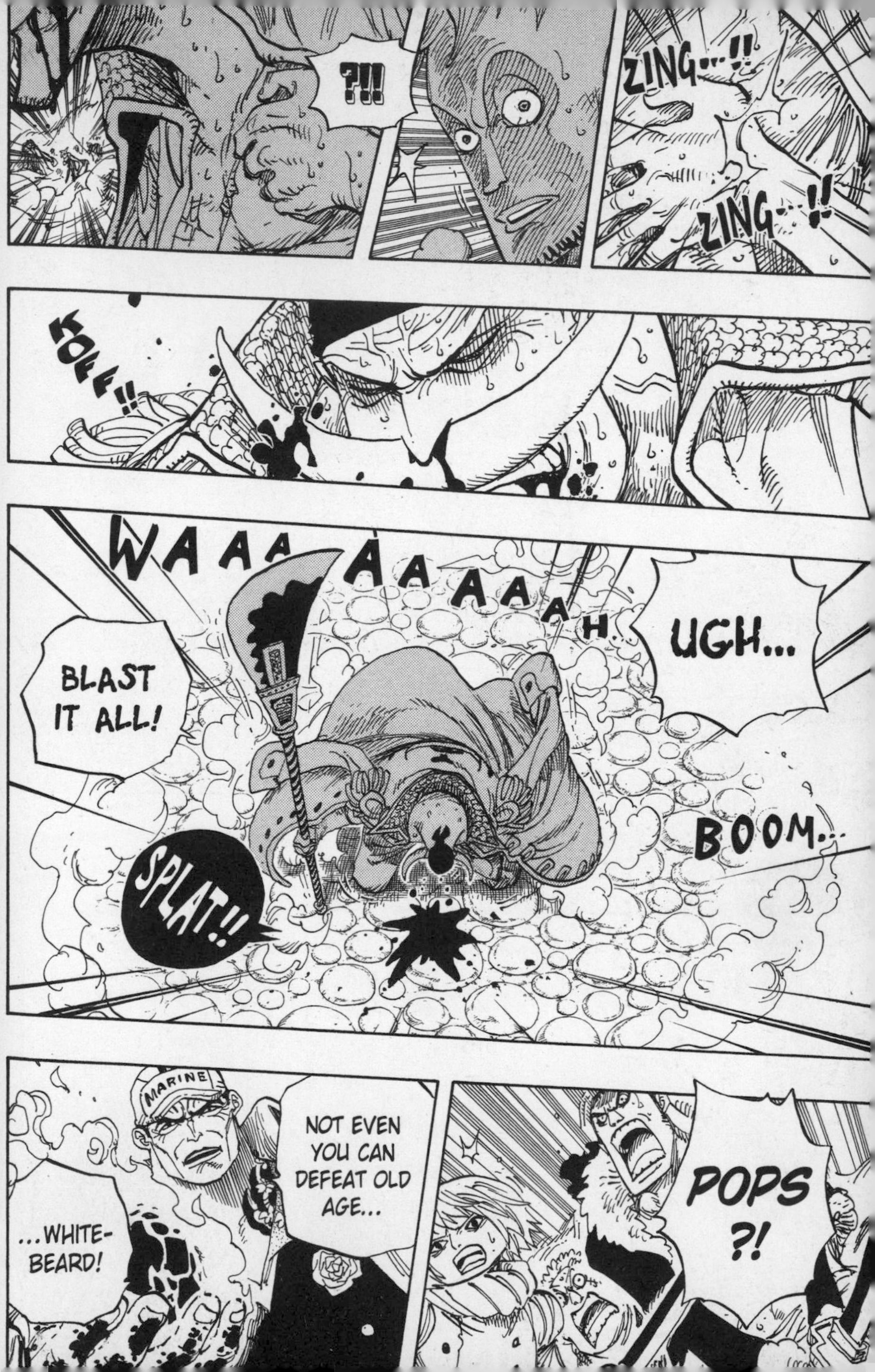
ZING...!!
ZING...!!
?!!
KOFF!!
UGH...
WAAAAAAAAH...
BLAST IT ALL!
BOOM...
SPLAT!!
POPS ?!
NOT EVEN YOU CAN DEFEAT OLD AGE...
...WHITE-BEARD!
MARINE

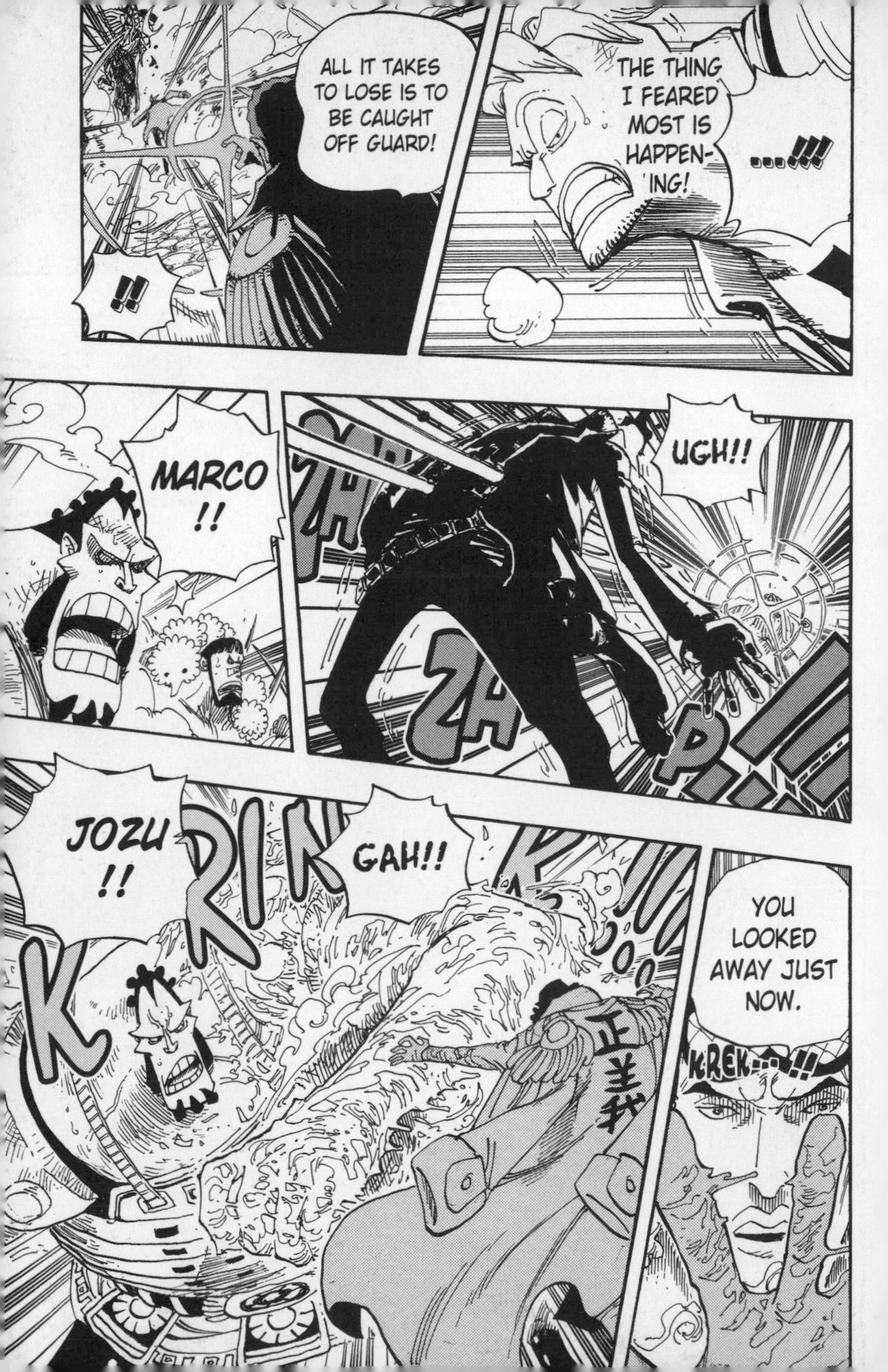
THE THING I FEARED MOST IS HAPPENING!
...!!!
ALL IT TAKES TO LOSE IS TO BE CAUGHT OFF GUARD!
!!
UGH!!
ZAH
ZAH
MARCO!!
YOU LOOKED AWAY JUST NOW.
KREK...!!
GAH!!
JOZU!!

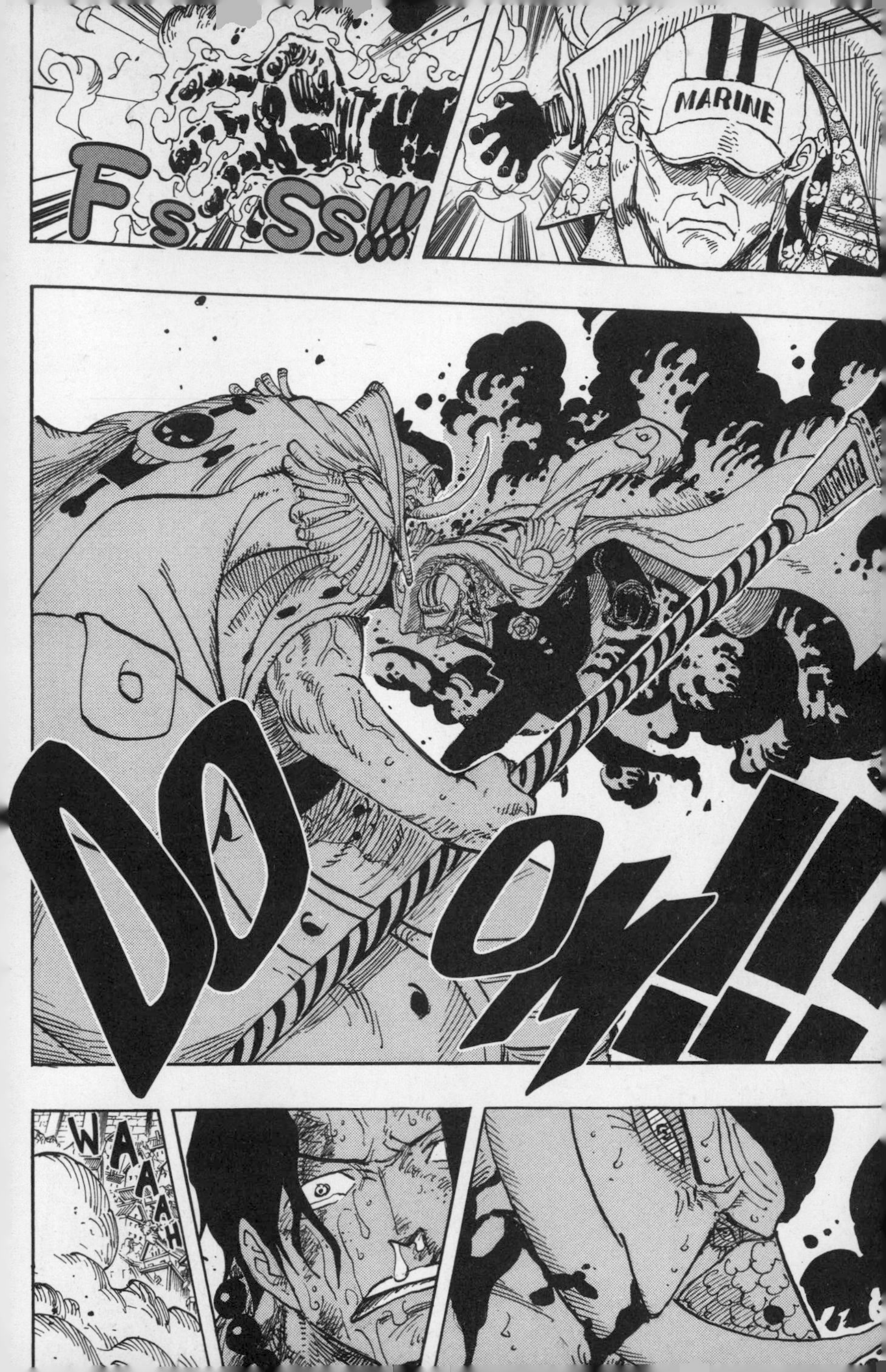
MARINE
FSSS!!!
DOON!!!
WAAAAH

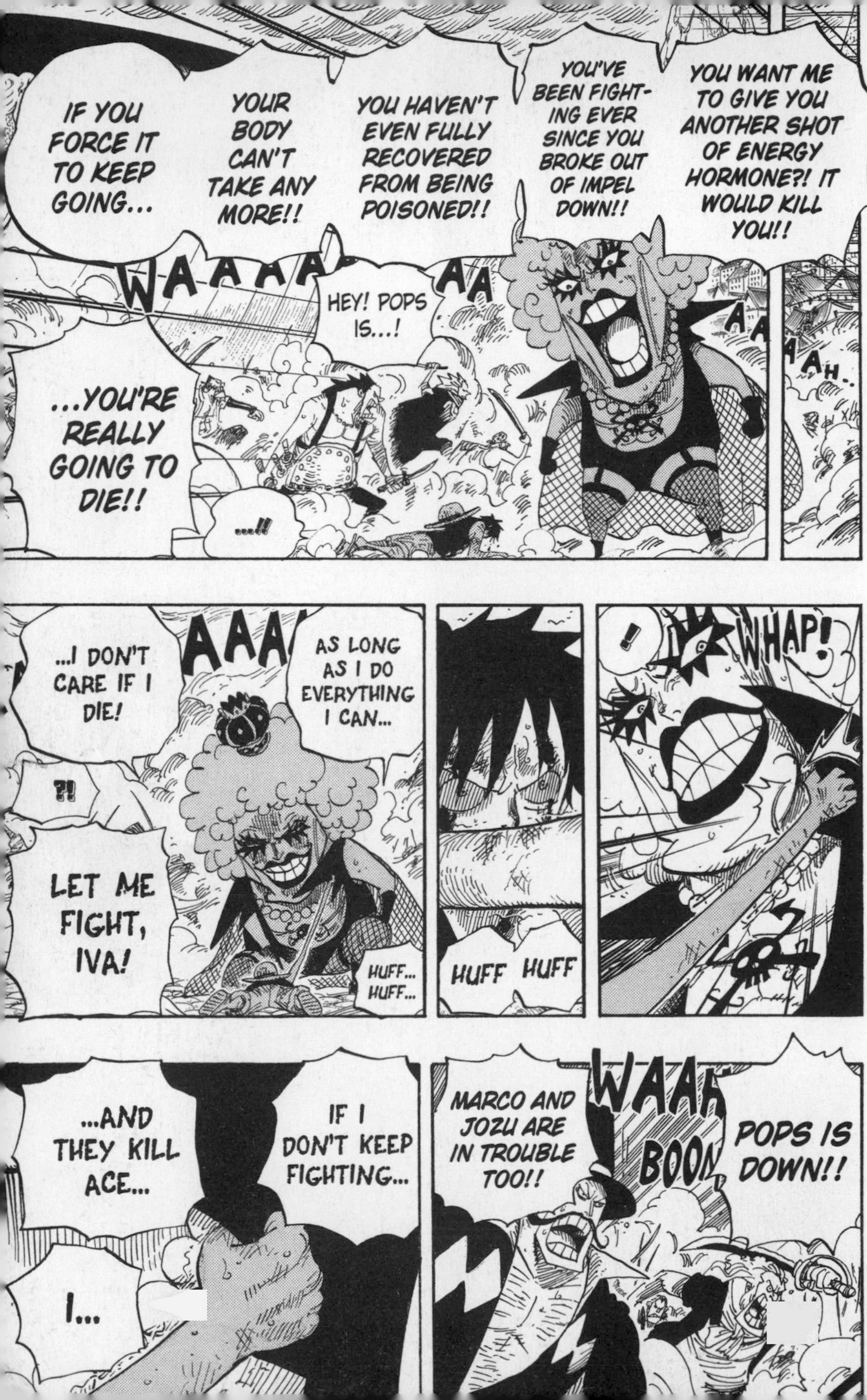
YOU WANT ME TO GIVE YOU ANOTHER SHOT OF ENERGY HORMONE?! IT WOULD KILL YOU!!
YOU'VE BEEN FIGHT-ING EVER SINCE YOU BROKE OUT OF IMPEL DOWN!!
YOU HAVEN'T EVEN FULLY RECOVERED FROM BEING POISONED!!
YOUR BODY CAN'T TAKE ANY MORE!!
IF YOU FORCE IT TO KEEP GOING...
AAAAH..
AA
HEY! POPS IS...!
WAAAA
...YOU'RE REALLY GOING TO DIE!!
...!!
!
WHAP!
HUFF HUFF
AS LONG AS I DO EVERYTHING I CAN...
AAA
...I DON'T CARE IF I DIE!
?!
LET ME FIGHT, IVA!
HUFF... HUFF...
POPS IS DOWN!!
WAAA
BOO
MARCO AND JOZU ARE IN TROUBLE TOO!!
IF I DON'T KEEP FIGHTING...
...AND THEY KILL ACE...
I...

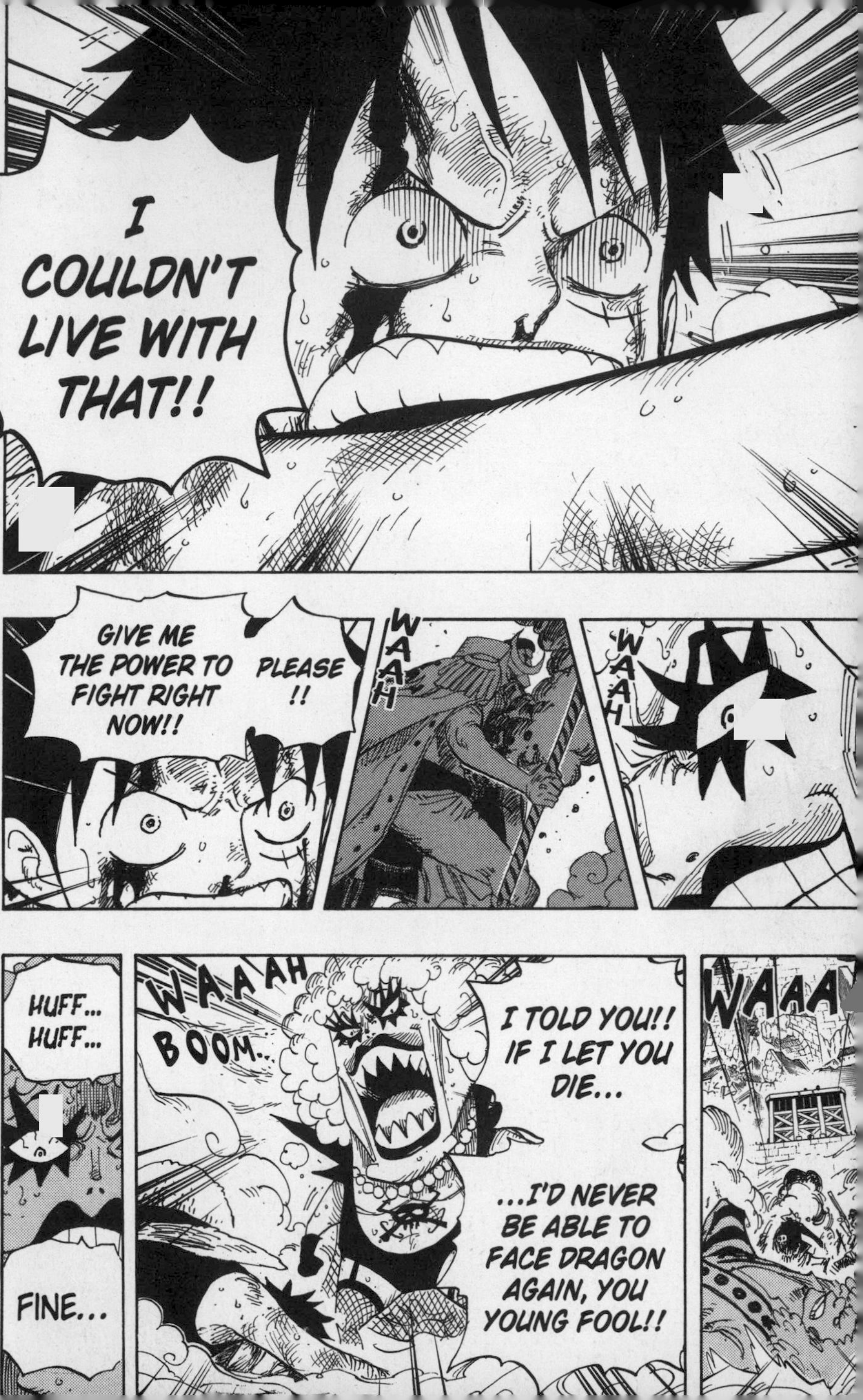
I COULDN'T LIVE WITH THAT!!
WAAAH
WAAAH
GIVE ME THE POWER TO FIGHT RIGHT NOW!! PLEASE!!
WAAA
I TOLD YOU!! IF I LET YOU DIE...
WAAAH
BOOM...
...I'D NEVER BE ABLE TO FACE DRAGON AGAIN, YOU YOUNG FOOL!!
HUFF... HUFF...
FINE...

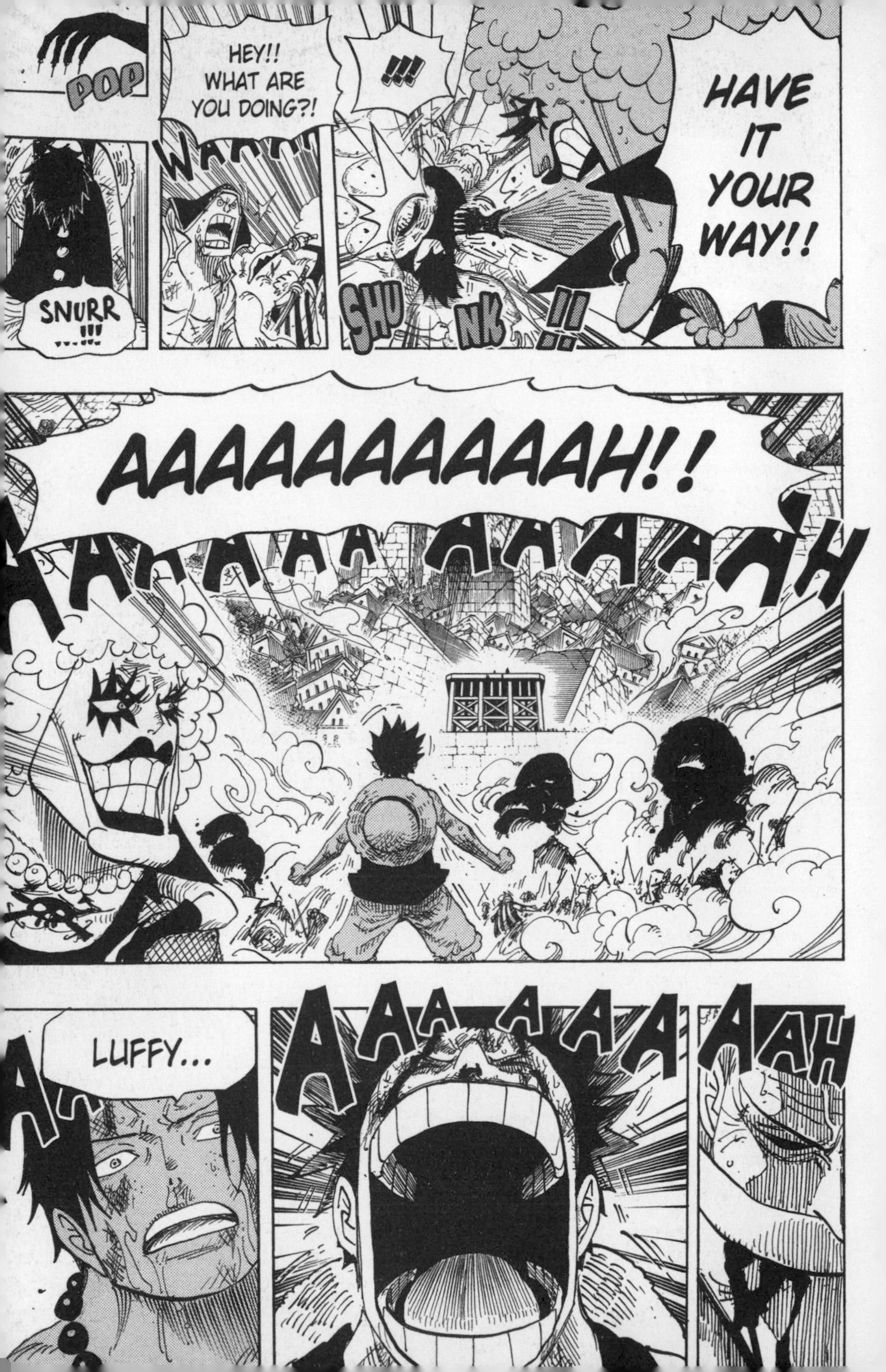
HAVE IT YOUR WAY!!
!!!
SHUNK!!
HEY!! WHAT ARE YOU DOING?!
POP
SNURR...!!!
AAAAAAAAAAH!!
AAAAAAAAAAH
AAAAAAAAAH
LUFFY...

SBS Question Corner

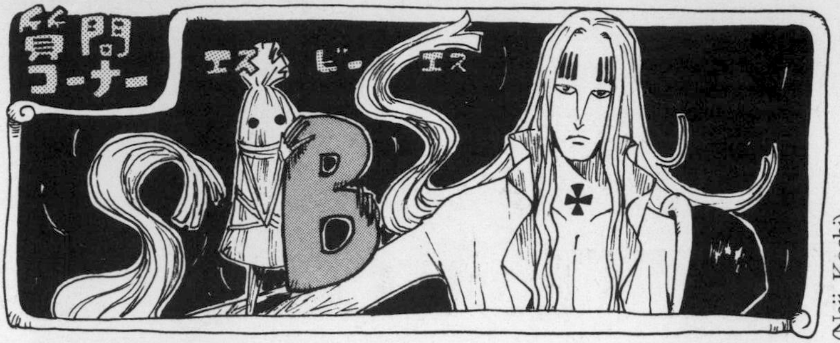
質問コーナー
エス ビー エス
B

(Naji, Kochi)

Q: Mr. Oda! I have someone that promised that we'd get married if you let me get on SBS, so please post this letter!♡ You have to make my day, Odacchi!♡♡

--☆Shogo Michihata

A: Sure thing. There. It's posted. Now who's the lucky man?! You better keep your promise!

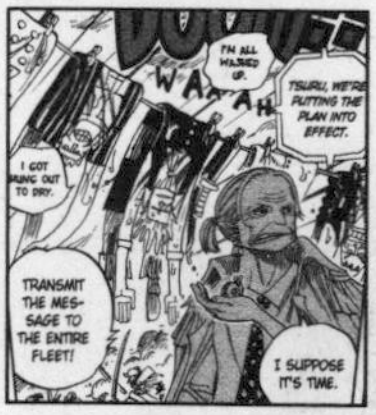
TSURU, WE'RE PUTTING THE PLAN INTO EFFECT.
I'M ALL WASHED UP.
WAAAH
I GOT HUNG OUT TO DRY.
I SUPPOSE IT'S TIME.
TRANSMIT THE MES-SAGE TO THE ENTIRE FLEET!

Q: I have a question. In chapter 556 of volume 57, there were a few pirates behind Tsuru that were being hung and dried. Who did that to them? Tsuru? And I'm wondering why they were hung there in the first place. And since Mr. 3 has been doing so well recently, can you explain it by talking like him?!

--Daddy of Two

A: You're right about them being hung out to dry! And you're right about the Naval Vice Admiral Tsuru being the culprit! Her Devil Fruit is the Wash-Wash Fruit! A "Washer Human"! She washes and dries any evildoer, cleaning up even their hearts just a little bit! Being able to wash away evil hearts, pirates find her to be quite a formidable foe! We must be careful!

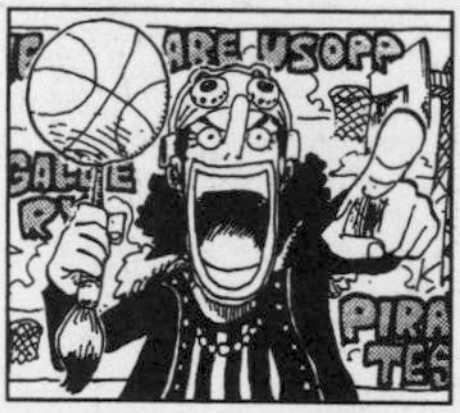
ARE USOPP
PIRA TES

Q: Hello, Odacchi! I have a 10 percent serious question. You know how there are some people that keep getting on Usopp Gallery Pirates in the Japanese volumes? Does that mean you're not the one picking and choosing which ones to post?! Or you're not even picking them seriously?! I really wonder about this! Answer me in exactly three lines!

--Sweet Strawberry

A: I am serious when I pick which ones to post! Wait, that didn't even take one line. I'll give you the long answer to this then. For every volume, we hold a meeting with my graphic novel editor Yokoyama, Usopp, and me. We decide which ones we'll post during that meeting. To me, I think that section should be composed of artists' works that my readers and I can fully enjoy. Just simply having your work posted isn't the end-all. I want their works to continually be posted so that you can have the readers enjoy it. I want their works to keep that motivation. That's why, if it's good, it'll get posted. Even if the person's art has been posted before. But in exchange, I won't give the grand prize to the same person twice. I really enjoy being a judge for this each time.

Chapter 569:
WHITE MONSTER

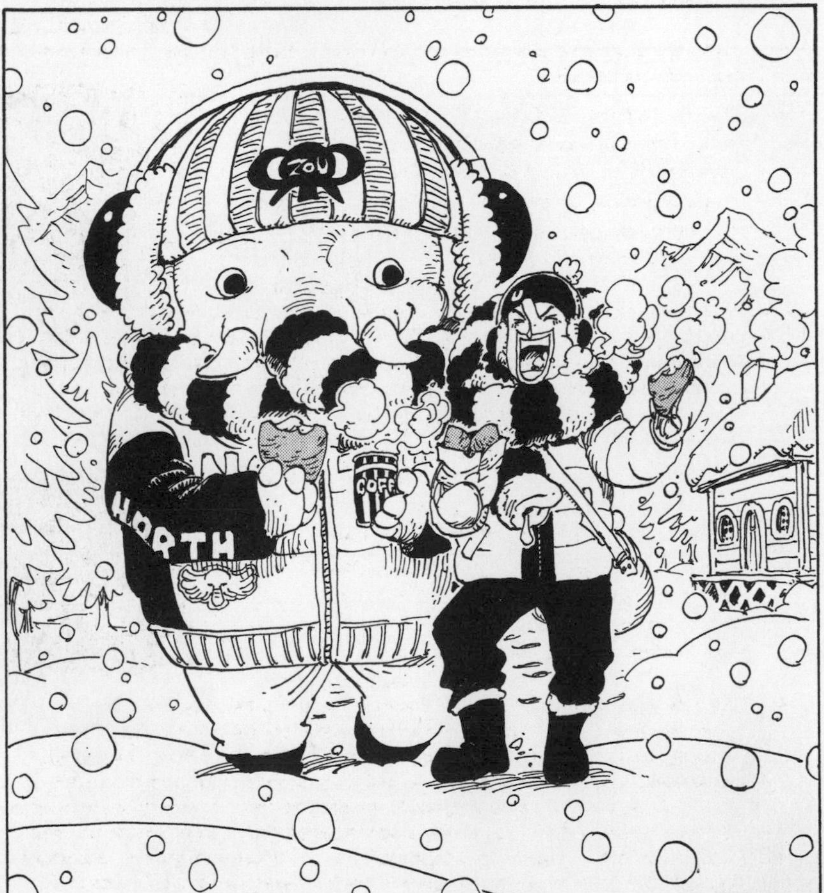
ZOU
NORTH
COFF

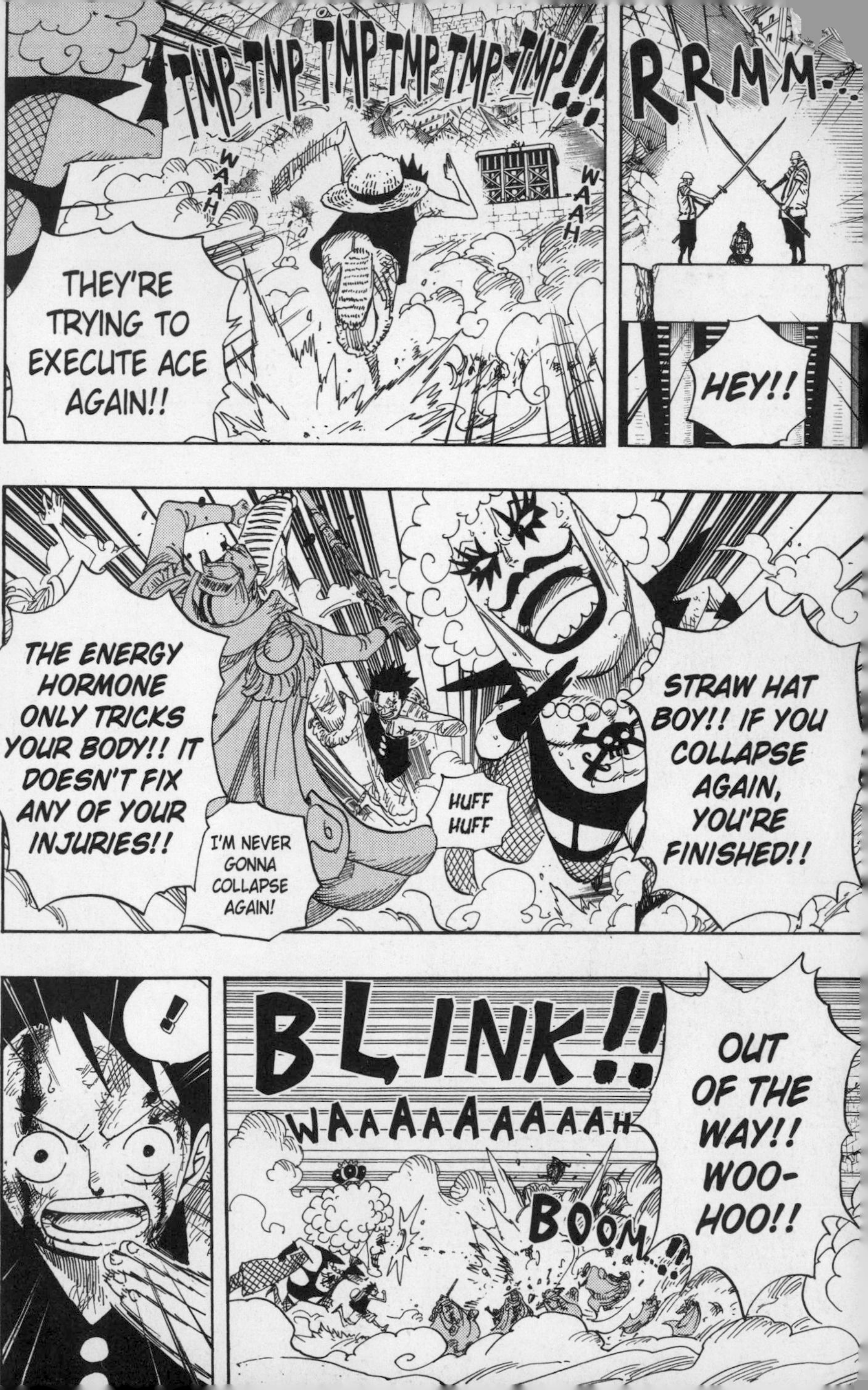
RRMM...
HEY!!
TMP TMP TMP TMP TMP TMP!!
WAAH
WAAH
THEY'RE TRYING TO EXECUTE ACE AGAIN!!
STRAW HAT BOY!! IF YOU COLLAPSE AGAIN, YOU'RE FINISHED!!
HUFF HUFF
THE ENERGY HORMONE ONLY TRICKS YOUR BODY!! IT DOESN'T FIX ANY OF YOUR INJURIES!!
I'M NEVER GONNA COLLAPSE AGAIN!
OUT OF THE WAY!! WOO-HOO!!
BLINK!!
WAAAAAAAAAAH
BOOM..!!
!

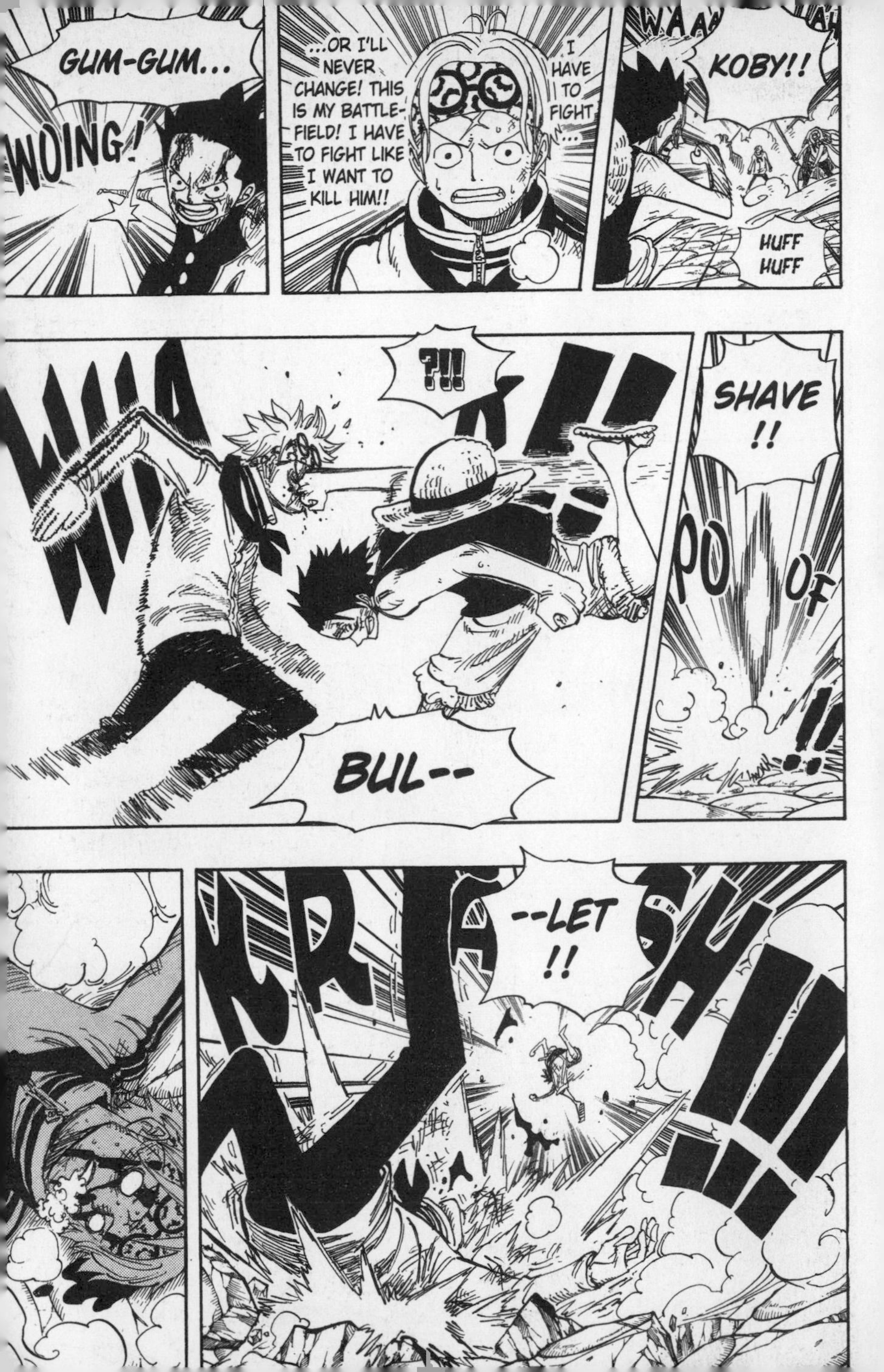
KOBY!!
HUFF HUFF
I HAVE TO FIGHT...
...OR I'LL NEVER CHANGE! THIS IS MY BATTLE-FIELD! I HAVE TO FIGHT LIKE I WANT TO KILL HIM!!
GUM-GUM...
WOING!
SHAVE!!
POOF!!
?!!
BUL--
--LET!!
KRASH!!

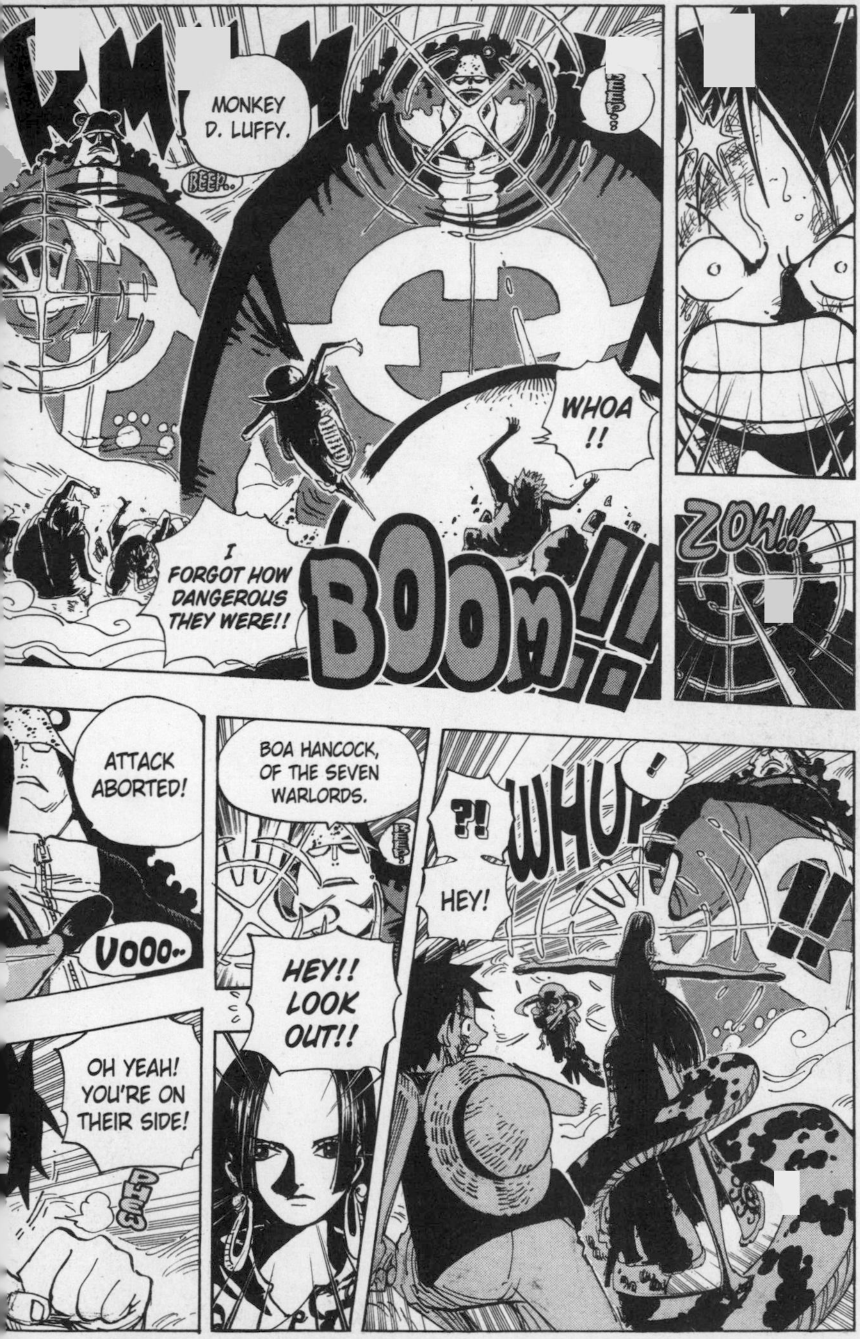
ZOW!!
MONKEY D. LUFFY.
BEEP..
WHOA !!
BOOM!!
I FORGOT HOW DANGEROUS THEY WERE!!
!
WHUP!!
?!
HEY!
BOA HANCOCK, OF THE SEVEN WARLORDS.
ATTACK ABORTED!
VOOO..
HEY!! LOOK OUT!!
OH YEAH! YOU'RE ON THEIR SIDE!

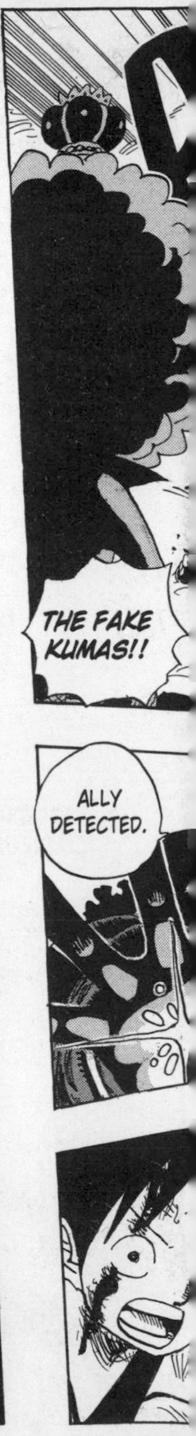
THE FAKE KUMAS!!
ALLY DETECTED.

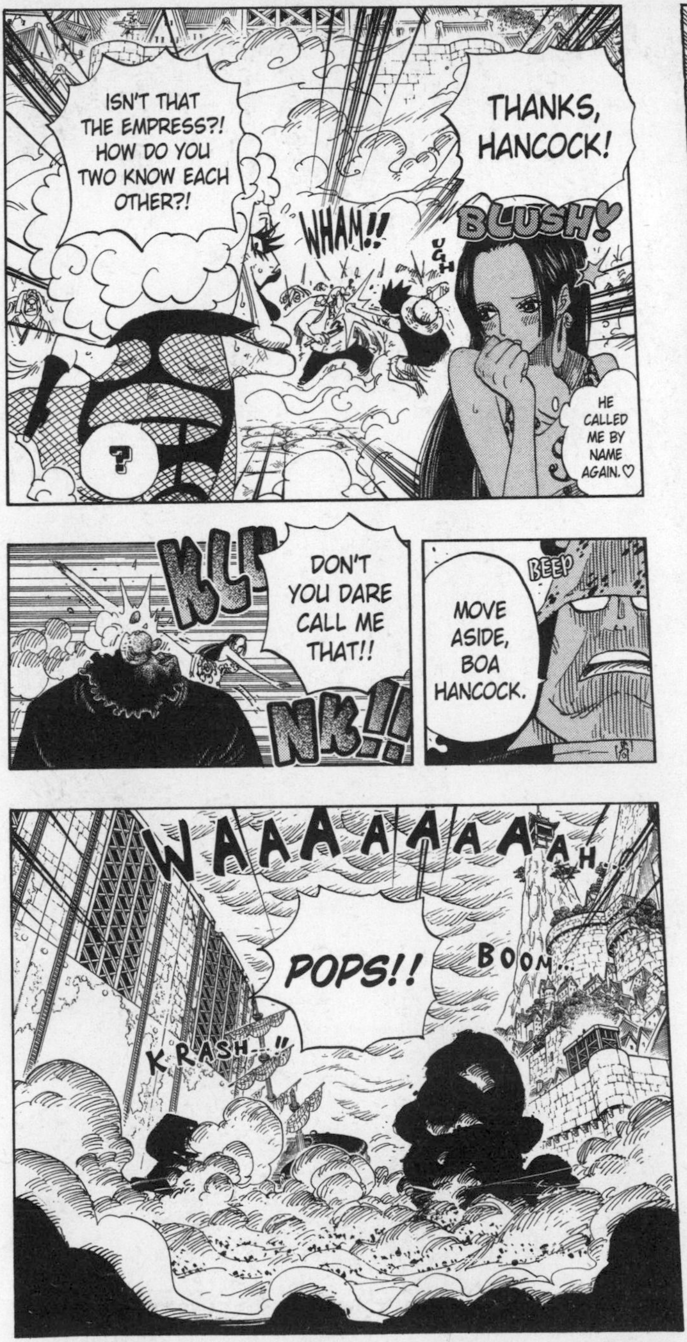
THANKS, HANCOCK!
BLUSH!
HE CALLED ME BY NAME AGAIN.♡
UGH
WHAM!!
ISN'T THAT THE EMPRESS?! HOW DO YOU TWO KNOW EACH OTHER?!
?
BEEP
MOVE ASIDE, BOA HANCOCK.
DON'T YOU DARE CALL ME THAT!!
KLUNK!!
WAAAAAAAAH...
POPS!!
BOOM...
KRASH...!!

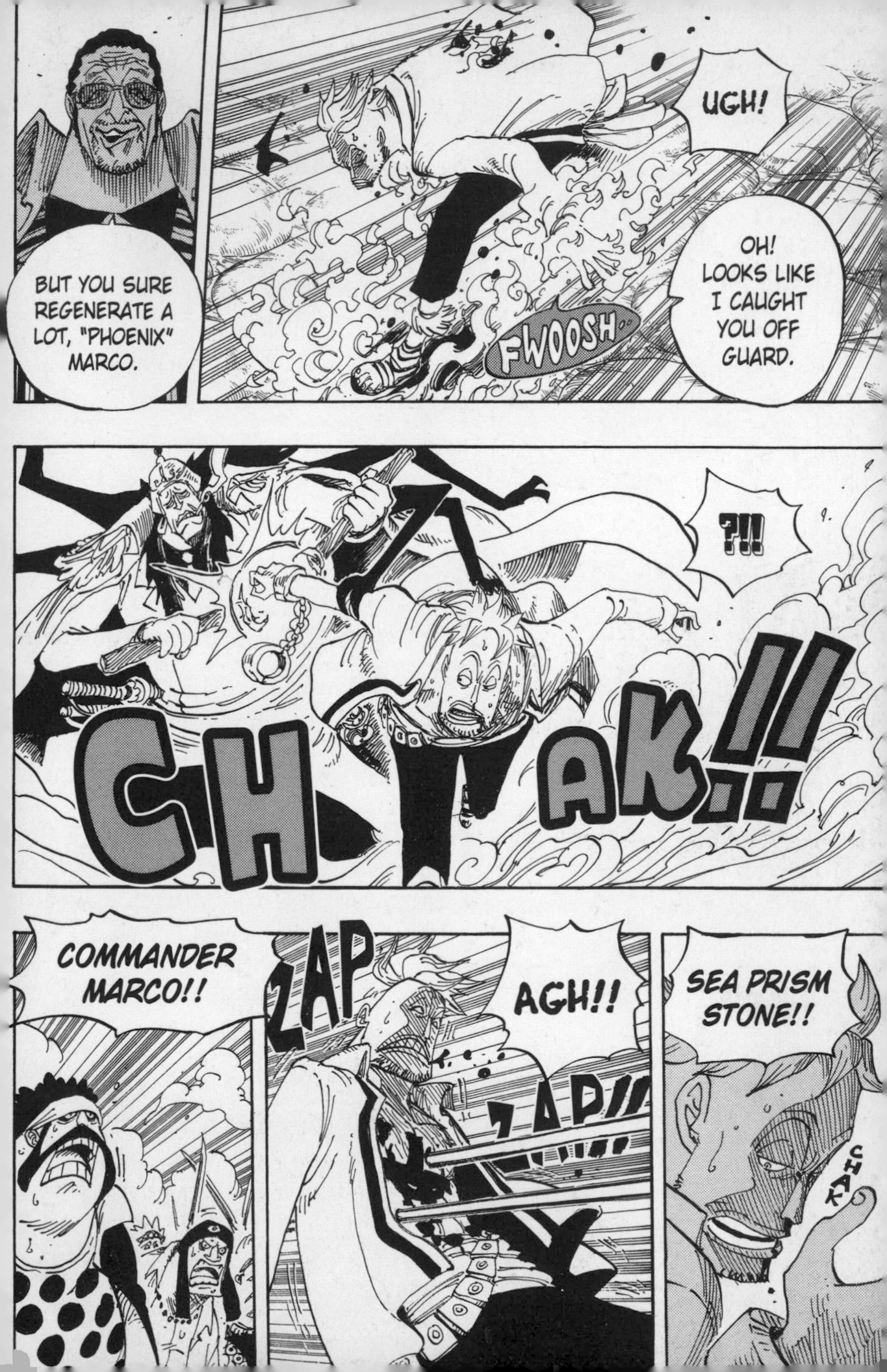
UGH!
OH! LOOKS LIKE I CAUGHT YOU OFF GUARD.
FWOOSH
BUT YOU SURE REGENERATE A LOT, "PHOENIX" MARCO.
?!!
CHAK!!
SEA PRISM STONE!!
CHAK
AGH!!
ZAP
COMMANDER MARCO!!

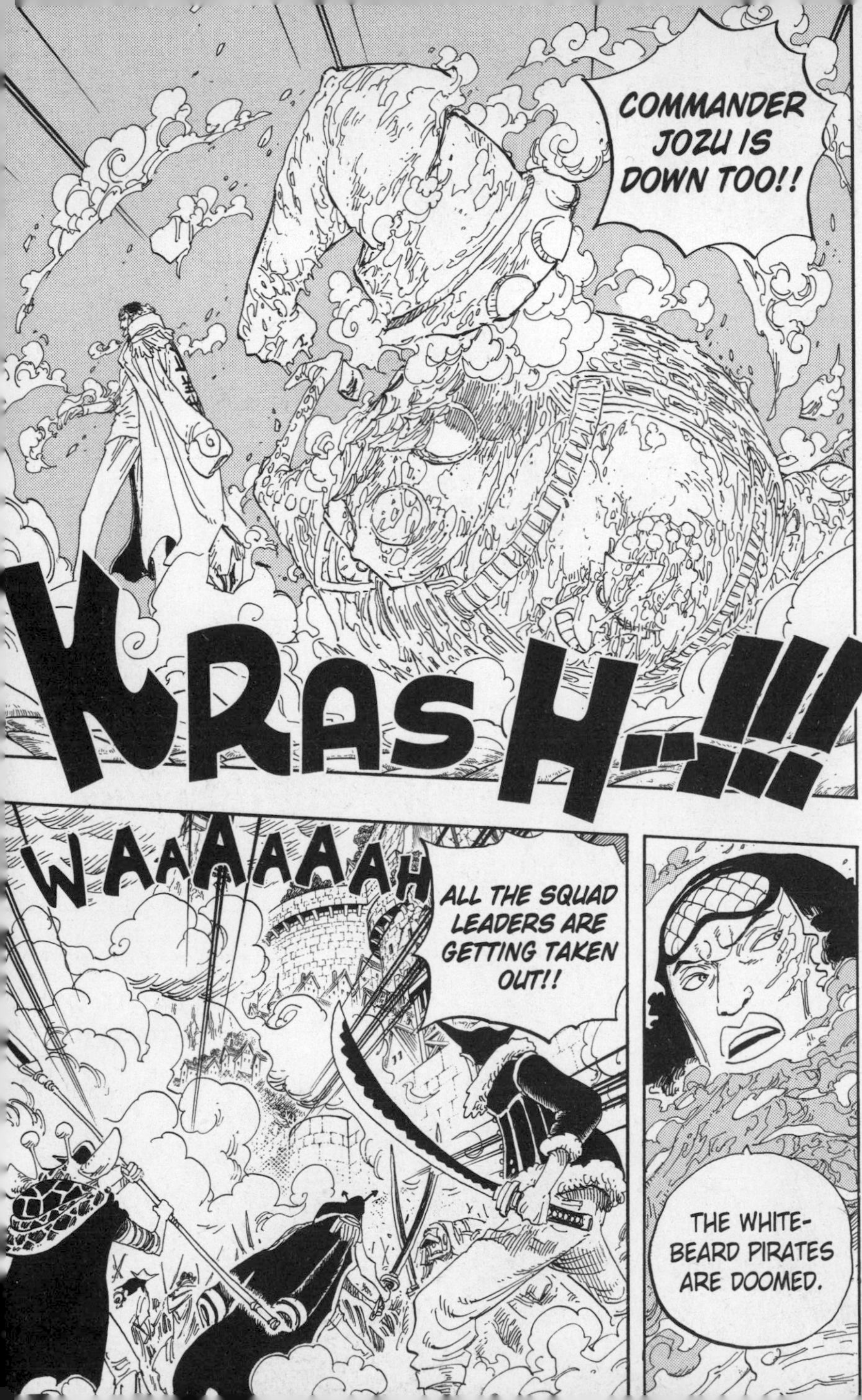
COMMANDER JOZU IS DOWN TOO!!
KRASH!!!
THE WHITE-BEARD PIRATES ARE DOOMED.
WAAAAAAAH
ALL THE SQUAD LEADERS ARE GETTING TAKEN OUT!!

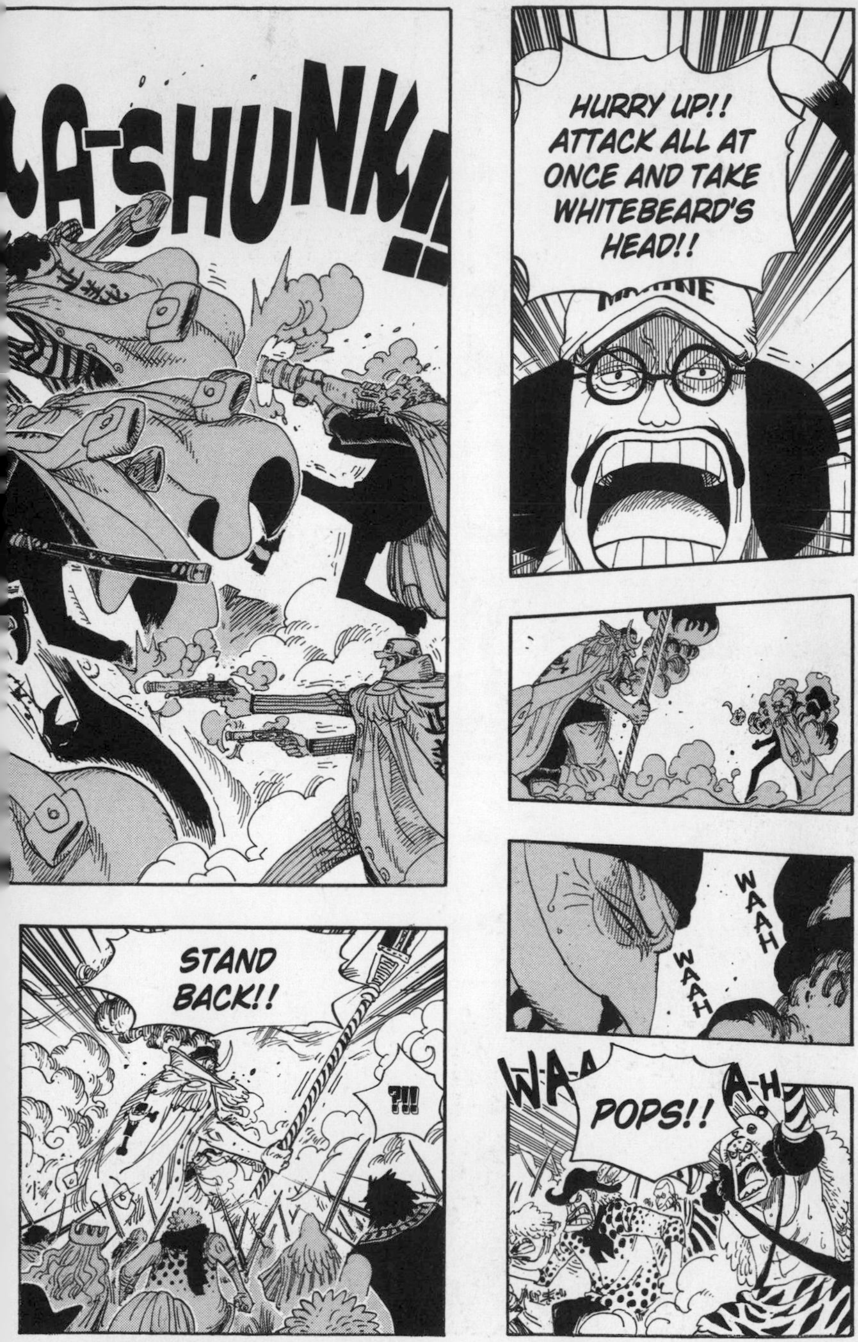
HURRY UP!! ATTACK ALL AT ONCE AND TAKE WHITEBEARD'S HEAD!!
KA-SHUNK!!
WAAH
WAAH
WA-A-A-H
POPS!!
STAND BACK!!
?!!

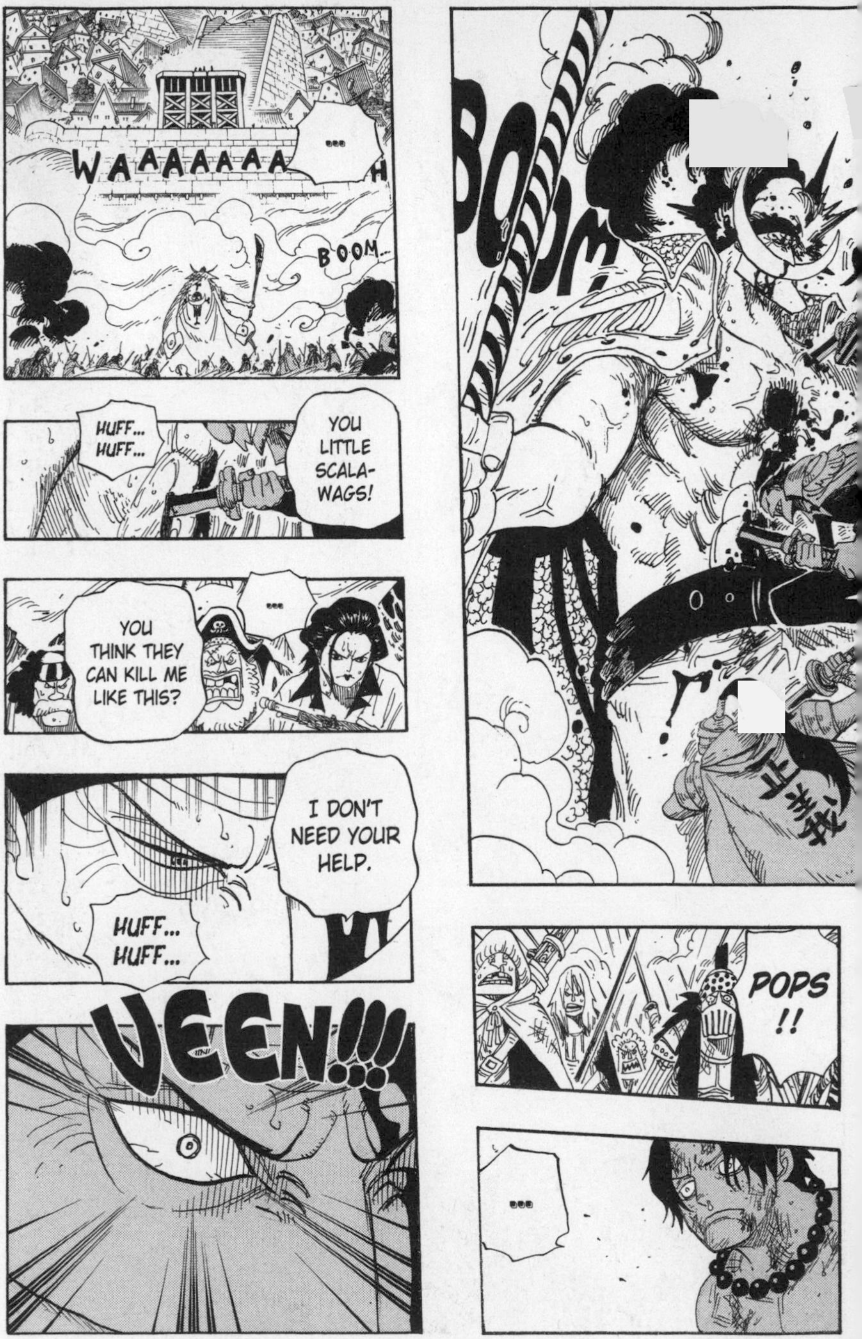
BOOM
POPS !!
...
...
WAAAAAAAH
BOOM...
YOU LITTLE SCALA-WAGS!
HUFF... HUFF...
...
YOU THINK THEY CAN KILL ME LIKE THIS?
I DON'T NEED YOUR HELP.
HUFF... HUFF...
VEEN!!!

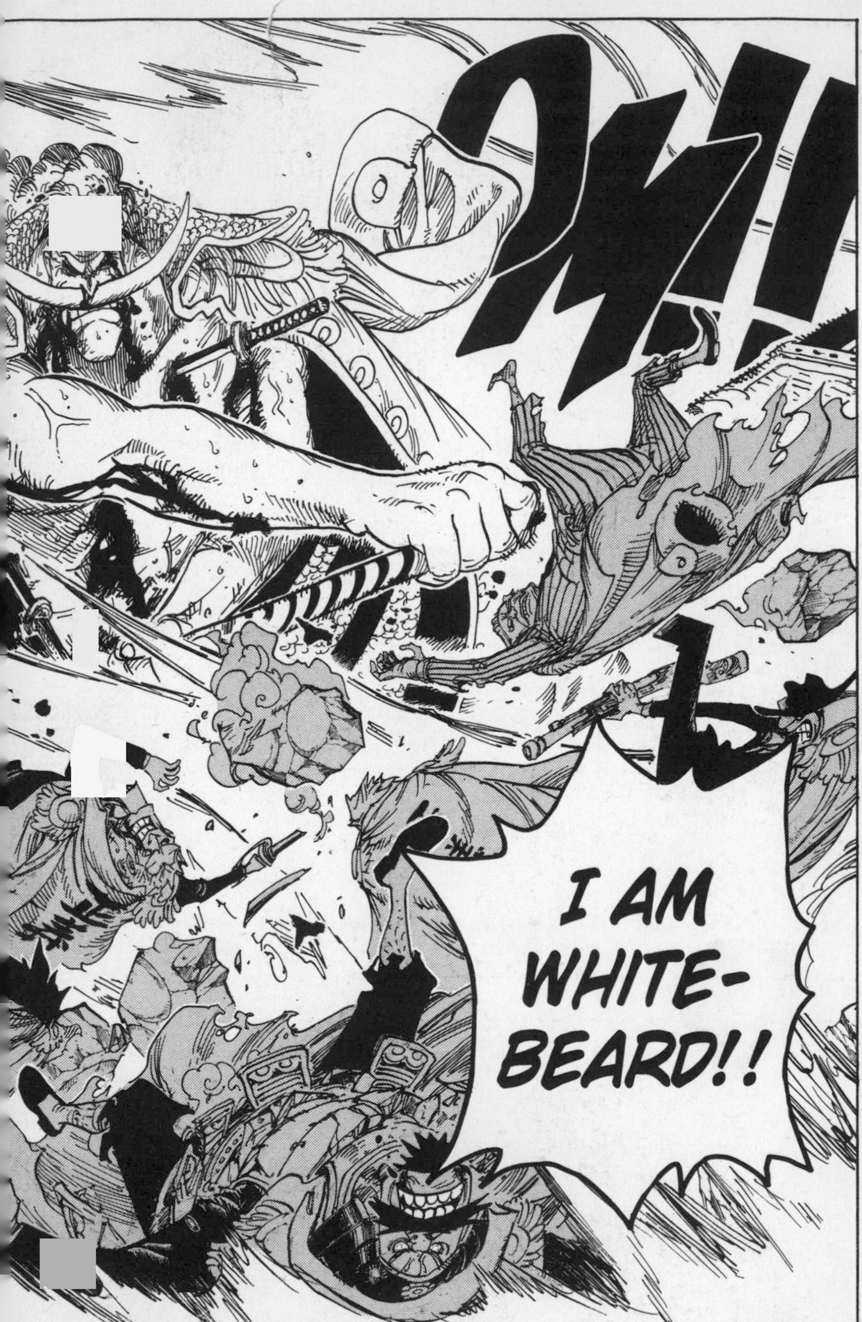
OW!!
I AM WHITE-BEARD!!

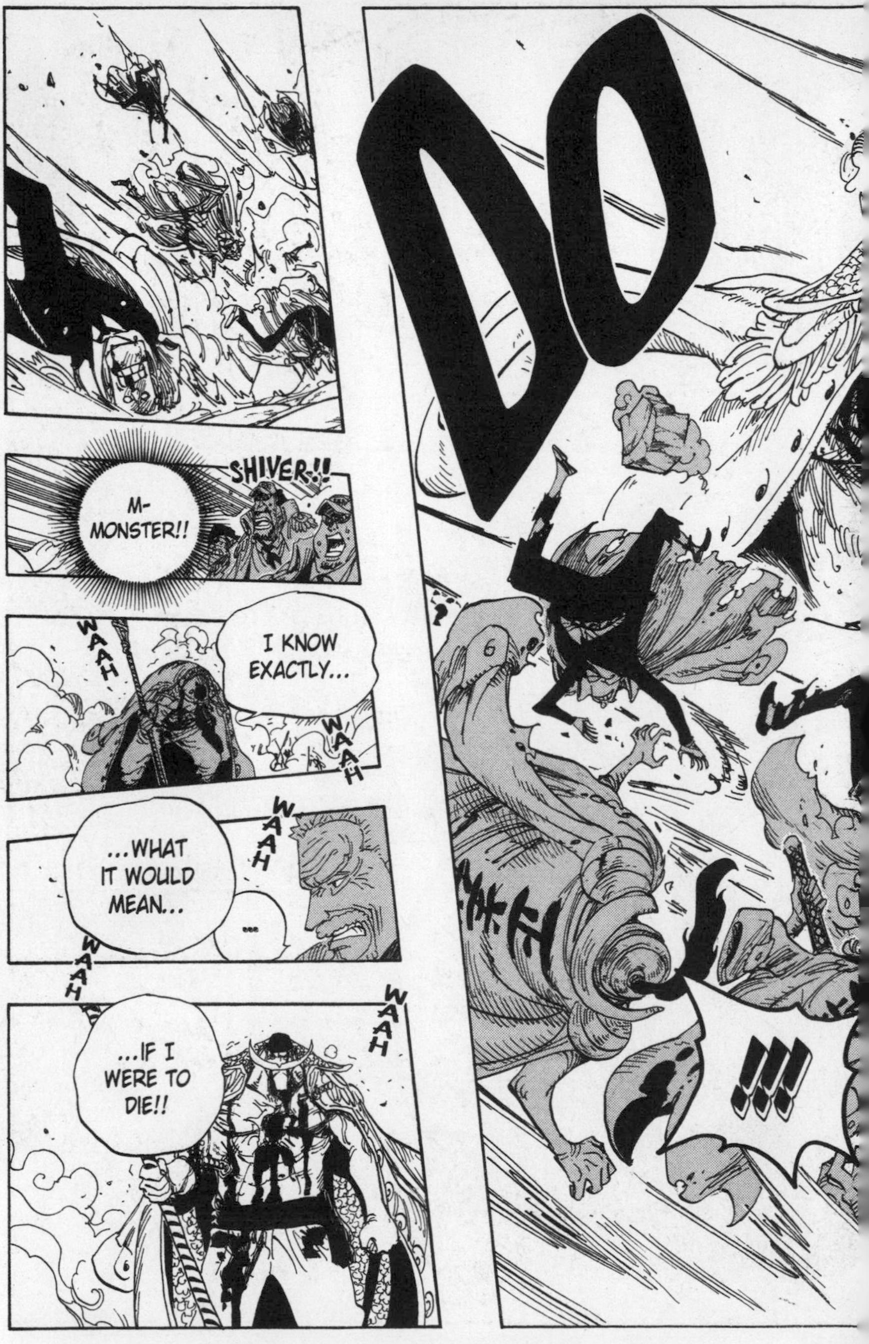
DO
!!!
SHIVER!!
M-MONSTER!!
WAAH
I KNOW EXACTLY...
WAAH
WAAH
...WHAT IT WOULD MEAN...
...
WAAH
WAAH
...IF I WERE TO DIE!!

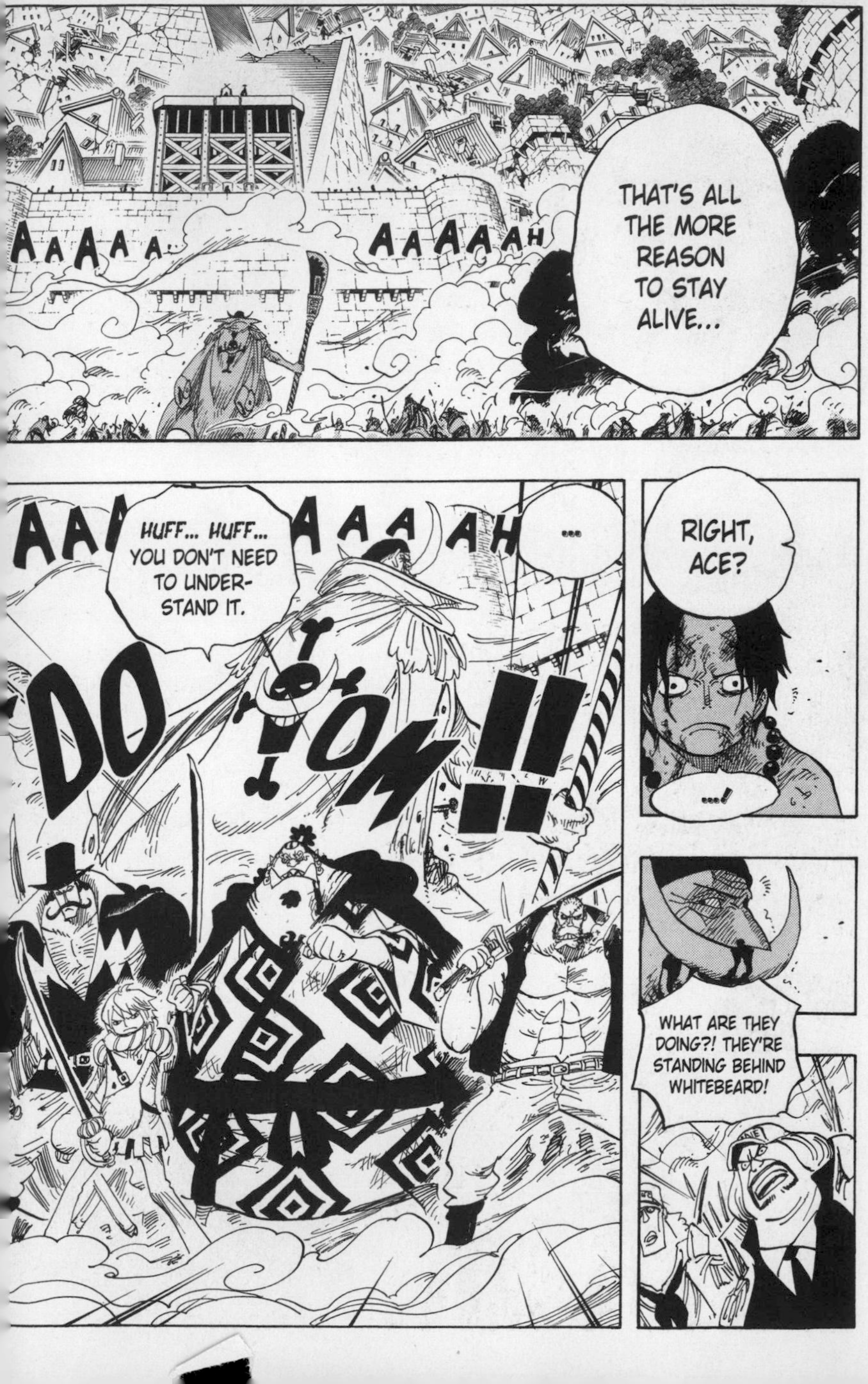
THAT'S ALL THE MORE REASON TO STAY ALIVE...
AAAAAH
AAAAA...
RIGHT, ACE?
...!
WHAT ARE THEY DOING?! THEY'RE STANDING BEHIND WHITEBEARD!
...
AAAAAH
HUFF... HUFF... YOU DON'T NEED TO UNDER-STAND IT.
DOOM!!

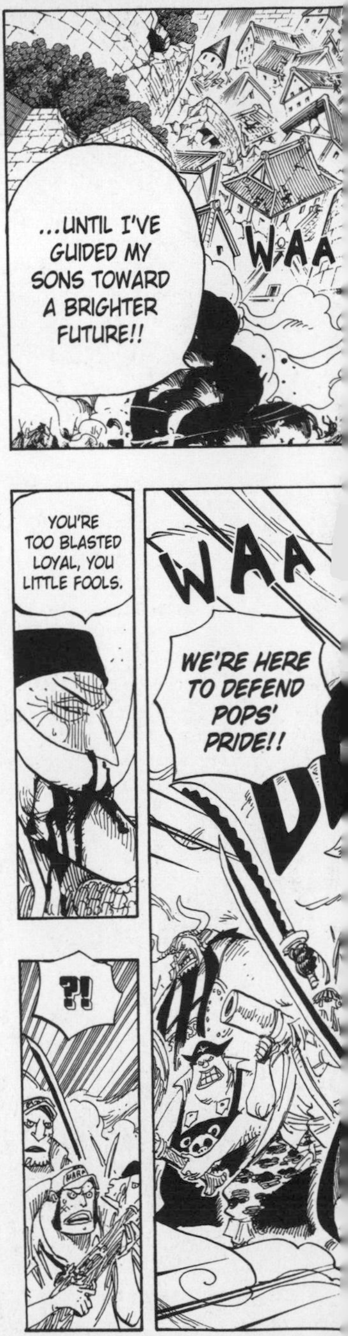
...UNTIL I'VE GUIDED MY SONS TOWARD A BRIGHTER FUTURE!!
WAA
WAA
WE'RE HERE TO DEFEND POPS' PRIDE!!
YOU'RE TOO BLASTED LOYAL, YOU LITTLE FOOLS.
?!!
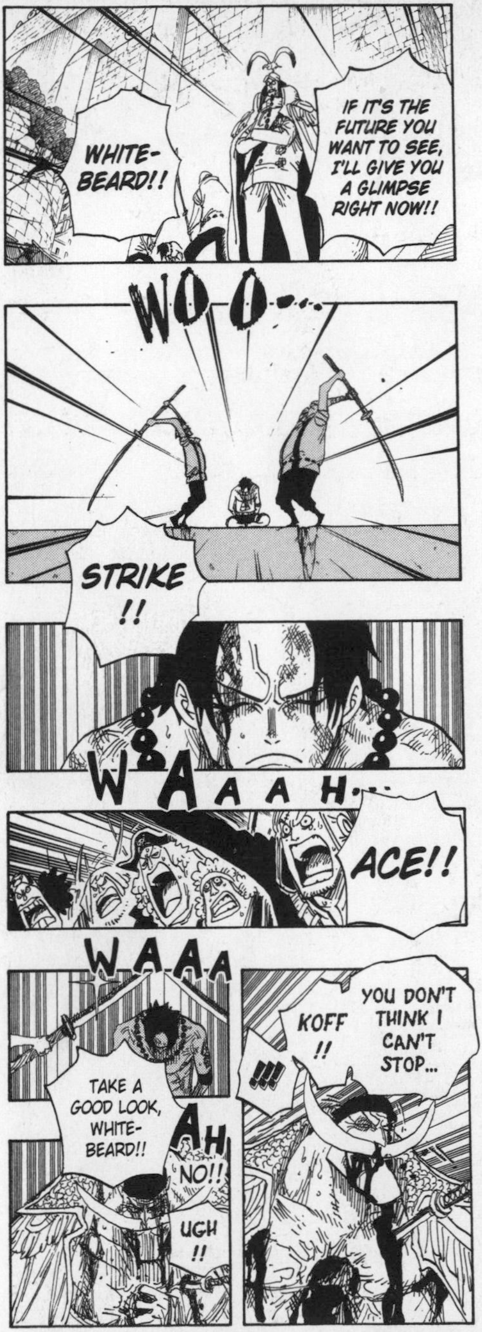
IF IT'S THE FUTURE YOU WANT TO SEE, I'LL GIVE YOU A GLIMPSE RIGHT NOW!!
WHITE-BEARD!!
WOO-...
STRIKE!!
WAAAH...
ACE!!
YOU DON'T THINK I CAN'T STOP...
KOFF!!
!!!
WAAA
TAKE A GOOD LOOK, WHITE-BEARD!!
AH
NO!!
UGH!!

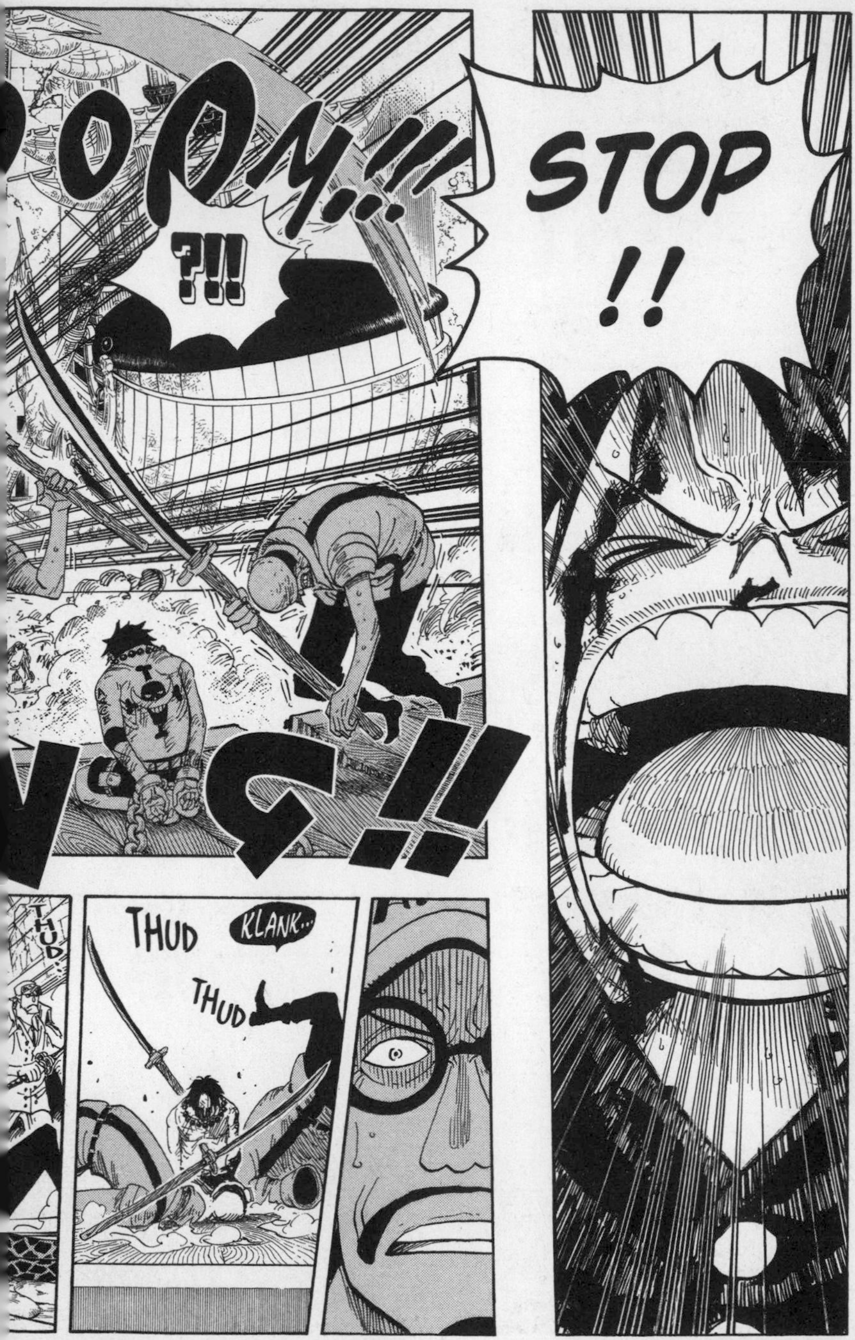
STOP !!
OOM..!!
?!!
NG!!
KLANK...
THUD
THUD
THUD

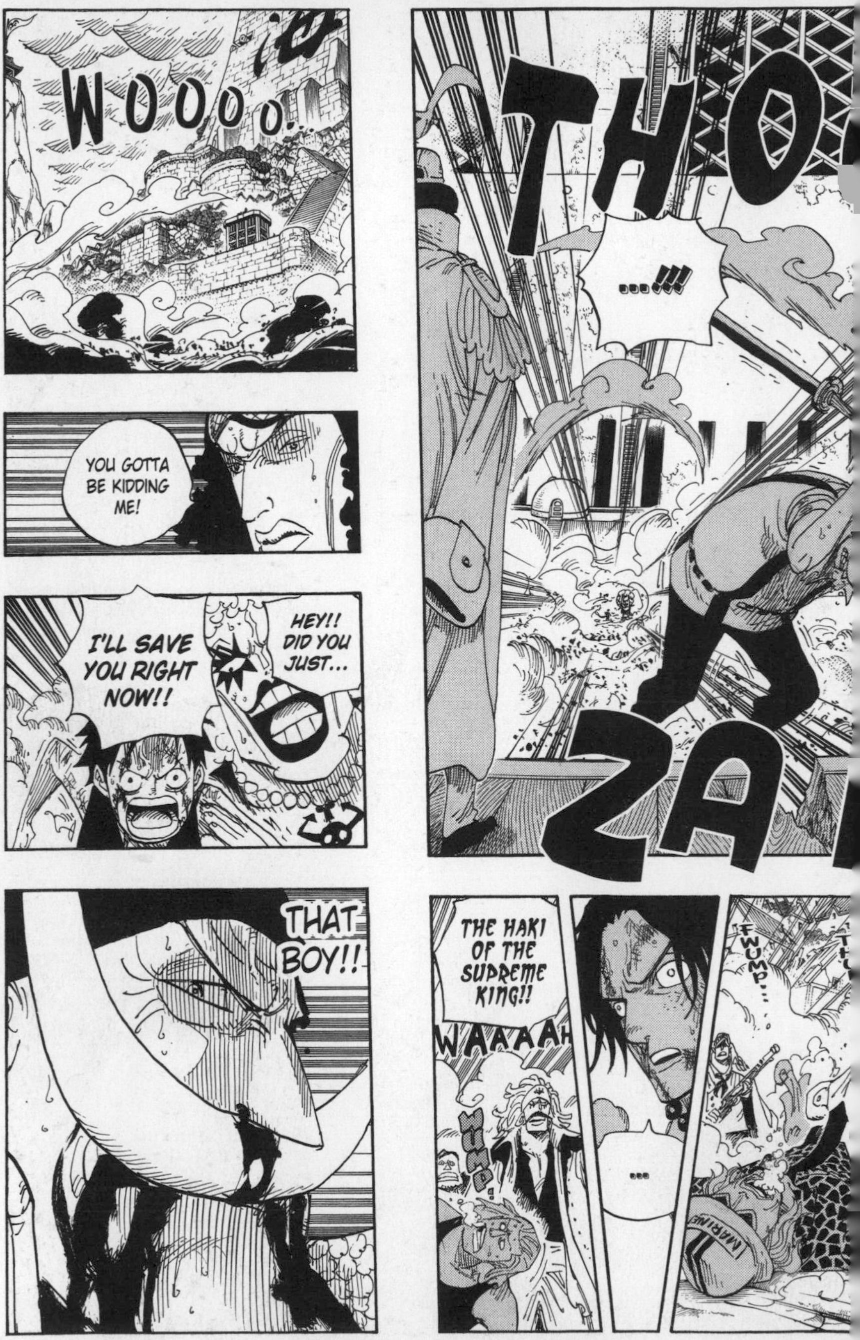
THO
...!!!
ZA
WOOOO...!!
YOU GOTTA BE KIDDING ME!
HEY!! DID YOU JUST...
I'LL SAVE YOU RIGHT NOW!!
FWUMP...
...
THE HAKI OF THE SUPREME KING!!
WAAAAH
THAT BOY!!

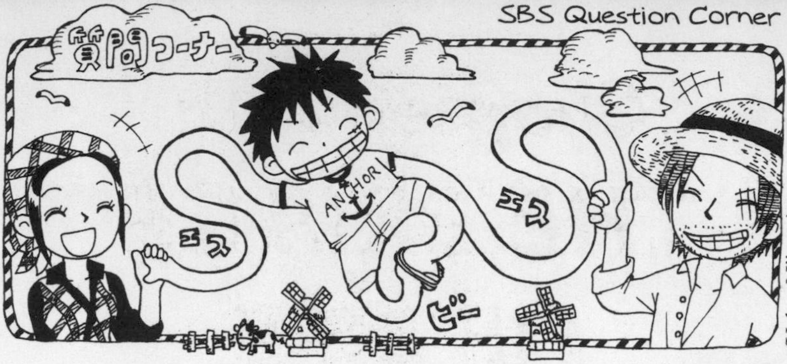
質問コーナー
ANCHOR
(Yoko, Niigata)

Q: Hello, Mr. Oda! There's something I really want to know. Please tell me the names of all the division commanders that Whitebeard leads! I'm especially wondering about the person carrying the giant iron ball and the samurai-like person!

--Semaru

A: Okay. There's so many questions about the behind-the-scenes stuff about the war this time! Anyway, I'm only answering because you asked. Stuff that's talked about in SBS really doesn't need to be remembered for the main story. I don't talk about certain things in the main story because I omitted them on purpose. I think that too much unnecessary information will only confuse the readers. So please enjoy the stuff in SBS strictly as an extra. Now here are the division leaders of the Whitebeard Pirates.

Captain of the Whitebeard Pirates
Edward Newgate

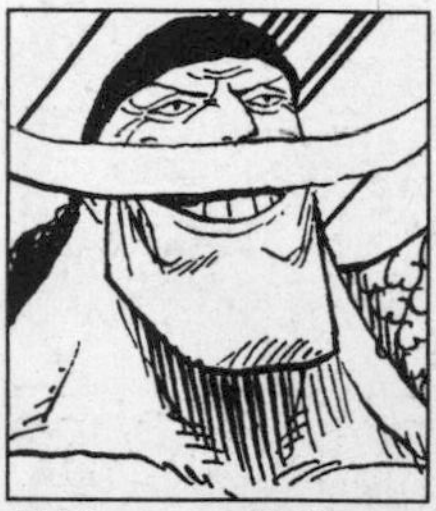

Division One Leader
Marco

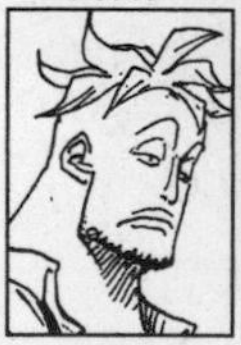

Division Two Leader
Ace

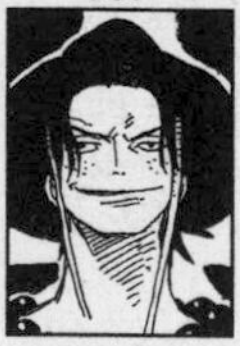

Division Three Leader
Jozu

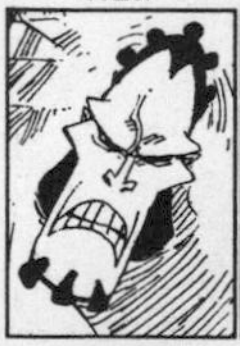

Division Four Leader
Thatch

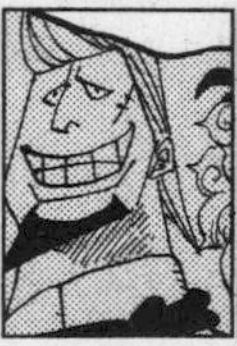

Division Five Leader
Vista

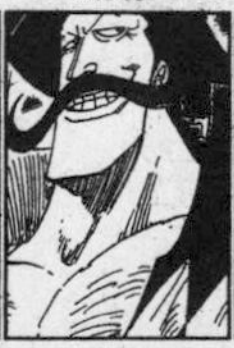

Division Six Leader
Blamenco

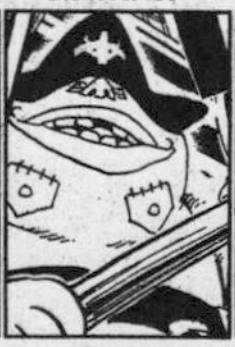

Division Seven Leader
Rakuyo

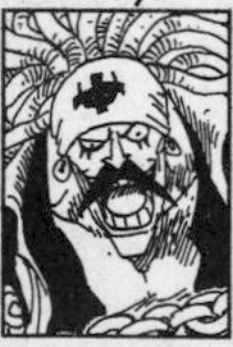

Division Eight Leader
Namule

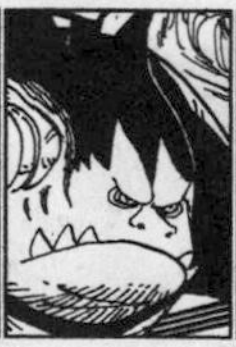

Division Nine Leader
Blenheim

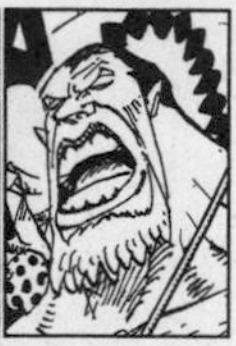

Division Ten Leader
Curiel

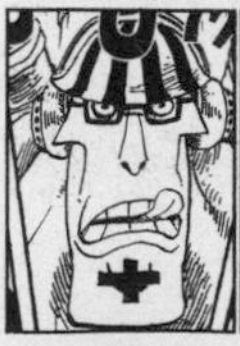

Division Eleven Leader
Kingdew

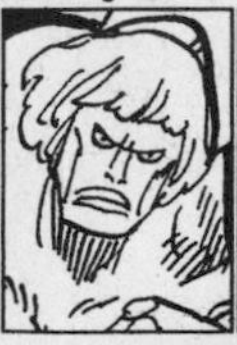

Division Twelve Leader
Haruta

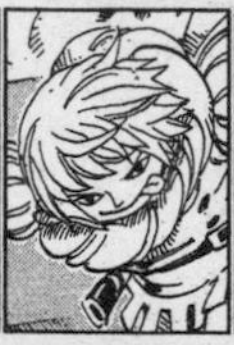

Division Thirteen Leader
Atmos

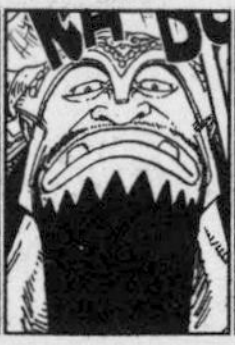

Division Fourteen Leader
Speed Jil

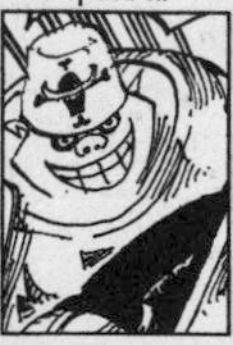

Division Fifteen Leader
Fossa

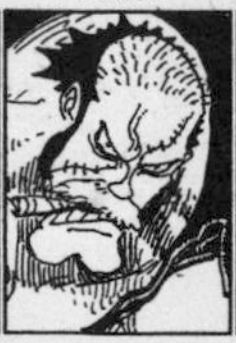

Division Sixteen Leader
Izo

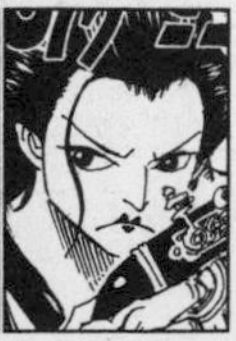

Chapter 570:
THE BRIDGE OF LIFE

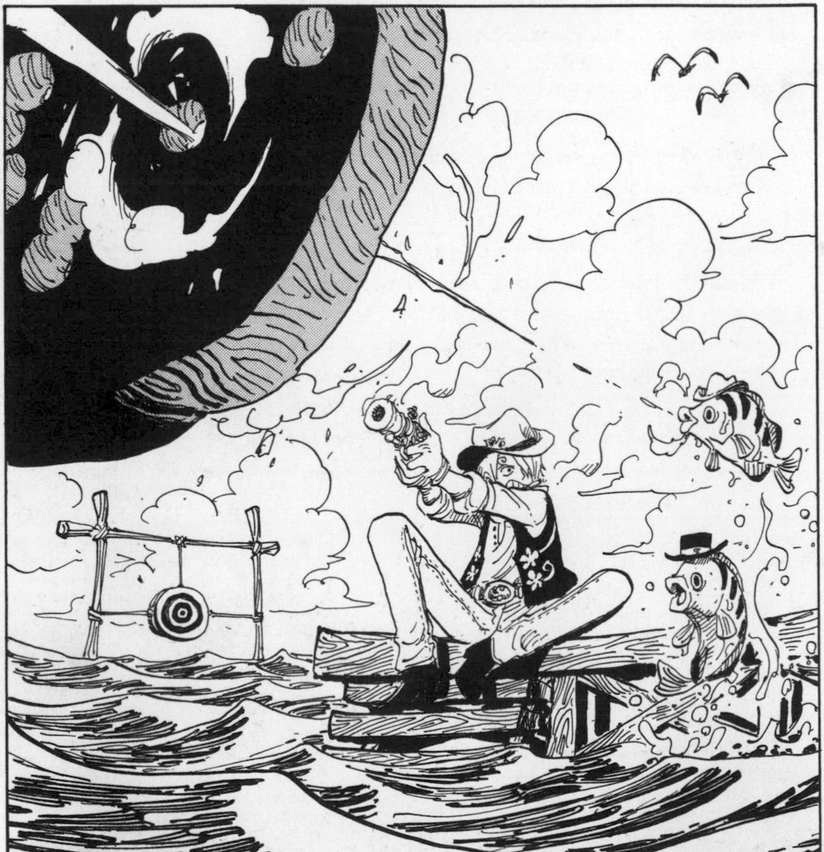

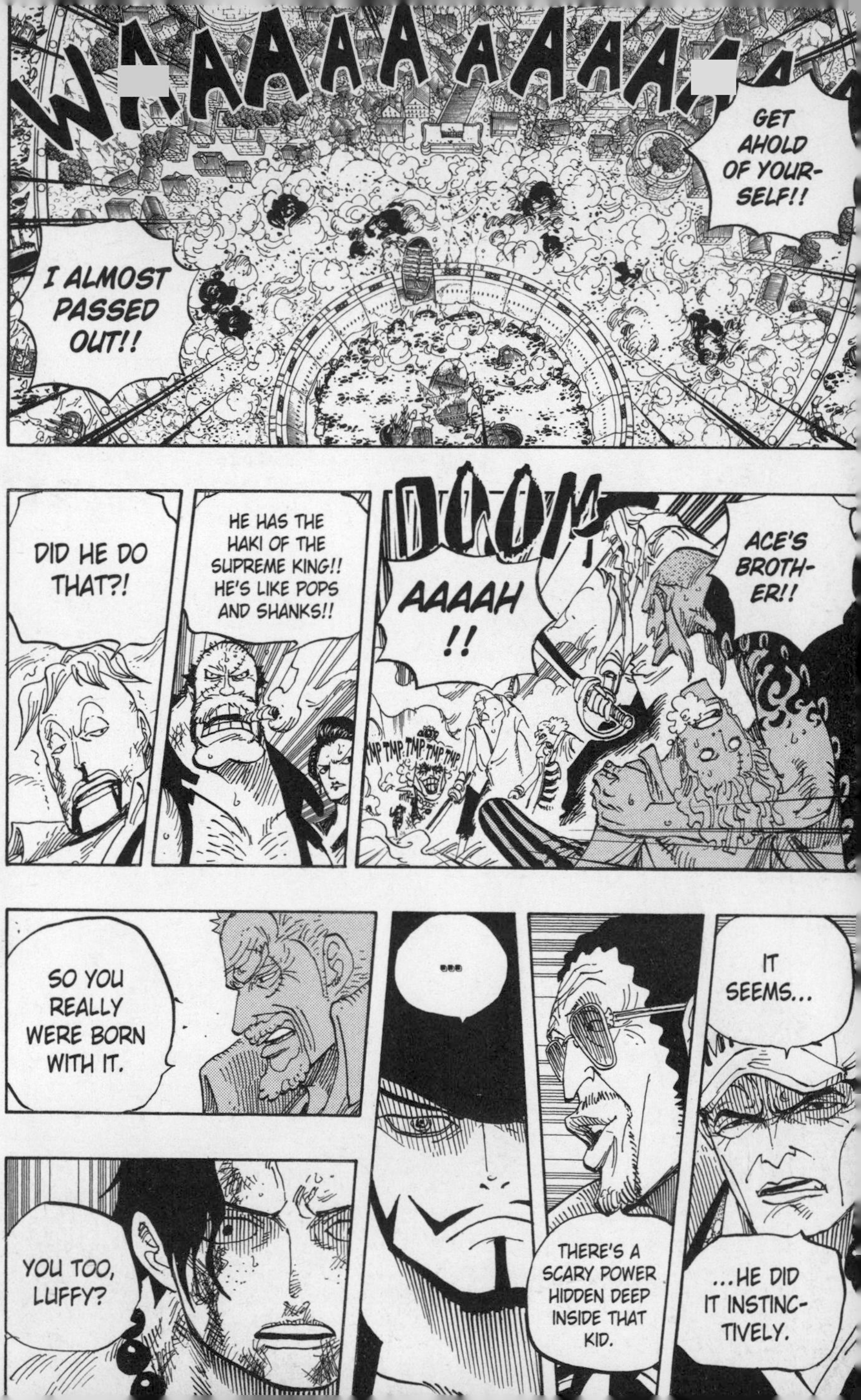
WAAAAAAAAA
GET AHOLD OF YOURSELF!!
I ALMOST PASSED OUT!!
ACE'S BROTHER!!
DOOM
AAAAH!!
TMP TMP TMP TMP TMP
HE HAS THE HAKI OF THE SUPREME KING!! HE'S LIKE POPS AND SHANKS!!
DID HE DO THAT?!
IT SEEMS...
...HE DID IT INSTINCTIVELY.
THERE'S A SCARY POWER HIDDEN DEEP INSIDE THAT KID.
...
SO YOU REALLY WERE BORN WITH IT.
YOU TOO, LUFFY?

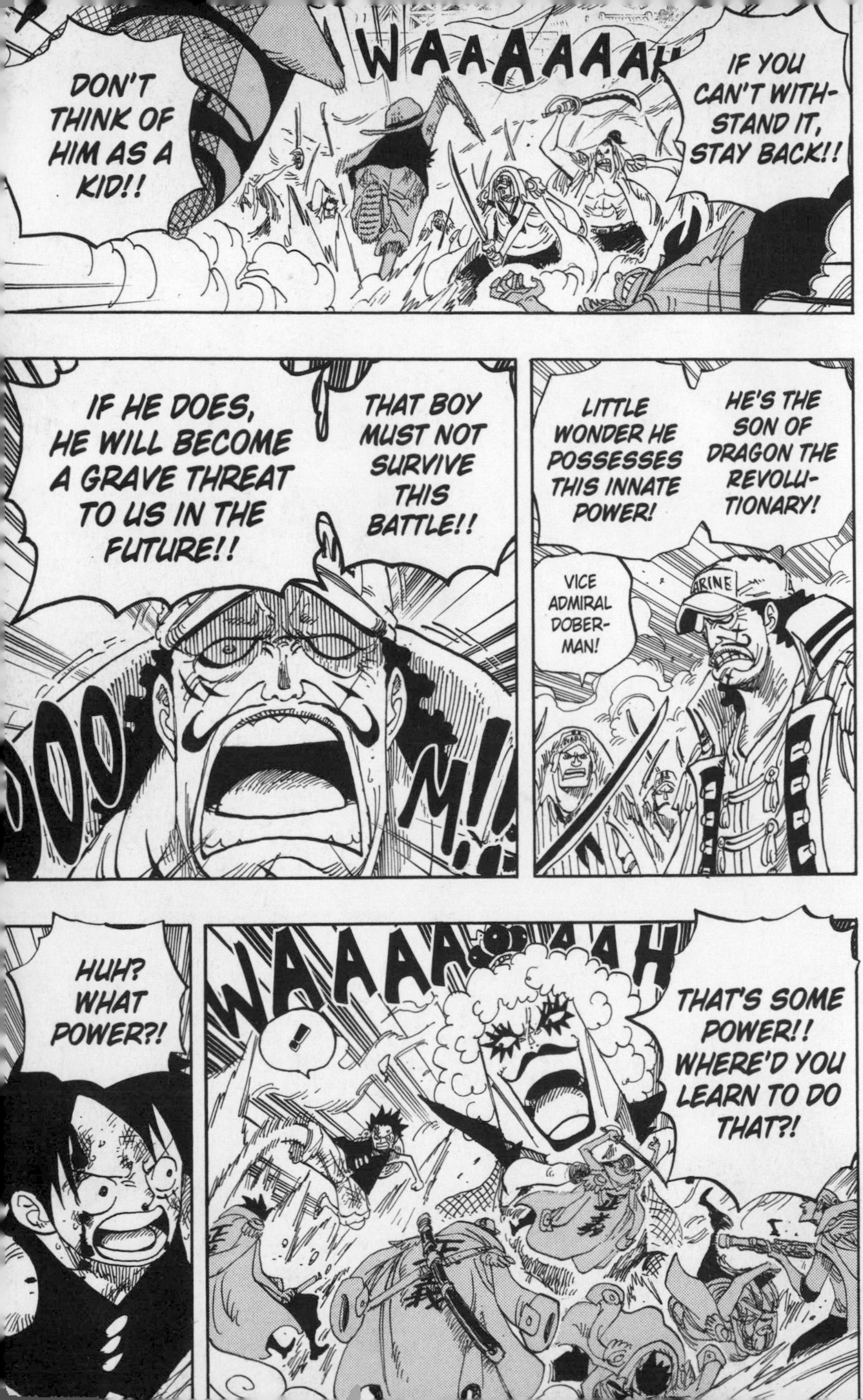
IF YOU CAN'T WITH-STAND IT, STAY BACK!!
WAAAAAAH
DON'T THINK OF HIM AS A KID!!
HE'S THE SON OF DRAGON THE REVOLU-TIONARY!
LITTLE WONDER HE POSSESSES THIS INNATE POWER!
VICE ADMIRAL DOBER-MAN!
THAT BOY MUST NOT SURVIVE THIS BATTLE!!
IF HE DOES, HE WILL BECOME A GRAVE THREAT TO US IN THE FUTURE!!
THAT'S SOME POWER!! WHERE'D YOU LEARN TO DO THAT?!
!
HUH? WHAT POWER?!

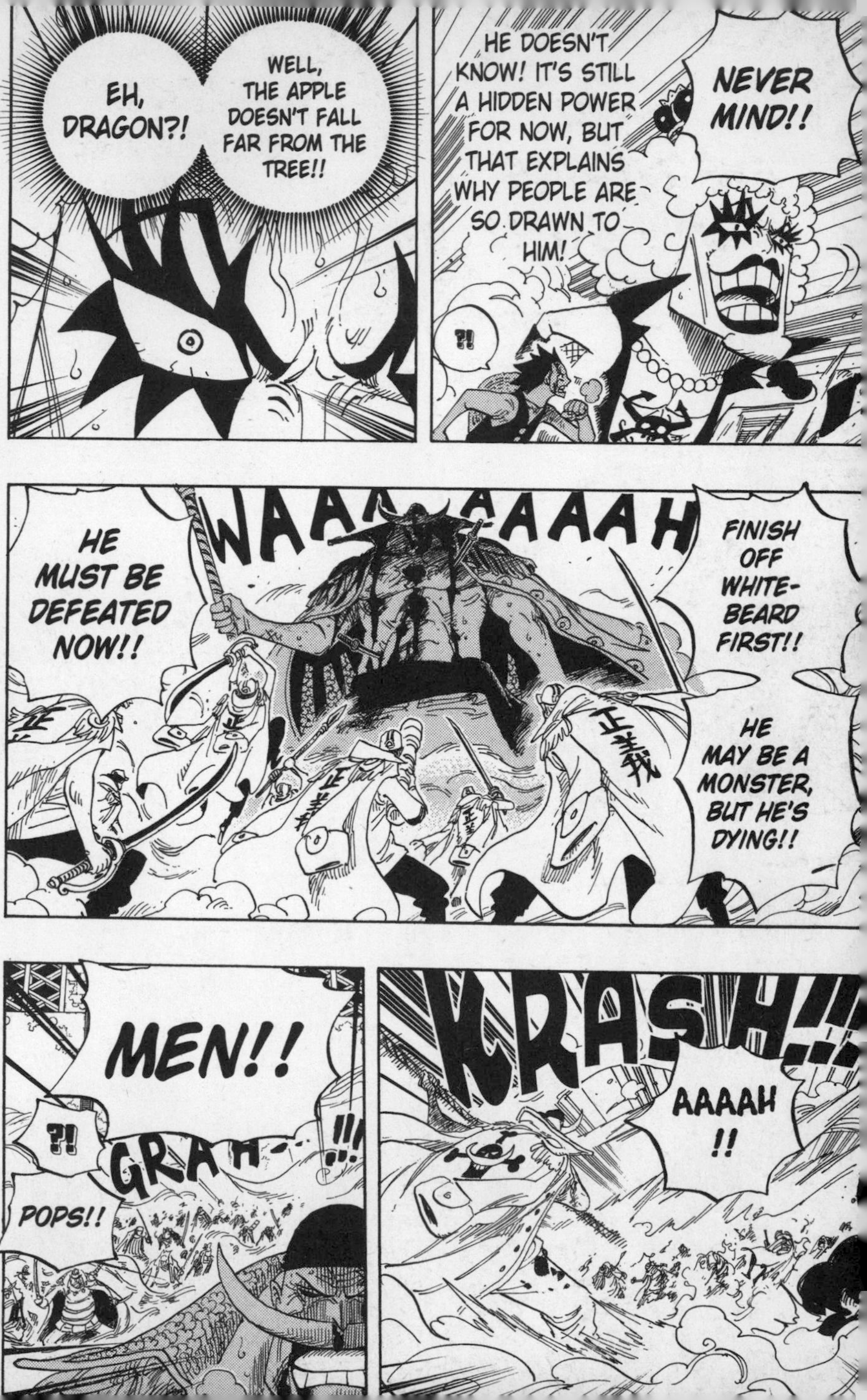

NEVER MIND!!
HE DOESN'T KNOW! IT'S STILL A HIDDEN POWER FOR NOW, BUT THAT EXPLAINS WHY PEOPLE ARE SO DRAWN TO HIM!
?!
WELL, THE APPLE DOESN'T FALL FAR FROM THE TREE!!
EH, DRAGON?!
FINISH OFF WHITE-BEARD FIRST!!
WAAA AAAAH
HE MUST BE DEFEATED NOW!!
HE MAY BE A MONSTER, BUT HE'S DYING!!
KRASH!!!
AAAAH !!
MEN!!
GRAH-- !!!
?!
POPS!!

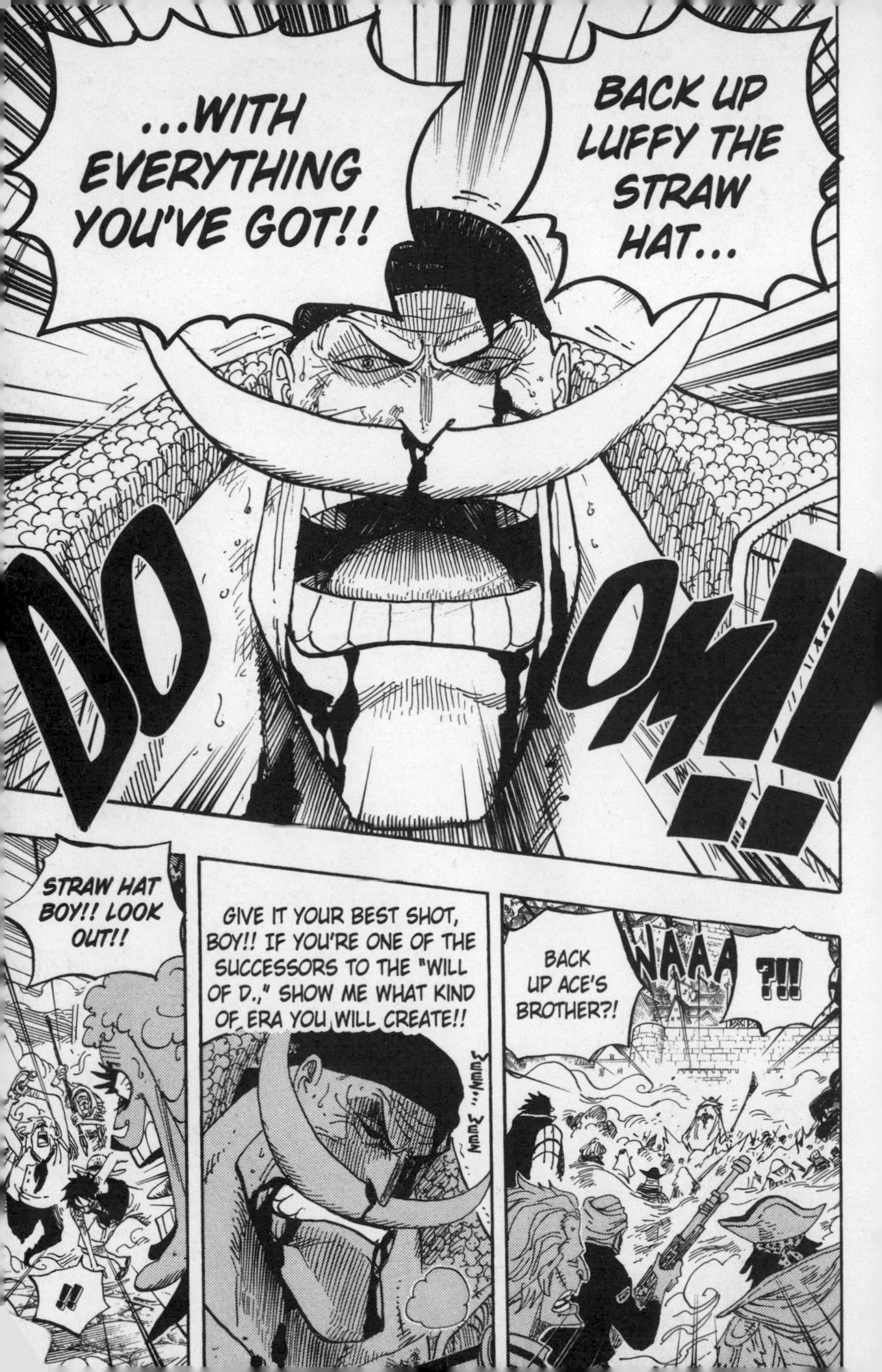
BACK UP LUFFY THE STRAW HAT...
...WITH EVERYTHING YOU'VE GOT!!
DOOM!!
WAAA ?!!
BACK UP ACE'S BROTHER?!
GIVE IT YOUR BEST SHOT, BOY!! IF YOU'RE ONE OF THE SUCCESSORS TO THE "WILL OF D.," SHOW ME WHAT KIND OF ERA YOU WILL CREATE!!
WEWN... WEWN
STRAW HAT BOY!! LOOK OUT!!
!!

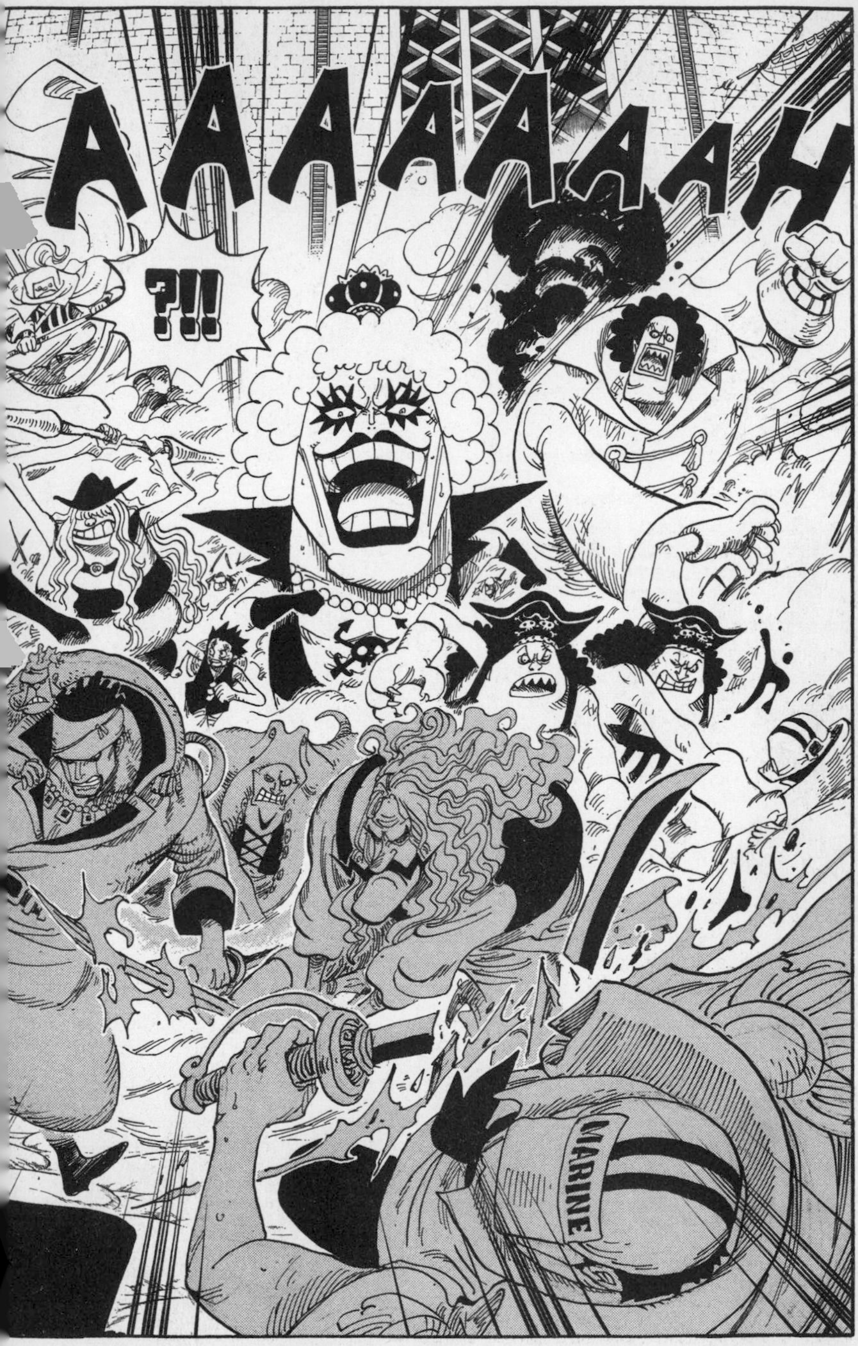

AAAAAAAAH
?!!
MARINE

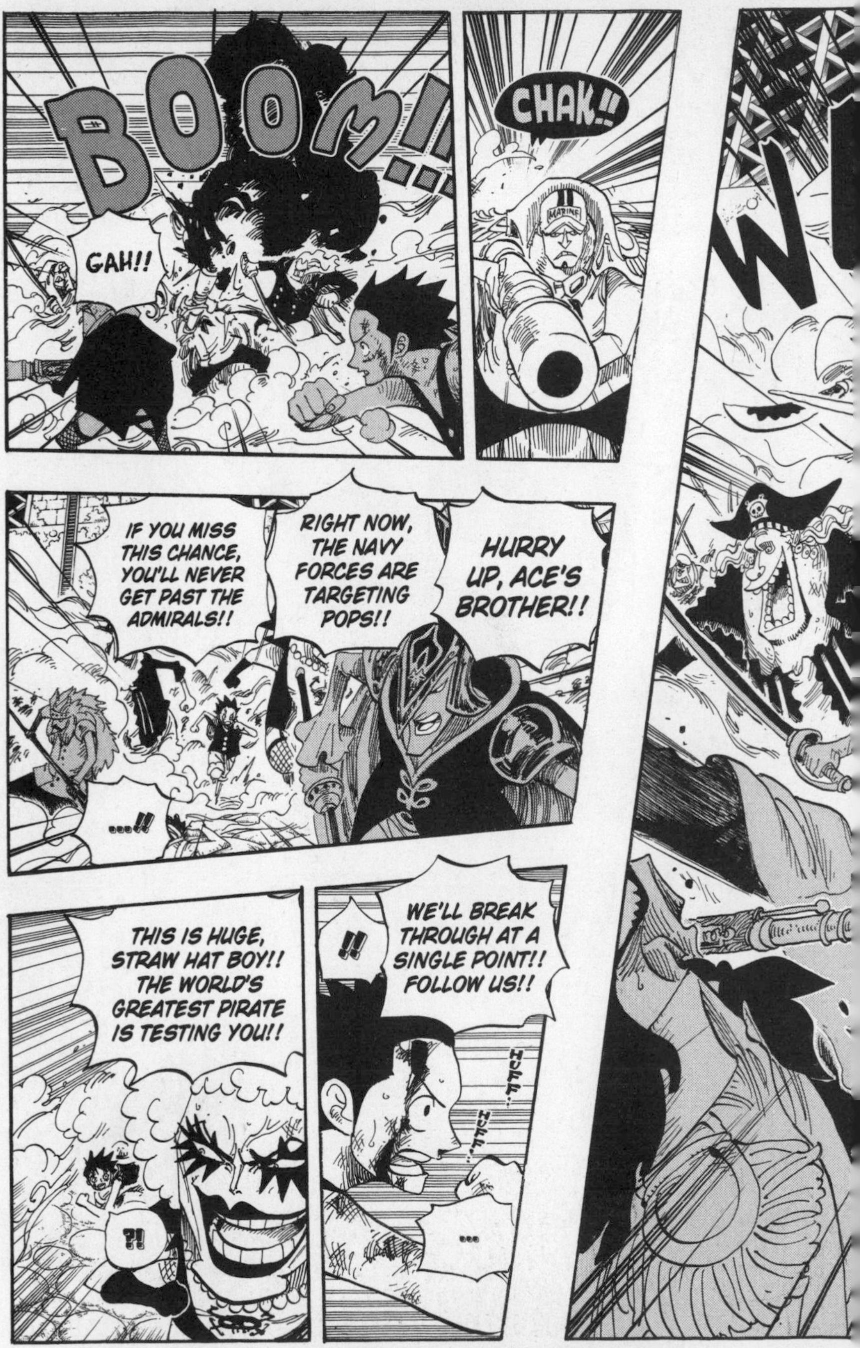
CHAK!!
BOOM!!...
GAH!!
HURRY UP, ACE'S BROTHER!!
RIGHT NOW, THE NAVY FORCES ARE TARGETING POPS!!
IF YOU MISS THIS CHANCE, YOU'LL NEVER GET PAST THE ADMIRALS!!
...!!
WE'LL BREAK THROUGH AT A SINGLE POINT!! FOLLOW US!!
!!
HUFF...
HUFF...
...
THIS IS HUGE, STRAW HAT BOY!! THE WORLD'S GREATEST PIRATE IS TESTING YOU!!
?!!

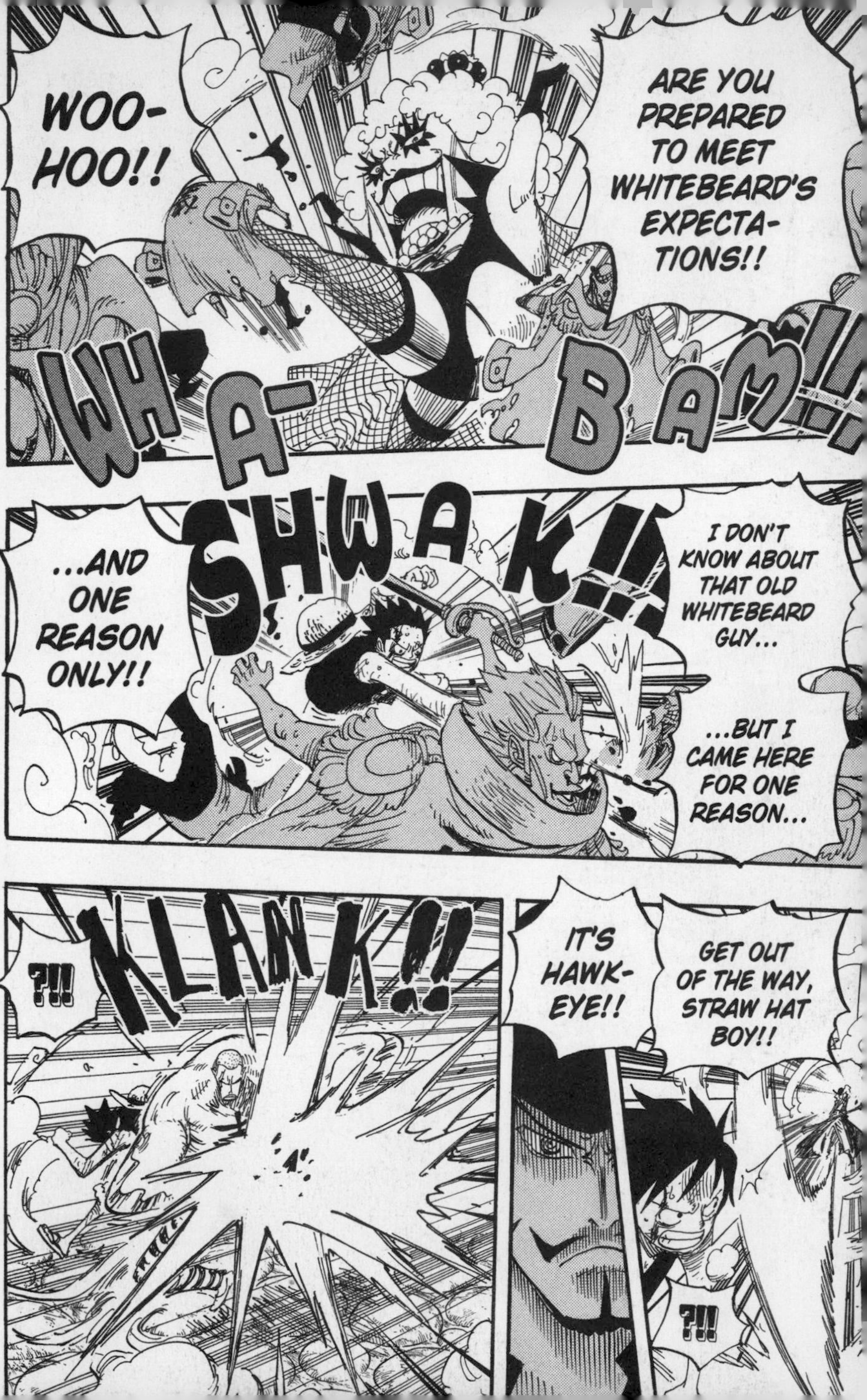
ARE YOU PREPARED TO MEET WHITEBEARD'S EXPECTA-TIONS!!
WOO-HOO!!
WHA-BAM!!!
I DON'T KNOW ABOUT THAT OLD WHITEBEARD GUY...
...BUT I CAME HERE FOR ONE REASON...
SHWAK!!
...AND ONE REASON ONLY!!
GET OUT OF THE WAY, STRAW HAT BOY!!
IT'S HAWK-EYE!!
?!!
KLANK!!
?!!

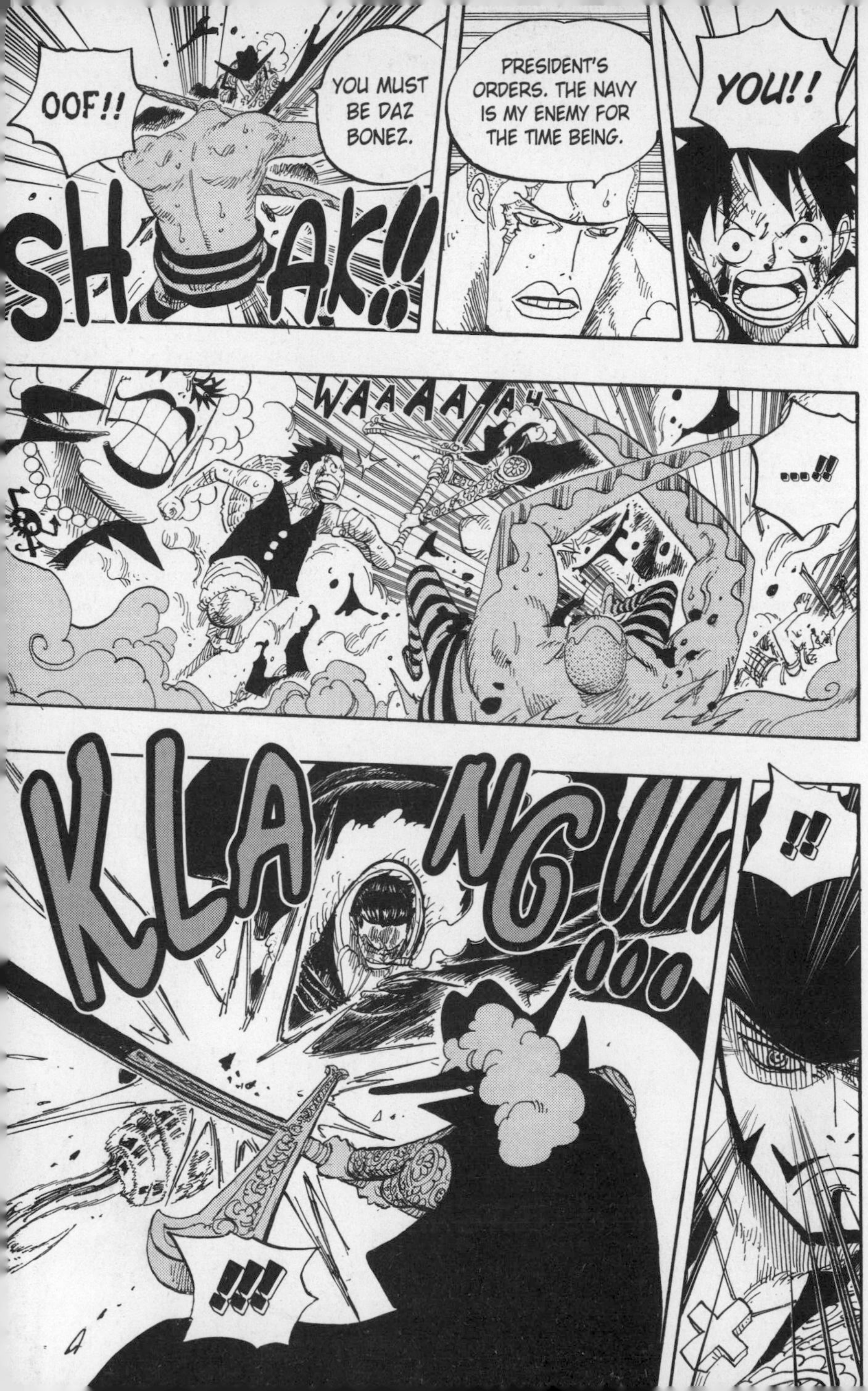
YOU!!
PRESIDENT'S ORDERS. THE NAVY IS MY ENEMY FOR THE TIME BEING.
YOU MUST BE DAZ BONEZ.
OOF!!
SHAK!!
...!!
WAAAAAAU
!!
KLANG!!...
!!!

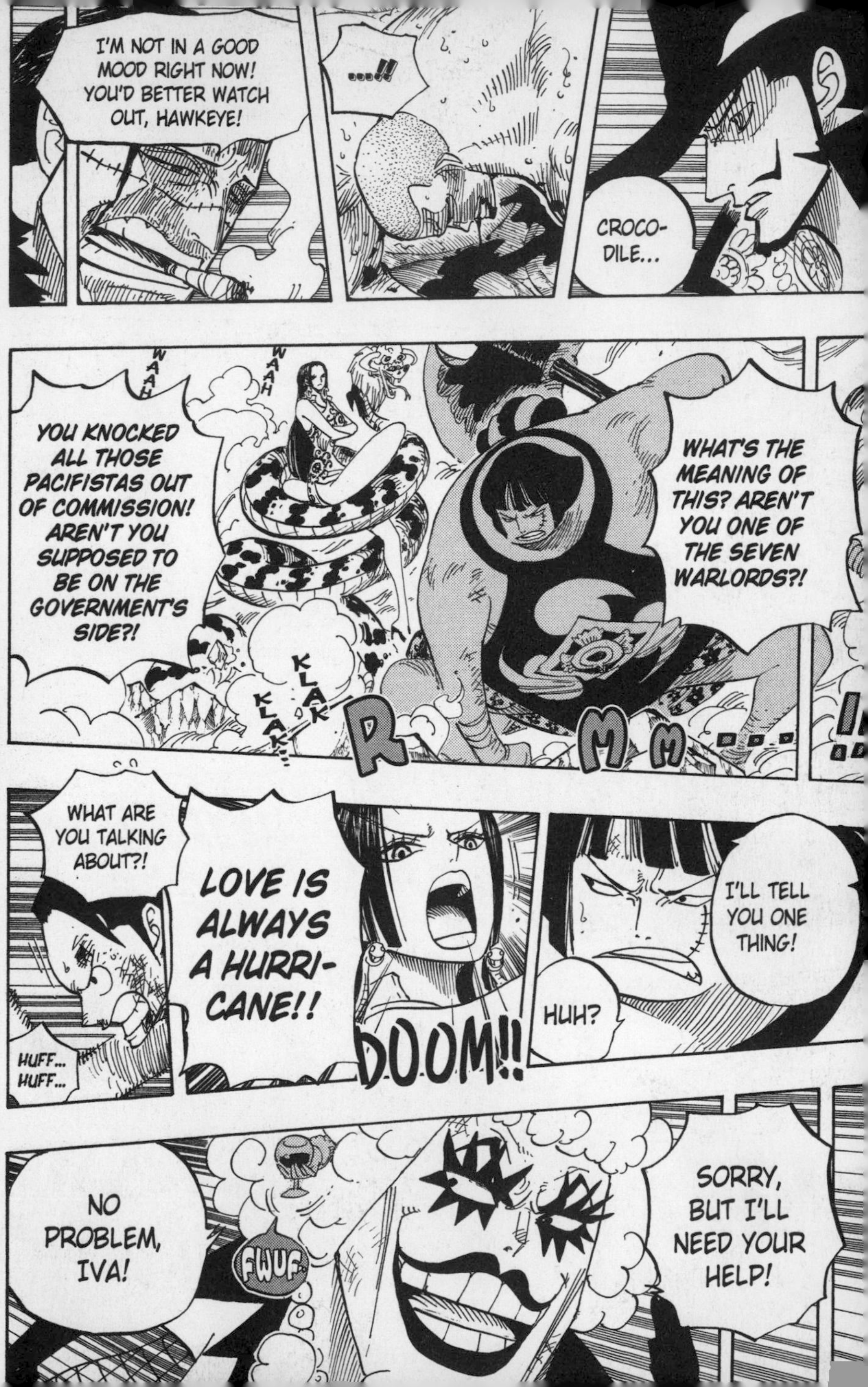
CROCO-DILE...
...!!
I'M NOT IN A GOOD MOOD RIGHT NOW! YOU'D BETTER WATCH OUT, HAWKEYE!
WHAT'S THE MEANING OF THIS? AREN'T YOU ONE OF THE SEVEN WARLORDS?!
WAAH
WAAH
YOU KNOCKED ALL THOSE PACIFISTAS OUT OF COMMISSION! AREN'T YOU SUPPOSED TO BE ON THE GOVERNMENT'S SIDE?!
KLAK KLAK
RMM...!!
I'LL TELL YOU ONE THING!
HUH?
LOVE IS ALWAYS A HURRI-CANE!!
DOOM!!
WHAT ARE YOU TALKING ABOUT?!
HUFF... HUFF...
SORRY, BUT I'LL NEED YOUR HELP!
FWUF
NO PROBLEM, IVA!

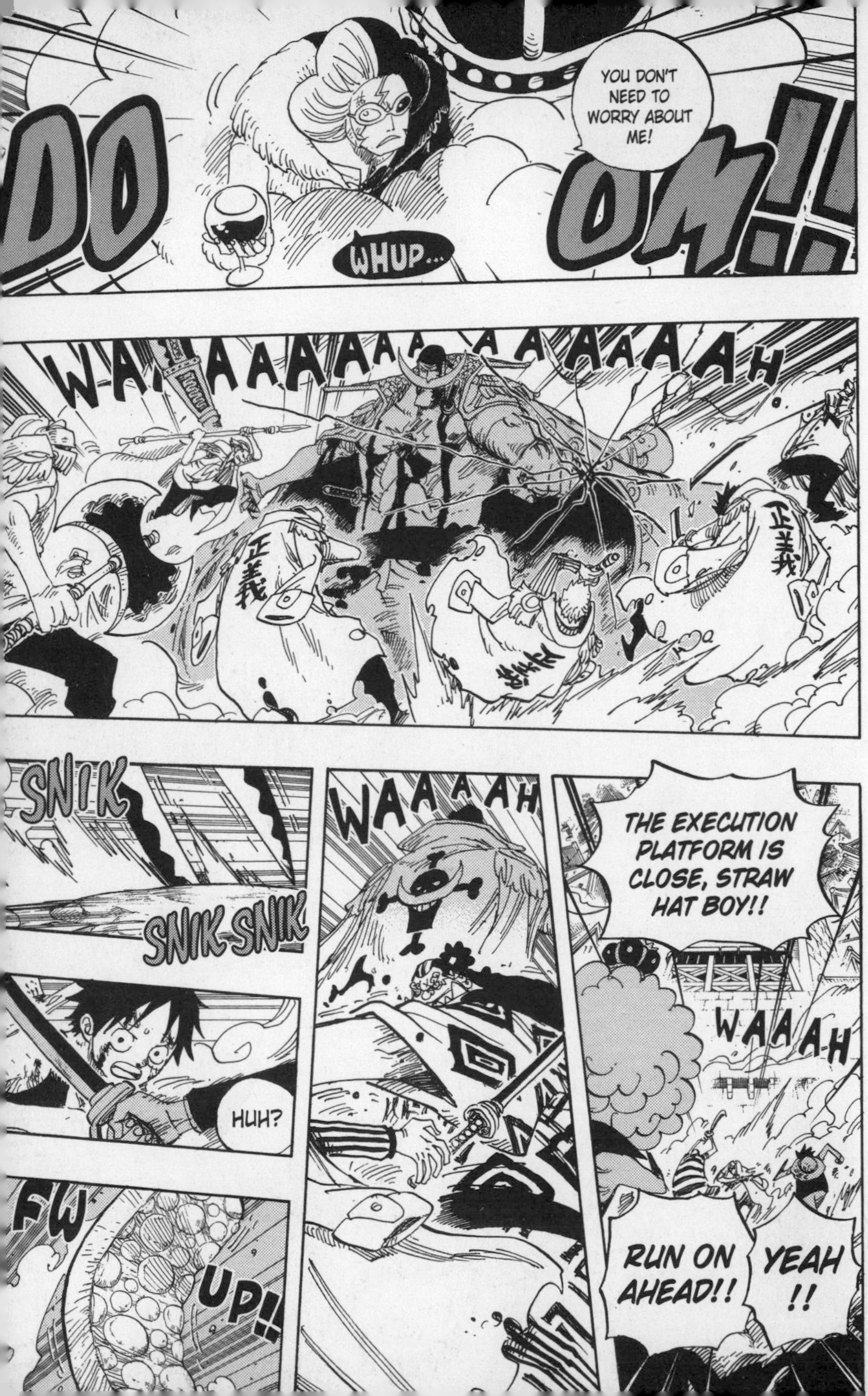
YOU DON'T NEED TO WORRY ABOUT ME!
DOOM!!
WHUP...
WAAAAAAAAAAAAAH
THE EXECUTION PLATFORM IS CLOSE, STRAW HAT BOY!!
WAAAH
YEAH!!
RUN ON AHEAD!!
WAAAAH
SNIK
SNIK-SNIK
HUH?
FWUP!!

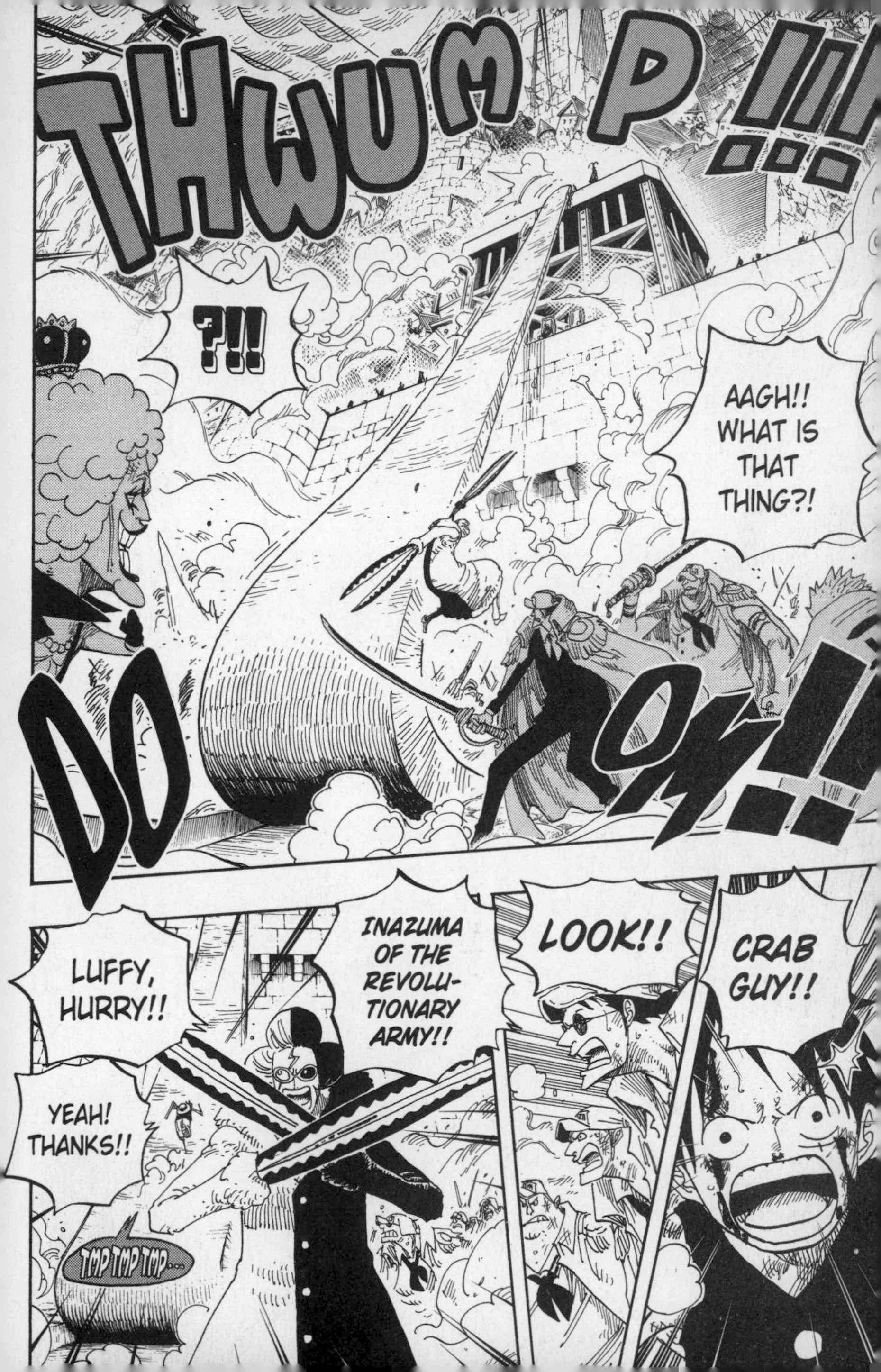
THWUMP!!!
AAGH!! WHAT IS THAT THING?!
?!!
DOON!!
CRAB GUY!!
LOOK!!
INAZUMA OF THE REVOLUTIONARY ARMY!!
LUFFY, HURRY!!
YEAH! THANKS!!
TMP TMP TMP...

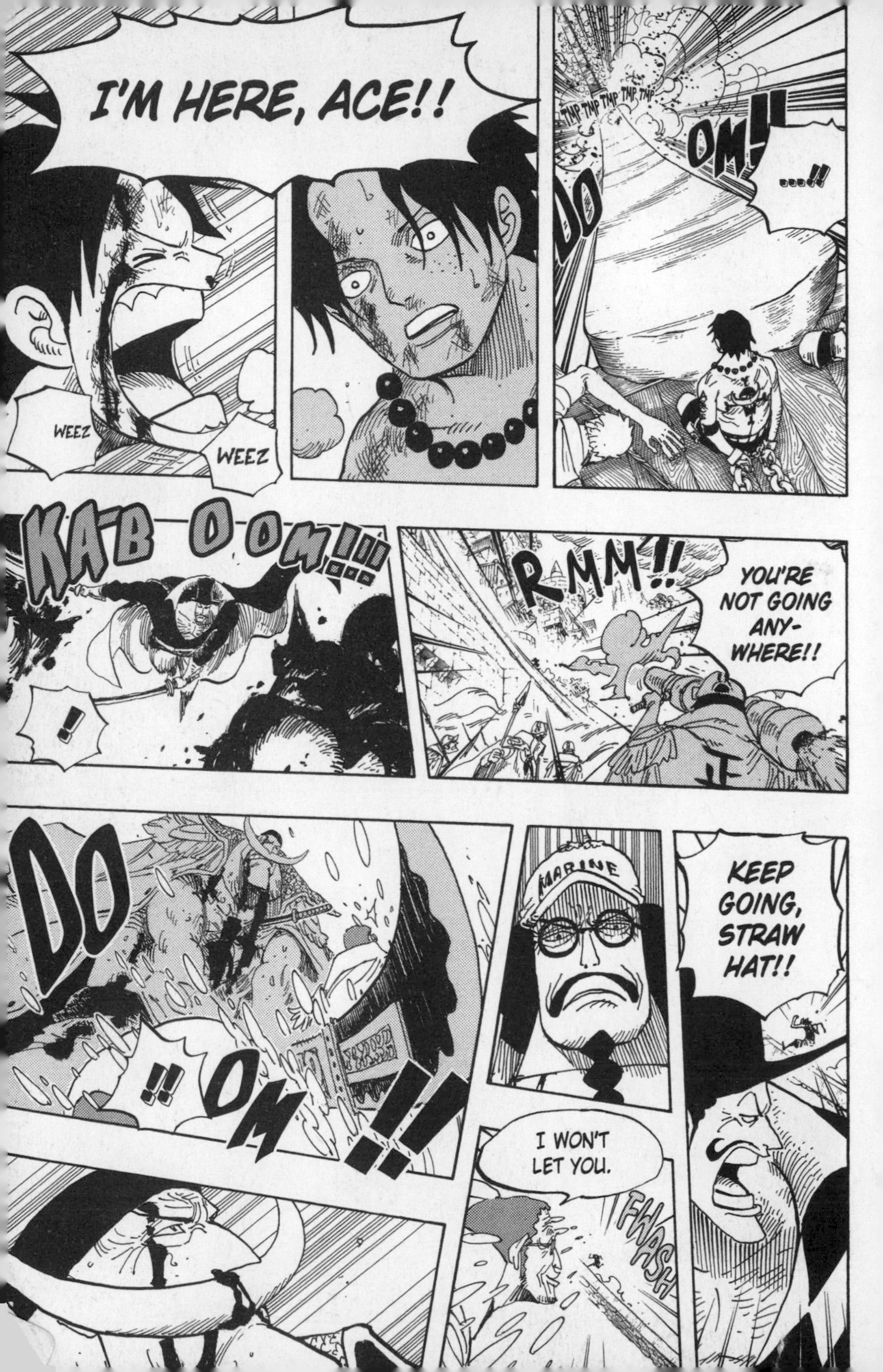
TMP TMP TMP TMP TMP
DO
OM!!
...!!
I'M HERE, ACE!!
WEEZ
WEEZ
RMM!!
YOU'RE NOT GOING ANY-WHERE!!
KA-B OOM!!!!
!
KEEP GOING, STRAW HAT!!
I WON'T LET YOU.
FWASH
DO
!!OM!!

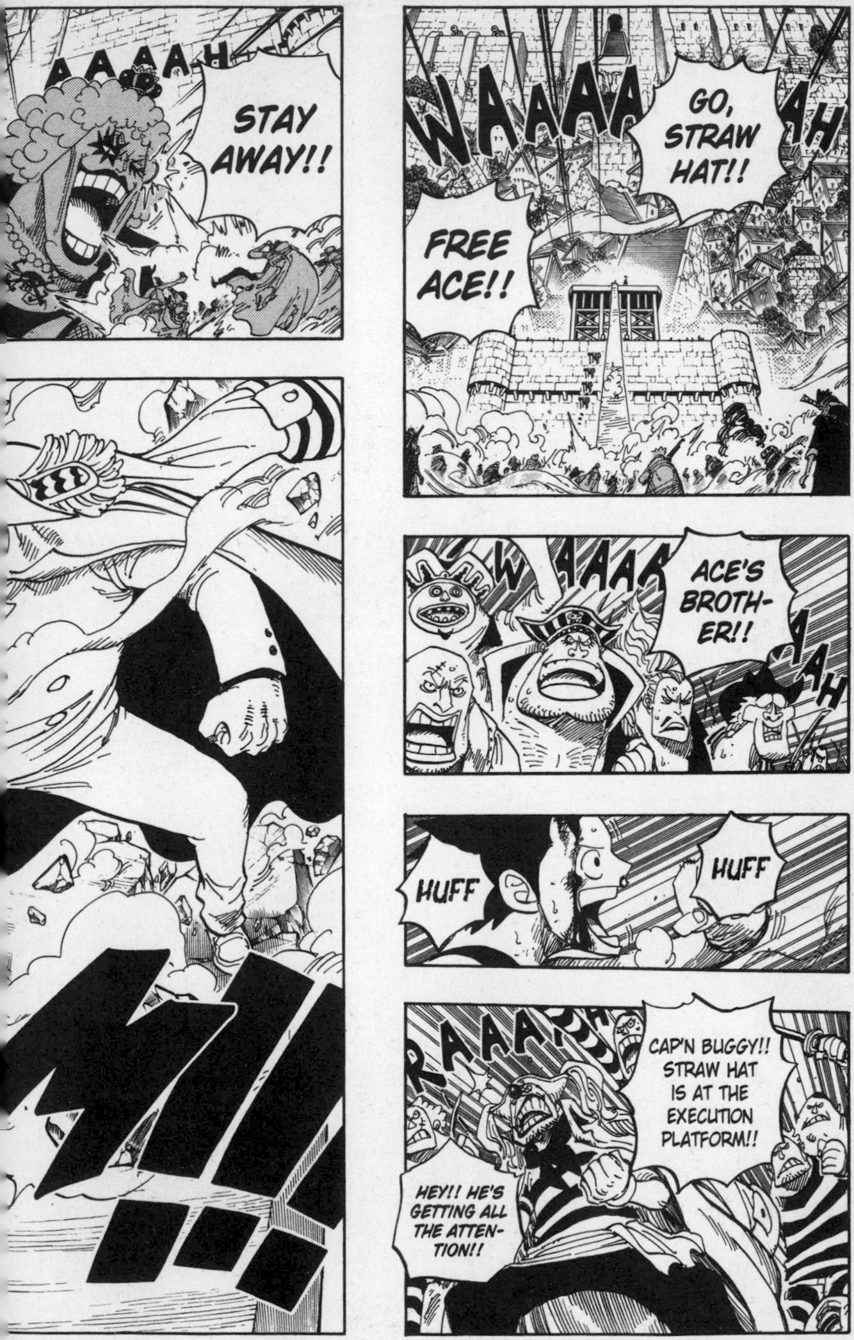
WAAAAAH
GO, STRAW HAT!!
FREE ACE!!
AAAAH
STAY AWAY!!
WAAAAAH
ACE'S BROTH-ER!!
HUFF
HUFF
RAAAAH
CAP'N BUGGY!! STRAW HAT IS AT THE EXECUTION PLATFORM!!
HEY!! HE'S GETTING ALL THE ATTEN-TION!!

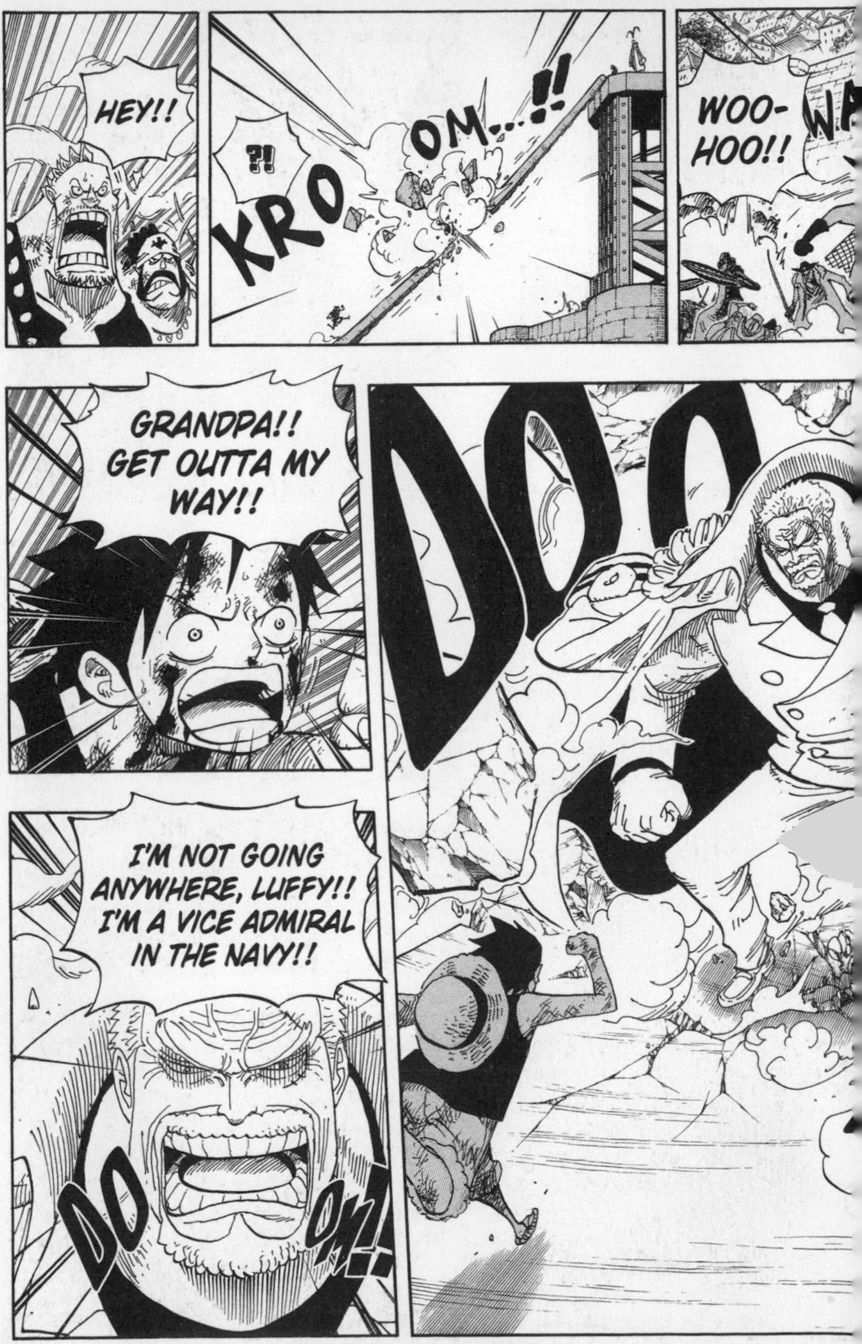
WOO-HOO!!
WA
?!
KRO OM...!!
HEY!!
DO
GRANDPA!! GET OUTTA MY WAY!!
I'M NOT GOING ANYWHERE, LUFFY!! I'M A VICE ADMIRAL IN THE NAVY!!
DO OM..!!

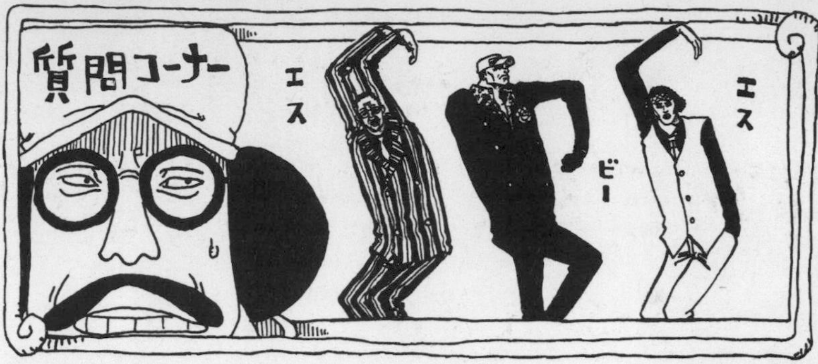
質問コーナー
エス
ビー
エス

(Kota Hidaka, Gifu)

Q: I just learned how to use Haki recently. My friends around me are collapsing left and right. What should I do?

--New Year's Man

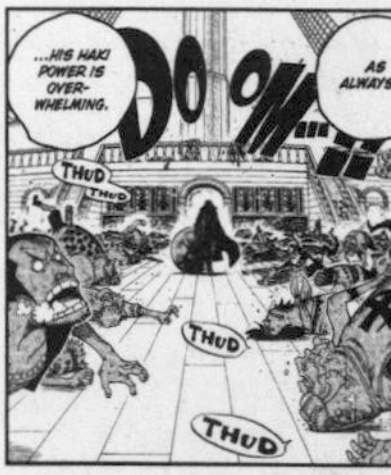
...HIS HAKI POWER IS OVER-WHELMING.
AS ALWAYS...
DOOM
THUD
THUD
THUD
THUD

A: Uh-huh. That's amazing. If that Haki has the color of the supreme king, then you better learn how to control it quick. Or else your friends are going to suffer. The other possibility I can think of is that you stink so much that your friends are passing out. If that's the case, go take a bath.

Q: There was something I wanted to ask you so I picked up a ballpoint pen to write this to you. It's about Emporio Ivankov. He looks very similar to Dr. Frank-N-Furter of the Rocky Horror Picture Show. What do you think?

--I love Yu-kun ♡ Takashi

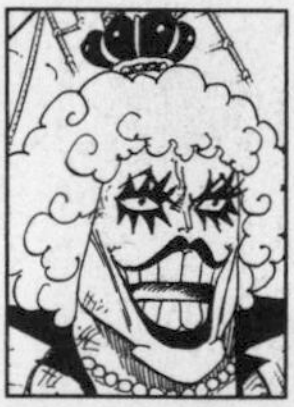

A: That's right. Rocky Horror Picture Show is a movie that all B-movie horror film lovers would know about. It's a very stupid film, but I love it to death. Kama Land is pretty much based on it. His looks are based on that character, but there's actually another person that I based Ivankov on. Despite having already brought out Bon Clay, that person made me want to create a REAL cross-dressing character! That person was in the same theater troupe as the voice actress for Luffy, Mayumi Tanaka. When I saw his theater performance, I was stunned! His name is Norio Imamura. Because his face looked like a rock, I mistakenly remembered his name as Iwamura, ["Iwa" means rock in Japanese.] which I then shortened to Iwa-san. On top of that, after Imamura found out that "Iva" was based on him, he rushed to the anime auditions for the character and was cast. In short, a real cross-dresser, Norio Imamura, who was the model for Iva, is playing Iva in the anime series! Stunning!

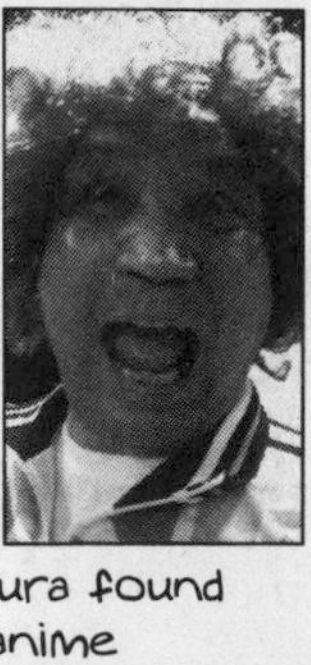

Chapter 571: THE EXECUTION PLATFORM

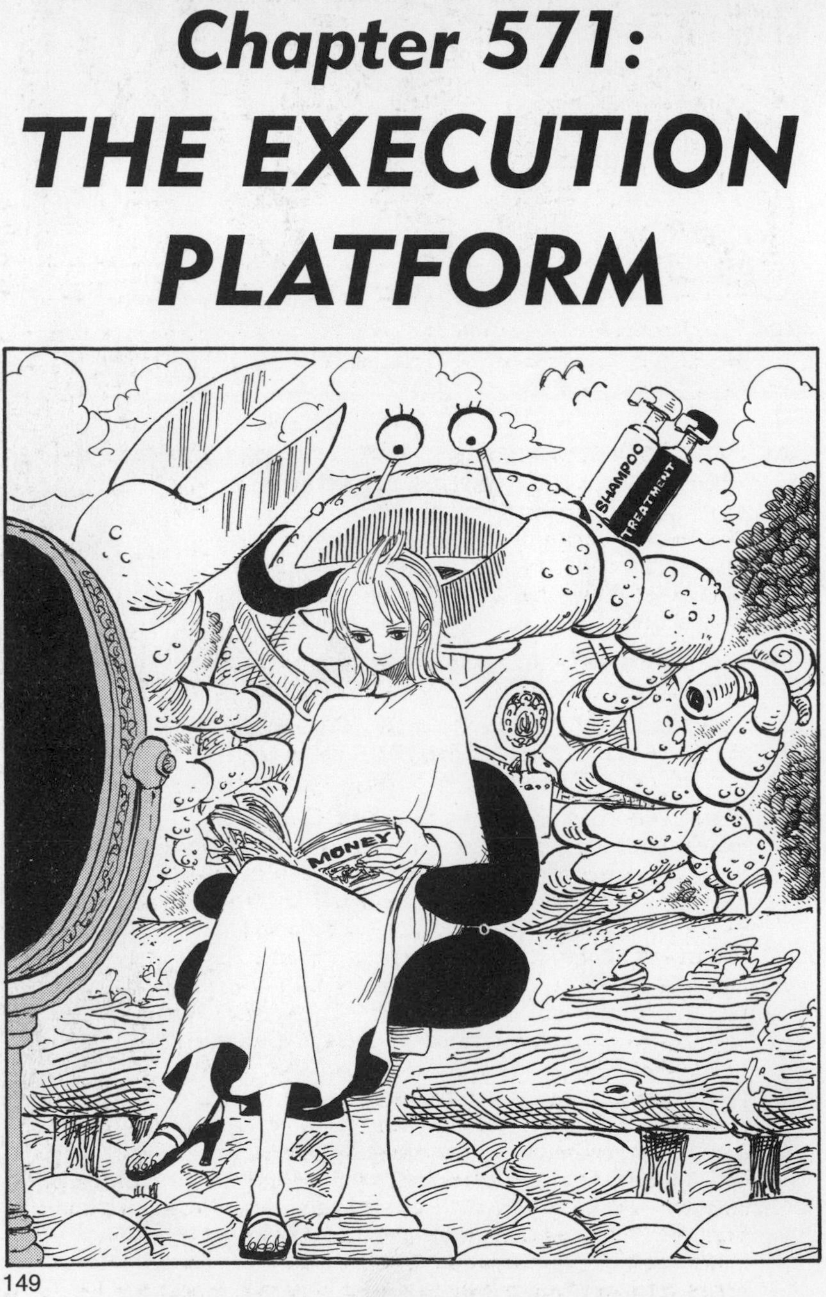

SHAMPOO
TREATMENT
MONEY

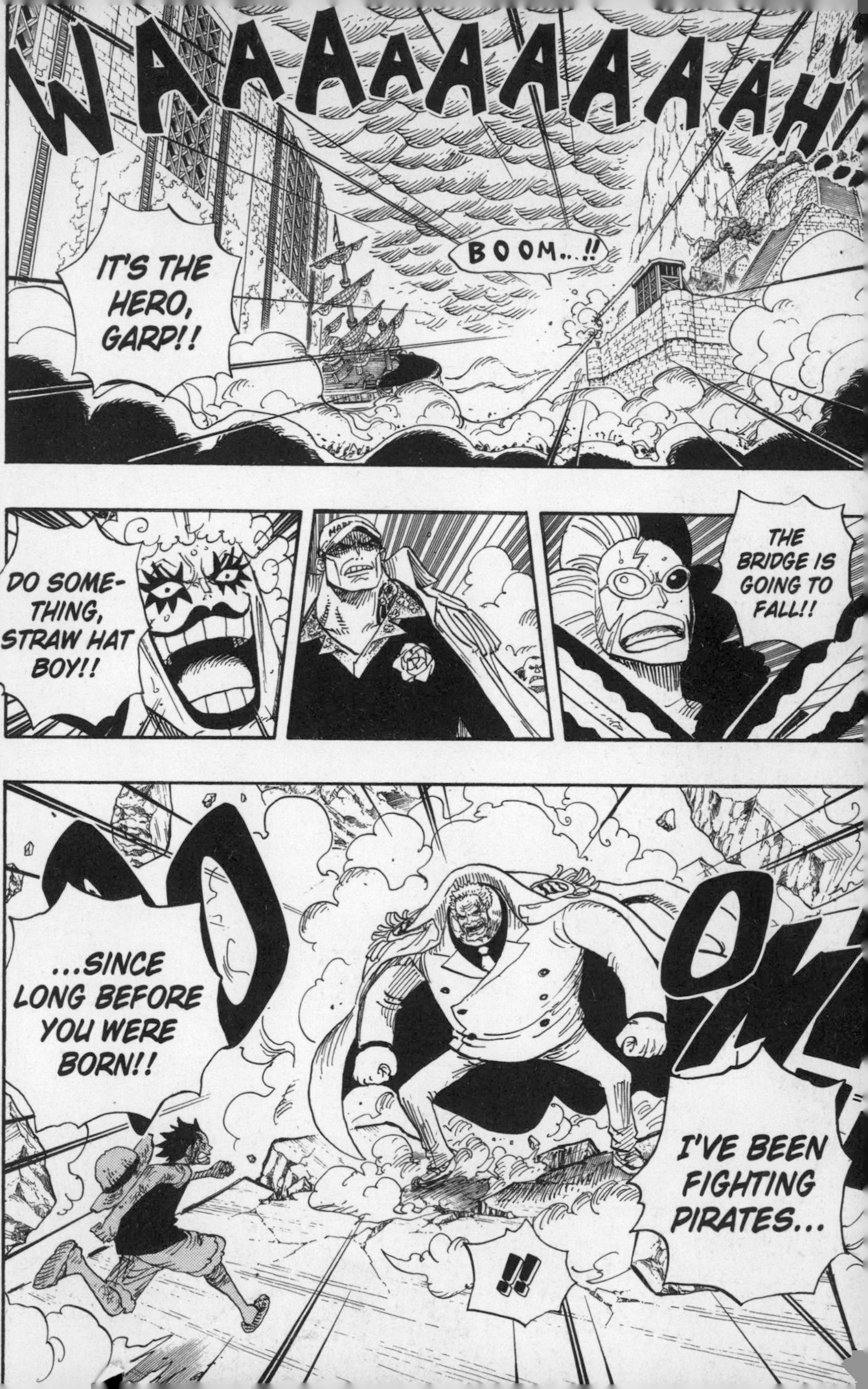
WAAAAAAAAAAH!!
BOOM...!!
IT'S THE HERO, GARP!!
THE BRIDGE IS GOING TO FALL!!
DO SOME-THING, STRAW HAT BOY!!
I'VE BEEN FIGHTING PIRATES...
!!
...SINCE LONG BEFORE YOU WERE BORN!!

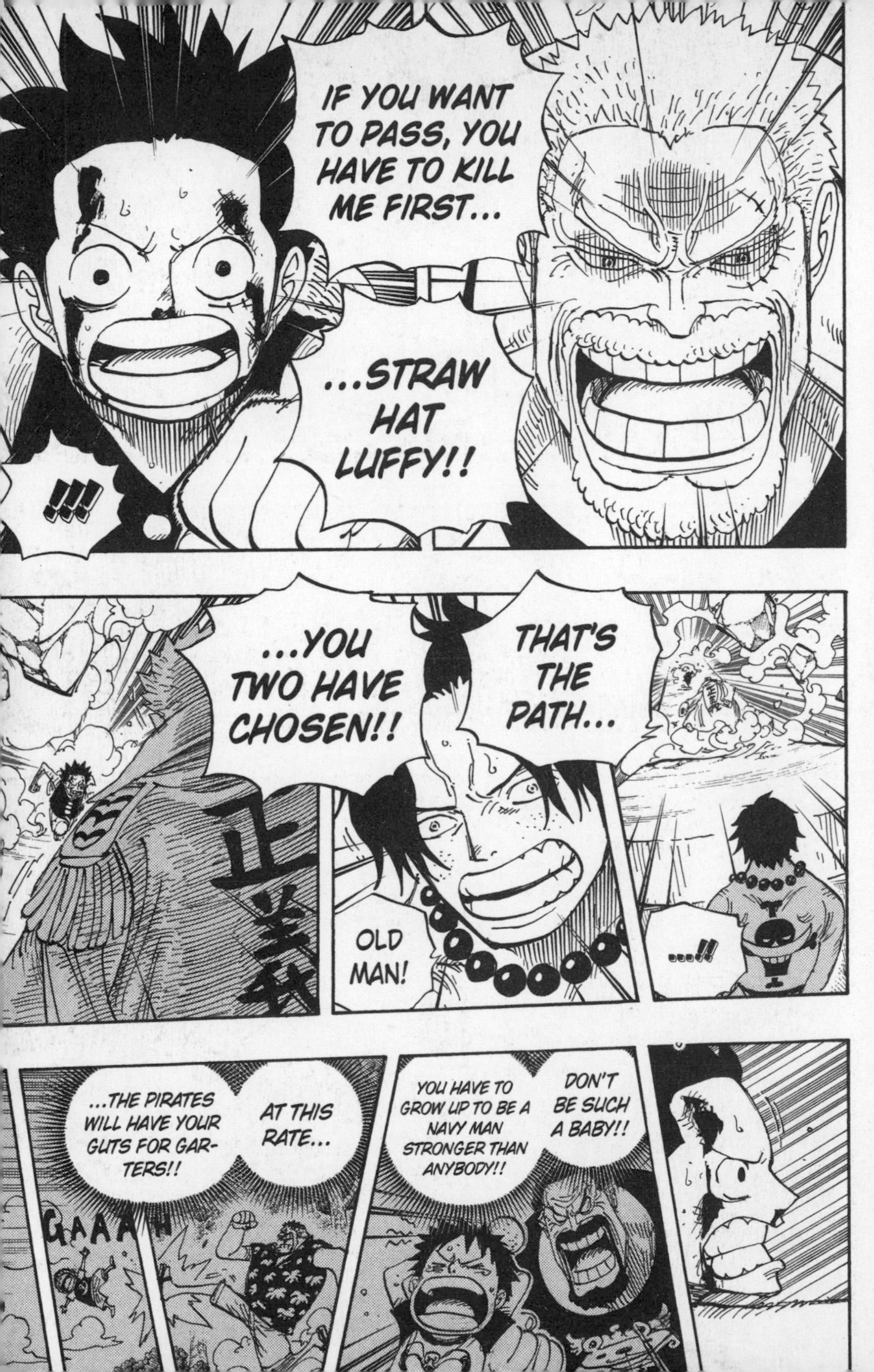
IF YOU WANT TO PASS, YOU HAVE TO KILL ME FIRST...
...STRAW HAT LUFFY!!
!!!
THAT'S THE PATH...
...YOU TWO HAVE CHOSEN!!
...!!
OLD MAN!
DON'T BE SUCH A BABY!!
YOU HAVE TO GROW UP TO BE A NAVY MAN STRONGER THAN ANYBODY!!
AT THIS RATE...
...THE PIRATES WILL HAVE YOUR GUTS FOR GAR-TERS!!
GAAAH

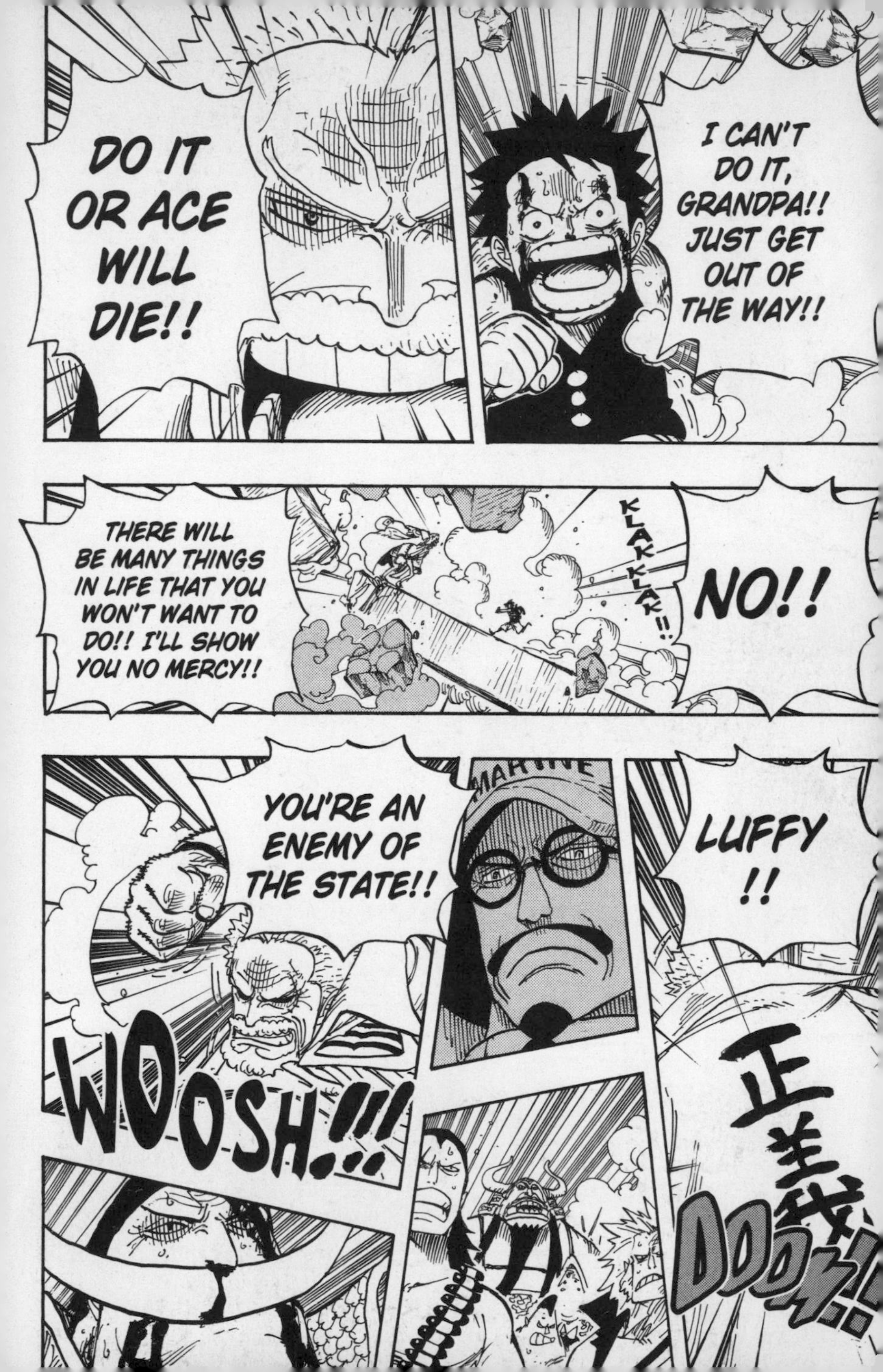
I CAN'T DO IT, GRANDPA!! JUST GET OUT OF THE WAY!!
DO IT OR ACE WILL DIE!!
NO!!
KLAK KLAK!!
THERE WILL BE MANY THINGS IN LIFE THAT YOU WON'T WANT TO DO!! I'LL SHOW YOU NO MERCY!!
LUFFY!!
YOU'RE AN ENEMY OF THE STATE!!
WOOSH!!!

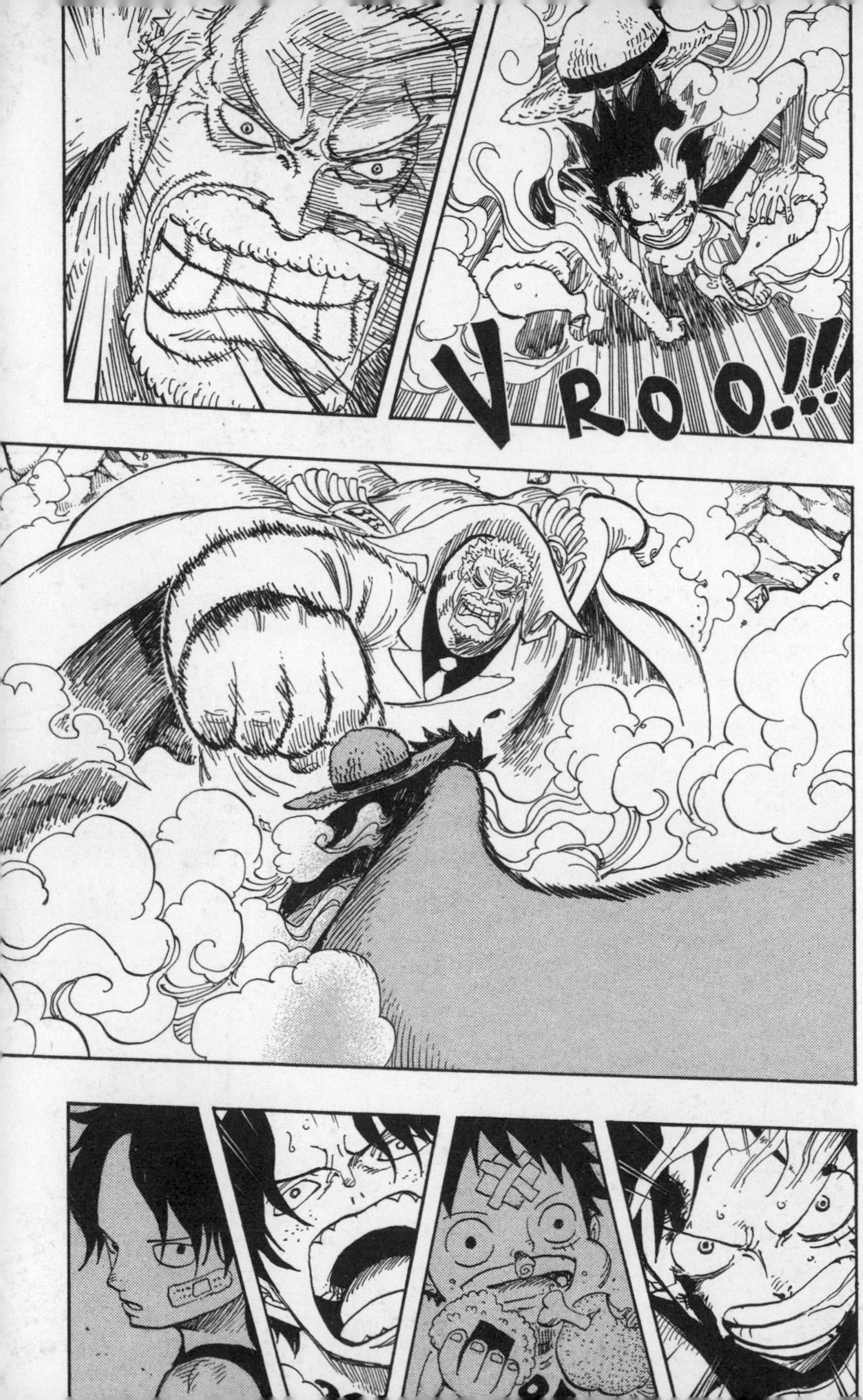
VROO!!!

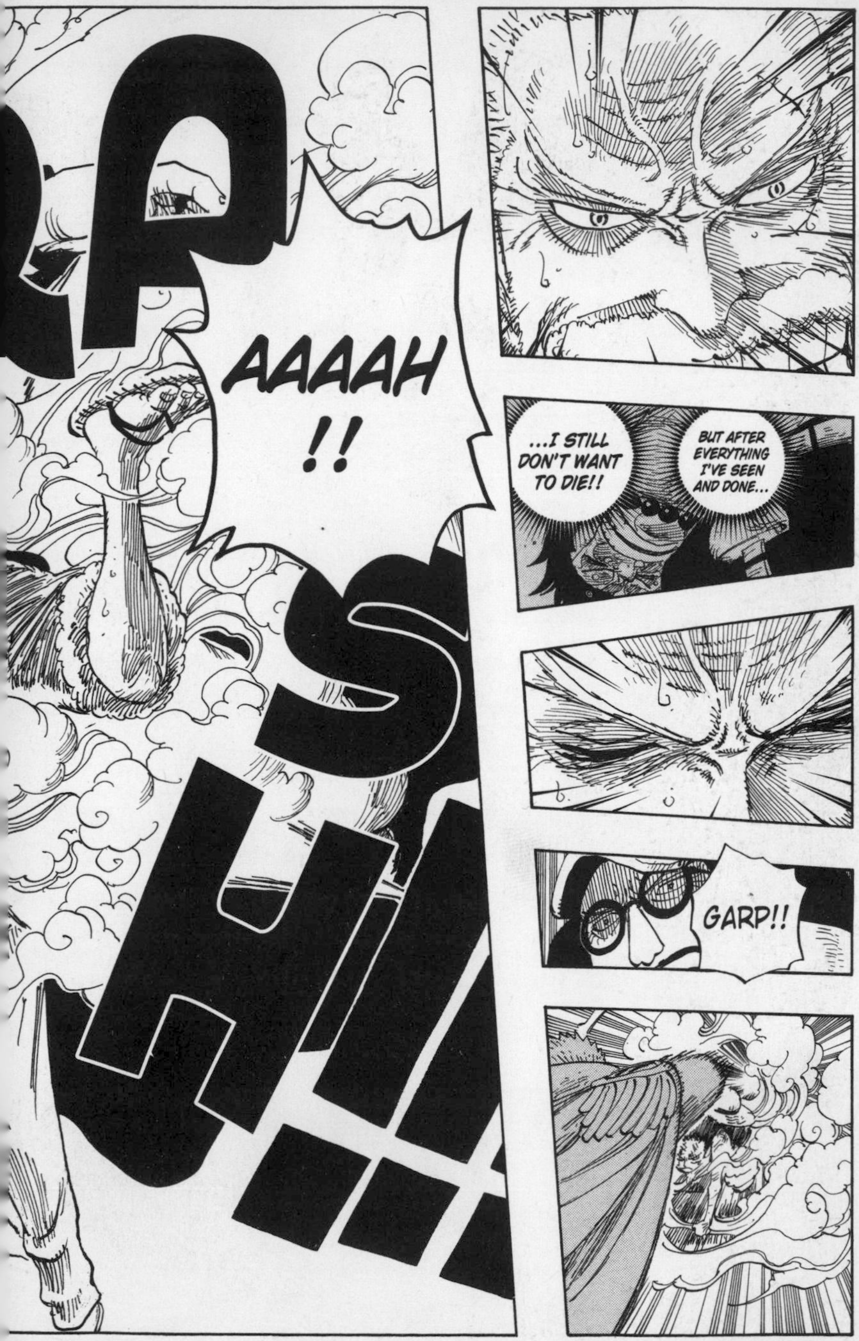
BUT AFTER EVERYTHING I'VE SEEN AND DONE...
...I STILL DON'T WANT TO DIE!!
GARP!!
AAAAH !!

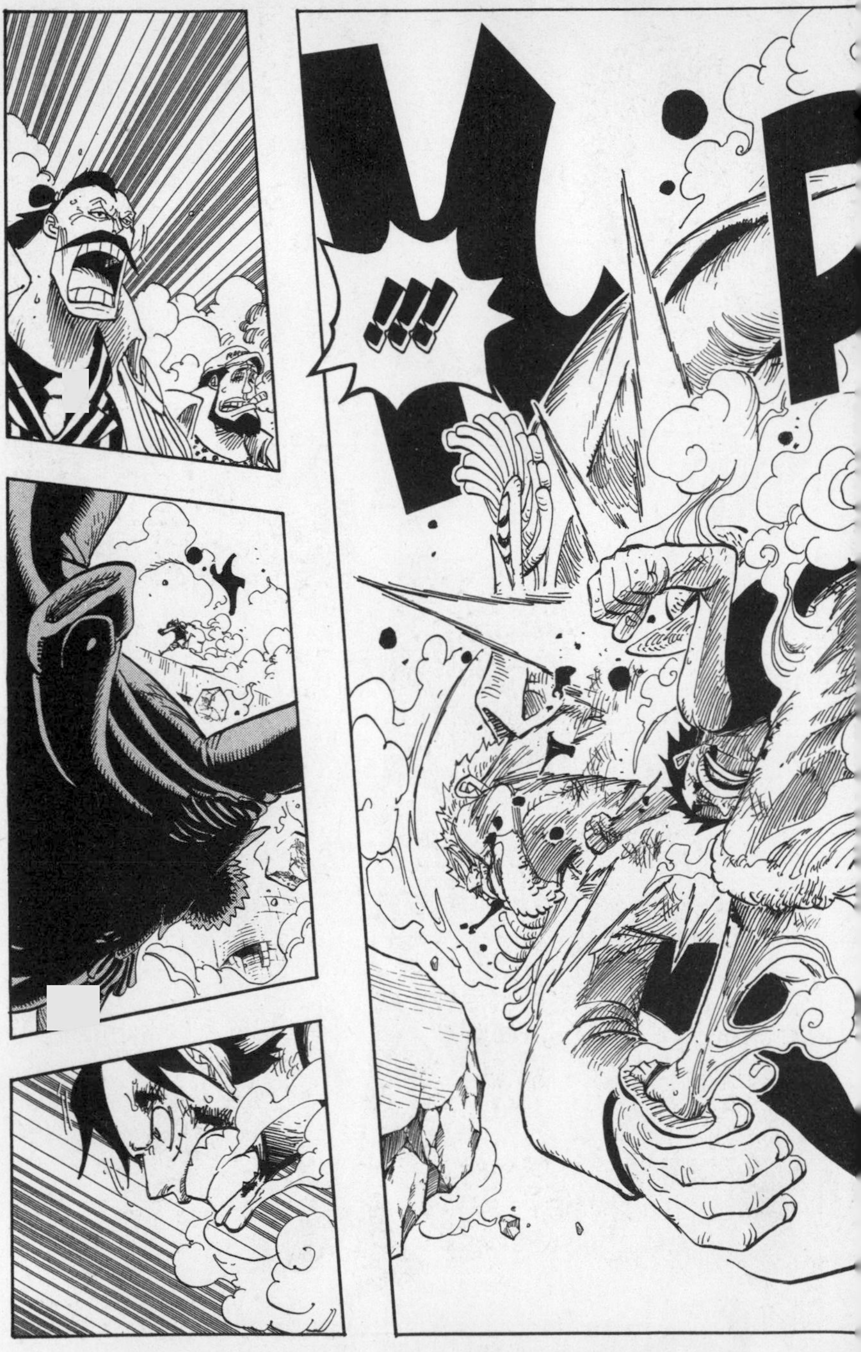
!!!

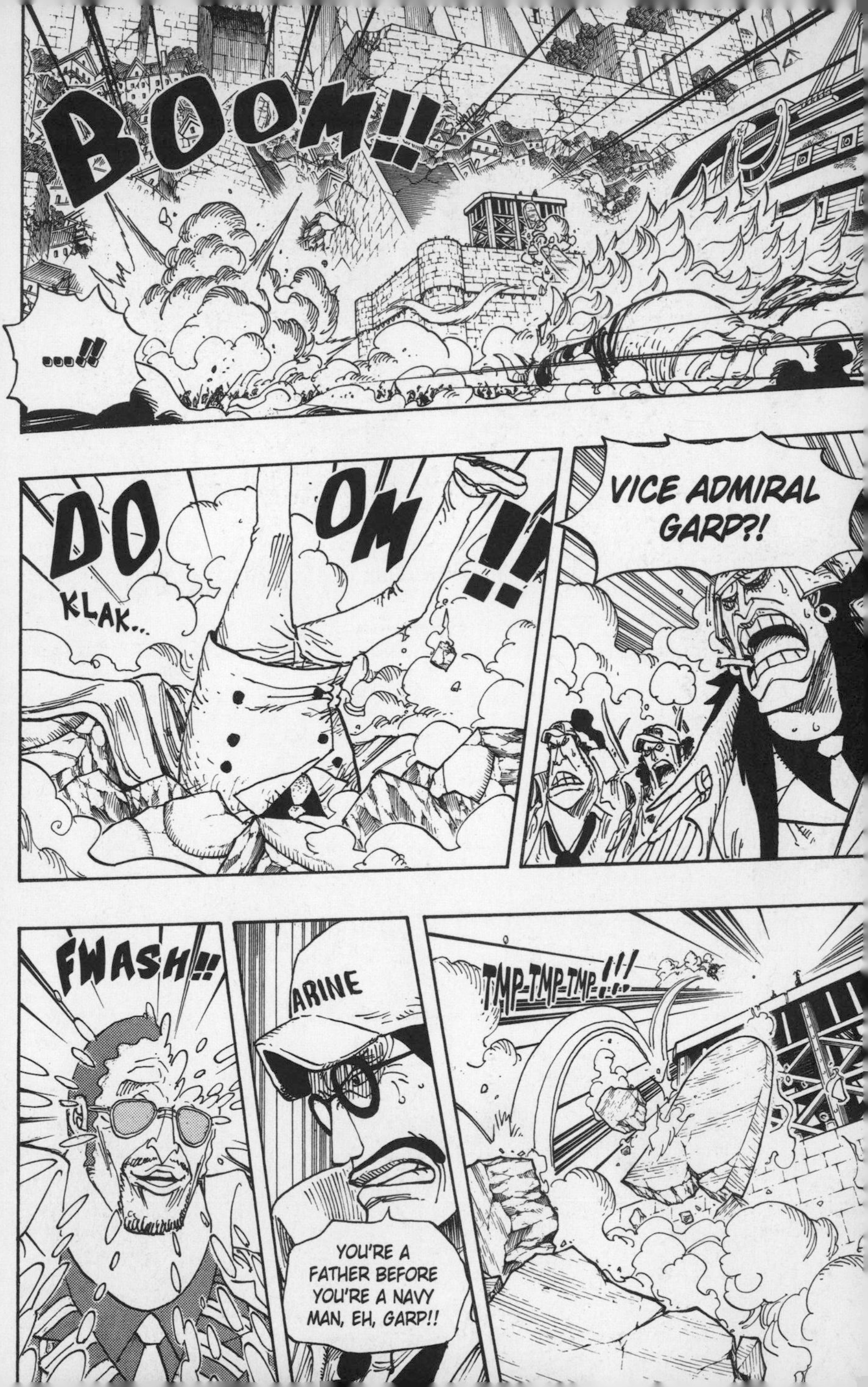
BOOM!!
...!!
VICE ADMIRAL GARP?!
DOOM!!
KLAK...
TMP-TMP-TMP!!!
ARINE
YOU'RE A FATHER BEFORE YOU'RE A NAVY MAN, EH, GARP!!
FWASH!!

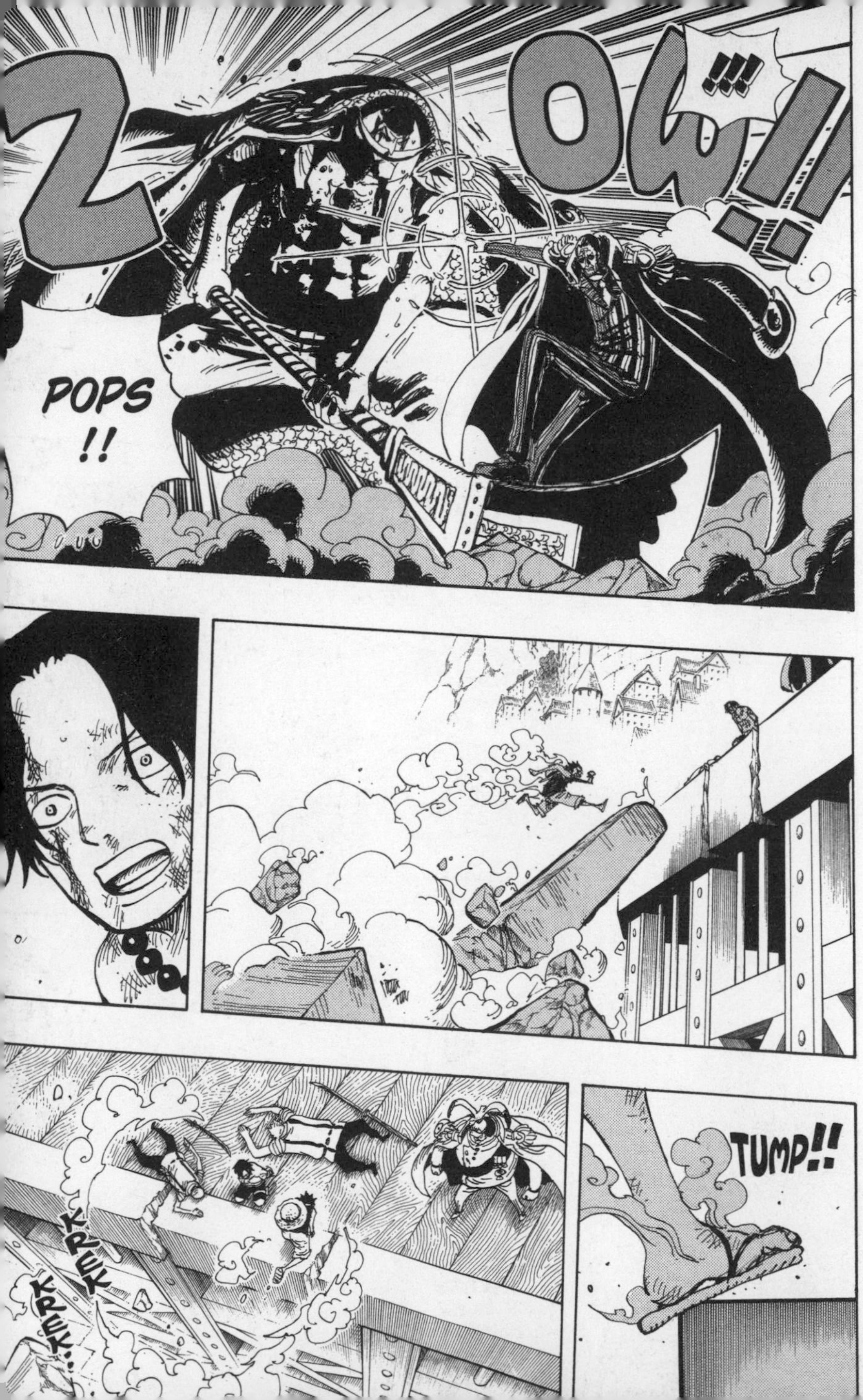
ZOW!!
!!!
POPS !!
TUMP!!
KREK
KREK...

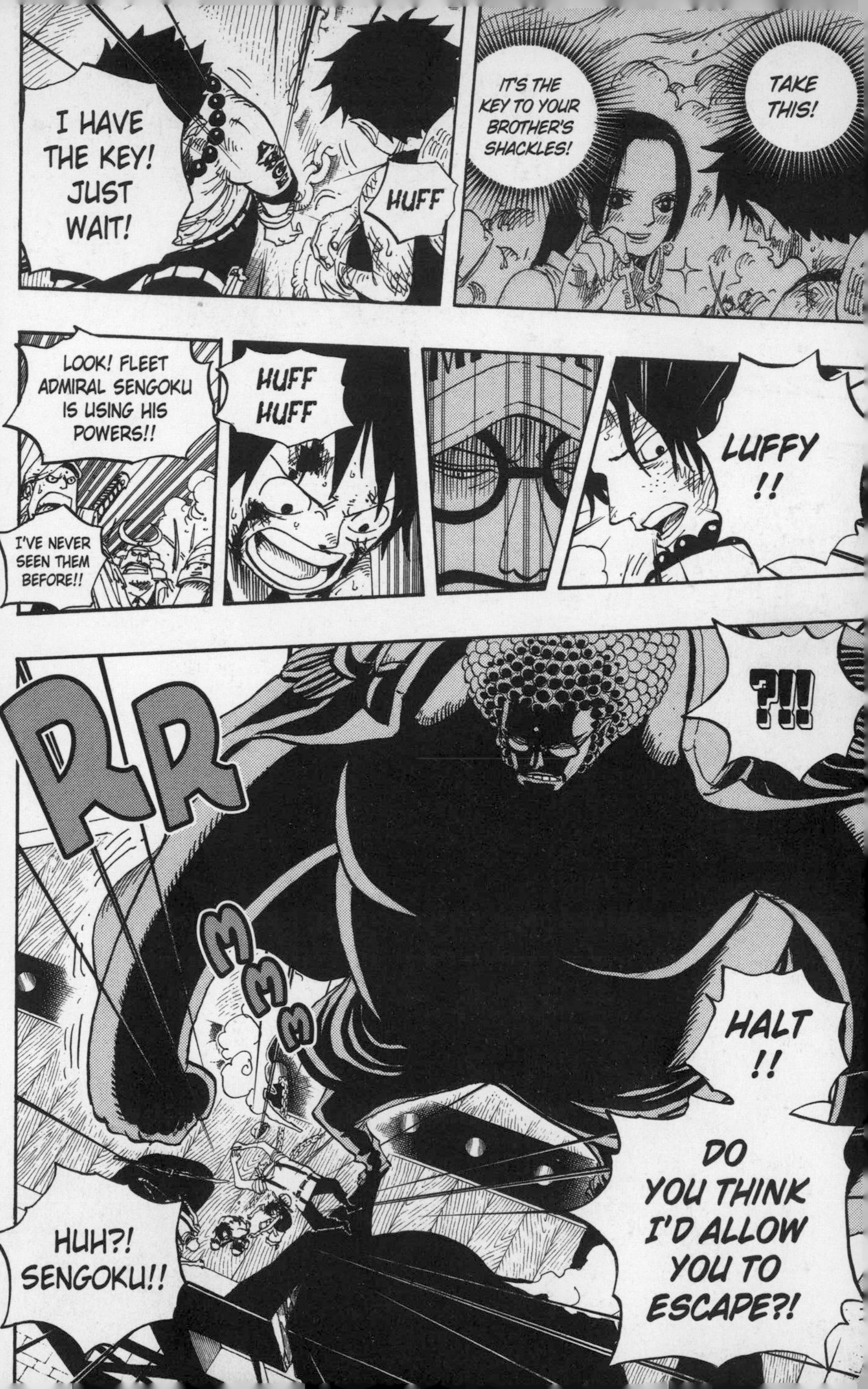
TAKE THIS!
IT'S THE KEY TO YOUR BROTHER'S SHACKLES!
I HAVE THE KEY! JUST WAIT!
HUFF
LUFFY!!
HUFF HUFF
LOOK! FLEET ADMIRAL SENGOKU IS USING HIS POWERS!!
I'VE NEVER SEEN THEM BEFORE!!
?!!
HALT!!
DO YOU THINK I'D ALLOW YOU TO ESCAPE?!
RR
MMMM
HUH?! SENGOKU!!

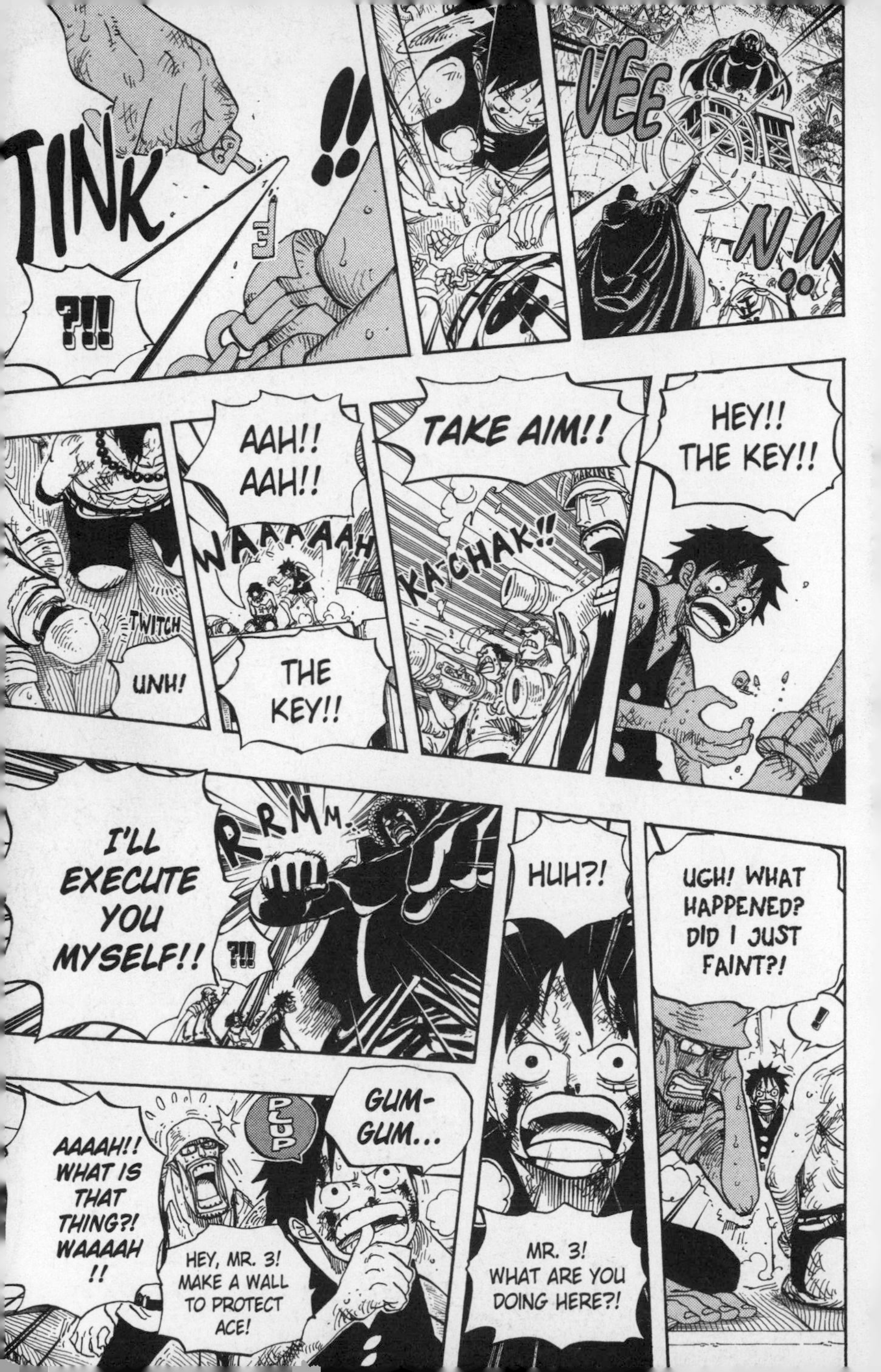
VEE
N!!
!!
TINK
?!!
HEY!! THE KEY!!
TAKE AIM!!
KACHAK!!
AAH!! AAH!!
WAAAAAH
THE KEY!!
TWITCH
UNH!
UGH! WHAT HAPPENED? DID I JUST FAINT?!
!
HUH?!
RRMM
I'LL EXECUTE YOU MYSELF!!
?!!
MR. 3! WHAT ARE YOU DOING HERE?!
GUM-GUM...
PLUP
HEY, MR. 3! MAKE A WALL TO PROTECT ACE!
AAAAH!! WHAT IS THAT THING?! WAAAAH!!

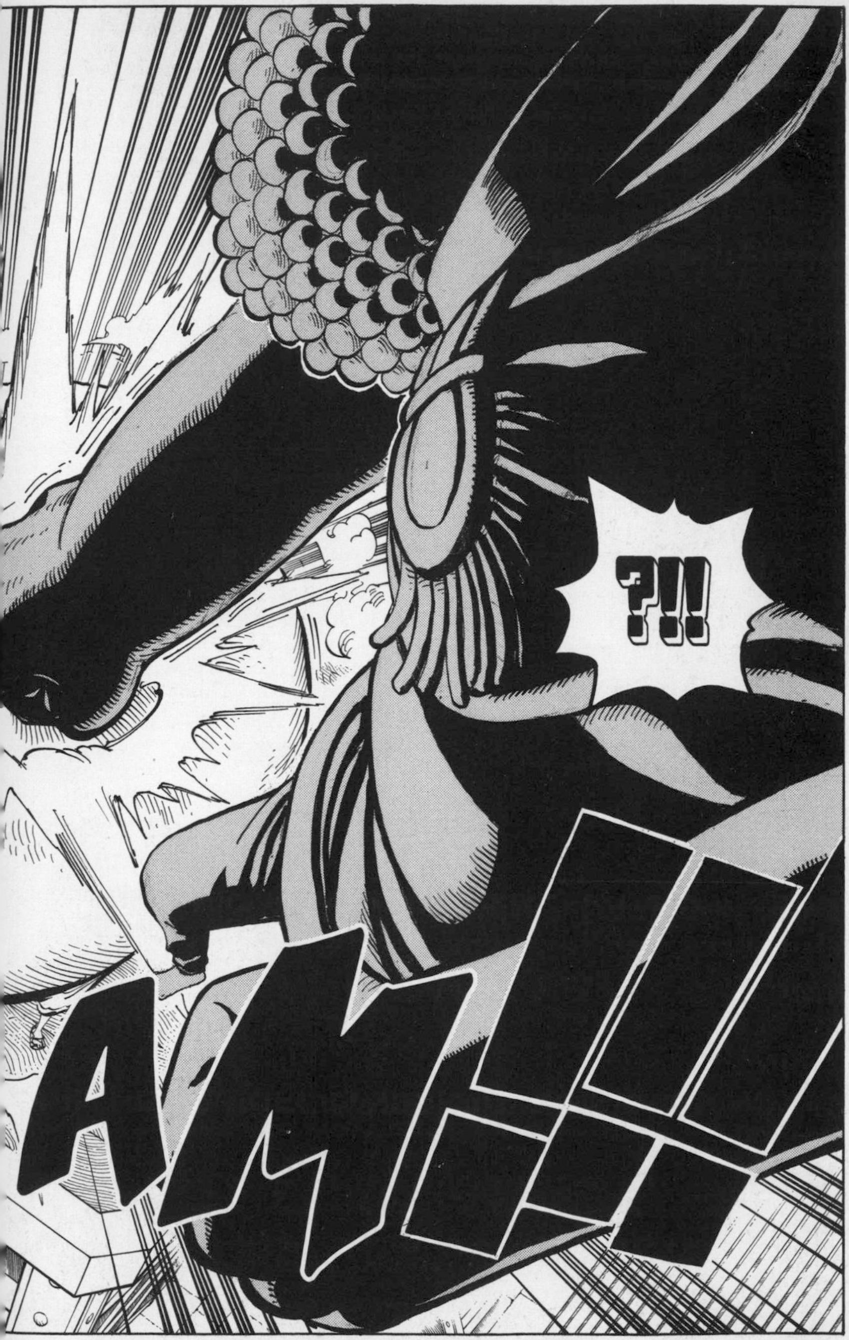
?!!
AM!!!

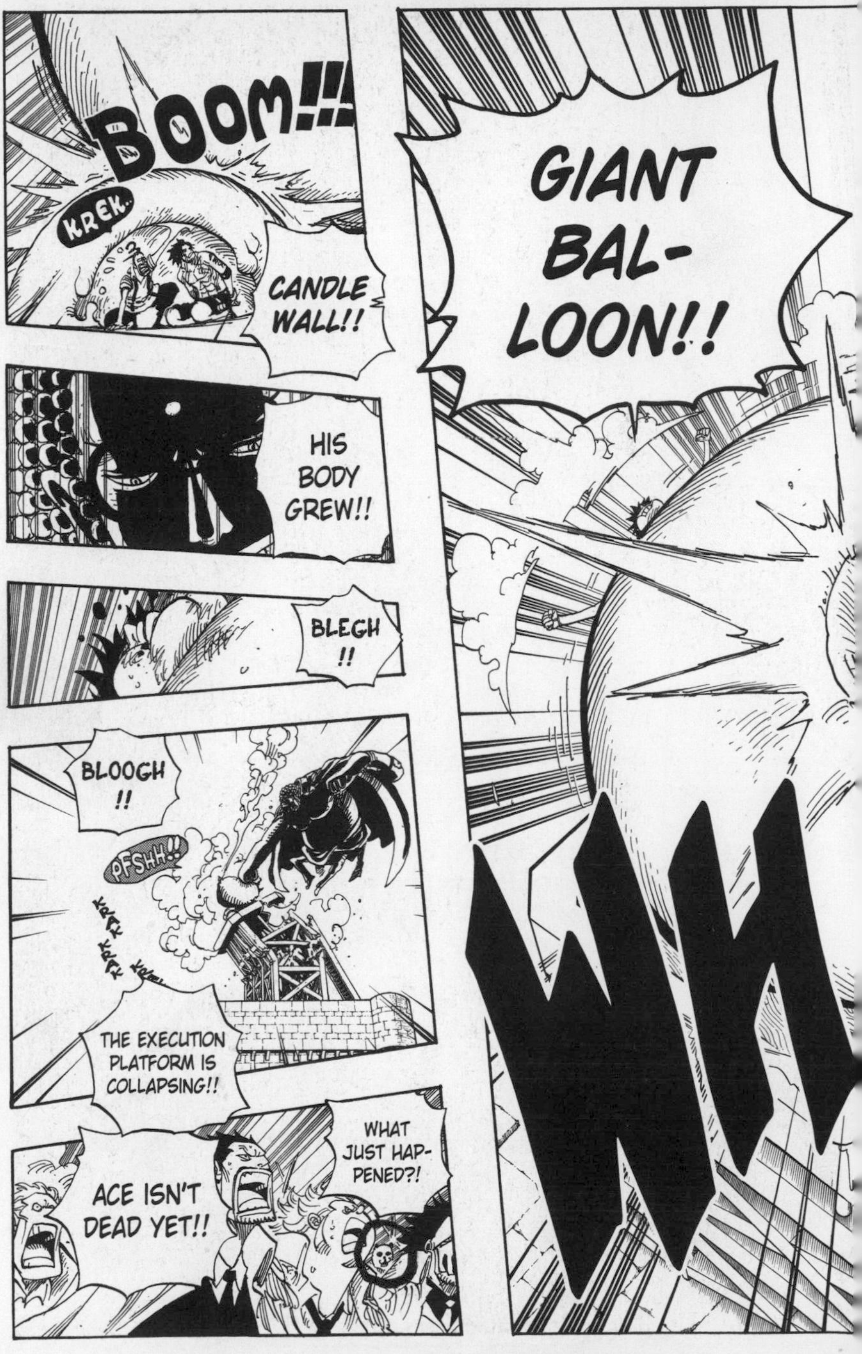
GIANT BAL-
LOON!!
WH
BOOM!!!
KREK..
CANDLE WALL!!
HIS BODY GREW!!
BLEGH !!
BLOOGH !!
PFSHH!!
KRAK KRAK KRAK
THE EXECUTION PLATFORM IS COLLAPSING!!
WHAT JUST HAP-PENED?!
ACE ISN'T DEAD YET!!

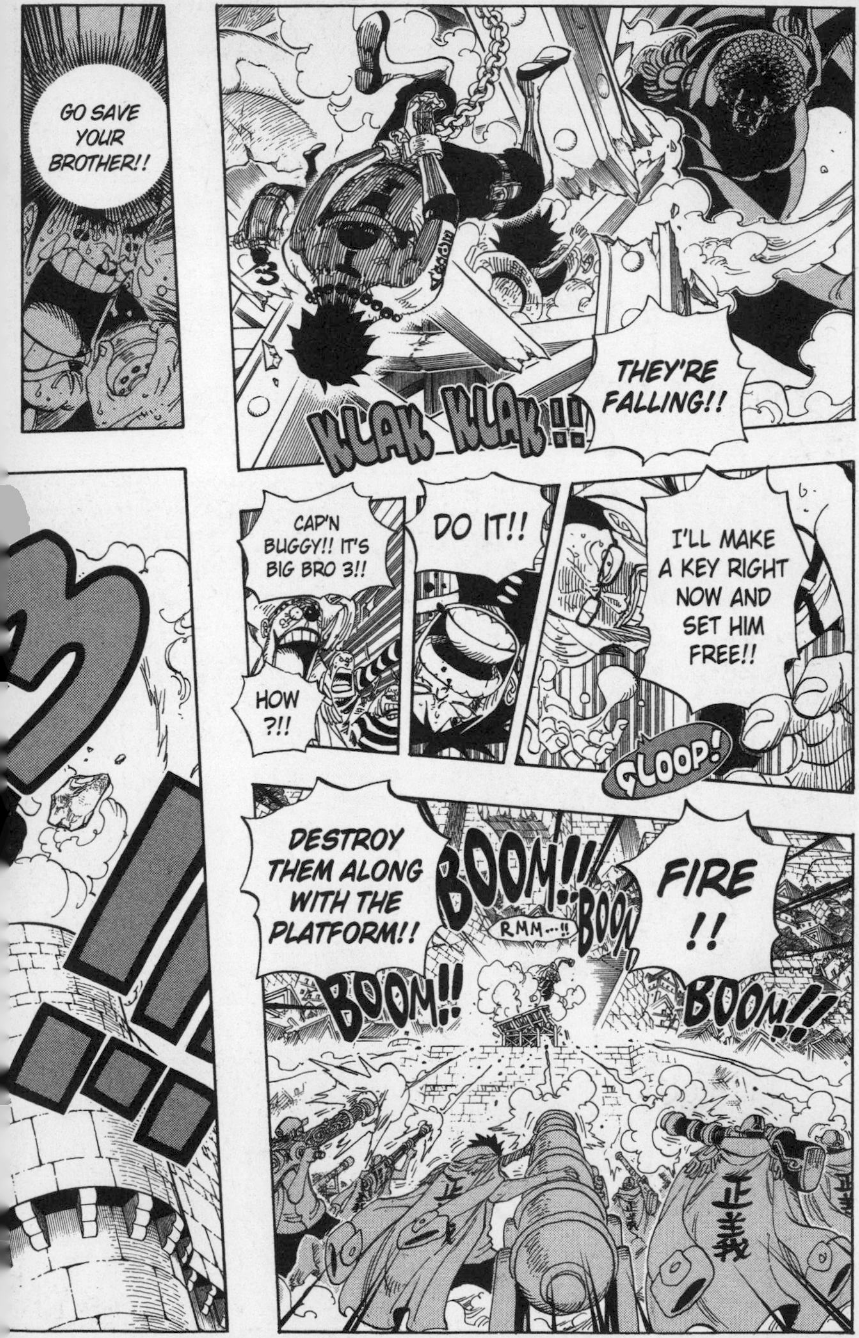
THEY'RE FALLING!!
KLAK KLAK!!
GO SAVE YOUR BROTHER!!
I'LL MAKE A KEY RIGHT NOW AND SET HIM FREE!!
GLOOP!
DO IT!!
CAP'N BUGGY!! IT'S BIG BRO 3!!
HOW ?!!
FIRE !!
BOOM!! BOOM
RMM...!!
DESTROY THEM ALONG WITH THE PLATFORM!!
BOOM!!
BOOM!!

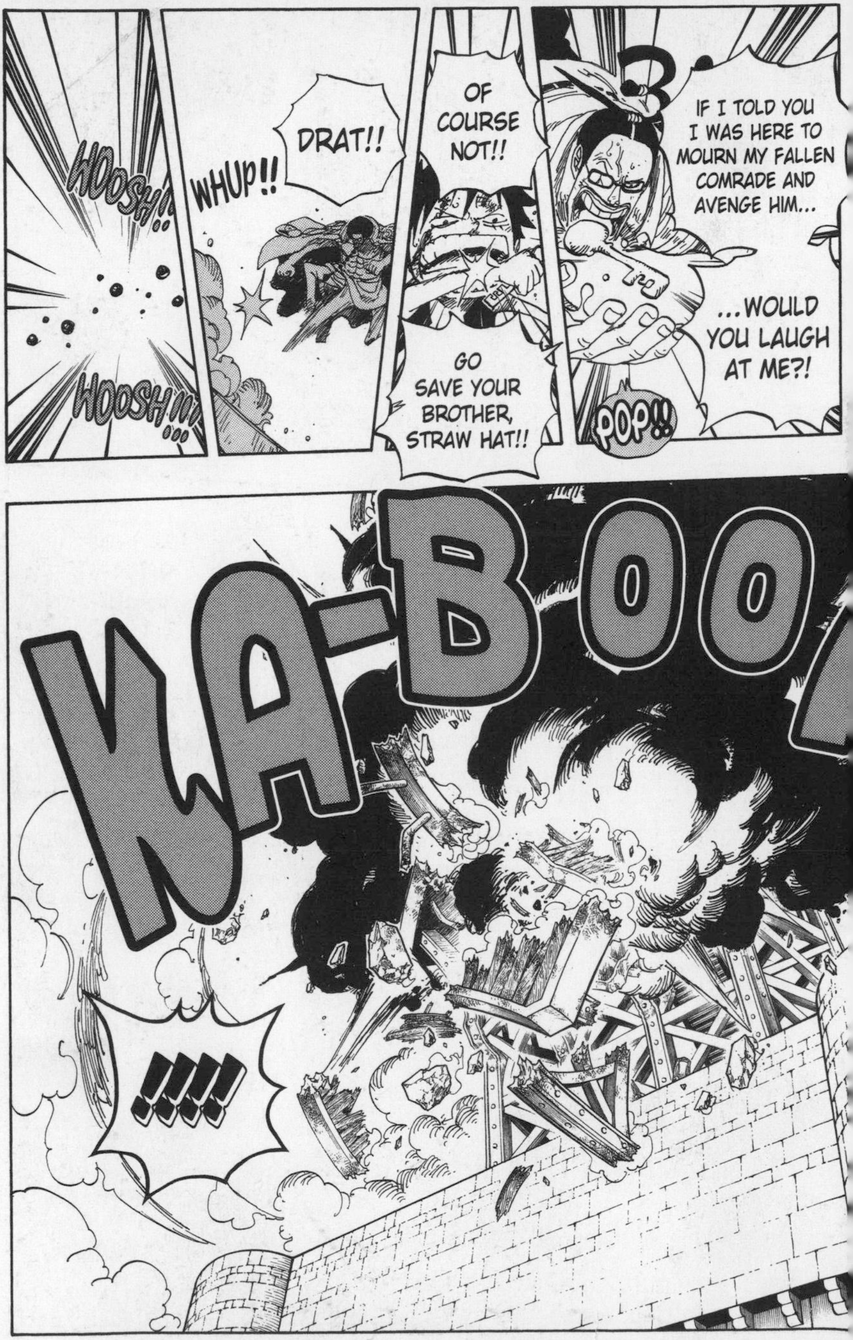
IF I TOLD YOU I WAS HERE TO MOURN MY FALLEN COMRADE AND AVENGE HIM...
...WOULD YOU LAUGH AT ME?!
POP!!
OF COURSE NOT!!
GO SAVE YOUR BROTHER, STRAW HAT!!
DRAT!!
WHUP!!
WHOOSH!!
WHOOSH!!!
KA-BOO
!!!!!

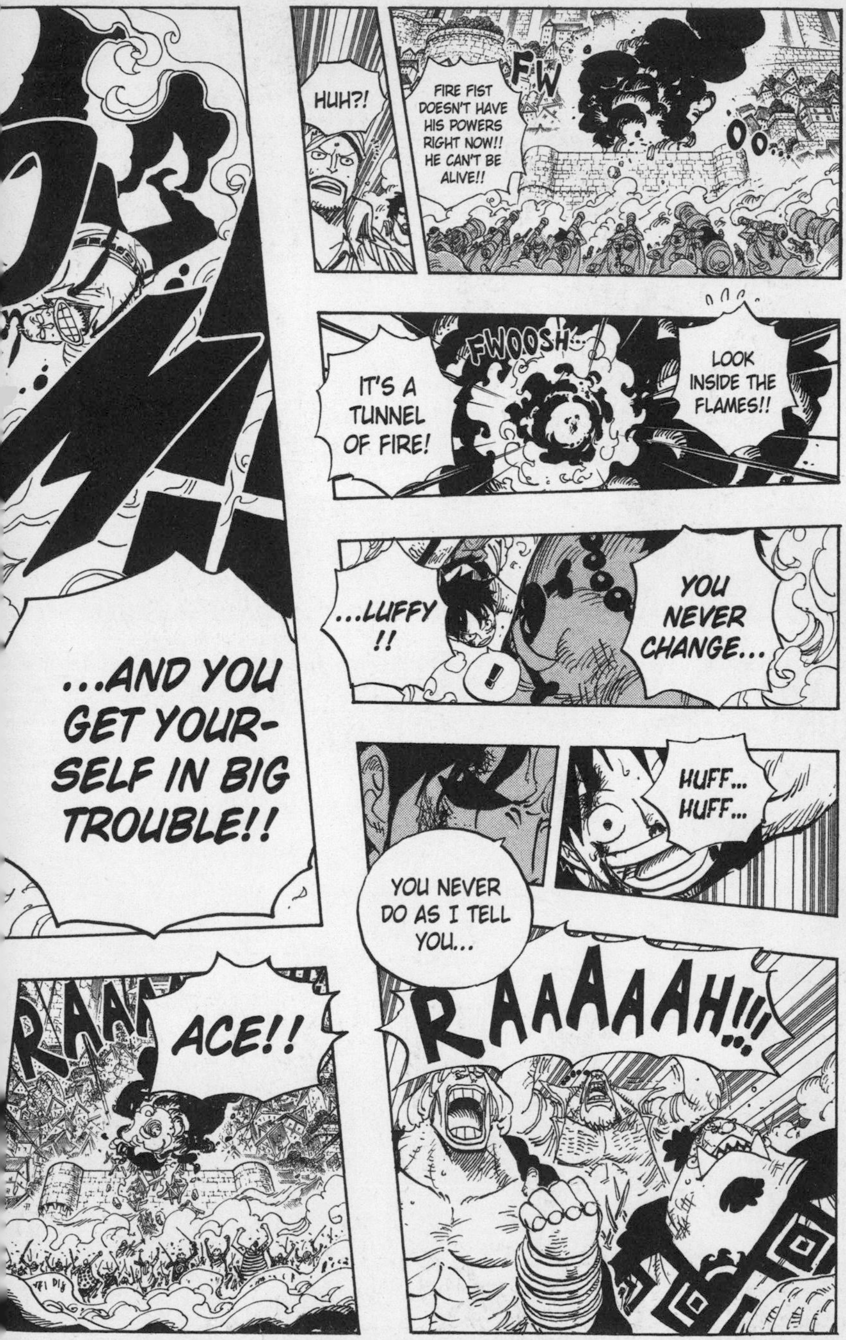
FW
FIRE FIST DOESN'T HAVE HIS POWERS RIGHT NOW!! HE CAN'T BE ALIVE!!
HUH?!
LOOK INSIDE THE FLAMES!!
FWOOSH
IT'S A TUNNEL OF FIRE!
YOU NEVER CHANGE...
...LUFFY!!
!
HUFF... HUFF...
YOU NEVER DO AS I TELL YOU...
...AND YOU GET YOUR-SELF IN BIG TROUBLE!!
RAAAAAH!!!
ACE!!

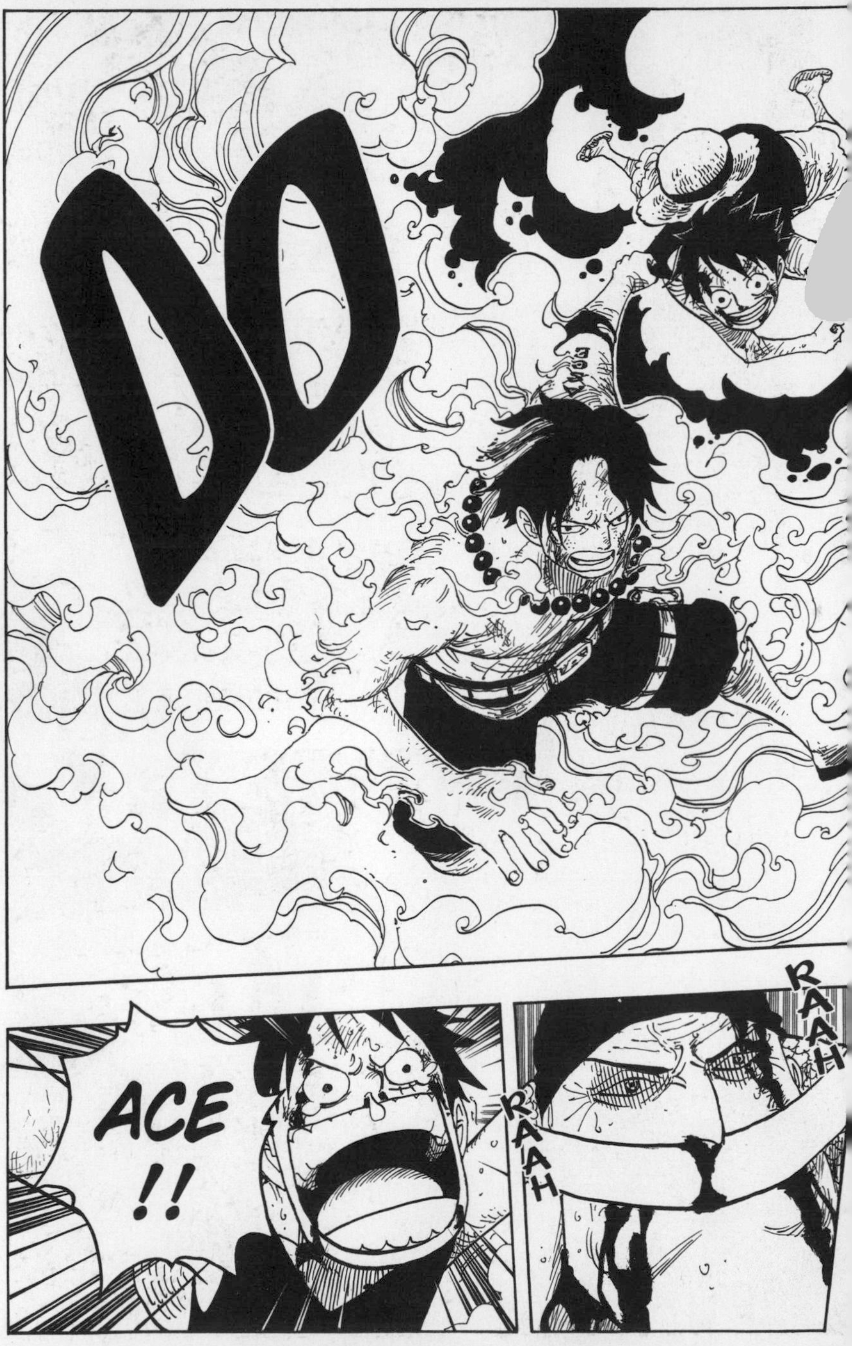
DO
RAAH
RAAH
ACE !!

SBS Question Corner

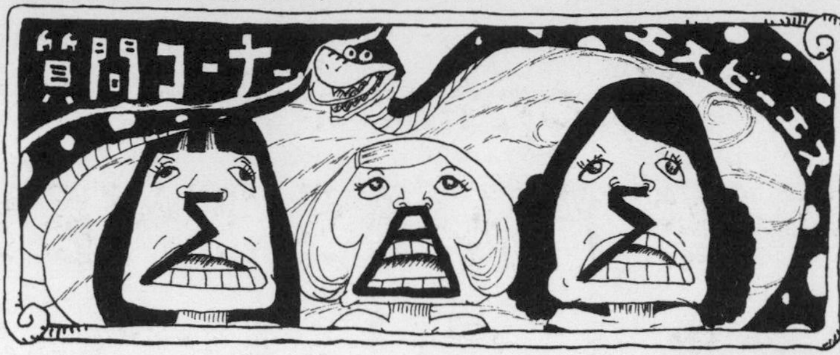
質問コーナー
エスビーエス
(Ako, Osaka)

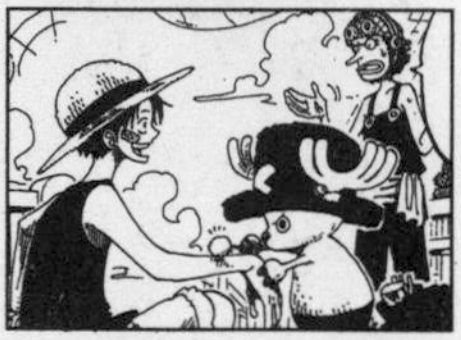

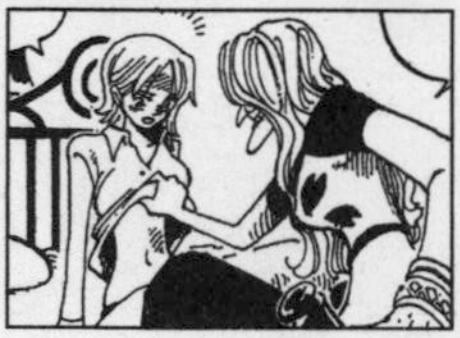

Q: I admired Chopper and went to medical school. Huh? What? You don't believe me? I-It's true. I-I got motivated from looking at Chopper treating his buddies… I-It's not because I wanted to do medical examinations on Nami!

--Shimizu Chamoroe

A: Shimizu Chamoroe!? When did you get out of prison?! Sheriff! Hurry up and catch him! He's a pervert that's always trying to mess up SBS (Refer to volume 55)! If he became a doctor, who knows what kind of freak accidents would happen!? What?! No, not me! Huh? What's wrong with being naked underneath my coat?!

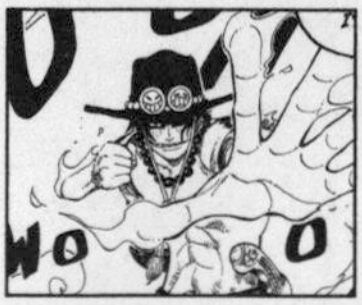

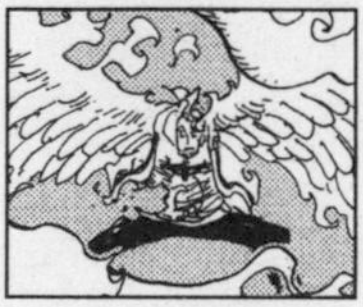

Q: Pleased to meet you, Mr. Oda. After reading volume 57, this came to my mind. I can't tell the difference between Marco the Phoenix's Mythical Zoan type, and Ace's Flame-Flame Fruit.

--CNY

A: I thought so. For this war arc, I omitted a lot of explanation to keep the pace going. To be more specific about Marco's powers, since he is a Zoan type, his body is still physical. But the Blue Flame of Revival is a power of the phoenix and can heal his wounds, nullifying most attacks. (But the healing has limitations.) It means the fire is for revival. But unlike real fire, it doesn't spread or give off heat of any sort, making it completely different from Ace's flames. This might come into play in the main story at a later time, so I'll leave it at that for now.

Q: Mr. Oda, in your SBS you say…perverted things, you know? (I'm sorry if that offends you.) Doesn't your wife complain? If she doesn't, she's like the perfect wife for manga artists. I'm impressed. No, seriously. I am.

--12 year old girl

A: I say even weirder things at home, so it's okay! This ends my SBS for this volume!

Chapter 572:
THE TIMES THEY ARE A-CHANGIN'

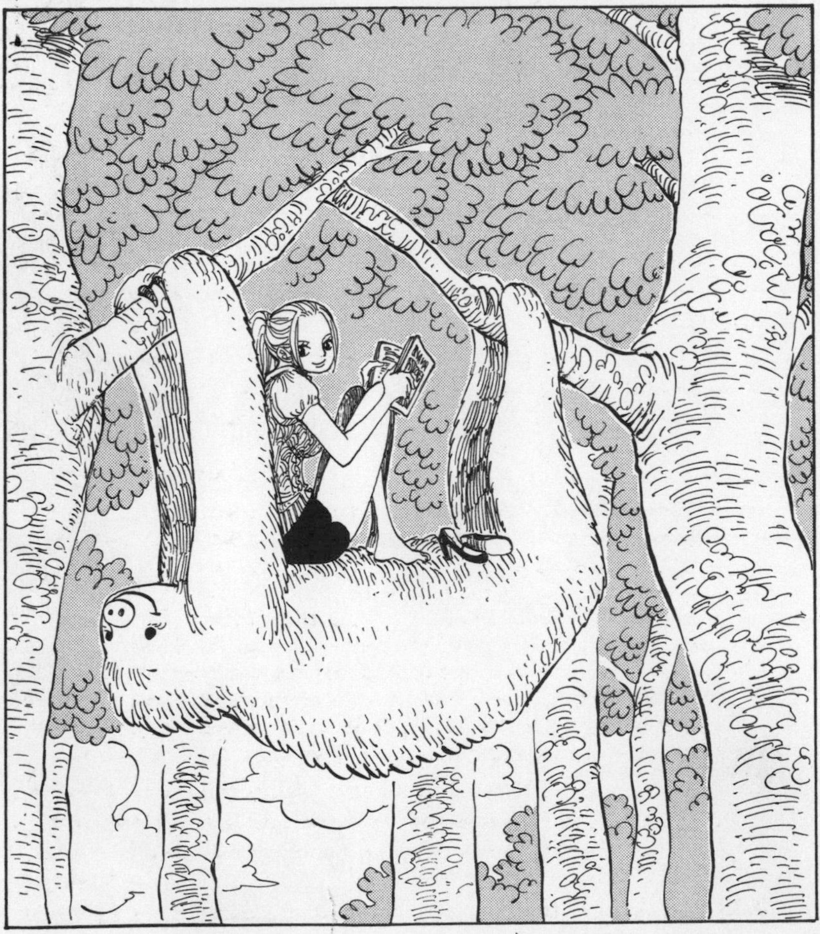

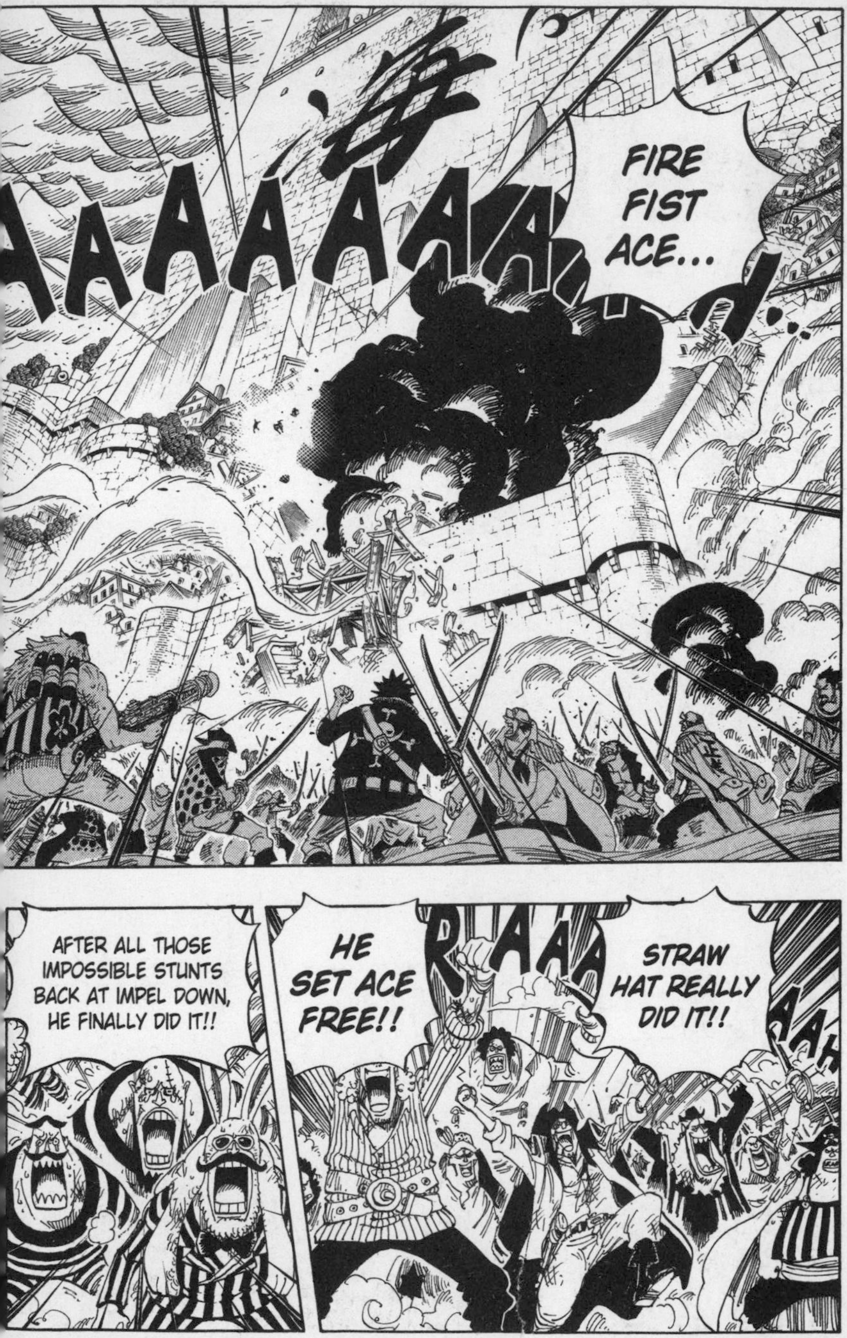
AAAAAAAA...
FIRE FIST ACE...
RAAAA
STRAW HAT REALLY DID IT!!
HE SET ACE FREE!!
AAAH
AFTER ALL THOSE IMPOSSIBLE STUNTS BACK AT IMPEL DOWN, HE FINALLY DID IT!!

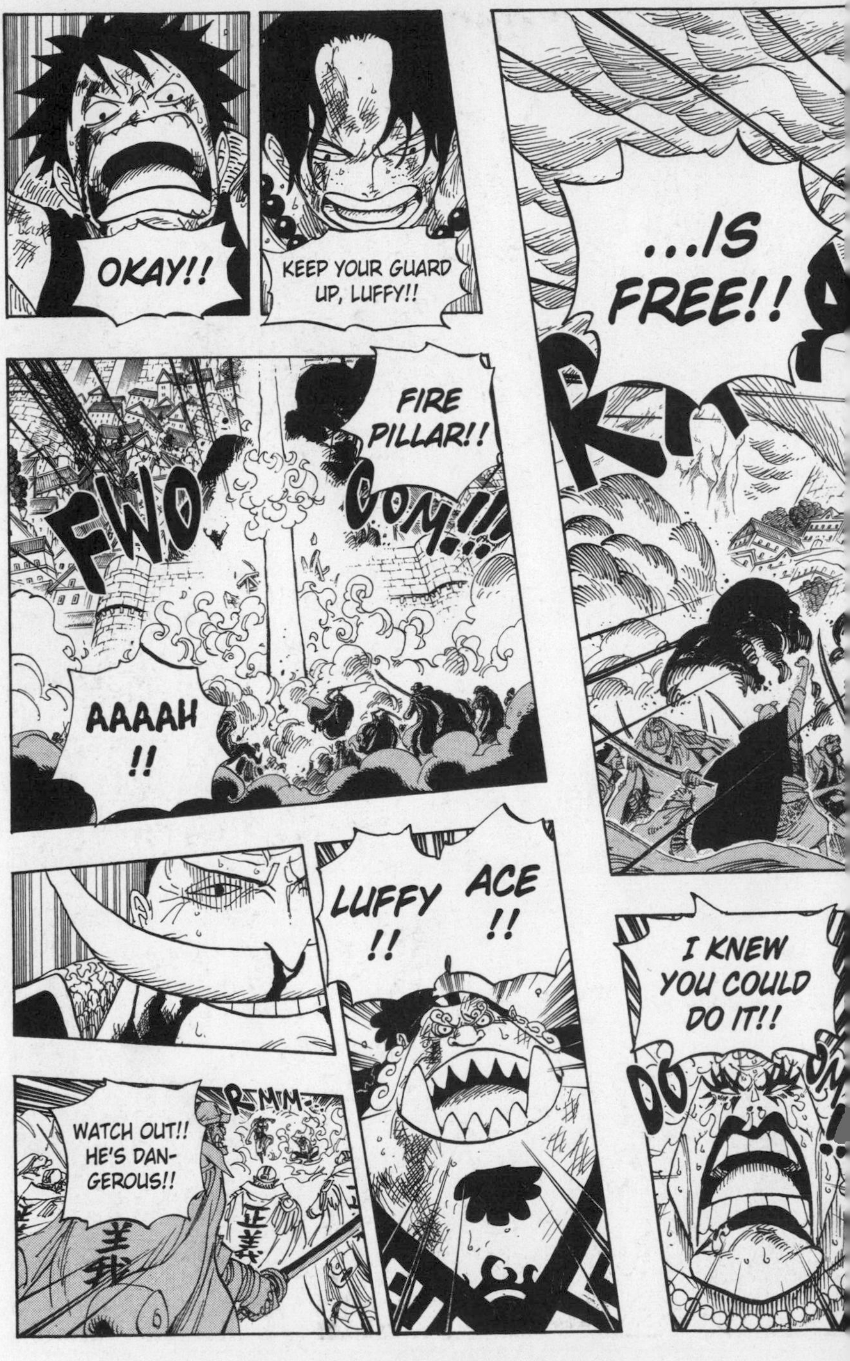
...IS FREE!!
RM
KEEP YOUR GUARD UP, LUFFY!!
OKAY!!
FIRE PILLAR!!
FWO
OOM!!!
AAAAH!!
I KNEW YOU COULD DO IT!!
DOOM
ACE!!
LUFFY!!
WATCH OUT!! HE'S DAN-GEROUS!!
RMM

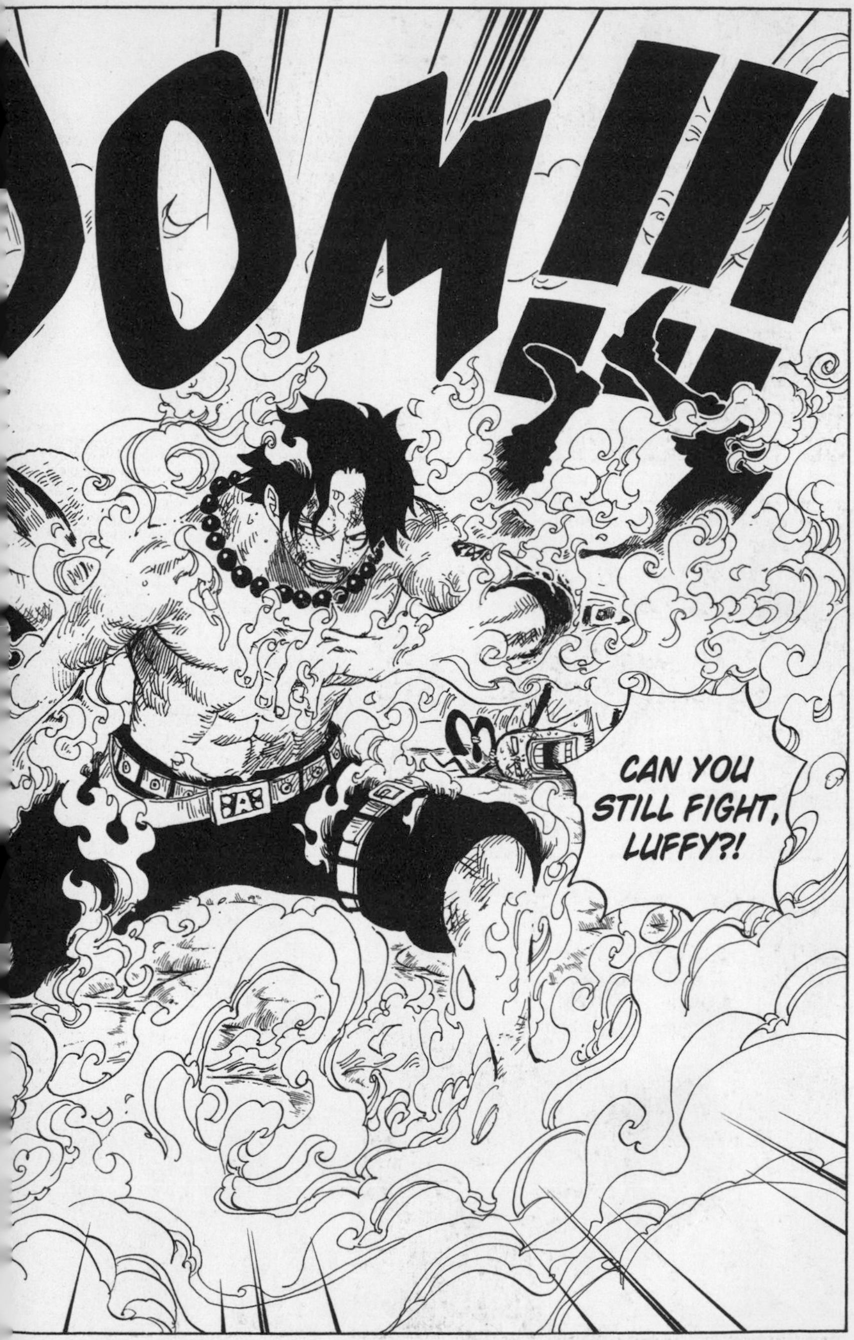
DOM!!!
CAN YOU STILL FIGHT, LUFFY?!

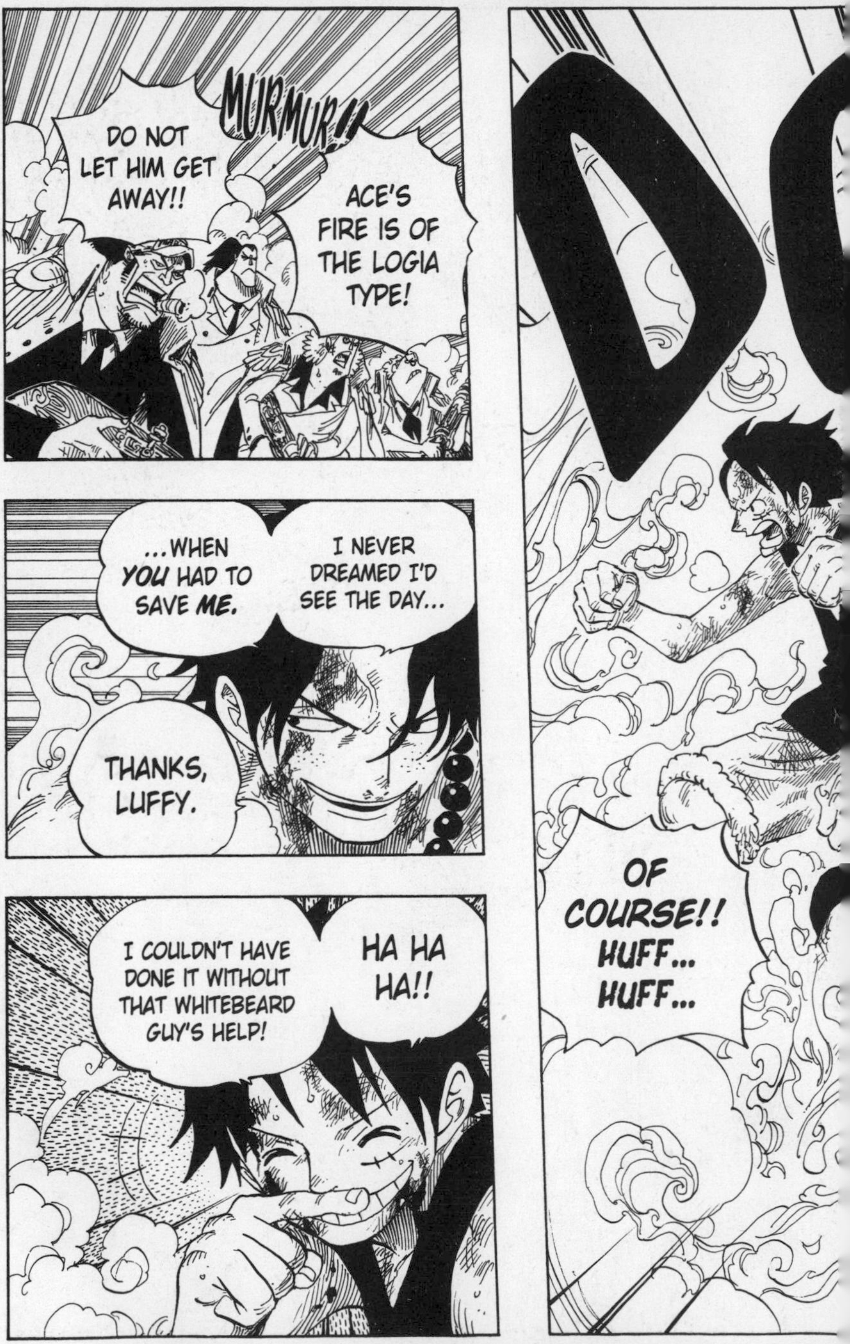
OF COURSE!! HUFF... HUFF...
MURMUR!!
ACE'S FIRE IS OF THE LOGIA TYPE!
DO NOT LET HIM GET AWAY!!
I NEVER DREAMED I'D SEE THE DAY...
...WHEN *YOU* HAD TO SAVE *ME*.
THANKS, LUFFY.
HA HA HA!!
I COULDN'T HAVE DONE IT WITHOUT THAT WHITEBEARD GUY'S HELP!

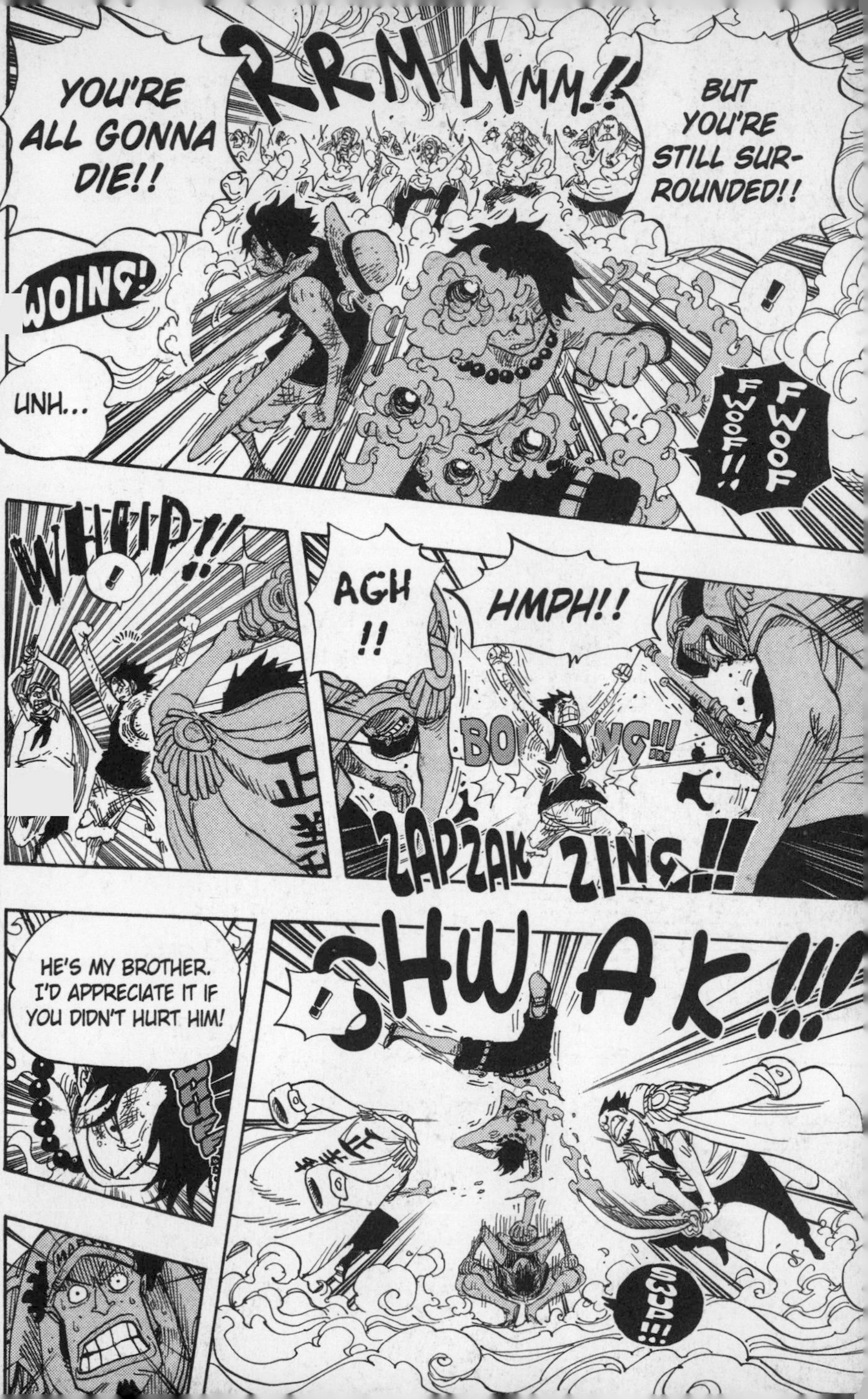
BUT YOU'RE STILL SUR-ROUNDED!!
RRMMMMM!!
YOU'RE ALL GONNA DIE!!
!
FWOOF FWOOF!!
WOING!
UNH...
HMPH!!
AGH !!
ZAP ZAK ZING!!
WHIP!!
!
SHWAK!!!
!
HE'S MY BROTHER. I'D APPRECIATE IT IF YOU DIDN'T HURT HIM!

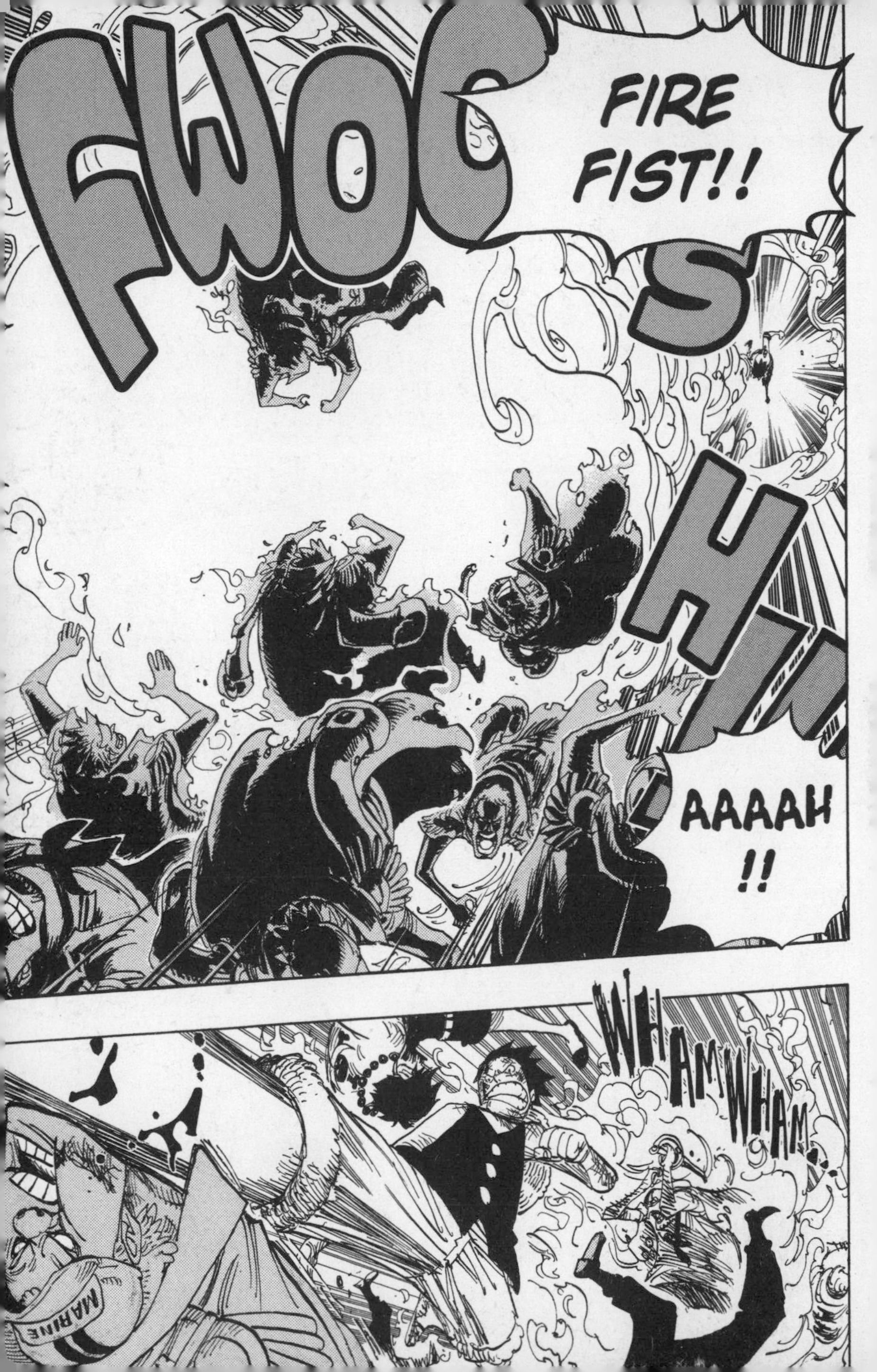
FIRE FIST!!
FWOOSH
AAAAH !!
WHAM WHAM

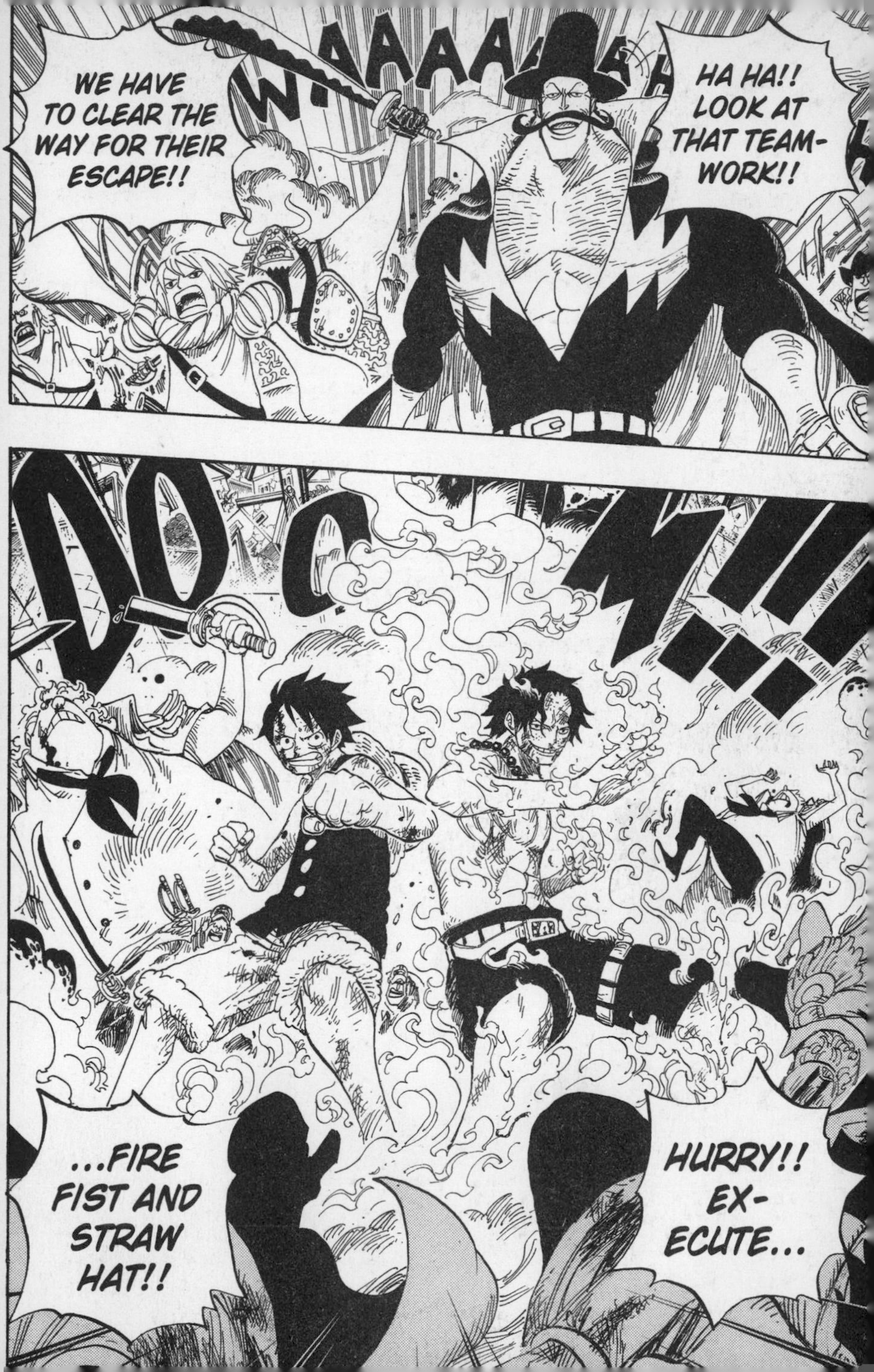
HA HA!! LOOK AT THAT TEAM-WORK!!
WE HAVE TO CLEAR THE WAY FOR THEIR ESCAPE!!
HURRY!! EX-ECUTE...
...FIRE FIST AND STRAW HAT!!

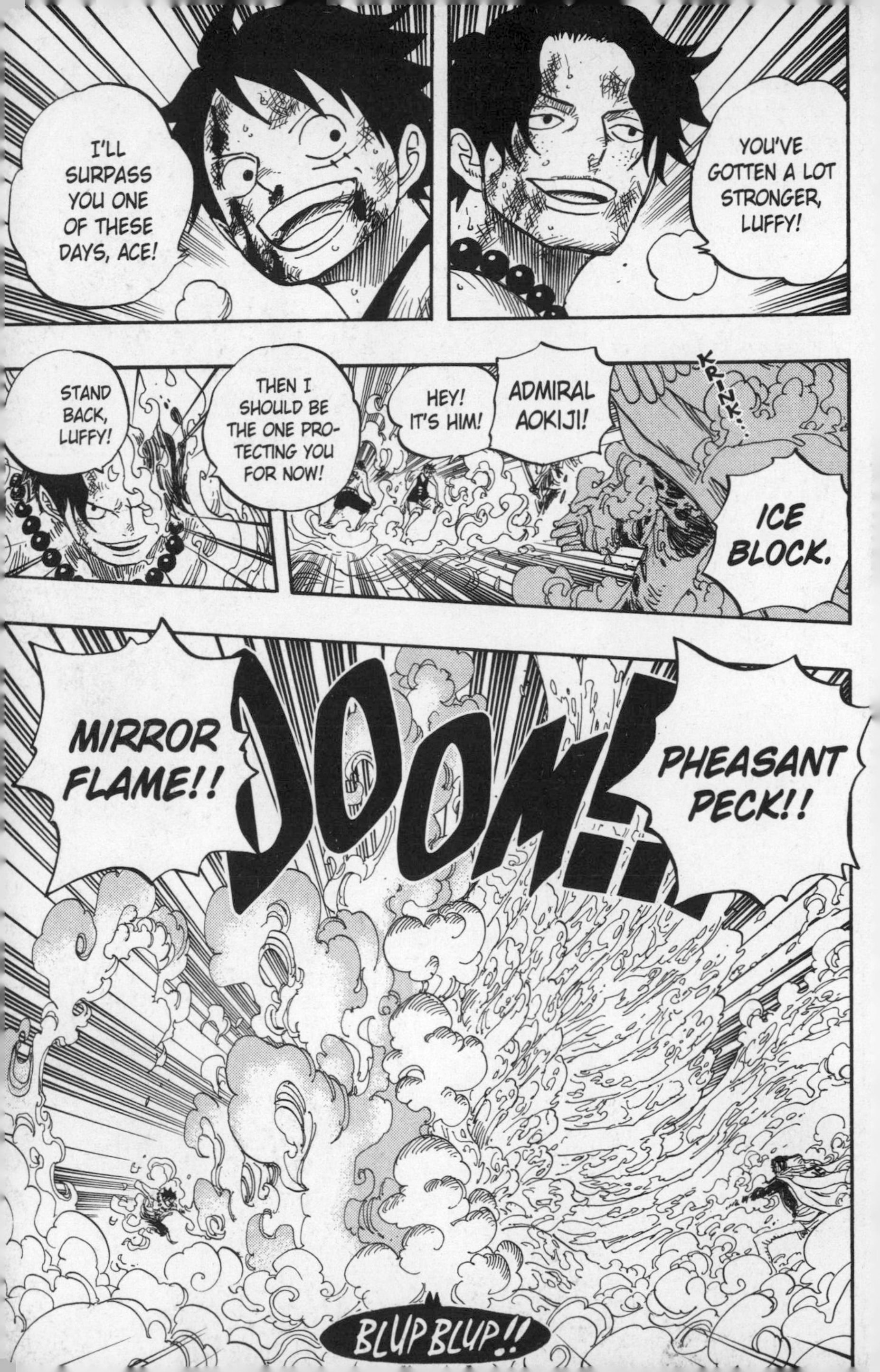
YOU'VE GOTTEN A LOT STRONGER, LUFFY!
I'LL SURPASS YOU ONE OF THESE DAYS, ACE!
KRINK...
ADMIRAL AOKIJI!
HEY! IT'S HIM!
ICE BLOCK.
THEN I SHOULD BE THE ONE PRO-TECTING YOU FOR NOW!
STAND BACK, LUFFY!
PHEASANT PECK!!
DOOM!!
MIRROR FLAME!!
BLUP BLUP!!

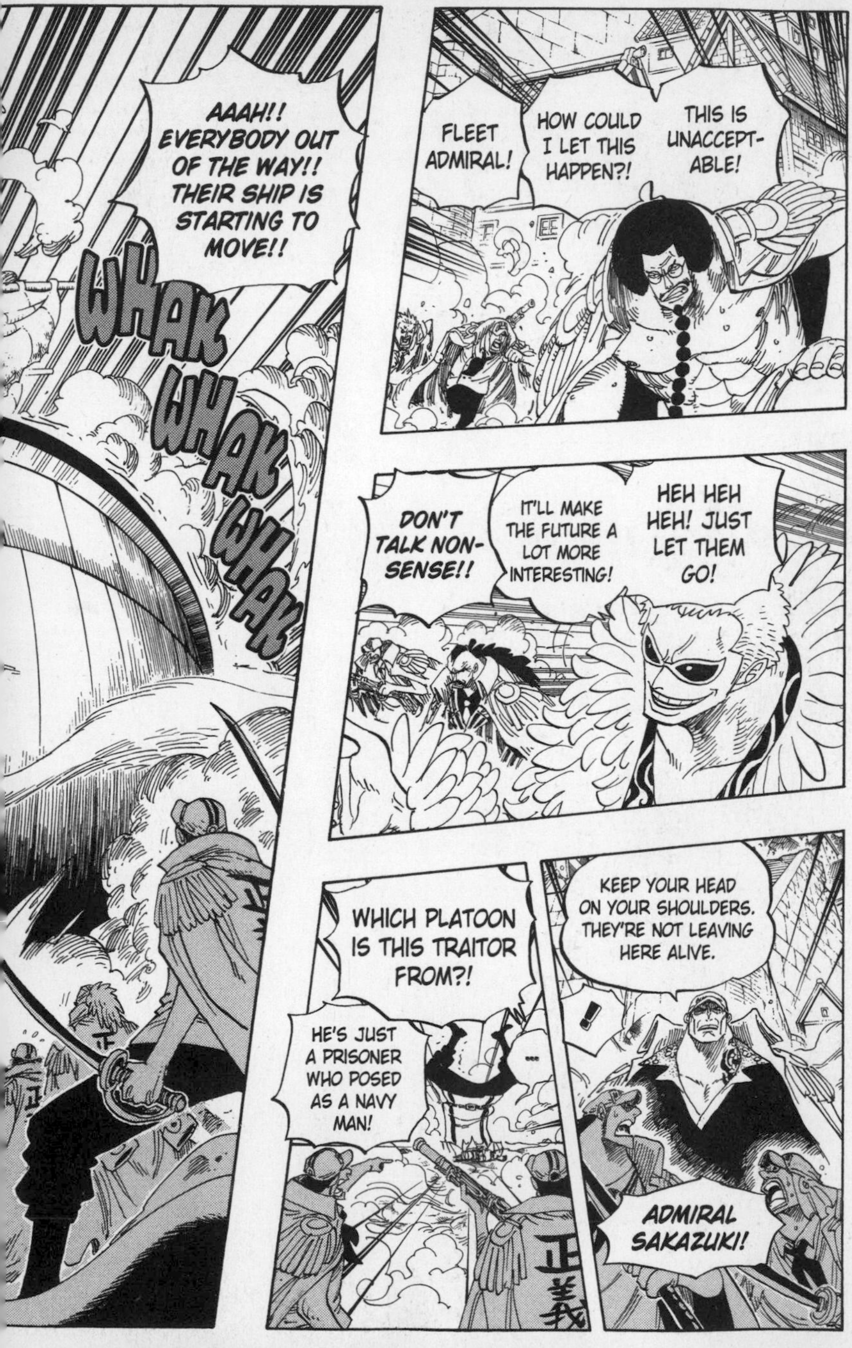
THIS IS UNACCEPT-ABLE!
HOW COULD I LET THIS HAPPEN?!
FLEET ADMIRAL!
HEH HEH HEH! JUST LET THEM GO!
IT'LL MAKE THE FUTURE A LOT MORE INTERESTING!
DON'T TALK NON-SENSE!!
KEEP YOUR HEAD ON YOUR SHOULDERS. THEY'RE NOT LEAVING HERE ALIVE.
!
ADMIRAL SAKAZUKI!
WHICH PLATOON IS THIS TRAITOR FROM?!
...
HE'S JUST A PRISONER WHO POSED AS A NAVY MAN!
AAAH!! EVERYBODY OUT OF THE WAY!! THEIR SHIP IS STARTING TO MOVE!!
WHAK
WHAK
WHAK

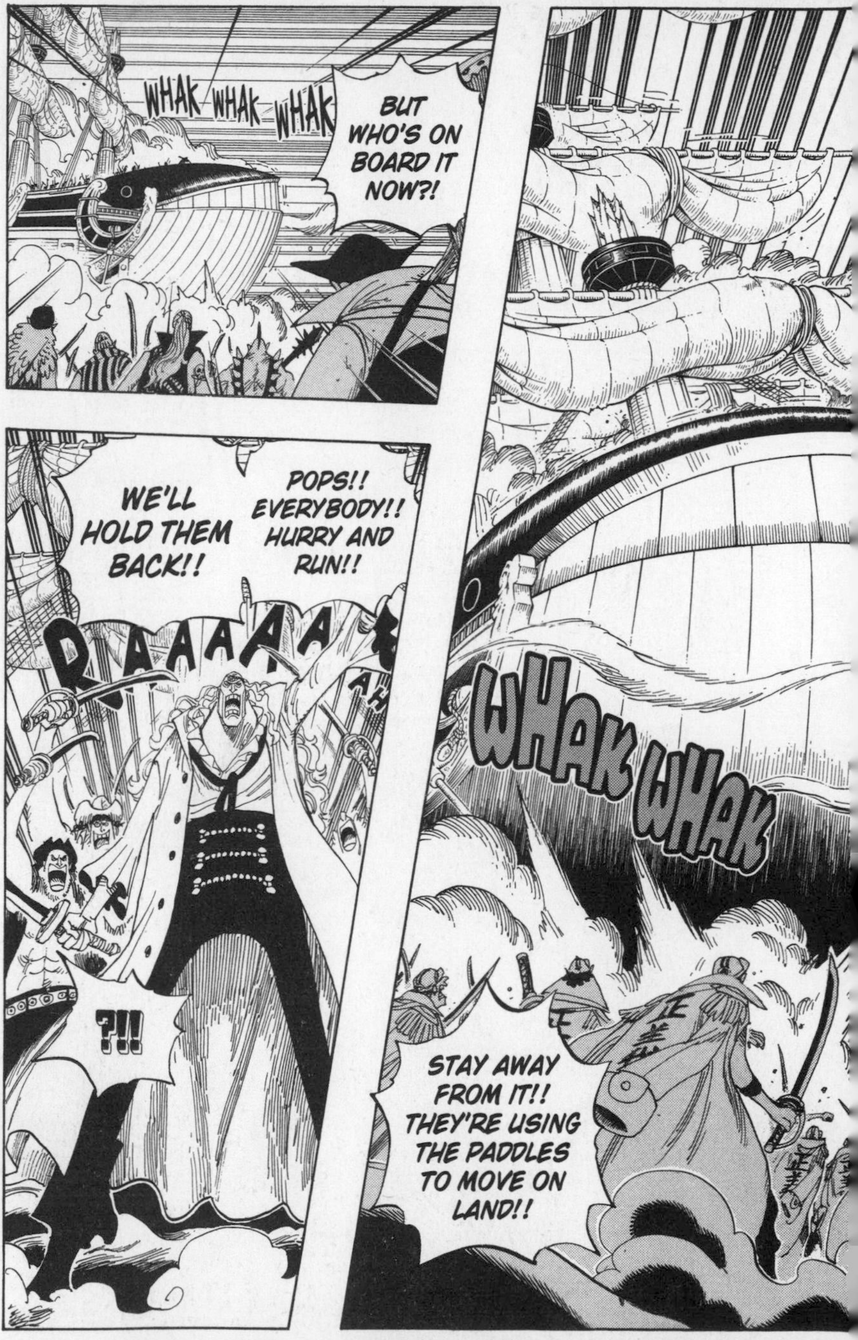
WHAK WHAK
STAY AWAY FROM IT!! THEY'RE USING THE PADDLES TO MOVE ON LAND!!
WHAK WHAK WHAK
BUT WHO'S ON BOARD IT NOW?!
POPS!! EVERYBODY!! HURRY AND RUN!!
WE'LL HOLD THEM BACK!!
RAAAAAAH
?!!

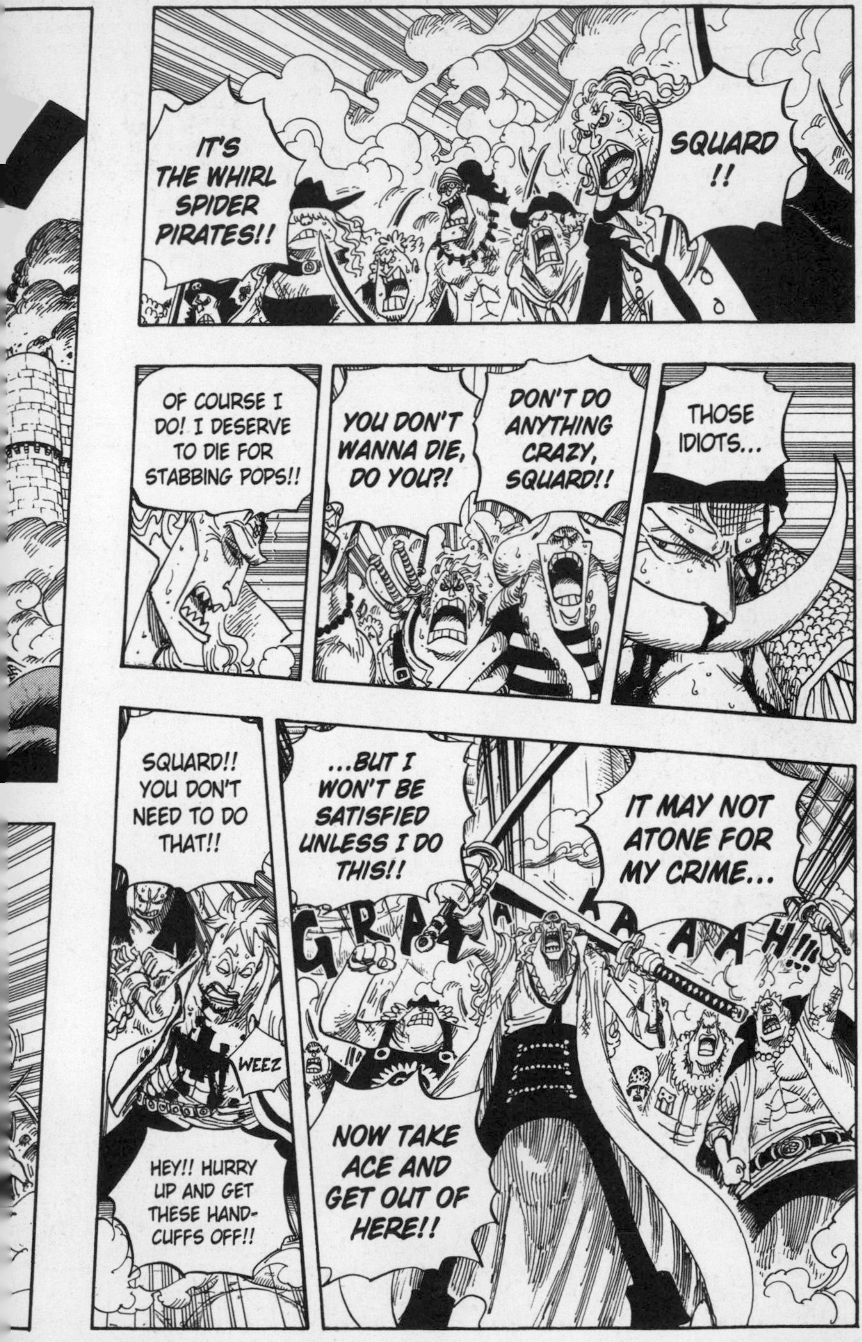
SQUARD!!
IT'S THE WHIRL SPIDER PIRATES!!
THOSE IDIOTS...
DON'T DO ANYTHING CRAZY, SQUARD!!
YOU DON'T WANNA DIE, DO YOU?!
OF COURSE I DO! I DESERVE TO DIE FOR STABBING POPS!!
IT MAY NOT ATONE FOR MY CRIME...
...BUT I WON'T BE SATISFIED UNLESS I DO THIS!!
GRAAAAAAH!!!
NOW TAKE ACE AND GET OUT OF HERE!!
SQUARD!! YOU DON'T NEED TO DO THAT!!
WEEZ
HEY!! HURRY UP AND GET THESE HAND-CUFFS OFF!!

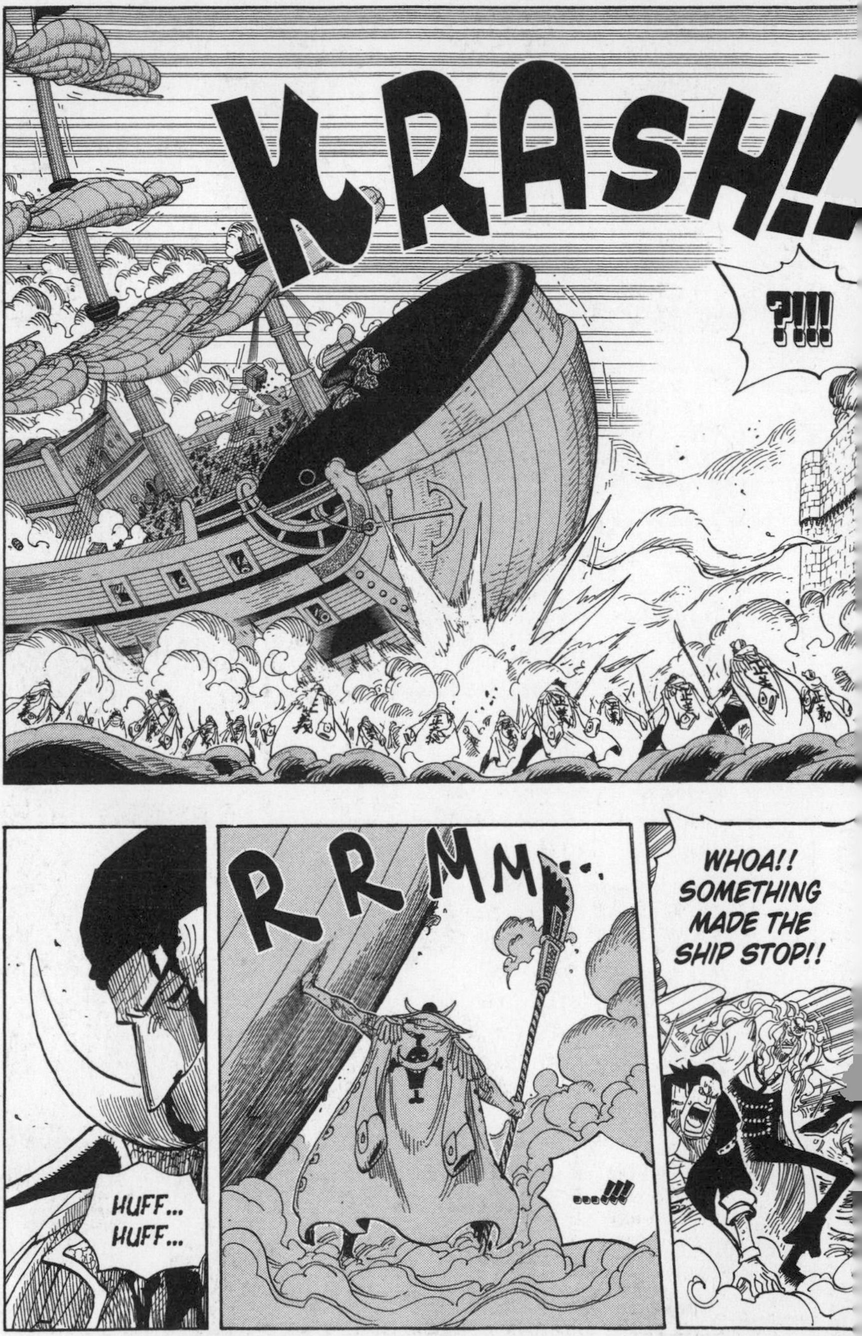
KRASH!!
?!!!
WHOA!! SOMETHING MADE THE SHIP STOP!!
RRMM..
...!!!
HUFF... HUFF...

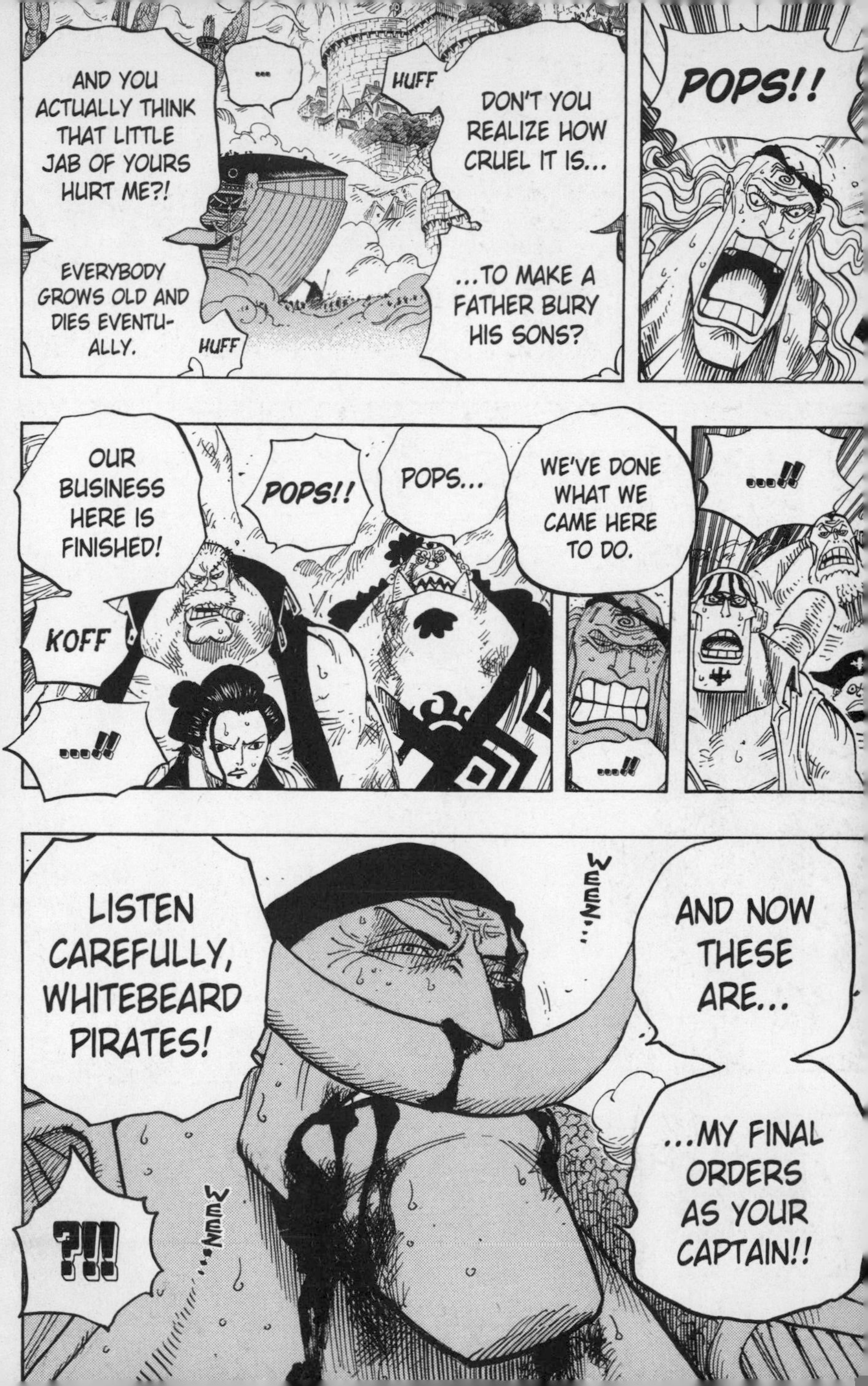

POPS!!
DON'T YOU REALIZE HOW CRUEL IT IS...
HUFF
...TO MAKE A FATHER BURY HIS SONS?
...
AND YOU ACTUALLY THINK THAT LITTLE JAB OF YOURS HURT ME?!
EVERYBODY GROWS OLD AND DIES EVENTU-ALLY.
HUFF
...!!
...!!
WE'VE DONE WHAT WE CAME HERE TO DO.
POPS...
POPS!!
OUR BUSINESS HERE IS FINISHED!
KOFF
...!!
AND NOW THESE ARE...
...MY FINAL ORDERS AS YOUR CAPTAIN!!
WEEN...
LISTEN CAREFULLY, WHITEBEARD PIRATES!
WEEN...
?!!

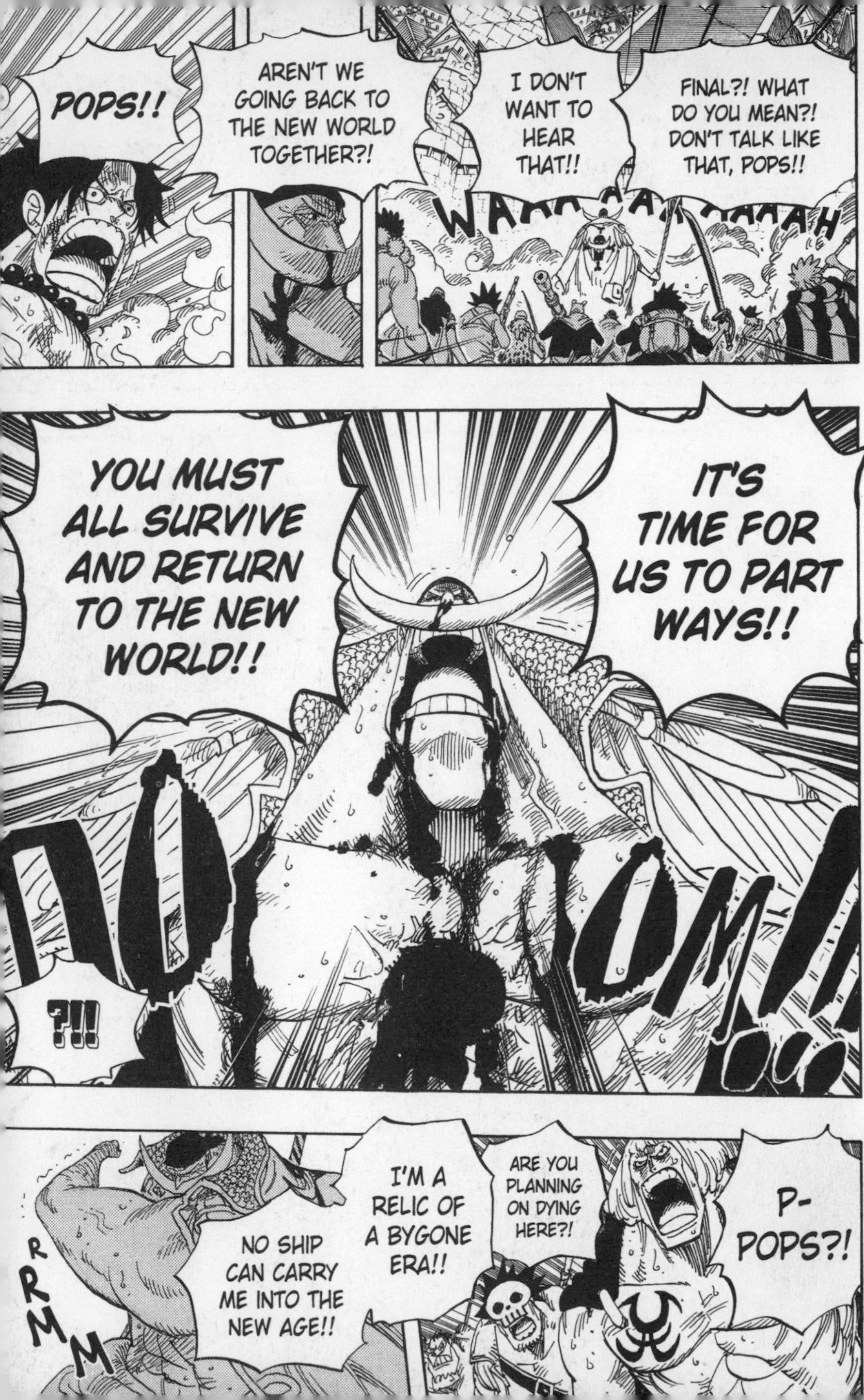
FINAL?! WHAT DO YOU MEAN?! DON'T TALK LIKE THAT, POPS!!
I DON'T WANT TO HEAR THAT!!
AREN'T WE GOING BACK TO THE NEW WORLD TOGETHER?!
POPS!!
IT'S TIME FOR US TO PART WAYS!!
YOU MUST ALL SURVIVE AND RETURN TO THE NEW WORLD!!
?!!
P-POPS?!
ARE YOU PLANNING ON DYING HERE?!
I'M A RELIC OF A BYGONE ERA!!
NO SHIP CAN CARRY ME INTO THE NEW AGE!!
RRMM

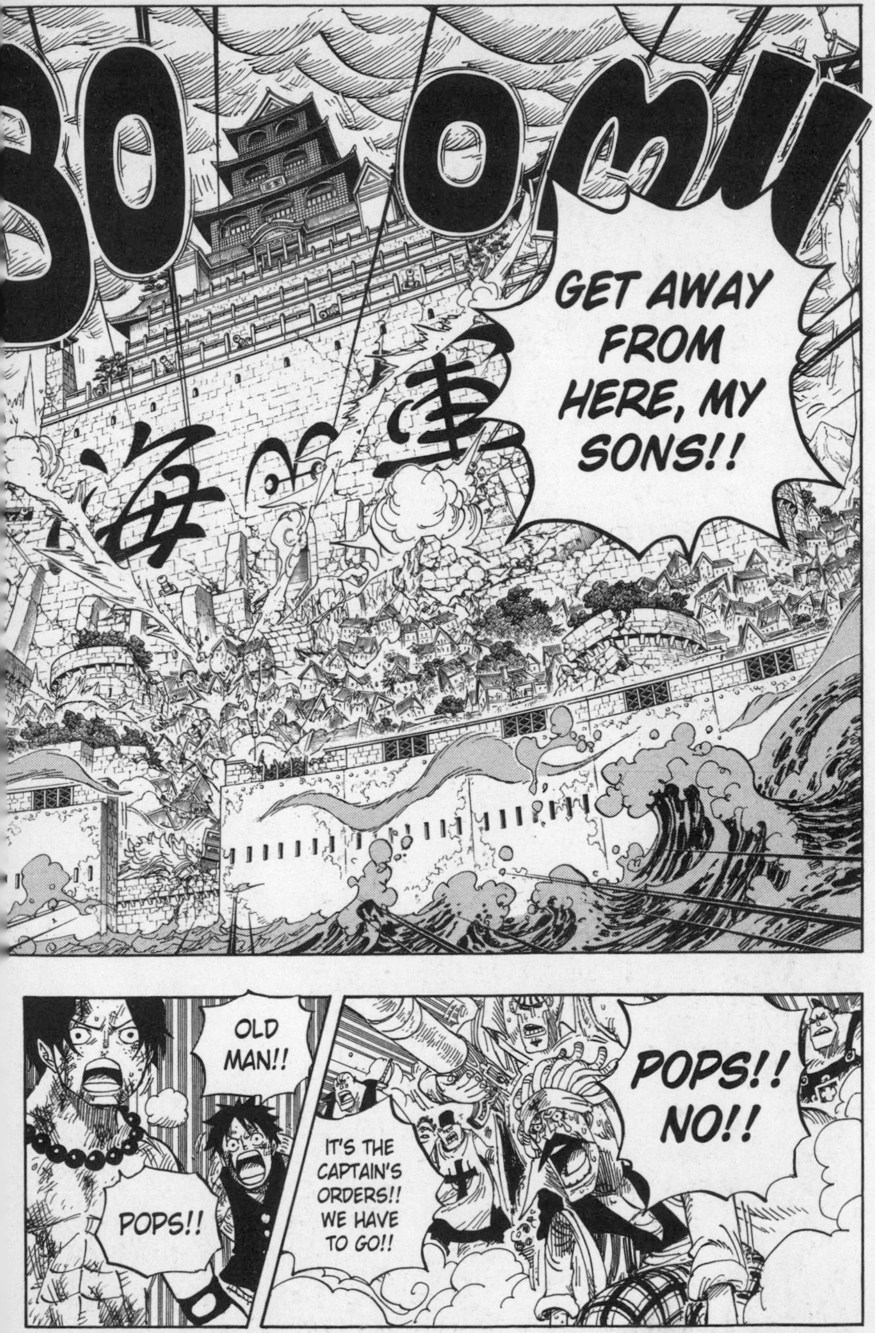
BOOM!!
海軍
GET AWAY FROM HERE, MY SONS!!
POPS!! NO!!
IT'S THE CAPTAIN'S ORDERS!! WE HAVE TO GO!!
OLD MAN!!
POPS!!

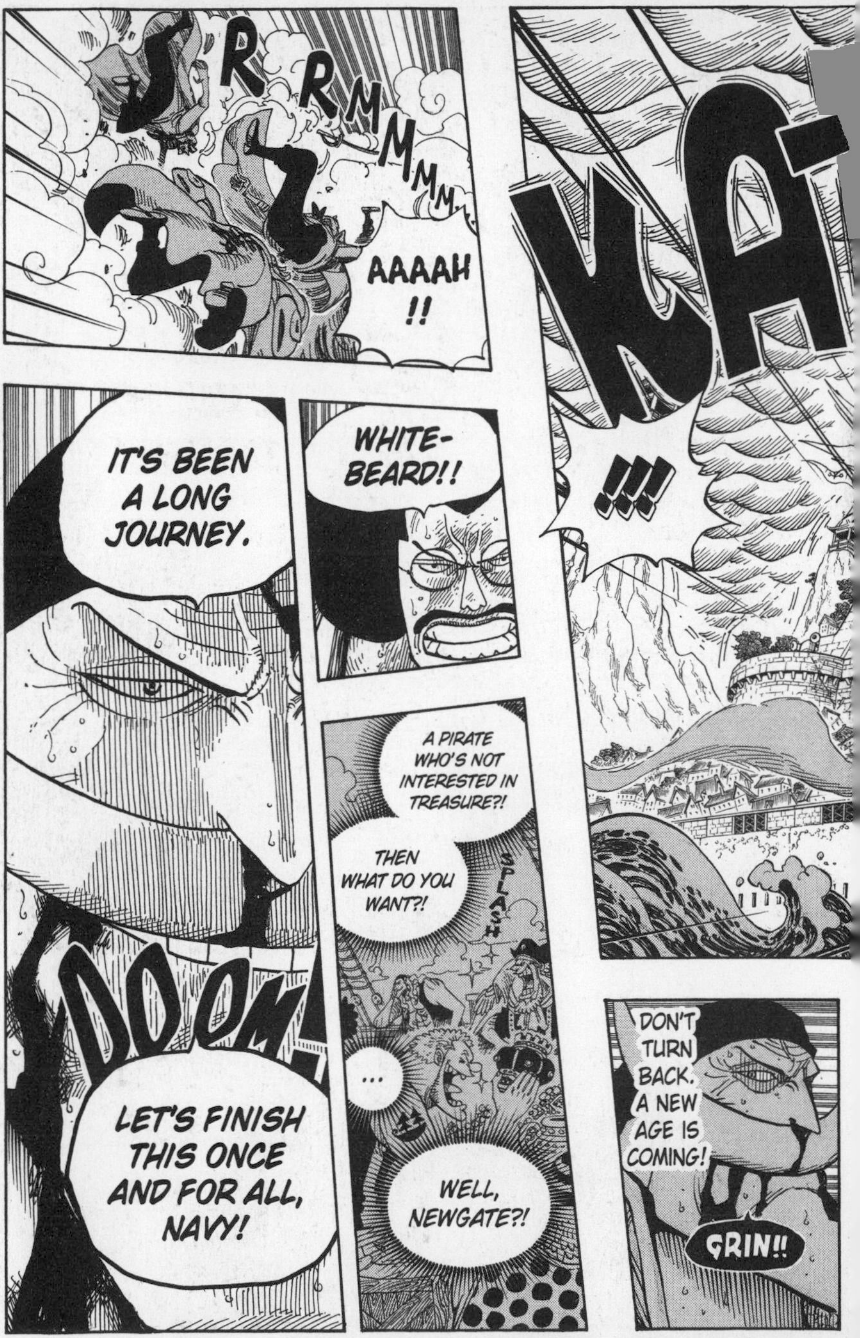
KWA
!!!!
RRRMMMMMM
AAAAH!!
DON'T TURN BACK. A NEW AGE IS COMING!
GRIN!!
WHITE-BEARD!!
A PIRATE WHO'S NOT INTERESTED IN TREASURE?!
THEN WHAT DO YOU WANT?!
SPLASH
...
WELL, NEWGATE?!
IT'S BEEN A LONG JOURNEY.
DOOM
LET'S FINISH THIS ONCE AND FOR ALL, NAVY!

CHOPPER'S VOICE ACTRESS, IKUE OTANI!

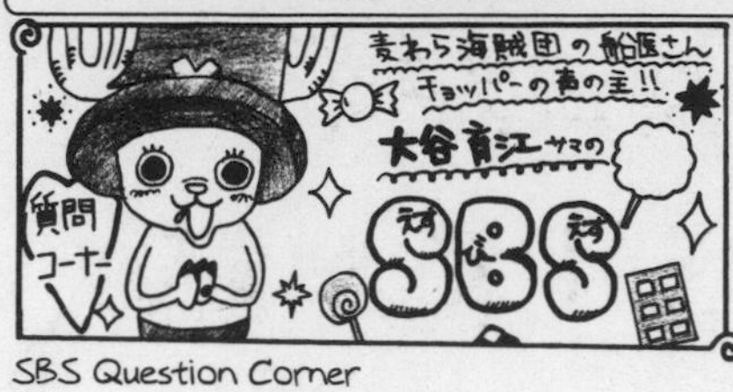
麦わら海賊団の船医さん
チョッパーの声の主!!
大谷育江サマの
SBS
質問コーナー

(L, Ibaraki)

SBS Question Corner

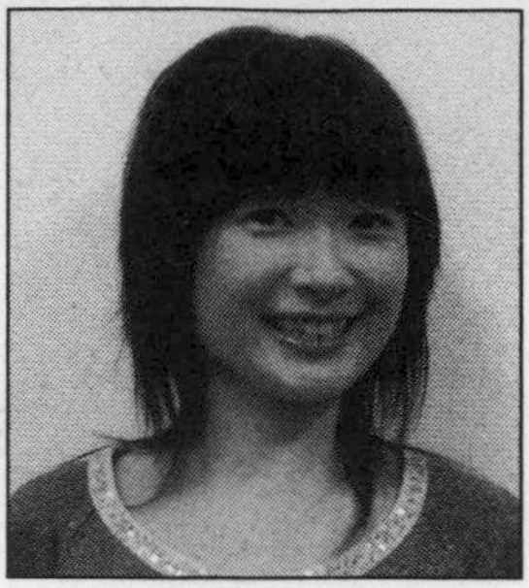

HDYD! (How do you do?!)
This is...how many times did we do this again? Oh yeah, six! This is our 6th voice actor/actress Question Corner! Let's start! She's the one who's voicing every single cute mascot character in Japan! No one can do cuter voices than she can! On top of that, she's one of the best actresses I've seen! Oh yeah, she's tiny and cute too! Here is the voice of our ship doctor, Chopper! The tiny Ikue Otani, in the house!

Oda (O): Now is everyone ready? Let's have her introduce herself! Here comes Ms. Otani!

Ikue (I): Yo.

O: That's so short! That really scared me!

I: Hey, Odacchi. Did you have to say "tiny" when you introduced me?

O: Oh, right. Sorry. Actually, I'm not sorry.

I: You should be!

O: Anyway, this is a question corner called SBS. Do you know what it stands for?

I: Of course I know.
(S)howing off my (B)ombshell rock, paper and scissors.
(S)o what's that?

O: That's what I want to know! So you don't know it. Here's a hint! You take questions and ask for submissions and...stuff.

I: Oh, I get it now!
(S)urprise! (B)lossoming! (S)unrise!

O: I'm the one being surprised! Whatever. I'll just leave it at that...

Otani's SBS continued on page 202! ☞

PREVIEW FOR NEXT VOICE ACTOR'S SBS

The next two will feature these two!

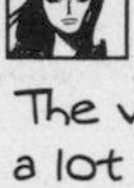 Robin (Yuriko Yamaguchi) 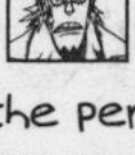 Franky (Kazuki Yao)

The very easygoing Yuriko and the perverted Yao. It should be a lot of fun! We'll be waiting for your nonsensical questions!

Chapter 573:
THE NAME OF THIS ERA IS "WHITEBEARD"

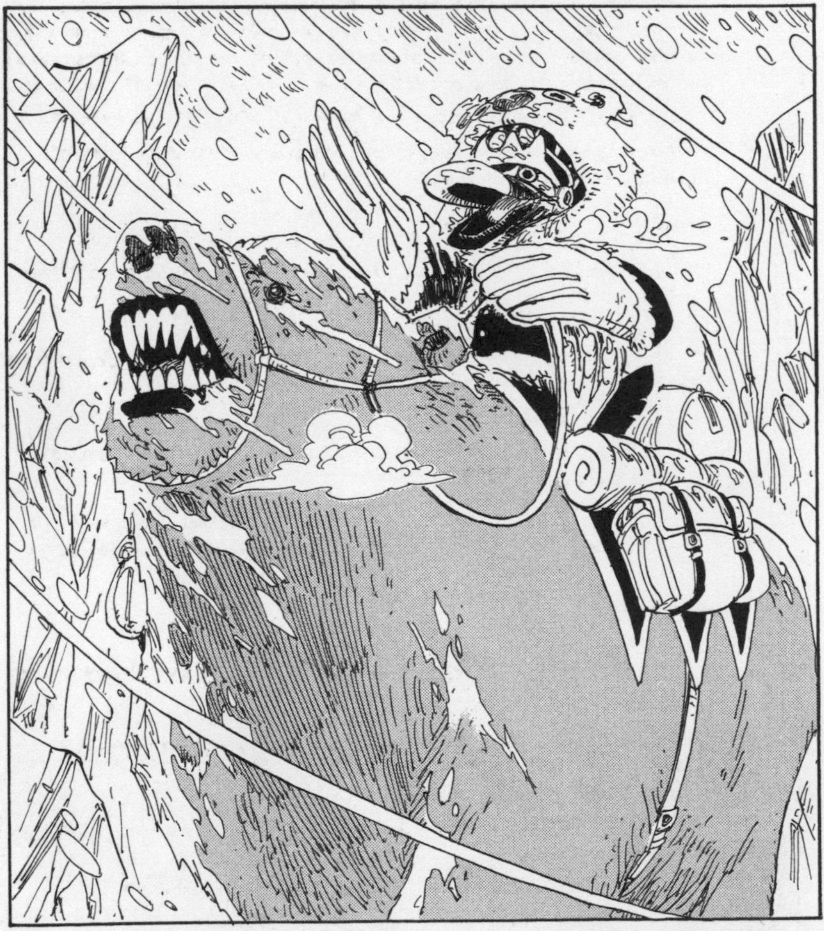

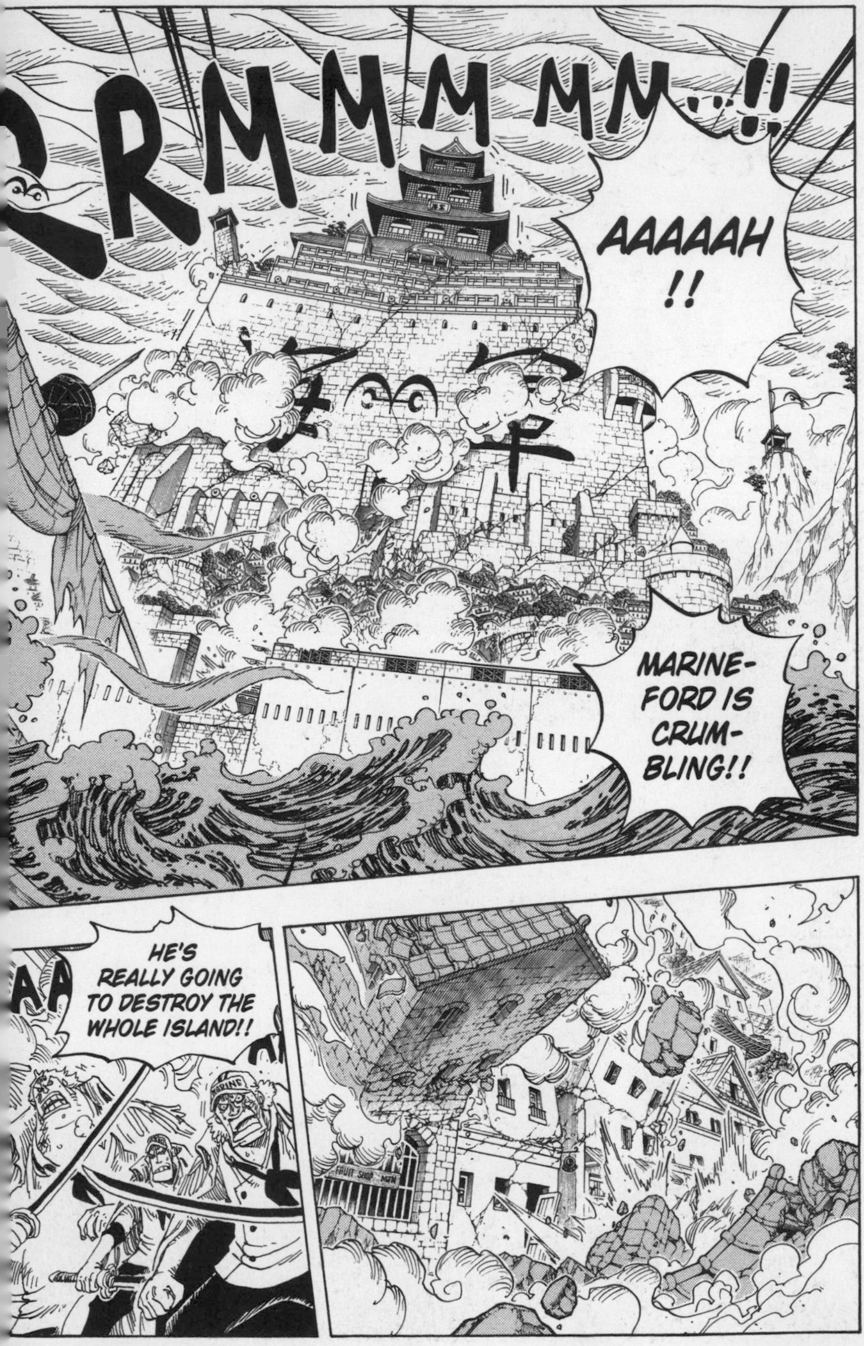
RMMM MM..!!
AAAAAH!!
MARINE-FORD IS CRUM-BLING!!
HE'S REALLY GOING TO DESTROY THE WHOLE ISLAND!!

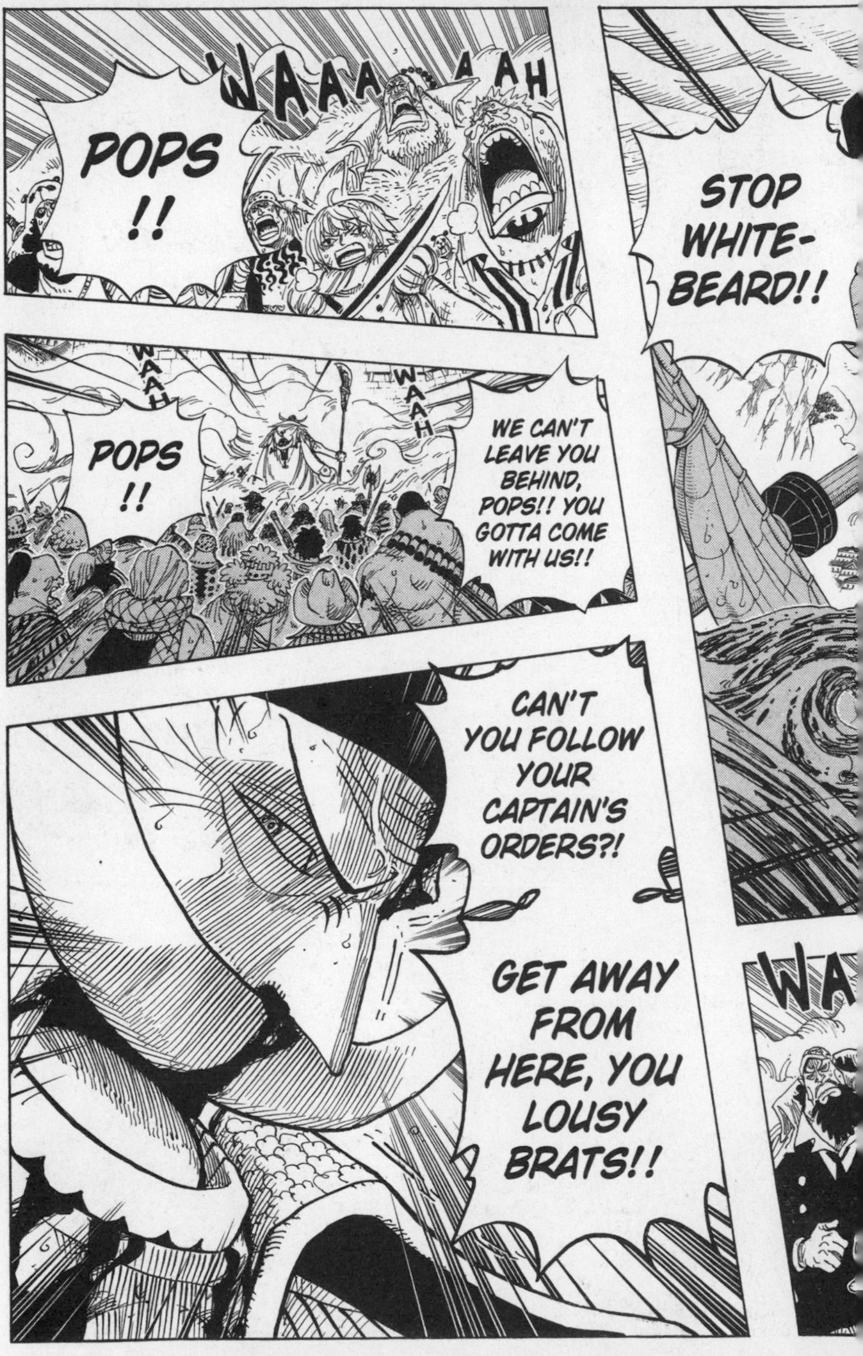
STOP WHITE-BEARD!!
WAAAAAAH
POPS!!
WAAH
WAAH
POPS!!
WE CAN'T LEAVE YOU BEHIND, POPS!! YOU GOTTA COME WITH US!!
WA
CAN'T YOU FOLLOW YOUR CAPTAIN'S ORDERS?!
GET AWAY FROM HERE, YOU LOUSY BRATS!!

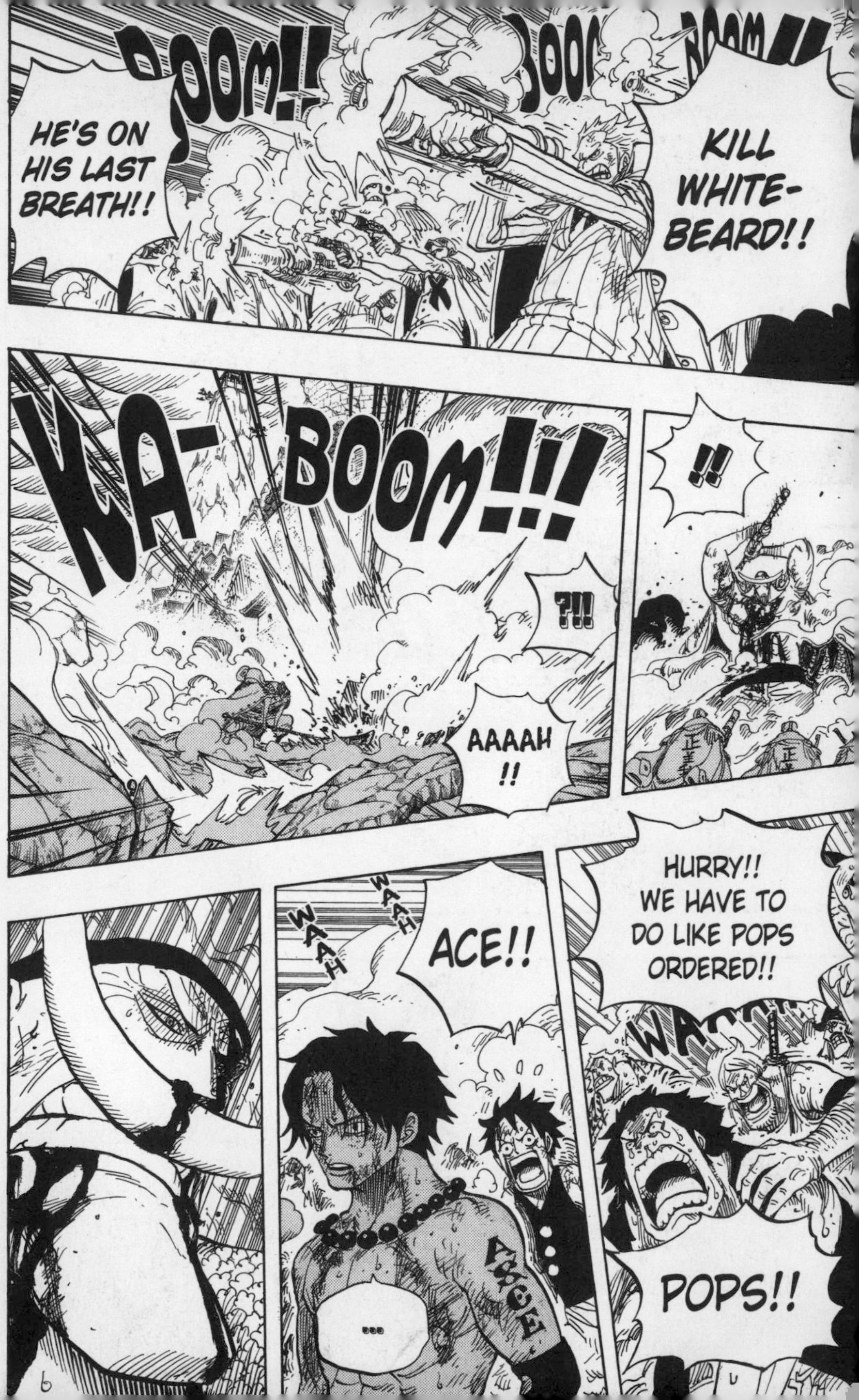
KILL WHITE-BEARD!!
HE'S ON HIS LAST BREATH!!
!!
KA-BOOM!!!
?!!
AAAAH !!
HURRY!! WE HAVE TO DO LIKE POPS ORDERED!!
POPS!!
WAAH
WAAH
ACE!!
...

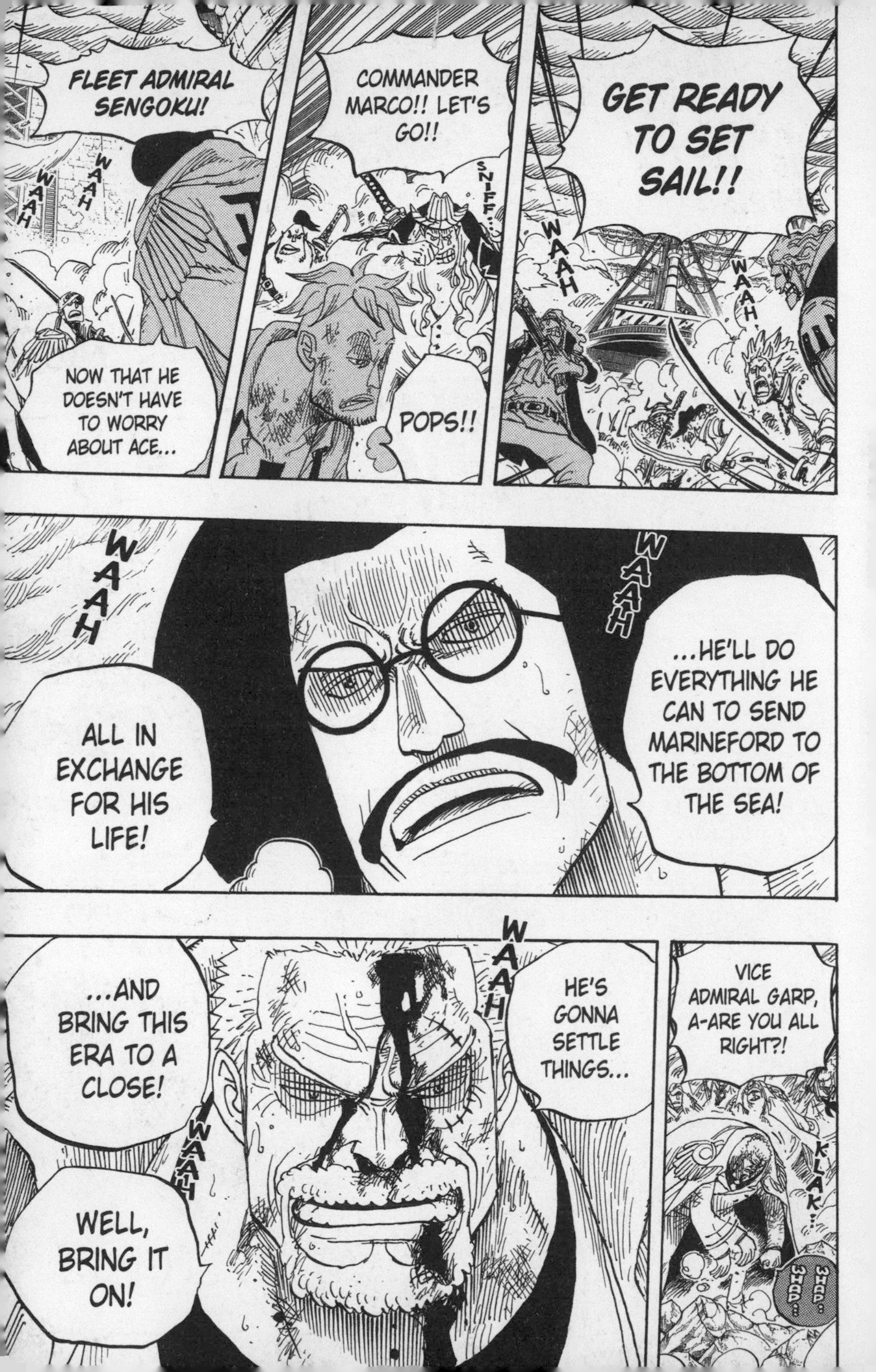
GET READY TO SET SAIL!!
WAAH
WAAH
COMMANDER MARCO!! LET'S GO!!
SNIFF...
POPS!!
FLEET ADMIRAL SENGOKU!
WAAH
WAAH
NOW THAT HE DOESN'T HAVE TO WORRY ABOUT ACE...
WAAH
...HE'LL DO EVERYTHING HE CAN TO SEND MARINEFORD TO THE BOTTOM OF THE SEA!
WAAH
ALL IN EXCHANGE FOR HIS LIFE!
VICE ADMIRAL GARP, A-ARE YOU ALL RIGHT?!
KLAK...
WHAP
WHAP
WAAH
HE'S GONNA SETTLE THINGS...
...AND BRING THIS ERA TO A CLOSE!
WAAH
WELL, BRING IT ON!

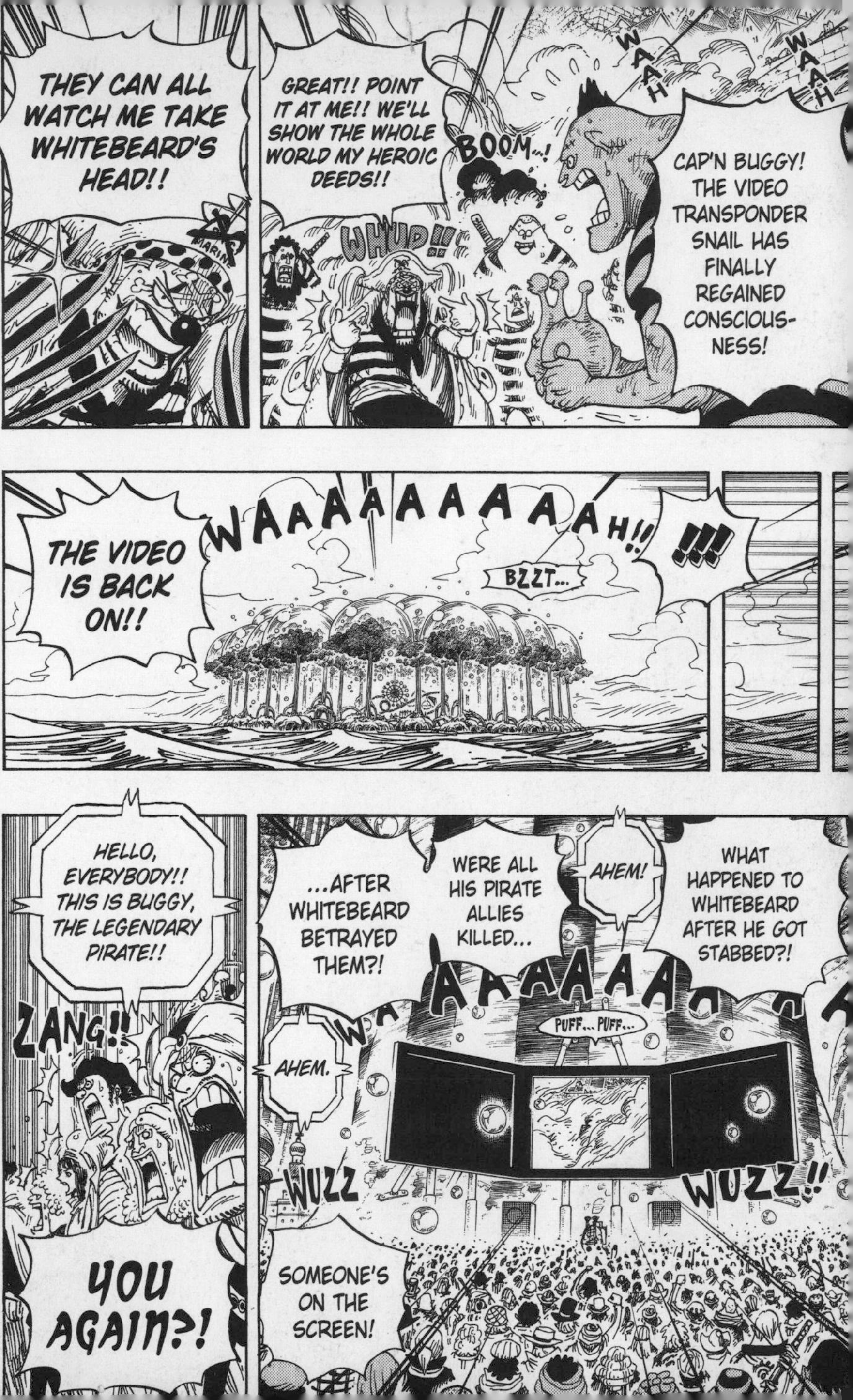
WAAH
WAAH
CAP'N BUGGY! THE VIDEO TRANSPONDER SNAIL HAS FINALLY REGAINED CONSCIOUS-NESS!
BOOM..!
GREAT!! POINT IT AT ME!! WE'LL SHOW THE WHOLE WORLD MY HEROIC DEEDS!!
WHUD!!
THEY CAN ALL WATCH ME TAKE WHITEBEARD'S HEAD!!
!!!
WAAAAAAAAAAH!!
BZZT...
THE VIDEO IS BACK ON!!
WHAT HAPPENED TO WHITEBEARD AFTER HE GOT STABBED?!
AHEM!
WERE ALL HIS PIRATE ALLIES KILLED...
...AFTER WHITEBEARD BETRAYED THEM?!
PUFF... PUFF...
AHEM.
WUZZ!!
WUZZ
SOMEONE'S ON THE SCREEN!
HELLO, EVERYBODY!! THIS IS BUGGY, THE LEGENDARY PIRATE!!
ZANG!!
YOU AGAIN?!

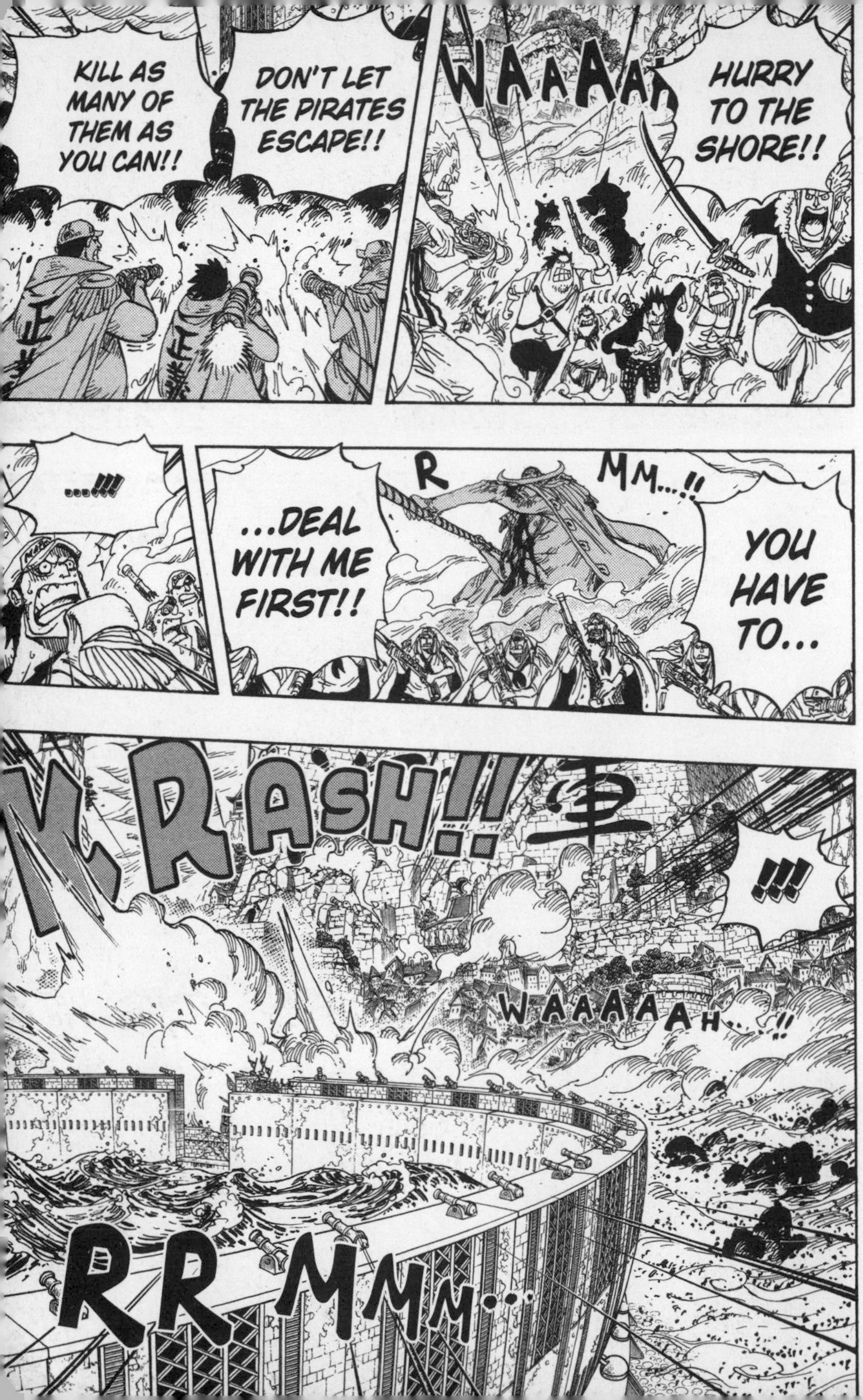
HURRY TO THE SHORE!!
WAAAA
DON'T LET THE PIRATES ESCAPE!!
KILL AS MANY OF THEM AS YOU CAN!!
YOU HAVE TO...
R MM...!!
...DEAL WITH ME FIRST!!
...!!!
RASH!!
!!!
WAAAAAH...!!
RR MMM...

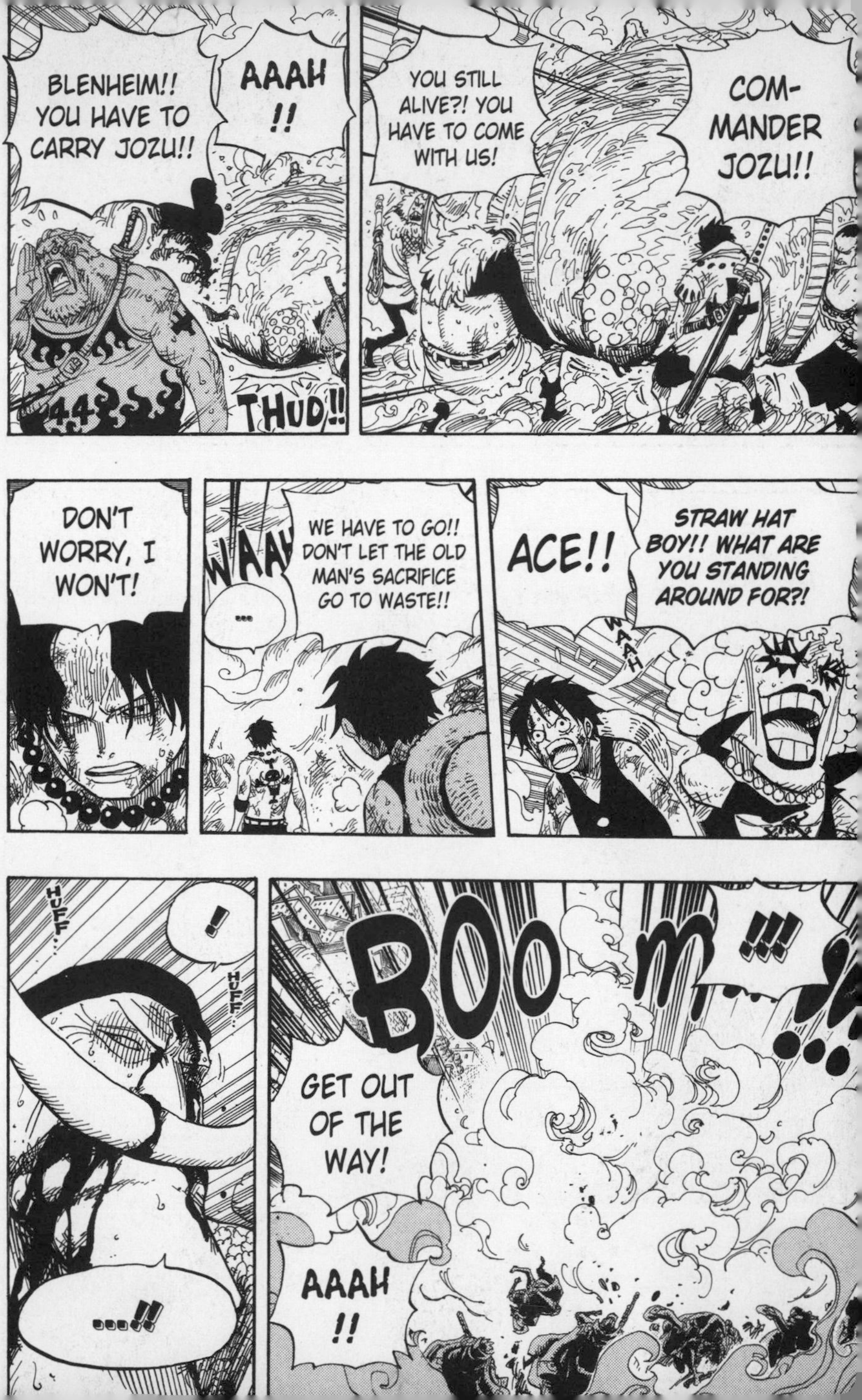
COMMANDER JOZU!!
YOU STILL ALIVE?! YOU HAVE TO COME WITH US!
AAAH !!
BLENHEIM!! YOU HAVE TO CARRY JOZU!!
THUD!!
STRAW HAT BOY!! WHAT ARE YOU STANDING AROUND FOR?!
WAAAH
ACE!!
WE HAVE TO GO!! DON'T LET THE OLD MAN'S SACRIFICE GO TO WASTE!!
...
DON'T WORRY, I WON'T!
BOOOM!!!
GET OUT OF THE WAY!
AAAH !!
!
HUFF...
HUFF...
...!!

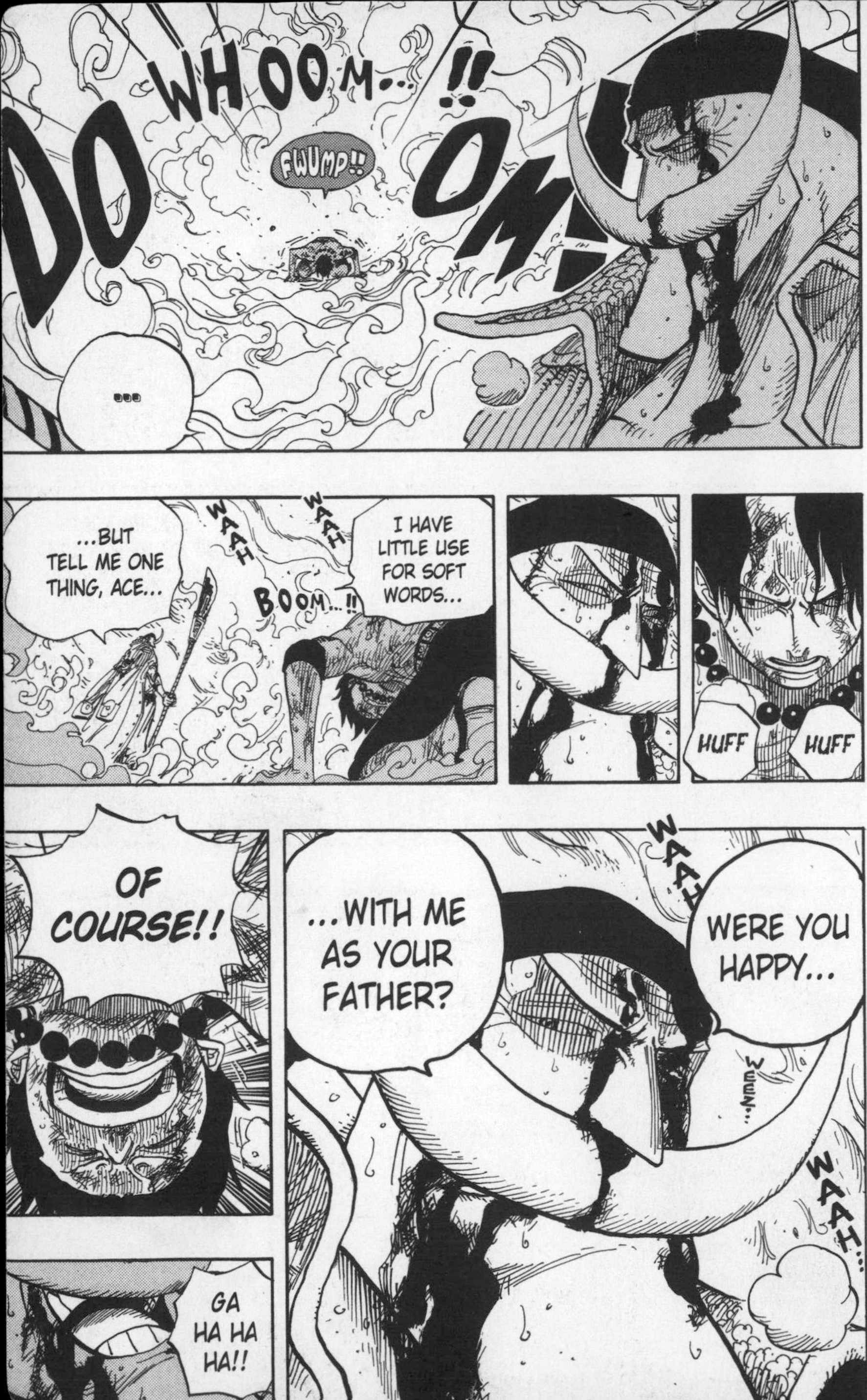
DO
WHOOM...!!
OM
FWUMP!!
...
HUFF
HUFF
I HAVE LITTLE USE FOR SOFT WORDS...
WAAH
WAAH
BOOM...!!
...BUT TELL ME ONE THING, ACE...
WAAH
WERE YOU HAPPY...
...WITH ME AS YOUR FATHER?
WEEN...
WAAH...
OF COURSE!!
GA HA HA HA!!

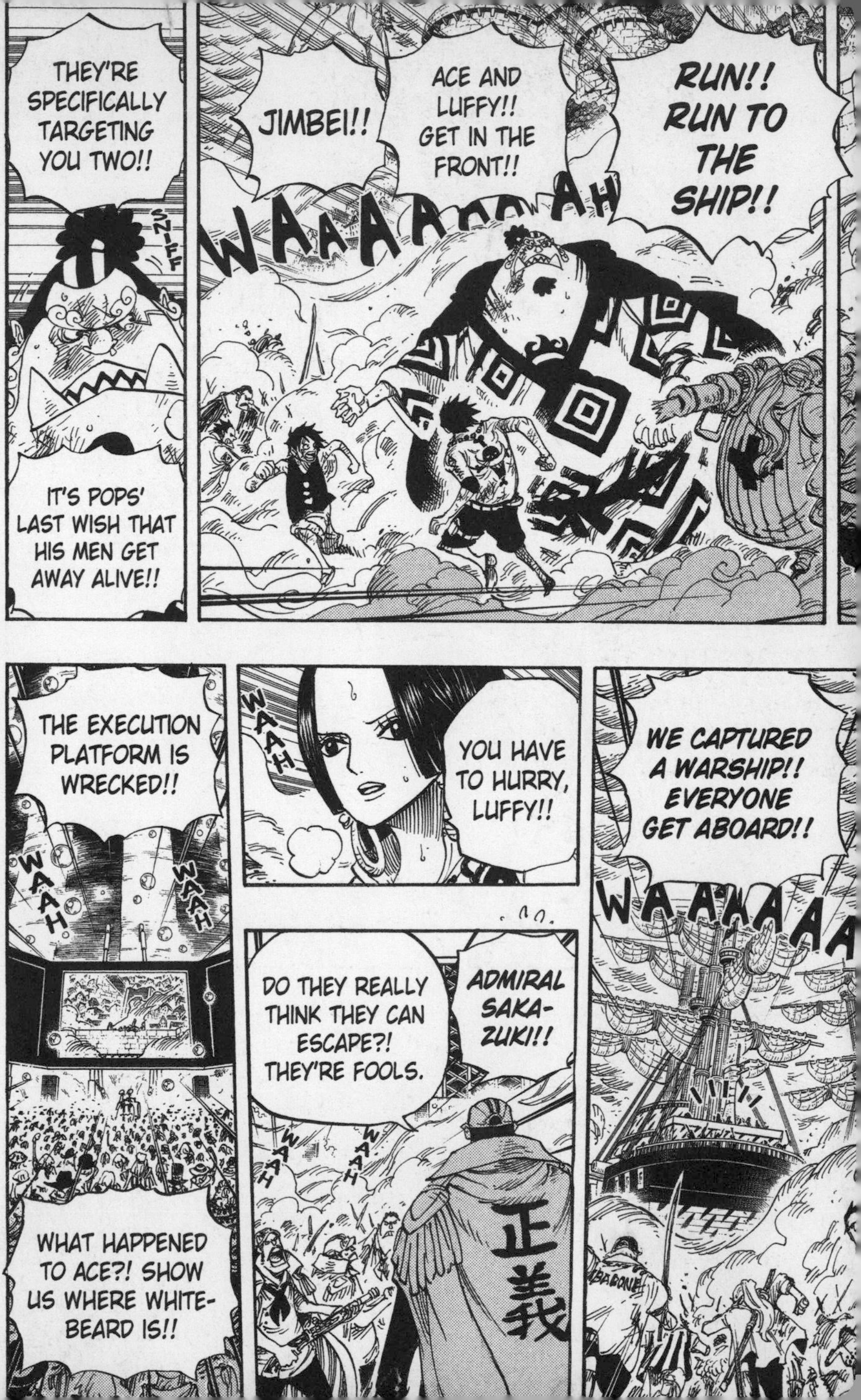
RUN!! RUN TO THE SHIP!!
ACE AND LUFFY!! GET IN THE FRONT!!
JIMBEI!!
WAAAAAAAH
THEY'RE SPECIFICALLY TARGETING YOU TWO!!
SNIFF
IT'S POPS' LAST WISH THAT HIS MEN GET AWAY ALIVE!!
WE CAPTURED A WARSHIP!! EVERYONE GET ABOARD!!
WAAAAAA
YOU HAVE TO HURRY, LUFFY!!
WAAAH
ADMIRAL SAKA-ZUKI!!
DO THEY REALLY THINK THEY CAN ESCAPE?! THEY'RE FOOLS.
WAAH
WAAH
正義
THE EXECUTION PLATFORM IS WRECKED!!
WAAH
WAAH
WHAT HAPPENED TO ACE?! SHOW US WHERE WHITE-BEARD IS!!

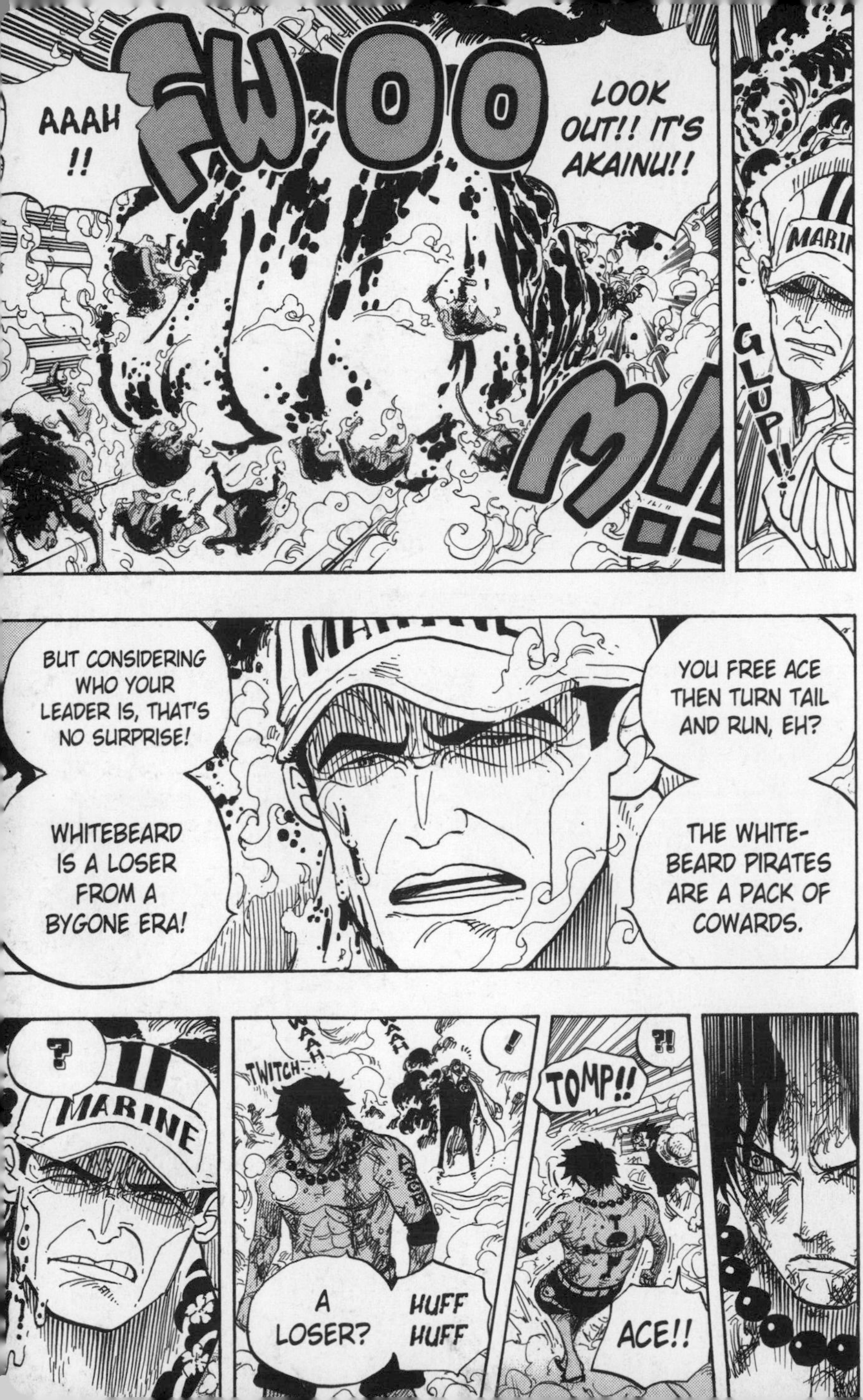
GLUP!!
LOOK OUT!! IT'S AKAINU!!
FWOOM!!
AAAH !!
YOU FREE ACE THEN TURN TAIL AND RUN, EH?
THE WHITE-BEARD PIRATES ARE A PACK OF COWARDS.
BUT CONSIDERING WHO YOUR LEADER IS, THAT'S NO SURPRISE!
WHITEBEARD IS A LOSER FROM A BYGONE ERA!
?!
TOMP!!
ACE!!
!
WAAH
TWITCH
HUFF HUFF
A LOSER?
?

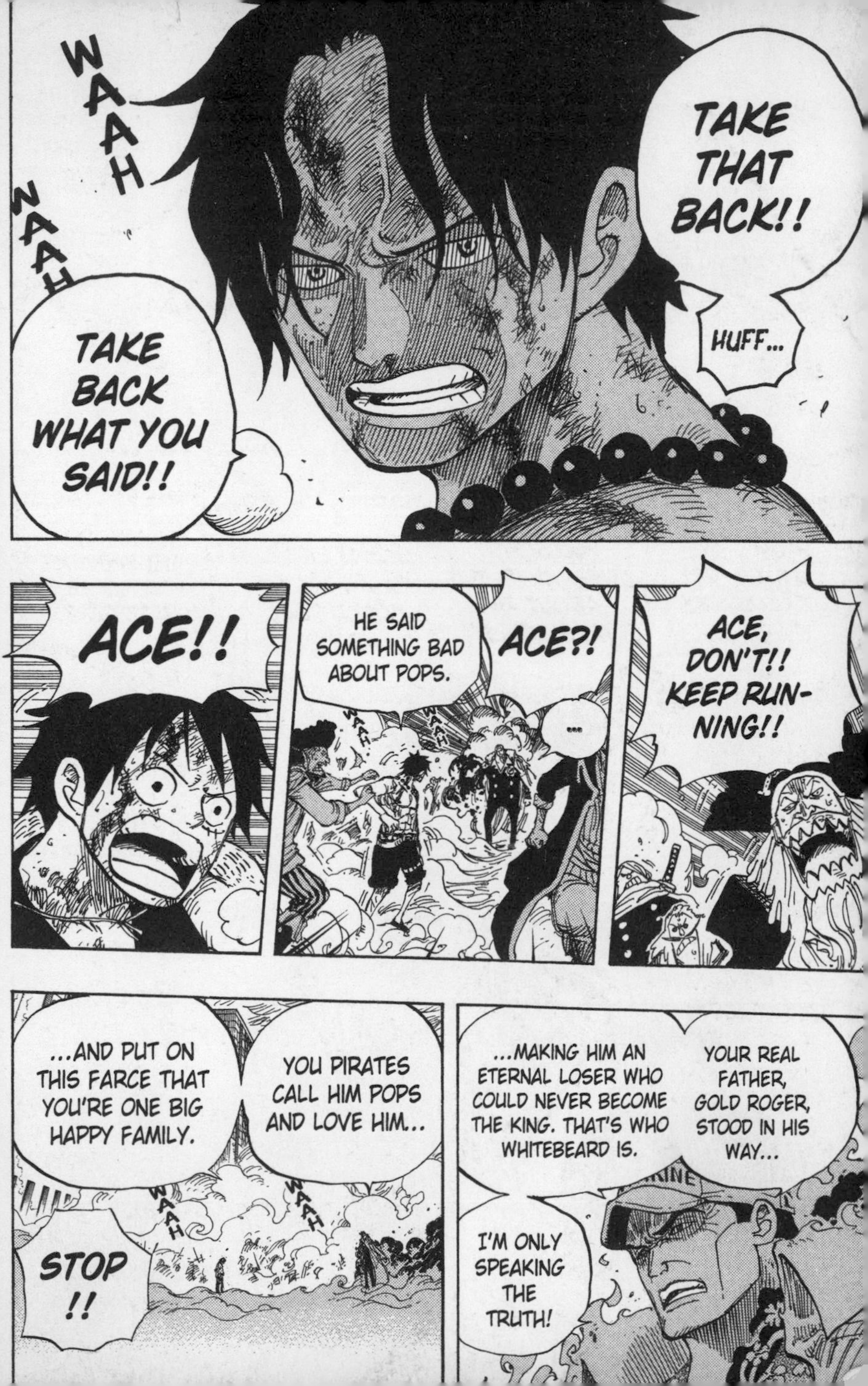
TAKE THAT BACK!!
HUFF...
WAAAH
WAAH
TAKE BACK WHAT YOU SAID!!
ACE, DON'T!! KEEP RUN-NING!!
ACE?!
...
HE SAID SOMETHING BAD ABOUT POPS.
WAAH
WAAH
ACE!!
YOUR REAL FATHER, GOLD ROGER, STOOD IN HIS WAY...
...MAKING HIM AN ETERNAL LOSER WHO COULD NEVER BECOME THE KING. THAT'S WHO WHITEBEARD IS.
I'M ONLY SPEAKING THE TRUTH!
YOU PIRATES CALL HIM POPS AND LOVE HIM...
...AND PUT ON THIS FARCE THAT YOU'RE ONE BIG HAPPY FAMILY.
WAAH
WAAH
STOP!!

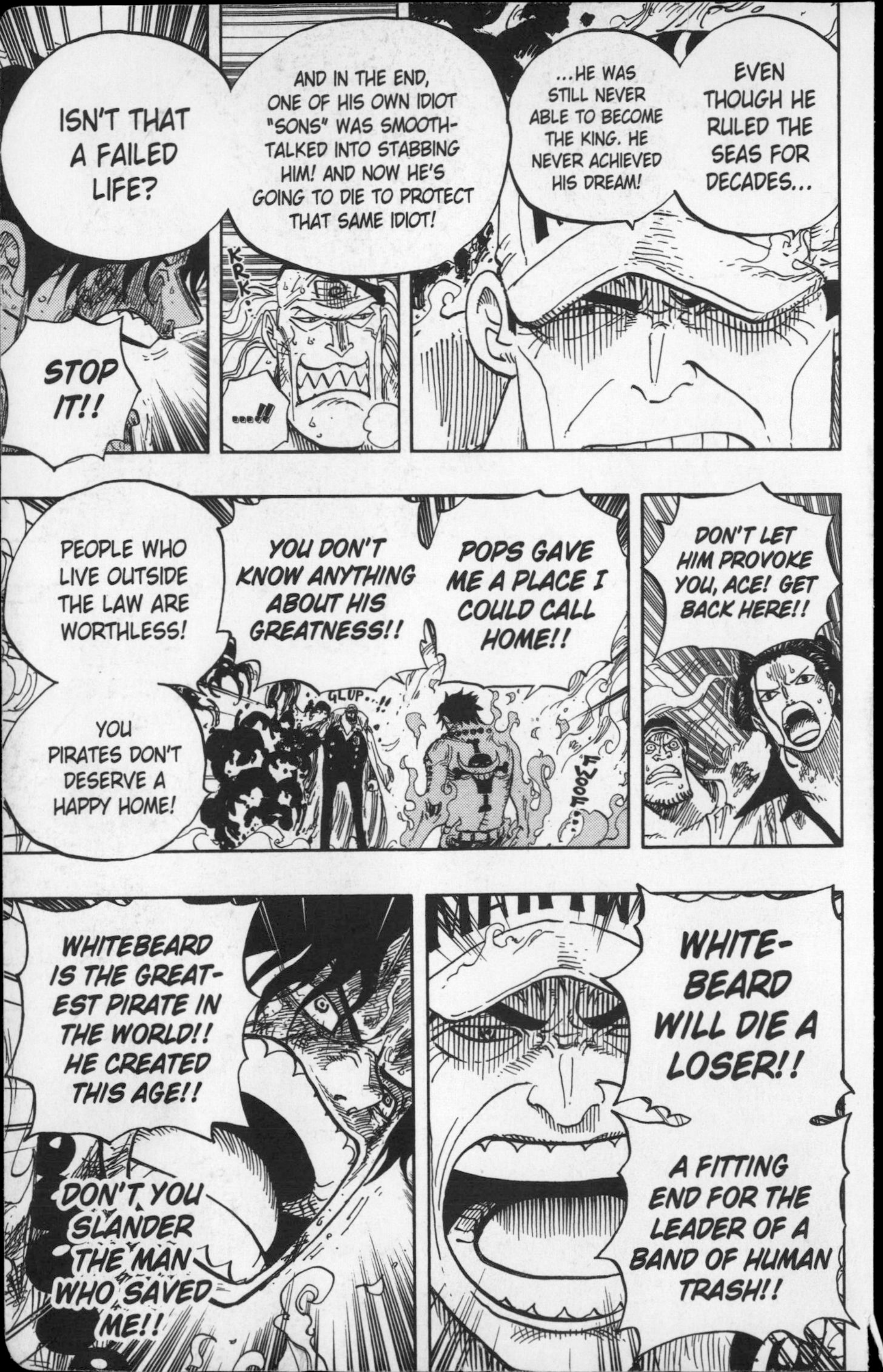
EVEN THOUGH HE RULED THE SEAS FOR DECADES...
...HE WAS STILL NEVER ABLE TO BECOME THE KING. HE NEVER ACHIEVED HIS DREAM!
AND IN THE END, ONE OF HIS OWN IDIOT "SONS" WAS SMOOTH-TALKED INTO STABBING HIM! AND NOW HE'S GOING TO DIE TO PROTECT THAT SAME IDIOT!
KRK
...!!
ISN'T THAT A FAILED LIFE?
STOP IT!!
DON'T LET HIM PROVOKE YOU, ACE! GET BACK HERE!!
POPS GAVE ME A PLACE I COULD CALL HOME!!
YOU DON'T KNOW ANYTHING ABOUT HIS GREATNESS!!
GLUP...!!
PEOPLE WHO LIVE OUTSIDE THE LAW ARE WORTHLESS!
YOU PIRATES DON'T DESERVE A HAPPY HOME!
WHITE-BEARD WILL DIE A LOSER!!
A FITTING END FOR THE LEADER OF A BAND OF HUMAN TRASH!!
WHITEBEARD IS THE GREAT-EST PIRATE IN THE WORLD!! HE CREATED THIS AGE!!
DON'T YOU SLANDER THE MAN WHO SAVED ME!!

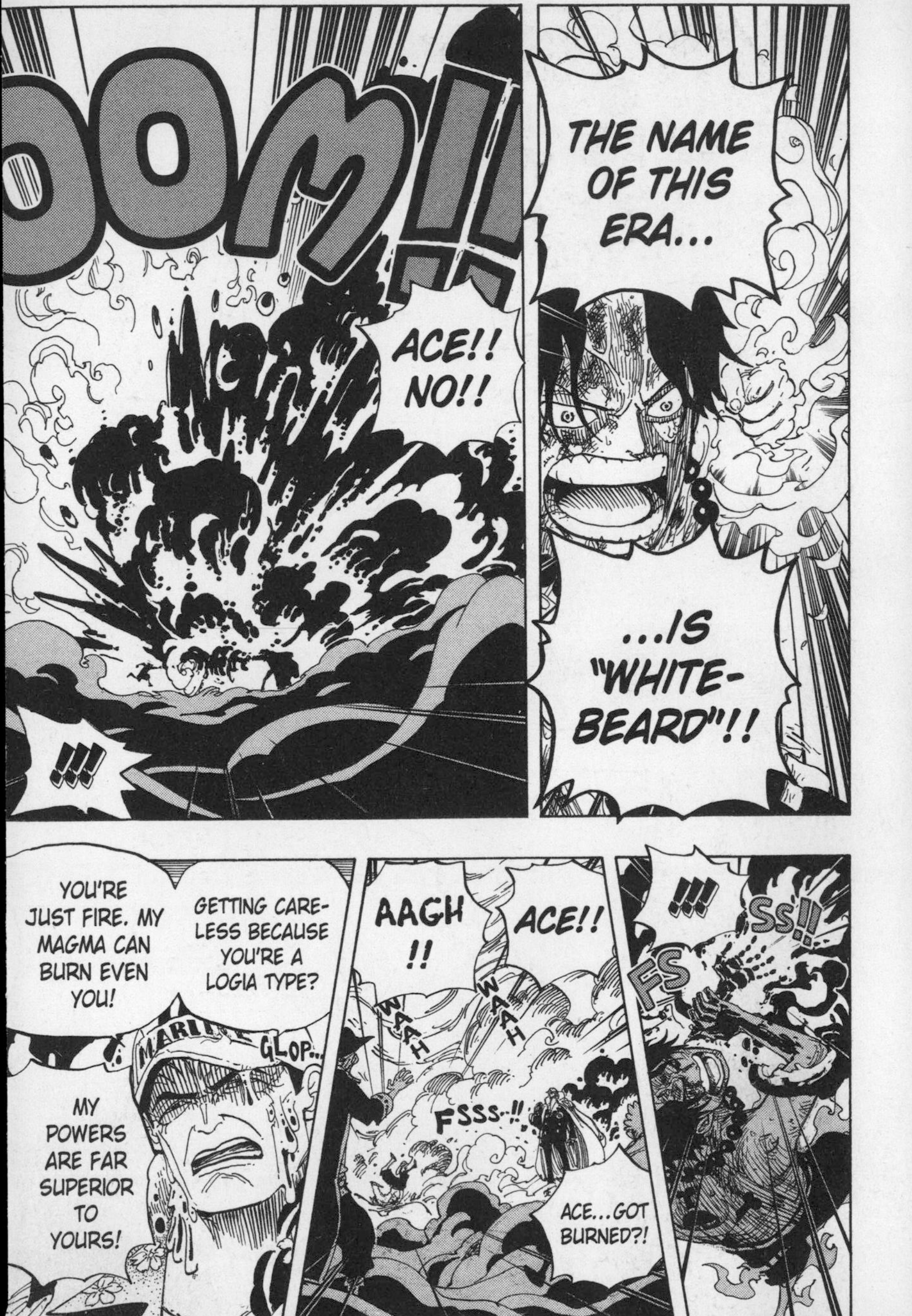
THE NAME OF THIS ERA...
...IS "WHITE-BEARD"!!
OOM!!
ACE!! NO!!
!!!
!!!
SS!!
FS
ACE!!
AAGH !!
WAAH
WAAH
FSSS..!!
ACE...GOT BURNED?!
GETTING CARE-LESS BECAUSE YOU'RE A LOGIA TYPE?
YOU'RE JUST FIRE. MY MAGMA CAN BURN EVEN YOU!
GLOP...
MY POWERS ARE FAR SUPERIOR TO YOURS!

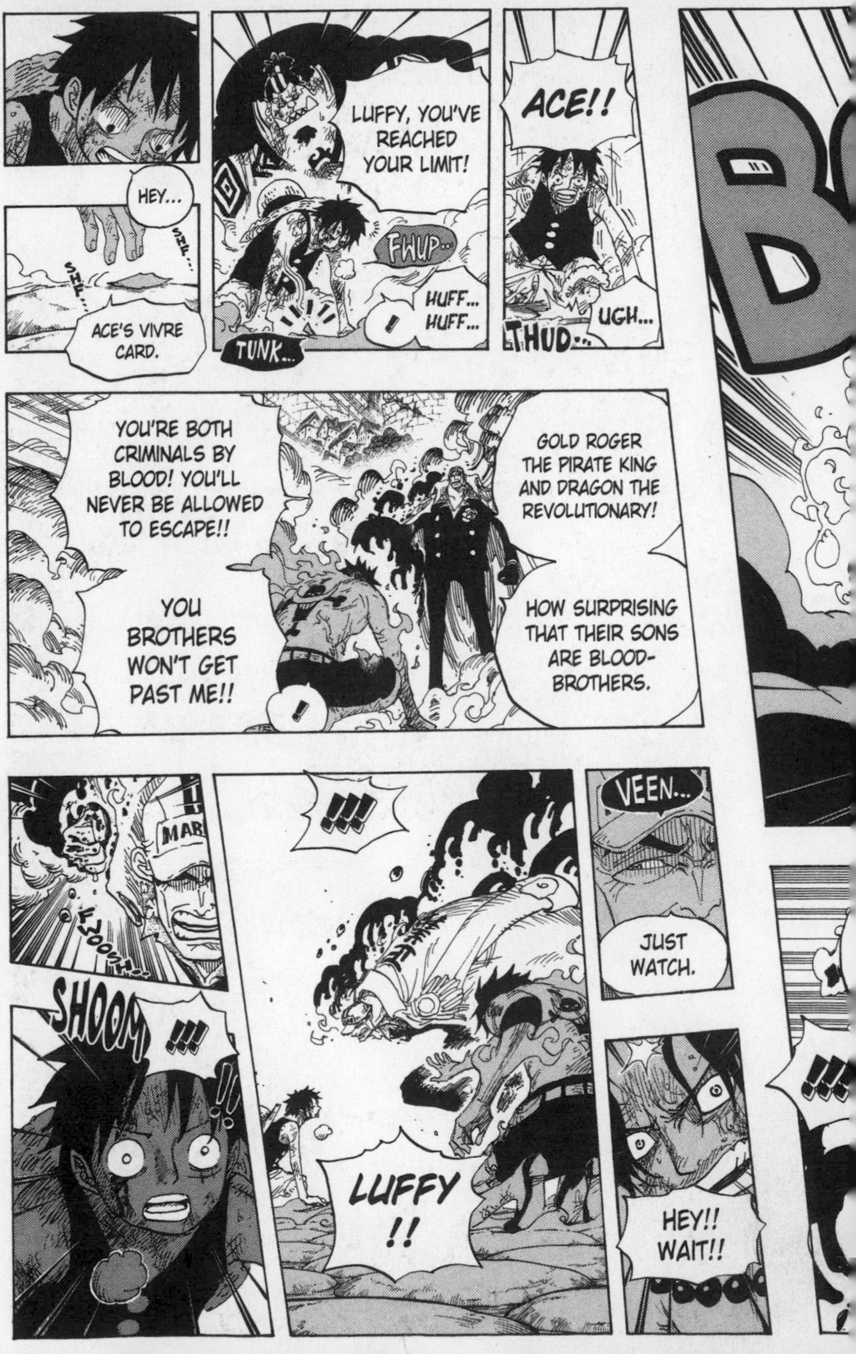
ACE!!
UGH...
THUD...
LUFFY, YOU'VE REACHED YOUR LIMIT!
FWUP..
HUFF... HUFF...
!
TUNK...
HEY...
SHF...
SHF...
ACE'S VIVRE CARD.
GOLD ROGER THE PIRATE KING AND DRAGON THE REVOLUTIONARY!
HOW SURPRISING THAT THEIR SONS ARE BLOOD-BROTHERS.
YOU'RE BOTH CRIMINALS BY BLOOD! YOU'LL NEVER BE ALLOWED TO ESCAPE!!
YOU BROTHERS WON'T GET PAST ME!!
!
VEEN...
JUST WATCH.
HEY!! WAIT!!
!!!
LUFFY !!
WOOSH...
SHOOM
!!!

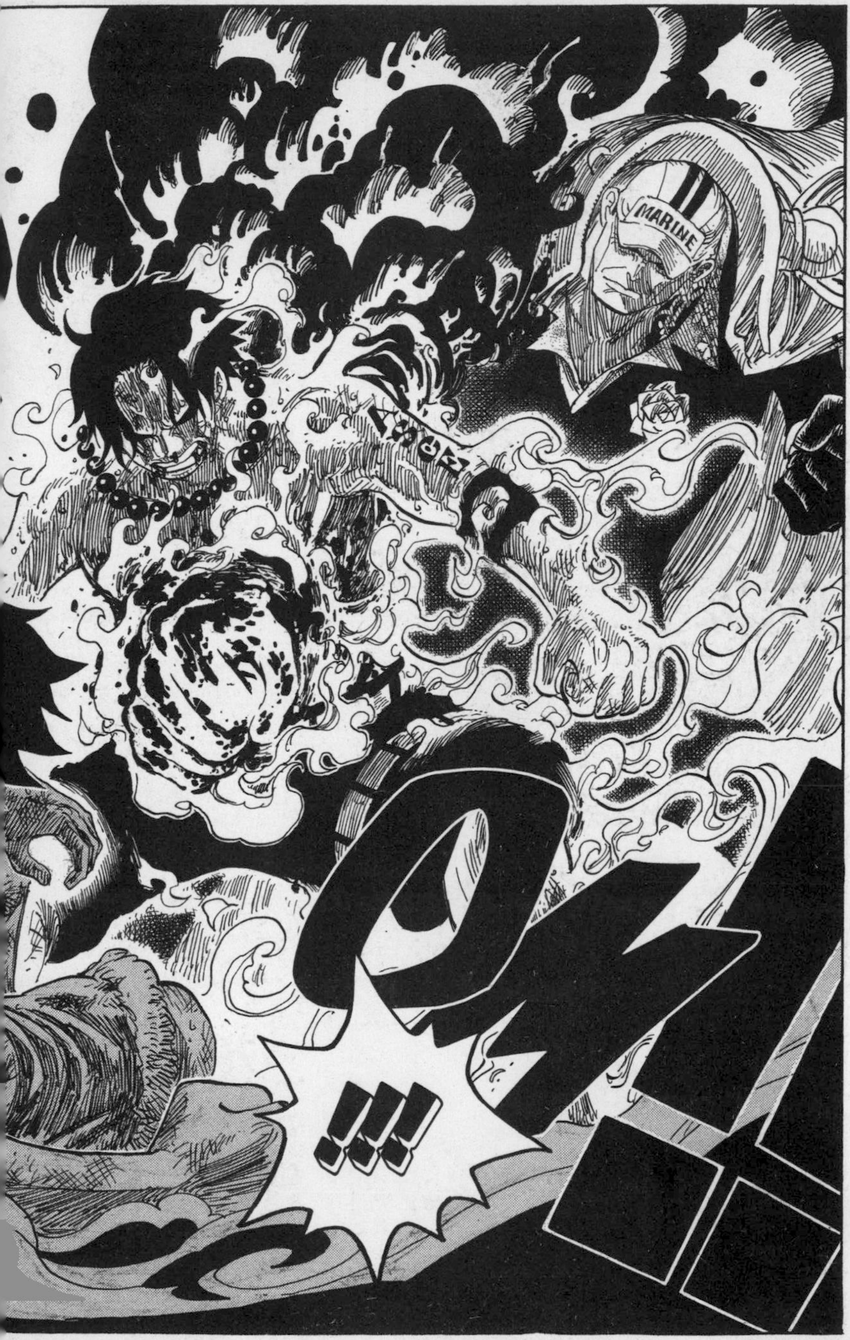
MARINE

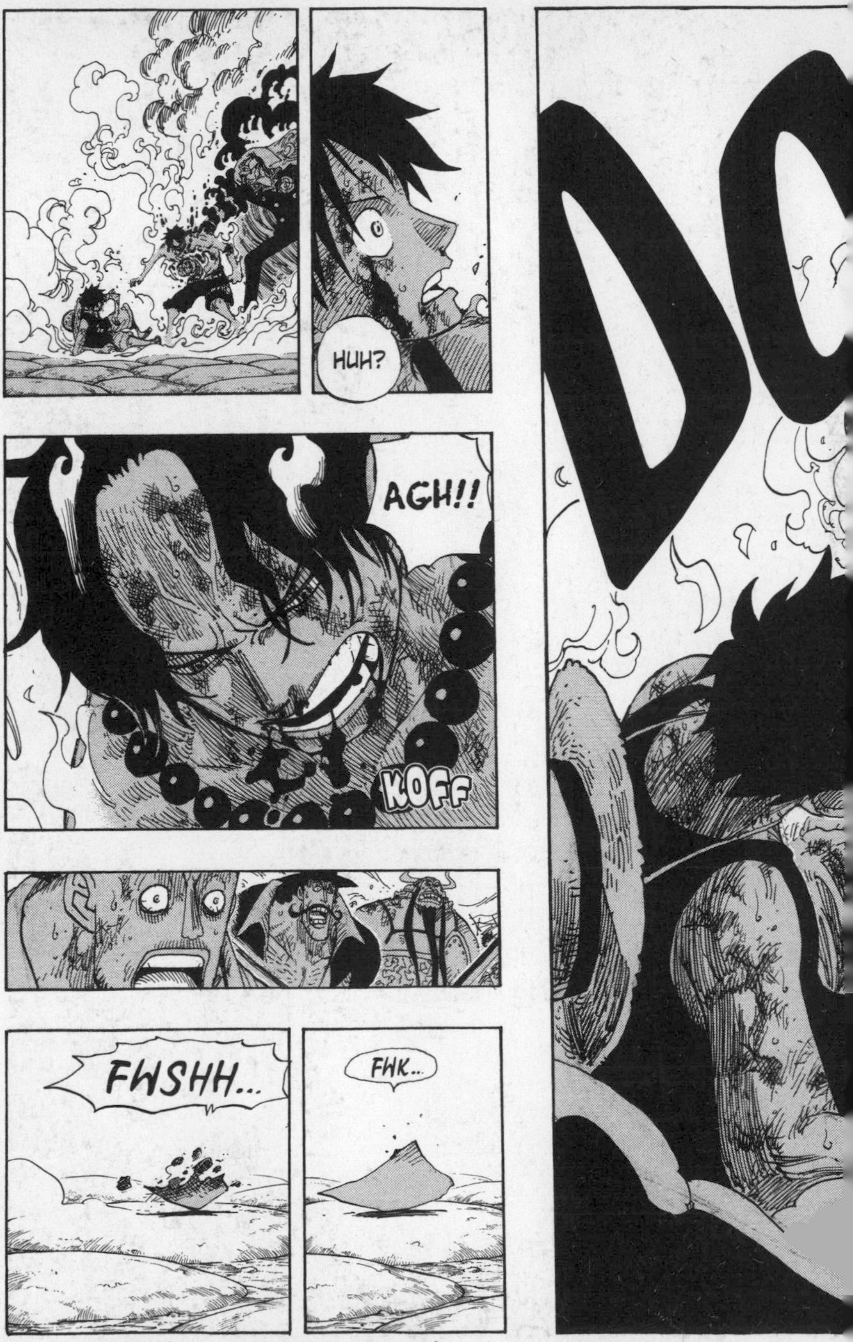
HUH?
AGH!!
KOFF
FWK...
FWSHH...

TO BE CONTINUED IN *ONE PIECE*, VOL. 59!

OUR SHIP DOCTOR, IKUE OTANI!

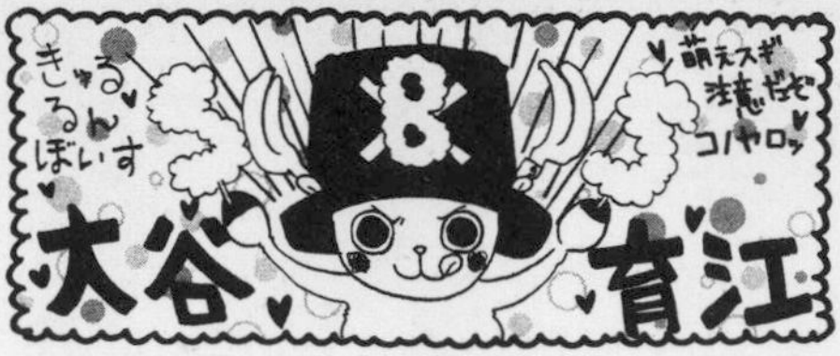
きゅるるんぼいす
萌えスギ注意だぜコノヤロッ
太谷育江
(Haruka, Osaka)

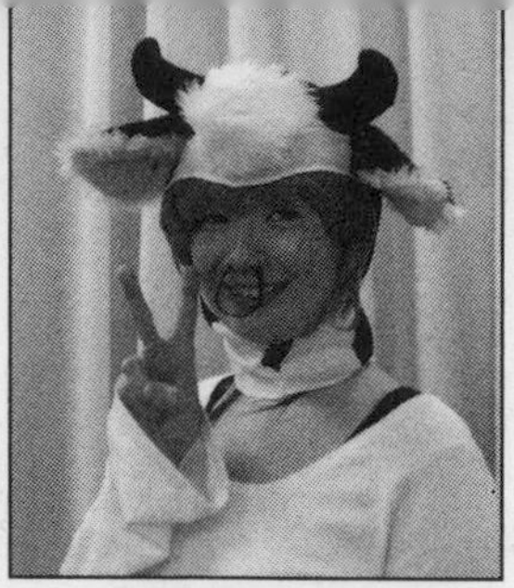

Reader(Q): Ms. Ikue Otani, do you also do Chopper's voice when he's big?

--Karen

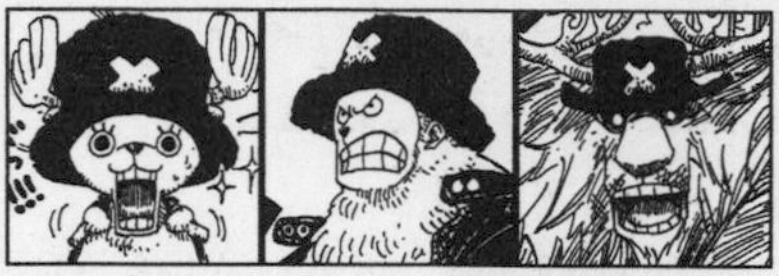

Ikue(I): That's right. My voice when he's in berserk mode has production effects on it, but I do all of Chopper's voices.

Q: How do you do! ☼ When Chopper gets big, do you get big too? I heard you're a voice actress that goes for realism!

--Macherie

I: Nope. I'm always big. But since I'm playing the part of the tiny Chopper, I have to shrink most of the time. BECAUSE I GO FOR REALISM.

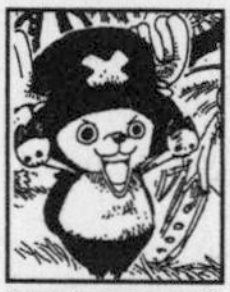

Q: So, give it to me straight. Which one is bigger? A life-sized Chopper, or you.

--Funako

I: What?! You're unsure about that?!

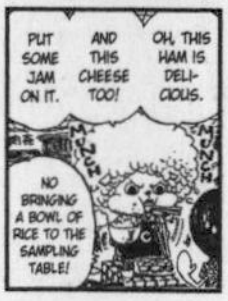
OH, THIS HAM IS DELICIOUS.
AND THIS CHEESE TOO!
PUT SOME JAM ON IT.
NO BRINGING A BOWL OF RICE TO THE SAMPLING TABLE!

Q: Ms. Otani! Is it true that you put jam on everything?!

--Mihon

I: Yup. I even put jam on jam.

Q: Hello, Ms. Ikue Otani! ⤴⤴ I have a question. Among the other voice actors and actresses, who is the one that you're the closest ♡ with? And who is the funniest? Please tell me! ☆≡

--Eikichi

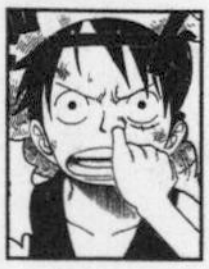

I: It's hard to say which one. But I think the funniest one is the Captain! I'm really impressed at how many pranks she comes up with.

Q: Can you think of a new technique for Chopper?

--Redbeard

I: Doctor's Orders!

Q: Ms. Otani, do you also have seven crazy transformations?

--Don't Mind Sekiguchi

I: Yeah, something like that.

Q: Can you try drawing Chopper's hat without looking at any reference material? You can, right?
　　　　--Don't Mind Sekiguchi

I: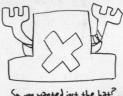

So, you wanted just the hat?

Q: Tell me what happens, when you, Ms. Otani, eat three Rumble Balls. Please draw it.
　　　　--Chappie

I:

Like this

Regular people

Q: Ms. Otani! I always love your cute voice! So for you... Take this!

Cotton Candy Attack!　　　--Captain Chopper

I: Ugh. Chew. Chew. Okay. You can come at me again! ♡

Q: I have a question for Chopper. ☆ Please cure my illness called "love sickness"!　　　　--Sugacchi

I: Let me have a go at this. Okay. Try finding me first.

Q: When Chopper gets surprised, his hat jumps off his head along with his antlers. When you get surprised, Ms. Otani, what jumps?　　　　--MASA

I: My heel.

Q: Otani! Take this! **Negative Hollow!**
(Sorry about that.)　　　　--Perona V

I: I'm so sorry I couldn't grow to be big even after eating so much...

Q: To Ms. Ikue Otani. I'm always watching you (on TV)! Chopper's voice is just too cute! ♡ I always try to impersonate Chopper. So how do you bring out Chopper's voice anyway? Do you have any advice for me to get better at impersonating your voice?　　　　--Pepper's Sister

I: If you maintain his motto of "Be a man," anyone can impersonate his voice.

Q: Ms. Otani! I'll be honest with you! May I have your voice?! ♡
　　　　--Reindeer Nakai

I: Sure. Here you go! ♡

Oda: Time's up, Ms. Otani! Thank you. Huh? Did your voice just change? What? You gave your voice to Reindeer Nakai?! Hmm, that's bad... So, Reindeer Nakai. Do you think you can make it to the recording session next week?! You can? That's great! (Is it?!)
See you all next volume! Oh, no! Ms. Otani is now unemployed!

COMING NEXT VOLUME:

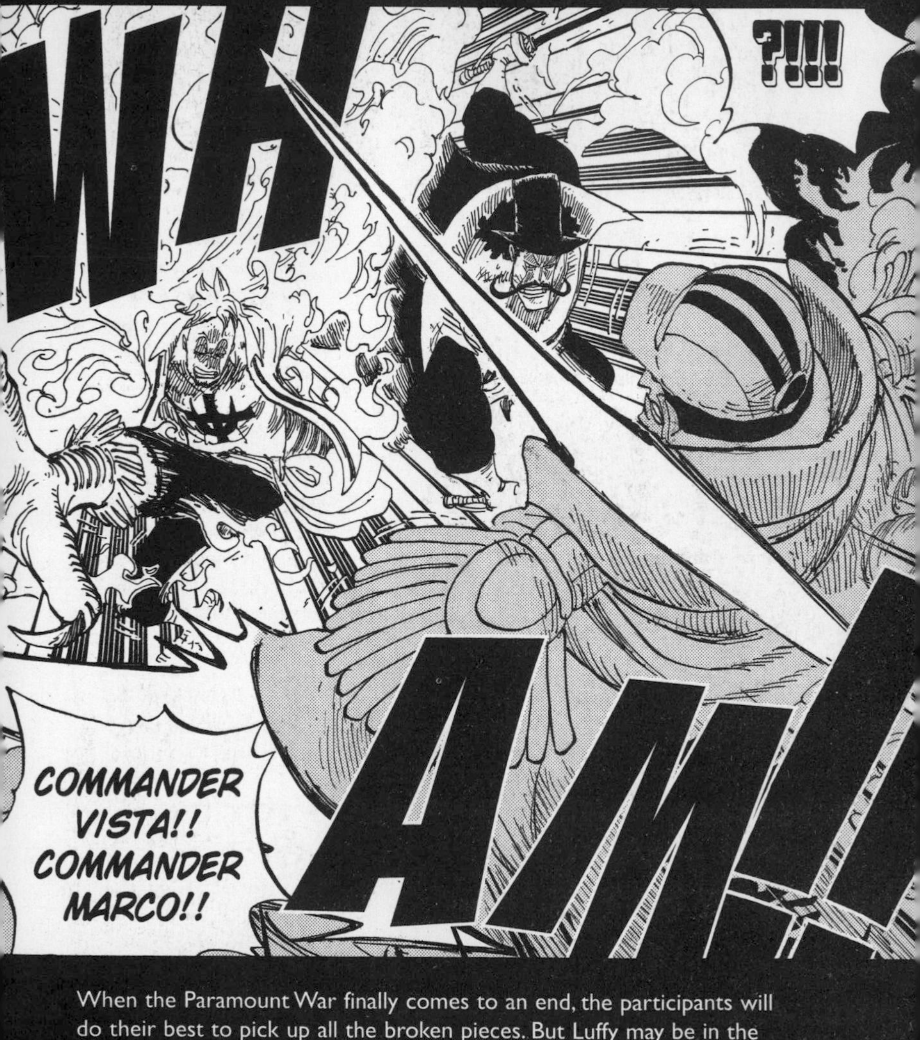
?!!!
COMMANDER VISTA!! COMMANDER MARCO!!

When the Paramount War finally comes to an end, the participants will do their best to pick up all the broken pieces. But Luffy may be in the toughest shape of all. Can he ever hope to recover from the tragic conclusion to this epic battle…?

ON SALE FEBRUARY 2012!

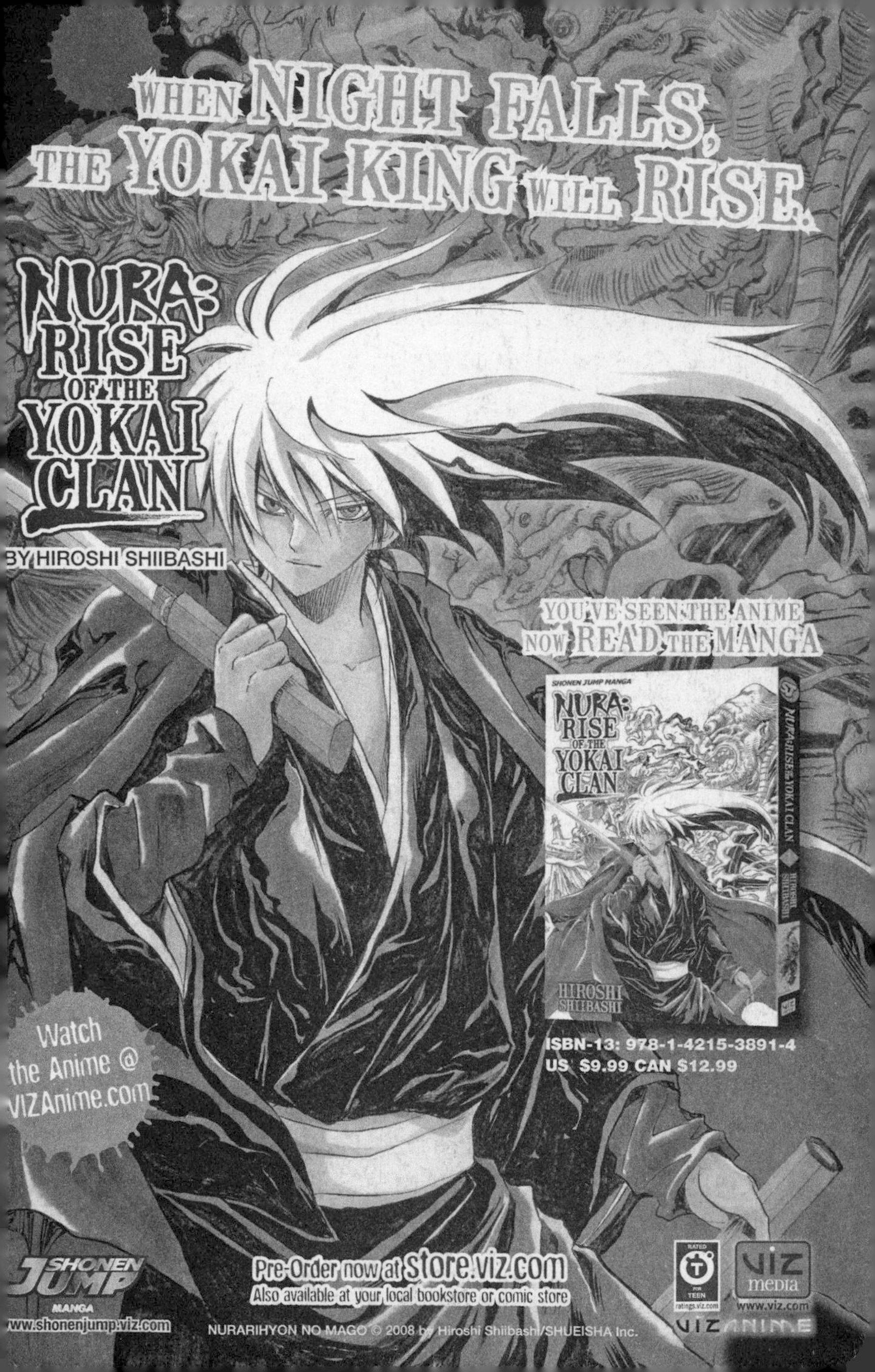
WHEN NIGHT FALLS, THE YOKAI KING WILL RISE.
NURA: RISE OF THE YOKAI CLAN
BY HIROSHI SHIIBASHI
YOU'VE SEEN THE ANIME NOW READ THE MANGA
SHONEN JUMP MANGA
NURA: RISE OF THE YOKAI CLAN
HIROSHI SHIIBASHI
ISBN-13: 978-1-4215-3891-4
US $9.99 CAN $12.99
Watch the Anime @ VIZAnime.com
SHONEN JUMP MANGA
www.shonenjump.viz.com
Pre-Order now at Store.viz.com
Also available at your local bookstore or comic store
RATED T FOR TEEN
ratings.viz.com
VIZ media
www.viz.com
VIZ ANIME
NURARIHYON NO MAGO © 2008 by Hiroshi Shiibashi/SHUEISHA Inc.

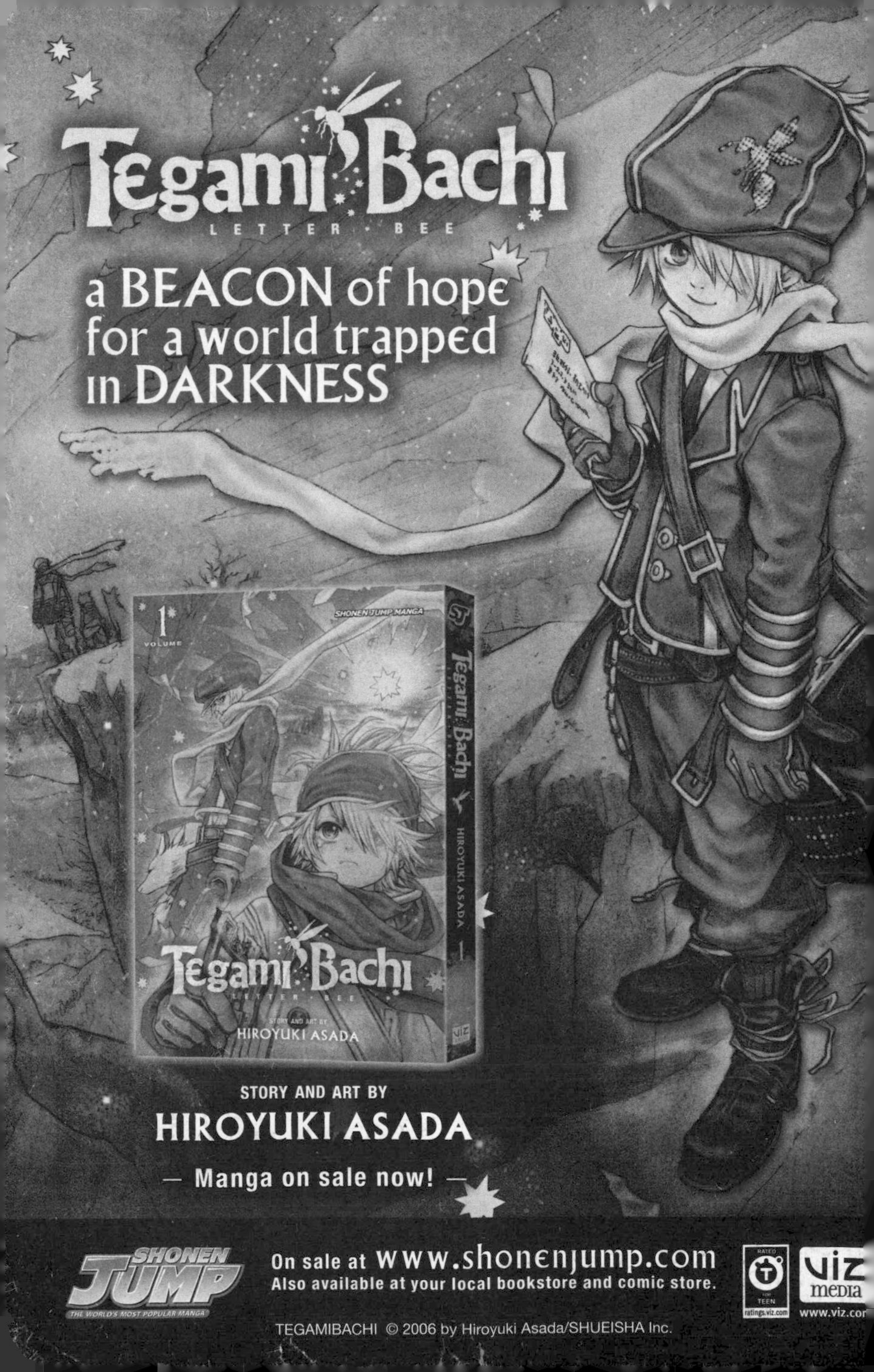
Tegami Bachi
LETTER BEE
a BEACON of hope for a world trapped in DARKNESS
1 VOLUME
SHONEN JUMP MANGA
Tegami Bachi
LETTER BEE
STORY AND ART BY
HIROYUKI ASADA
STORY AND ART BY
HIROYUKI ASADA
— Manga on sale now! —
SHONEN JUMP
THE WORLD'S MOST POPULAR MANGA
On sale at www.shonenjump.com
Also available at your local bookstore and comic store.
RATED T TEEN
ratings.viz.com
viz media
www.viz.com
TEGAMIBACHI © 2006 by Hiroyuki Asada/SHUEISHA Inc.